W9-BPO-778

WITHDRAWN

**SPEECH: DYNAMIC COMMUNICATION**
*Second Edition*

**MILTON DICKENS**

UNIVERSITY OF SOUTHERN CALIFORNIA

# Speech
## DYNAMIC COMMUNICATION

## SECOND EDITION

HARCOURT, BRACE & WORLD, INC.
NEW YORK / CHICAGO / BURLINGAME

# PREFACE

The philosophy underlying this second edition is the same as that in the first edition. Speechmaking is presented as a dynamic process uniting speaker and listeners, not as a static one-sided performance by the speaker. This view has been reinforced by adding a new chapter on theories of communication.

Public speaking is described as enlarged conversation, and this approach has been strengthened by adding a chapter on group discussion, a chapter that attempts to bridge the gap between what is ordinarily called informal conversation and what is ordinarily called formal public speaking.

Speechmaking is viewed as an interdependent mixture of attitudes, knowledge, and skills. I have tried to keep all three ingredients in balance and to avoid overemphasizing any one of them. I think that the balance in this edition is better than in the first because of the addition of a chapter on the speaker's responsibility. Since undergraduates tend to shrug off pious platitudes, I have focused this new chapter on recent research.

While trying to improve the presentation of a basic philosophy of speech I have tried to avoid the changing of a basic philosophy of teaching speech. For example, I believe that a textbook for a beginning course should be held to a moderate length so that teachers may supplement the text by using a project workbook, a sourcebook for speech topics and ideas, or readings from newspapers and periodicals of significant contemporary speeches. Therefore in adding chapters I have sought to compensate by deleting, condensing, or combining other chapters.

I have made changes in the chapter sequence, such as moving up the chapters on speech outlining from the second to the first half of the book. These changes reflect recent trends in curricula and pedagogy as reported by numerous teachers using the first edition. I realize, however, that speech teachers often assign the chapters of any text in changing sequences to conform with the special needs of different classes. I have tried to facilitate such desirable flexibility by tight internal chapter organization so that each chapter is a self-contained unit which may be logically and conveniently assigned in any of several combinations.

Users of the first edition strongly recommend that I retain the idea of including in the appendix suggested schedules of classroom projects, together with instructions and criticism charts. I have endeavored to broaden the usefulness of these materials by providing a schedule for a one-semester terminal course, as well as for two semesters of a year course.

A teachable text in beginning speech requires, of course, examples from contemporary speakers. These examples, verbal or pictorial, are perishable. In updating I have sought to adhere to the policy that all examples must be related to the students' experience and that pictorial examples must be illustrative of the text, not merely decorative.

In the preface to the first edition I said, "I hope you will treat the book kindly, yet give me your criticism for improvement." Both of these hopes have been fulfilled, and this revision has given me the chance to make the book more useful to more of its users.

My greatest indebtedness in preparing this revision is to Frederick Williams of the University of Wisconsin who assisted me in almost all phases of the work and who should be credited as collaborator on the new Chapter 20. Penetrating criticisms of various portions of the book were generously given by William Schrier of Hope College, Ted W. Benedict of Pacific Union College, and Randall C. Ruechelle of Colorado State University. Useful suggestions on many specific points were provided by Harold J. Borden of El Camino College, W. Charles Redding of Purdue University, Sydney Kessler of Valley College, Howard Russell of Pierce College, and James Linn of the University of Hawaii. Advice and encouragement were unstintingly given by my colleagues at the University of Southern California, especially Forrest L. Seal, William B. McCoard, Gale Richards, and James H. McBath. Invaluable help on the photography was provided by Fenwick and Melvin English. Efficient assistance on typing, proofreading, and indexing was provided by Joan Williams. Useful suggestions on English usage were made by Marcay Dickens.

I find it impossible to acknowledge specifically my indebtedness to the many persons who have influenced my thinking through the years. Former teachers, colleagues, friends, and students have helped to shape my concepts of speech. I do want to acknowledge specifically the influence of the late Percy Marks who read and criticized the entire manuscript of the first edition; I can only hope that some of his teaching will be reflected in this second edition.

Jennette Dickens, my wife, again gave many practical suggestions about the book, and again gave patient and wise encouragement.

MILTON DICKENS

*Los Angeles, California*
*January 1963*

PART ONE
GETTING STARTED


PART TWO
CONSTRUCTING THE SPEECH

# CONTENTS

**PART THREE
DELIVERING THE SPEECH**


**PART FOUR
SECURING AUDIENCE RESPONSES**


**PART FIVE
DEVELOPING A PHILOSOPHY OF SPEECH**


**APPENDIXES**

**SPEECH: DYNAMIC COMMUNICATION**
*Second Edition*

# PART ONE

# GETTING STARTED

*A speech is neither an act, nor a solo, nor an exhibition. A speech is an enlarged conversation between speaker and audience.*

Whether speaking with a small group of students or participating in the inauguration of the President of the United States, poet Robert Frost thinks of himself and his listeners as a single group.

TOPICAL PREVIEW

# 1

# APPROACHING THE STUDY OF SPEECH

Words, words, words—you are bombarded with them. The bombardment begins on some days the moment you wake up and continues with but minor interruptions until you go to bed. You talk with family, friends, colleagues, and teachers during personal conversations, class meetings, group discussions, and telephone calls. You listen to newscasters, political candidates, and advertisers who reach you through television, radio, and motion pictures. You may conclude that "what this country needs is not more speech but better speech."

Better speech is your goal in studying this textbook. You will study not only the skills but also the principles of effective speaking. You will learn that effective speech is not a "thing" but an interaction that occurs among people when both the speaker and the listeners are participating knowledgeably, responsibly, and communicatively.

Let us begin this study by analyzing a deceptively simple definition.

## A definition of speech

For our purposes speech may be defined as the communication of thought and emotion by means of voice, language, and/or bodily action. By speech we can mean conversation, discussion, public speaking, reading aloud, acting, or even booing, hissing, heckling, or sign language.

Effective speech occurs when both speaker and listener are participating knowledgeably, responsibly, and communicatively.

### Misconceptions about public speaking

It is remarkable that so many people's attitudes about public speaking are fifty years behind the times. To see if you too have picked up a few misconceptions, let us examine three of the most common and dangerous of them.

### *A simple secret to successful speaking?*

Almost no one expects to find an easy formula for playing the violin or performing surgical operations, or for figure skating or shooting golf in par. Yet thousands of people believe there is a simple secret for successful speechmaking. This belief is an ancient one and will doubtless flourish forever. The extent of the belief is indicated by the fact that certain so-called public speaking courses attract adults in amazing numbers. The advertisements for some of these courses make entertaining reading. They promise to reveal, almost magically, how to sway an audience, conquer fears, develop self-confidence, become a leader, improve one's personality, win friends, make more money, improve the memory, perfect one's voice, and radiate charm. Usually all these blessings are to be harvested in ten easy lessons, with a free demonstration and testimonial meeting preceding the organization of the class. Sometimes all the blessings can be bestowed simply by a series of lectures—completely painless since one does not have to make any speeches. Equally painless methods include correspondence courses, home study from phonograph records, or just reading a book.

In response to the demand, quack courses have evolved a fascinating collection of public speaking secrets. Sometimes the secret is physiological, glorifying breath control or the like. More commonly the nostrum is psychological, such as, "Just imagine that all the audience are sitting in their underwear." Then there are the trick-word formulas; for example, "There are just three rules for successful speaking. Stand up. Speak up. And shut up." Or, "Have something to say. Say what you mean. And mean what you say." And so on.

You learn better speech by critically watching and listening to experienced speakers.

STANDARD OIL

7

As a variation of the above attitude, the study of public speaking is sometimes viewed not so much as a single secret but as an accumulation of little ones—a bag of tricks that, once mastered, will enable one to make people believe that black is white.

Why are these widespread beliefs dangerous? First, they provide fertile ground for a flourishing crop of quacks. Second, they lead college students to bring misconceptions to a speech course. Such students expect that if they merely sit through most of the class meetings a metamorphosis will somehow occur, giving them an easy short cut to becoming good speakers. There is no such short cut. The road is interesting but neither short nor necessarily smooth. In another course—history, let us say—these same students would expect to dig in and earn their knowledge.

## Public speaking: an isolated activity?

There is a widespread feeling that public speaking is far removed from simply talking to a group. The phrase "making a speech" seems to carry the connotation that it is an act peculiarly isolated from the ordinary speaking and thinking that immediately precede and follow it. The incongruity of this attitude is the basis for the old gag, "Before beginning my *speech* tonight, there is something I want to *say*."

Professor J. A. Winans, an influential pioneer in modern methods of speech education, expressed the prevalent attitude delightfully:

> Some seem to look upon speaking in public as a strange and almost abnormal act; and although they have been talking to others all their lives, they either fear to make a speech, or if they do "rise to address an audience," they cease at once to be their normal selves, assume strange tones and speak in stilted language.[1]

That such an attitude would be an obstacle to your progress in the study of speech is surely evident. Many people have been afraid even to start the study of speech because of such false fears. The attitude sets false goals and conceals the true nature of the course.

## An exhibition of platform virtuosity?

For more than half a century following the Civil War it was fashionable to view public speaking and oral reading as pretty fancy performances. Those were the days of elocutionists and "grand-style" orators. Elocution has been pleasantly defined as the art of saying nothing well. Professional elocutionists traveled about the country giving recitals and elocution lessons. Pulpit

---

[1] James A. Winans, *Speech-Making*, D. Appleton-Century, 1938, p. 11. Reprinted by permission of Appleton-Century-Crofts, Inc.

speaking and reading were characterized by the artificial ministerial chant. Political oratory was all too frequently of the Senator Foghorn type: "And so I say unto you that the *future* of these United States—yes, every one of these fifty far-flung states, and we love them all—that *future*, I repeat, rests [dramatic pause] with the *youth* of today!"

Fourth of July orations and high school declamation contests have now disappeared almost entirely. But not quite. There is still the inevitable social lag. Some older speakers, readers, and teachers have not kept pace with the changing times and are still performing. And many out-of-date attitudes toward speech are still widely held—even perhaps by you.

Well, you ask, what harm is there in thinking of speechmaking as a display of platform skills? To answer this question we must recall how powerful any attitude is. It predetermines or colors our responses to all relevant stimuli. Thus if you believe that making a speech means performing some kind of solo, or act, that attitude will influence almost everything you undertake in this course. Furthermore, the influence will be harmful. As examples, consider the following three dangers:

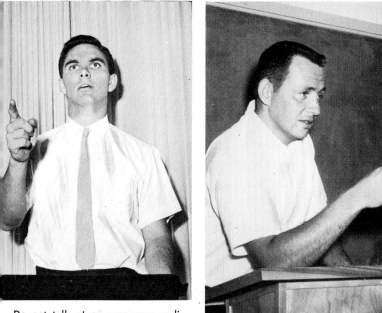

Do not talk *at* or *over* your audience.

Talk *to* and *with* your audience.

FREDERICK WILLIAMS

**9**

*1. Emotional maladjustment.* Stage fright involves a large element of self-consciousness. When you believe that making a speech is an exhibition of platform virtuosity, you are obviously putting yourself on the spot. You believe that you, as the speaker, are the focus of all attention, and that the audience is critically observing your posture, gestures, choice of words, and tone of voice. Naturally you become acutely conscious of yourself; you make it almost impossible for you to be conscious of anything else.

*2. Indirectness.* During a speech you should be more concerned with your listeners' reactions than with your own sensations. But if you view the speech as a solo performance, to you the audience becomes merely a group witnessing your act. You are up there in splendid isolation. You may manage to keep your eyes turned toward the audience but you see them only as a hazy mass. And they soon become aware of your nonseeing, faraway look. The total effect is one of indirectness, that of talking *at* them or *over* them, never, as you should, *to* them or *with* them.

*3. Artificiality.* When you believe that the how-you-say-it is the ultimate in speech training, you glorify means into ends. You make polished gestures more important than sincerity. You believe a resonant voice more desirable than straight thinking. You replace factual content with high-sounding phraseology. The total effect is of too much polish, too much grace, and too much glibness. Your mechanics stick out. You are artificial. Even when people praise you as a clever speaker, you fail.

### Useful attitudes toward public speaking

We now have three examples of common misconceptions about speech-making. There are a good many other misconceptions, of course, but these three should suffice to illustrate the effects of harmful attitudes. If these are samples of undesirable attitudes, what are the desirable ones? The remainder of this chapter will begin to answer that question.

### Progress must be earned

Sometimes a true story fits into a fictional pattern too neatly. Albert Walker's story fits so neatly that it sounds fictional, yet every detail of it is true.

Al was the poor boy from across the tracks. He learned to use his fists early, and he learned to use them well—so well that he became a national amateur boxing champion. His athletic ability earned him a university scholarship; he was intelligent, and he was determined to make the most of his great opportunity. Eventually he discovered the importance of speech training and naïvely supposed that he ought to try out for the debate team.

There he stood for his tryout speech—a prize fighter trying to be a speaker.

He took a boxer's stance, left foot forward, feet far apart—and attempted to gesture with his right hand. His lips, stiff with scar tissue, could not form some sounds distinctly, and his broken nose, flat itself, flattened his tones. His articulation was bad, his grammar and pronunciation worse. He even talked out of the side of his mouth and scowled at his audience as if it were an opponent in the ring. He fought his speech, and the speech won the fight.

Al made the squad for this paradoxical reason: he was the worst prospect the coach had ever seen. The coach wanted to put speech training to its severest test, figuring that if Al could develop into a debater, practically anybody could.

Al became a debater. By the end of the year he had helped win several major debates; in addition, he had competed in the annual senior speaking contest and placed second. True to the American success-story pattern, he had gone from rags to riches.

Al's success was attained not merely by working hard in debating practice or in the classroom, though he did work determinedly in both. Actually, he worked every time he opened his mouth to speak. He learned to think about what he was saying and how he said it. He learned to listen to his pronunciation, to the grammar he used, to the very sounds he made. He suffered intensely from self-consciousness for a time, of course, but as his speaking experience increased, his self-consciousness faded.

It is not surprising that Al places great value on his speech training. As he is the first to admit, his later success as a businessman would have been impossible without it. It is all right to talk like a pug in the ring, but where else?

You almost certainly do not talk like a pug. Almost as certainly you have few, if any, of Al's handicaps. What he did you can do more easily, but not without work. If you are as determined as he was to succeed, you will succeed—that is, if you will try as he did.

With the resolve to pitch in and work, you are off to a healthy start in this course. You start by setting goals for yourself, with the knowledge that you can make definite progress toward those goals. But you expect no royal road, no mysterious secret, no bag of tricks, no snap course. You expect to get out of it just what you put into it. Speechmaking is a complex mixture of attitudes, knowledge, and skill, and progress must be earned.

## Public speaking as enlarged conversation

An important contribution to speech education was made when J. A. Winans, many years ago, reminded his colleagues that there are no fundamental differences between conversation and public speaking. Suppose, he suggested, you and one of your friends arrive early for a class. Your friend has just returned from a trip with the football team and begins telling you about the big intersectional game. This, you would say, is a conversation. As he talks two more members of the class arrive and join you in listening to the account of the game. Let us imagine that others continue to arrive by twos and threes and that all are eager to get the exciting details. Your friend is so engrossed in his story that as more students join the group he simply raises his voice and continues to talk. Now at what point does your friend's report cease to be conversation and become a speech? Would it be when the fifth person joins the group? Or the tenth, the thirteenth, the twenty-fifth? Obviously, there is no arbitrary point at which the change occurs.

**1. DIFFERENCES BETWEEN PUBLIC SPEAKING AND CONVERSATION** Consider the photographs on pages 12 through 14. Notice the progressive sequence from the conversation between the two students by the window to the public address at a political convention. Are there fundamental differences among these speech situations?

The most obvious difference is the increasing number of people. As we have already seen, however, the increase is not really fundamental. An audience comprises one or more persons. The pictures are alike, then, in that all contain audiences, although of different sizes.

*When does conversation become public speaking?*

Two students are chatting between classes. This is conversation. • Next you see four students enjoying a coffee break. Is this still a conversation? • A professor conducts a seminar of eight students. Is it still conversation? • A professor conducts an informal class of sixteen students who often interrupt with questions or comments. When the professor or a student talks, is he conversing or is he making a speech?

COLBY COLLEGE

FREDERICK WILLIAMS

UNIVERSITY OF SOUTHERN CALIFORNIA

NEW YORK UNIVERSITY

A citizen expresses his views during a New England town meeting. Is he conversing or is he making a speech? • A major address is being given at a national political convention. You would probably say that this is a clear example of making a public speech.

STANDARD OIL

*Consider the preceding six photographs in sequence. When does conversation turn into public speaking?*

With an increase in size of the group, a speaker will probably talk louder and slower. Likewise, the seating arrangements will probably be changed in order to make it easier for the speaker to be seen and heard. But these differences are neither inevitable nor profound.

In the first and second photographs all the members of the groups talk and listen alternately. By the time we reach the last picture one person is doing most of the talking.

We might go on to suggest other variables: the situations tend to become more formal, audience interests more varied, speaker preparation more thorough. All the foregoing variables are in terms of *more* or *less* and so they give added support to the proposition that the differences between conversation and public speaking are differences of degree only, not of kind.

**2. RESEMBLANCES BETWEEN PUBLIC SPEAKING AND CONVERSATION**   All speaking situations, such as those illustrated by the photographs, have the fundamental characteristics described in our definition of speech. In each situation thought and emotion are communicated by speaker to listener through the same media (light and sound waves) and by the same techniques (voice, language, and bodily action). Or, to use a traditional classification, each speaking situation includes: a speaker, a speech, an audience, and an occasion.

Understanding public speaking as enlarged conversation provides you with the best possible basic approach to learning public speaking. You are not taking this course to learn to perform some new or strange or frightening activity. You are here to learn to enlarge your conversation. Now, at your best, you are already probably a pretty good conversationalist. Think over a few conversations where you know you were most effective. Would it not be relatively easy to duplicate that effectiveness in a slightly larger or more formal group—say, a committee meeting or panel discussion? It certainly would be *if* you could just retain a conversational attitude while at the same time making a few adaptations. Stop thinking in terms of making a speech, and begin thinking in terms of talking with a group of your fellows. Begin now to pay attention to your daily conversations and to use them as a laboratory for practice. Search out opportunities to serve on committees or to join with small discussion groups. Approach the study of public speaking as a gradual process, beginning with good conversation, and progressing by natural stages through other less familiar speech situations. As Henry Ford once remarked, "Nothing is particularly difficult if you divide it into small jobs."

Not only does the conversational approach help us visualize a natural and gradual way of learning public speaking, but it also sets useful standards.

Most of the characteristics of good conversation are also the characteristics of good public speaking: animation, directness, and interesting ideas.

## Public speaking as communication

In our definition of speech (page 5) the key word was *communication*. The most important implication of this term is that speaking and listening combine to form the process. To show how they do we may roughly summarize the principal steps in a complete act of oral communication.

1. THE ACT OF ORAL COMMUNICATION   *a. The speaker has an idea.* Somebody has to have an idea to begin with—otherwise there is nothing to communicate. So the process starts with neural impulses racing about in the prospective speaker's brain and nervous system. From his entire storehouse of thoughts and emotions he must choose that portion he wishes to communicate. If his thinking is confused, or if his choice of what to say is poor, he is foredoomed to failure.

*b. The speaker puts the idea into words.* Having selected an idea to be communicated, the prospective speaker must next translate it into words. He is confronted with the fact that any idea can be expressed in different ways. None of these ways can correspond precisely to his idea because words are not the actual things or experiences—words only stand for them. So he chooses what he hopes will be the best possible set of words. If his choice is poor, the communication process is going to be disturbed.

*c. The speaker transmits.* Next the speaker uses vocal and other physical movements to put sound waves and light waves into motion. These may reach the listener directly, or they may be transmitted electronically by such means as television, radio, or telephone.

At this juncture it will be instructive to recall the common misconceptions, described earlier in this chapter, that speechmaking is primarily self-expression, or display, or an isolated act. According to such a viewpoint, vocalization concludes the process, or is, at least, the last step of any importance. Just how much is overlooked or slighted by that viewpoint is suggested by the remaining items of our analysis.

*d. The listener hears and sees.* Now the listener joins the process. The sound and light waves impinge on sensory receptors so that the listener hears and sees. If the speaker does not speak loudly enough or if his bodily action is inadequate the communicative process may suffer a breakdown at this stage.

*e. The listener perceives.* Assuming that he is able to hear the words or see the bodily actions, the listener attaches meaning to them. Probably he can never attach exactly the same meaning to the symbols as the speaker does. So we know that the speaker's idea is not "delivered" as a parcel is delivered, nor is it transferred from one brain to the other, nor does the speaker's thought become the listener's. What happens can be more accurately described as the arousing or stirring up of thought. The speaker hopes that the thought thus aroused in the listener will correspond approximately to the thought that he expressed.

*f. The listener reacts.* In a conversation or group discussion the listener is likely to react promptly by talking. In a public speaking situation the audience's reactions are not so readily apparent, but they are there just the same. Listeners may smile, laugh, applaud, nod, or yawn. If a speaker is oblivious to such clues, or misinterprets them, he is not likely to communicate effectively.

*g. The speaker responds to the listeners' reactions.* A good conversationalist is a responsive listener and constantly adapts his remarks to the responses of his listeners, and so does a good public speaker. While speaking he "listens" to his audience mostly with his eyes and "hears" them reply through their facial expressions, movements, or lack of movements. He adapts his whole mood and manner to them.

Think back over the act of oral communication. Apply the seven steps to the last conversation you heard, and to the last class lecture. Do not be satisfied with merely learning them. Instead, learn to think in terms of them.

2. THE COMMUNICATIVE ATTITUDE   A speaker has a communicative attitude when he thinks of himself and his listeners as participating in a single group. He does not think in terms of "they, the audience" and "I, the speaker." He has the "you and I" attitude toward each speaking situation. When you are speaking you want your listeners to feel that they are as much a part of the process as you are. You want to create the feeling that "all of us here are thinking this through together." The ability to heighten the listeners' awareness of their participation may be termed *communicativeness.*

If a speaker has a communicative attitude it will always show. His whole mood and manner will reveal it in a dozen unconscious ways. For example, he will tend to choose and prepare his subject matter with the idea of having something to share. While he is speaking his bodily alertness, his facial expression, and the variations in his voice will all be subtly improved if he speaks for communication. In addition to relying on these unconscious signs, however, a speaker can deliberately practice two specific sets of speaking habits to enhance his communicativeness. The first of these is *eye contact* (often called directness); the second is *references to audience.*

*a. Eye contact.* Beginning speakers often try to avoid the eyes of their listeners. Instead of looking at the audience, they keep their eyes glued to their notes, the floor, the walls, or the ceiling. Consider, for example, the pictures on pages 9 (left), 19 (left), and 21. For illustrations of effective eye contact study the pictures on pages 9 (right), 19 (right), and 20.

In general, the rule is this: While you are speaking maintain direct eye contact with your listeners, looking from one individual to another, unless you have reasons for looking elsewhere. Usually you should look about slowly; if your eyes keep darting rapidly from place to place, the effect may seem furtive or shifty. If the audience is fairly large or scattered, be careful to include persons from all parts of the group. Do not form the habit of concentrating most of your attention on one side of the room, for instance, or on just the first rows.

On some occasions, of course, there is good reason for looking away from your audience. Perhaps you are describing a tall building; so you look upward as a gesture to convey the effect of height. Perhaps you are telling a story and you wish to mimic somebody whose eyes were downcast or glazed. Perhaps you want to cite statistics or give a quotation, and to emphasize your accuracy, you may read from your notes. Thus communicativeness does not require that you should never look away from your audience.

Some students complain that catching someone's eye distracts them and causes them to forget what they are saying. The answer is: It all depends upon what you are used to doing. If you form the habit of maintaining eye contact, it seems distracting *not* to catch the listeners' eyes.

*b. References to audience.* Show your awareness of the audience's participation by mentioning it from time to time. Such references may take a variety of forms. You should adapt the expression of your own ideas in terms of your listeners' reactions. "Before the meeting I was talking with several members of your outfit and they convinced me that the . . ." "I see that some of you are looking puzzled—let me put my point another way. . . ." Sometimes you should refer to the name or the activities of the group. "I do not have to stress the importance of service to you members of Rotary. . . ." Sometimes you can even call individual members of the audience by name. "During dinner I was introduced to Dr. Kenneth Shanks, chairman of your membership committee, who told me that . . ." In your speech class it is good practice to name individuals occasionally. "Miss Williamson, you are an education major, and this means . . ." "As we all heard the other day, Fred Bowman loves trout fishing, so he will be especially interested to know that . . ." In general, it is wise to word your ideas in terms of "you and I," "we," "us," "our," "as you know," "let's think about this together," and the like.

Franklin D. Roosevelt was acknowledged, even by his political enemies, to have been the most effective American speaker of his generation. When trying to characterize his effectiveness, people often used the term "communicativeness." When he was talking in person to individuals or small groups, President Roosevelt was noted for his eye contact, facial animation (he was the news photographers' delight), and variety of voice. He retained his communicative qualities even when addressing huge crowds or broadcasting to millions via radio. This was shown not only in all aspects of his delivery, but also in his choice of ideas and illustrations and in his choice of words, especially in his audience references. Study the following typical excerpts from Roosevelt speeches.

. . . for I propose to follow my custom of speaking frankly to the nation concerning our common problems. . . .

We gave warning last November that we had only just begun to fight. Did some people really believe that we did not mean it? Well, I meant it, and you meant it. . . .

You and I owe it to ourselves individually, as a party and as a nation, to remove those doubts and difficulties. . . .

. . . to me, and I am sure to you. . . .

FREDERICK WILLIAMS R. GRAVES

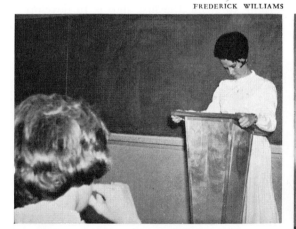

This undergraduate is notebound. She does not give her audience a sense of participation.

This graduate student talks directly to her audience. Her eyes seem to speak.

I feel a kinship between your business and mine. The backbone of the customers we are both trying to satisfy is the same. . . .

If I have spoken to you seriously tonight, it is because I believe that you too, are thinking of . . .

That is why I came to you . . . with a simple plea for your assistance . . . in working out our common problems. . . .

## Methods of studying speech

Your speech class will differ in several ways from most of your other courses. For example, in this class the students, rather than the instructor, will do most of the talking. Learning will be through expression more than impression. Emphasis will be more on practice than on theory. Probably this class will be smaller than your others; you will get to know your fellow students better. You will learn to give and take constructive personal criticism. Emphasis will be placed on your individual problems. For you the subject matter will be not just speech, but *your* speech. And you will learn to collaborate with the instructor in teaching yourself.

In many respects the task of learning public speaking may be compared with learning to swim. In learning to swim, the first step is to develop a liking for the water. If you have a fear of the water, you must overcome that

WAYNE DAVIS

In a speech class the students, rather than the instructor, do most of the talking.

fear. Thus in learning to swim the first stage is likely to be simply getting into the shallow end of the pool in order to become accustomed to the water. With greater confidence and a desire to learn, you might well consider three main helps: first, you might read a book about swimming; second, you might get a competent coach; third, you might watch other people swimming. All the steps just mentioned would be useful, but they would not necessarily teach you to swim. The final and essential step is *practice*.

It should be noted immediately, however, that while practice is the essential step, it should not be the only one. Anyone who undertakes to teach himself to swim by the single method of just practicing will take a long time to learn, will have unnecessary difficulties, and will acquire a good many bad swimming habits. He will have learned all right—learned to be a poor swimmer! If he wants to become a good one, he will have to start again, unlearn the bad habits, and *practice with guidance* as he systematically substitutes new habits for the old.

The major steps, outlined above, apply equally well to the learning process for public speaking.

## Reading

You will be expected to read this text not as something to be memorized in order to answer examination questions, but as a guide for your speaking practice. You will also be expected to do appropriate reading in order to

You improve your speech by watching
your classmates speaking.

FENWICK ENGLISH

**21**

prepare the subject matter for some of your talks. Finally, you should learn to read critically the texts of important current speeches, as reported in newspapers and periodicals.

## Observation

You will find that the thoughtful observation of others' speaking will provide many examples of what to do and what not to do. Look for such examples among your fellow students in campus speaking situations. Look for examples as you listen to more experienced speakers. Make use of the opportunities for observation provided by radio, television, motion pictures, and phonograph recordings.

## Criticism

You will expect to receive personal criticism in this course from your instructor and from your fellow students. You will take criticisms with a receptive

Not practice alone but *guided* practice is the most important method for learning better speech.

FENWICK ENGLISH

attitude, evaluate them thoughtfully, and be guided by them as you prepare your next talk.

As you progress you must become your own best critic. You must develop objectivity and insight. You must not condemn yourself when you have done your best. You must be willing, however, to face up to weaknesses or mistakes, and immediately plan how to correct these faults. A tremendous help in the development of self-criticism is the use of voice-recording equipment, which is now available to most students, and motion pictures if they can be utilized.

## Practice

You will have a chance to participate in a series of interesting speech projects in this course. But do not restrict your practice to the speech classroom. Articulation and pronunciation, for example, can best be practiced in conversation. If you are a member of extracurricular groups, seize every opportunity to speak before those groups for practice.

You will remind yourself, however, that practice is wasteful or even harmful unless it is guided and purposive. It is more accurate to say that practice makes permanent, rather than perfect. Therefore your reading, observation, and criticism should guide your practice.

## Summary

Early in the study of speech you will want to eliminate the misconceptions you may have and substitute constructive attitudes. For example, there is no simple secret in learning public speaking; progress must be earned. Public speaking is not isolated from normal activities; it is simply enlarged conversation. Public speaking is not an exhibition; it is communication. Thus in the future do not ask, "Did I make a good speech?" Say rather, "Did I communicate?" or better yet, "What did I communicate?"

In improving your speech the most important learning method is guided practice. Guidance is secured through a combination of reading, observation, and personal criticism.

## TOPICAL PREVIEW

I   The problem of stage fright

    A   How prevalent?

    B   How serious?

    C   How difficult?

II   Control of stage fright

III   A practice speaking program

    A   On days prior to the speech

    B   On the day of the speech

    C   While speaking

IV   The program in practice

    A   In class

    B   Outside class

    C   The right attitude

V   Summary

# 2

## GAINING CONFIDENCE AND POISE

### The problem of stage fright

*How prevalent?*

Early one semester a former combat flyer stood before his speech class for the first time and began sweating it out. He was a healthy, athletic-looking fellow but in obvious distress. He avoided looking at the audience, his knees shook, perspiration popped out on his forehead, and his words came haltingly. Finally, he bogged down completely; his mind went blank. With a stricken look he turned toward his instructor, and for all the world like a frightened child he said "Dr. Knox, I'm scared." Some of this student's friends later revealed that during the war he had flown on more than fifty combat missions and had been twice decorated for bravery.

The flyer's experience supports the common view that stage fright is a sort of universal disease uniting all men in a brotherhood of misery. A humorist knows the audience will appreciate it when he prefaces a speech with, "The human mind is a wonderful thing; it starts working at the moment of birth and never stops until we get up to deliver a speech." If you do not find stage fright a serious personal problem, you will read this chapter with only academic interest. If you are like most beginners, however, you will want a thorough treatment of the subject. You will want to know what scientific research has taught us about the causes, and you will cer-

This young lady talks animatedly with her friend because her mind is on her subject and her audience. If she thought she were "making a speech," she might freeze up, becoming stilted and nervous.

tainly want to know what experienced public speakers have to say about the cure.

If you are bothered by the expectation of stage fright, you have plenty of company. For example, Buehler gave a list of "elements which make for effective speaking" to 493 students about to begin a speech course. He asked them to rank the elements in order of importance—"self-confidence" was ranked first.[1] Baird and Knower surveyed various college groups, and reported that 60 to 75 per cent admitted their nervousness and 30 to 35 per cent of them considered it a serious problem.[2] Gilkinson gave a questionnaire to 420 beginning speech students and found that most of them answered "yes" to a variety of statements describing common stage-fright symptoms; only 6 per cent said that speaking was "a pleasurable experience unaccompanied by any fears or doubts."[3] Dickens and Parker secured pulse and blood pressure readings immediately before and immediately after two classroom speeches by fifty men and fifty women in a beginning college course. Approximately 94 per cent of all the readings showed fluctuations.[4]

Thus the problem of stage fright is common to most beginning speakers. It is usually a perfectly natural and normal response to a new, complex, and challenging social situation.

## How serious?

There are at least three ways of describing stage fright: how the speaker feels (confidence); how he looks and sounds to the audience (poise); and how his neuromuscular and glandular system behaves (physiological reaction). In Clevenger's words, "These may be thought of as the amount of fright a speaker says he has,[5] the amount his audience says he has, and the amount a meter says he has."

Dickens, Gibson, and Prall arranged for forty male college students whose speech experience and training varied greatly to give short speeches before an audience of sixty-one speech teachers. The teachers were asked to judge each student by marking a five-step rating scale which ranged from "virtually no observable degree of stage fright" through "extreme degree of stage fright." The students were asked to fill out a subjective inventory con-

[1] E. C. Buehler and Wil A. Linkugel, *Speech: A First Course*, Harper, 1962, pp. 388–91.
[2] A. Craig Baird and Franklin H. Knower, *General Speech*, McGraw-Hill, 1949.
[3] Howard Gilkinson, "A Questionnaire Study of the Causes of Social Fears Among College Speech Students," *Speech Monographs*, Vol. X (1943); also "Social Fears As Reported by Students in College Speech Classes," *Speech Monographs*, Vol. IX (1942).
[4] Milton Dickens and William R. Parker, "An Experimental Study of Certain Physiological, Introspective and Rating-Scale Techniques for the Measurement of Stage Fright," *Speech Monographs*, Vol. XVIII (November 1951).
[5] Theodore Clevenger, Jr., "A Synthesis of Experimental Research in Stage Fright," *The Quarterly Journal of Speech*, Vol. XLV (April 1959).

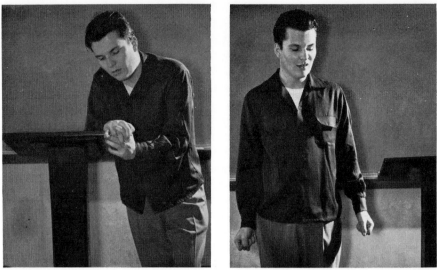

Here are two pictures taken during a classroom talk near the beginning of the course. As you might guess the student had no previous speech training. Now look at the photographs at the bottom of the next page.

sisting of 104 statements, each describing a common symptom of stage fright or of confidence. When the judges' ratings (one way of measuring poise) were statistically compared with the personal reports by the speakers (one way of measuring confidence), it was found that the two were related but by no means identical. Detailed comparisons revealed that the teachers overestimated the students' confidence more frequently than they underestimated it. In other words, you are likely to appear more poised than you feel, even when judged by experts.[6]

Dickens and Parker had fifty male and fifty female speakers fill out subject inventories after speaking, had classmates rate them for poise, and took pulse and blood pressure readings (one way of measuring physiological reaction of the speakers). They found that all three measurements were positively related but capable of wide independent variations. For example, your heart can pound faster without your necessarily feeling more fearful; furthermore, you will probably make a better speech in this condition than you would if your pulse remained completely placid.

These research results show that most beginning students are inclined to exaggerate the seriousness of the problem of stage fright. This fact was

[6] Milton Dickens, Francis Gibson, and Caleb Prall, "An Experimental Study of the Overt Manifestations of Stage Fright," *Speech Monographs,* Vol. XVII (March 1950).

vividly illustrated by a student who gave a talk during the third week of the term and afterwards wryly remarked, "Many a man has died feeling better than I did." Yet his was one of the best talks the class had thus far heard. His fellow students were marking a criticism chart, and they were unanimous in checking one item—"poised." Two months later the same student said, "I'm beginning to believe that stage fright is a blessing in disguise. I make a better speech when I come to class scared."

### How difficult?

Over two thousand years ago Plutarch recorded that when Demosthenes, the most famous orator of ancient Greece, first addressed the people he was afflicted by "weakness in his voice, a perplexed and indistinct utterance and a shortness of breath. . . . So that in the end, being quite disheartened, he forsook the assembly." And Cicero, most famous of the ancient Roman orators, confessed through the words of Crassus:

> Assuredly, just as I generally perceive it to happen to yourselves, so I very often prove it in my own experience, that I turn pale at the outset of every speech, and quake in every limb and in all my soul.

R. GRAVES

Here are two pictures of the same student shown on the preceding page. These were taken during the last two weeks of the course. Such improvement in poise and confidence is common in speech classes.

Similar testimony has been added throughout the subsequent centuries by famous speakers, actors, musicians, and other public performers. Contrary to popular belief, however, these testimonies appear to be the exceptions. Modern research indicates that very few prominent and experienced speakers regularly suffer severe stage fright.

Knisely, using a controlled interview technique, studied the stage-fright experiences of sixty highly experienced and successful speakers, all nationally prominent people. He found that fourteen of them (23.3 per cent) never experience stage fright.[7] Wrenchley, in an entirely independent study, probed the careers of thirty other experienced speakers and reported that seven (also 23.3 per cent!) had no stage fright.[8] Furthermore, Knisely found that of those who experienced stage fright the great majority described it as a mild nervous tension which disappeared soon after the beginning of a talk. Only three or four of the sixty could be said to find stage fright a difficult problem. They too, of course, were going ahead with regular and successful speaking engagements.

Knisely's study revealed an overwhelming trend toward diminution of stage fright as the speakers gained experience—a marked decline in both frequency and severity of occurrences. Three speakers (5 per cent) believed that they had never experienced any stage fright. Of the remaining fifty-seven, fifty reported that their fright had definitely declined. Of the remaining seven, four judged that their fright had never been severe. Only three felt that their fright was seriously distressing and had not improved. None, however, reported an increase in current severity or frequency of stage fright over that of his earlier speaking. Said Knisely:

> The one clear-cut and positive trend was that in fifty cases of the fifty-seven who had earlier experienced the problem, stage fright disappeared or diminished after the beginning of regular and frequent "practical" speaking careers. This phenomenon tended to occur regardless of the other known variables. In most cases, the results were reported as having occurred within less than a year after the beginning of intensive speaking series.

For many years speech teachers have occasionally conducted anonymous polls at the conclusion of speech classes to discover, among other things, how many students had gained confidence and poise. Favorable responses of from 60 to 90 per cent have always been found. The same results have

[7] Wade A. Knisely, "An Investigation of the Phenomenon of Stage Fright in Certain Prominent Speakers," unpublished doctoral dissertation, University of Southern California, 1950.
[8] Elma D. Wrenchley, "A Study of Stage Fright Attacks in a Selected Group of Experienced Speakers," unpublished Master's thesis, University of Denver, 1948.

been reported by members of organizations such as the Toastmaster and Toastmistress Clubs, where the members have banded together for the purpose of practicing public speaking without the regular guidance of professional teachers. Some of these many classes and clubs have practiced stage-fright therapies based on one theory, others based on another theory or combination of theories, and some have made no conscious effort to deal with stage fright at all; but they all provided opportunity for regular speaking practice. The key to the problem is repeated successful practice. But "successful" talks must be carefully prepared and rehearsed in advance. As Robinson says, "Confidence in and of itself is no substitute for good preparation and practice." [9]

Students frequently testify that in the beginning they overestimated the difficulty of the problem of stage fright. One such student is shown in the "before" and "after" candid camera shots on pages 28–29. The "before" pictures were taken during the first week of a semester; the "after," during the last week. He was asked at the first class meeting what he hoped to gain from the course, and he replied, "The most important thing is to learn to stand before an audience without being petrified." After giving his final speech, he exclaimed, "Four months ago I wouldn't have believed I could possibly do it!"

So, how difficult is the conquest of stage fright? Only as difficult as you make it.

## The control of stage fright

Before gaining much actual experience, some youthful would-be orators enjoy daydreams as charming as those in James Thurber's "The Secret Life of Walter Mitty." They envision some happy day when they will stride coolly and confidently before a huge and unruly crowd, deliver an eloquent address, and stand unmoved during the tremendous ovation that follows. With growing experience, however, they will learn that such a complete absence of emotion tends to make the speaker careless, listless, condescending, colorless, or dull. Speaking experience will teach you that a certain amount of the right kind of tension is helpful.

In visualizing yourself as you will become by the end of this course, you should picture a person who has made great strides in emotional adjustment while facing an audience. You will feel more confident. You will appear more poised. Do *not* visualize yourself as strolling nonchalantly in front of a group and addressing them with no more tension than you would feel

[9] Edward R. Robinson, "What Can the Speech Teacher Do about Students' Stage-fright?" *The Speech Teacher,* Vol. VIII (January 1959).

in saying, "Good morning," to your family as you join them for breakfast. Such a goal is possible but undesirable.

You want to *control* stage fright, not to eliminate it. You will learn to put your emotions to work, not to stifle them. Your nervous and emotional tension will be like the steam in a boiler. You will learn to release it so that it will give your speaking greater drive or punch.

Control involves more than a reduction of the frequency and severity of stage fright. There must be a qualitative change as well. It is difficult to express this change in written words, but we may suggest it by saying that, over a period of time, the before-speaking sensations undergo a transition from a feeling of panic to a feeling of being keyed up. This keyed-up feeling may be unpleasant or pleasant or a mixture of both. The speaker is unafraid; he notes his inner tensions objectively and with satisfaction, knowing they will make him more alert, more vigorous, and more dynamic. He knows that soon after getting his speech under way he will forget these tensions, and he may even experience an over-all sense of exhilaration.

Thus your objective in this class is not to become immune to the stimulus of an audience, but to develop emotional control. This objective may be usefully subdivided into three specific goals: (1) to effect a transition from the feeling of fear or panic to one of being keyed up; (2) to prevent the tension from becoming too severe immediately before speaking; (3) to learn how to release the tension effectively after the speech has begun.

## A practice speaking program

Having made a preliminary analysis of the problem, and having visualized the three goals, you will next want to plan a detailed and systematic program. Such a program comprises specific procedures, many of which have been successfully used by public speakers for centuries, and many of which you should make habitual by practice. You will, of course, adapt the following suggestions to your particular needs.

### On days prior to the speech

*1. Choose an interesting subject.* It is important to have something to say. Do you believe deeply in some cause? Why not make an honest plea for it? Have you come across information that has been of invaluable help to you? Why not share it with your classmates? If you can find a subject in which you are so interested that you are able to lose yourself in it, your stage-fright problem is whipped for that particular speech.

*2. Know your subject thoroughly.* Some insidious siren seems to beckon beginning speakers to the *Reader's Digest* for speech subjects and then impels them to limit their study of the subject to that one condensed article. The *Reader's Digest* was never intended for such use. Do not try to give a digest of a digest. In the beginning speak only about subjects upon which you have a background of personal experience. Personal experience should often be reinforced by additional study; for you want to begin your speech knowing more about your subject than anyone else present, and knowing that you know it. Naturally you should not try to tell everything you know in one short talk; but confidence springs from the very fact that you couldn't possibly tell all you know on the subject in the time allowed. One of the highest compliments anyone can pay a speaker is to say that he certainly knows what he's talking about. It is within your power to earn that compliment.

Begin your preparation early. Do not wait until a vacant period just before your speech class. Do not tire yourself by working far into the preceding night. You should give yourself several days for your speech so that your thinking on the subject will have time to mature. Talk about your subject with your friends; think about it while riding the bus; give it a chance to grow.

*3. Learn the idea sequence of your talk.* Out of all you know about a subject, you must make choices of which items to discard, which to use. Once chosen, the points must be arranged in sequence. Write them on a card and study them. You will soon learn that you cannot get lost as long as this card is available. It becomes your first important protection against the beginner's usual fear, "What if I should forget?"

*4. Practice aloud.* It is sometimes hard to convince a beginner that the best way to prevent forgetting is *not* to memorize. He thinks he would feel a lot safer if he wrote the entire speech and committed it to memory. Actually, that is the hard way. It stands to reason that if a set of words has not been memorized, it cannot be forgotten—there are no words to forget. "But," you object, "if I don't memorize, I won't be able to say anything." Actually, it doesn't work out that way.

Here is what you should do. Prepare your card with the sequence of ideas on it. Go to your room (or any place suitable for practicing aloud), and start talking that speech. You can simply talk to yourself or, as shown by the pictures on page 59, you may get a friend to listen, or you may even rig up something to remind you of an audience. Develop each of the ideas in the sequence. Talk loud enough so that you become used to your own voice. Give the entire speech. Perhaps when the ideas are spoken, they will not seem effectively arranged. If not, make the necessary changes. Then give the speech aloud again from the beginning. Do not try to use the same words you used before. In fact, it is good practice to try to use different words. On the second or third trial, time yourself. Keep on practicing aloud whenever you have a few minutes and a convenient place. You will use the card to guide you at first, but presently you will find that you hardly need refer to the notes. Practice in this fashion until you find that, within your time limit, you can cover all the points without a serious hitch. If it will ease your mind at first, write out and memorize the opening sentence and the closing thought. You are then ready.

## On the day of the speech

*1. Chat with others.* If you are scheduled to speak in class today, come a bit early and sit down next to an acquaintance. Talk with him and keep your mind off your speech. Talk with people as they arrive. Keep your mind on them. Such talk will remind you that public speaking is simply enlarged conversation. Chat with friends individually or in small groups before you make your talk; you will do exactly the same thing a little later when you make it.

*2. Concentrate on the proceedings.* When the class or the meeting comes to order, there will be remarks by the instructor or chairman, and possibly by other speakers, before you are introduced. Follow these proceedings with interest. Pay attention and be genuinely absorbed in what is said and done. Above all, watch carefully for something that you can use as part of your opening remarks. This watching serves a dual purpose. It keeps your mind off yourself, preventing the build-up of undue tension, and it provides you with the best possible type of opening remarks.

*3. Stretch and yawn.* If you feel "butterflies" fluttering during this period, watch for an opportunity to stretch. The muscles of the arms, shoulders, and neck can always be tensed and relaxed energetically in this fashion without attracting attention. And usually it is possible to yawn once or twice surreptitiously behind your hand or handkerchief. Yawning relaxes the jaws and throat, and will improve your voice quality when you begin.

*4. Breathe slowly and regularly.* You can always force yourself to breathe slowly, a little more deeply than usual, and *regularly*. Regular breathing results in a notable calming effect on the whole body.

*5. Walk to the platform confidently.* When you have been called upon or introduced, do not drag toward the platform as if it were a scaffold, but walk briskly. Regardless of how you think you feel, walk as though you were completely poised and confident.

*6. Pause before starting.* Approach the spot from which you plan to speak so that your last step will be toward the audience. Then pause, take a comfortable stance, look directly at one or two friends or acquaintances in the group, smile at them, and greet the audience.

## While speaking

*1. Look at individuals.* Do not try to look at your audience as a whole; keep on looking at and talking to the several individuals whom you know —possibly the same ones with whom you were chatting just before the meeting. Talk loud enough to be heard but make the talk enlarged conversation.

*2. Move about.* Plan to move about a good deal during the first minute or so. Find easy, natural things to do. Readjust the speaker's stand; open and close a book; if you can make use of a simple chart, walk to the chalkboard and draw one; use gestures to describe the shape or size of some object you have mentioned. The best way to relax is through purposeful physical action. Do not forget to use it. During the first one or two talks, if it will make you feel at home, lounge upon the speaker's stand. Of course, you will want to discard such crutches as soon as possible, but at first get rid of pent-up energy. Don't allow yourself to "freeze."

*3. Concentrate on your subject and audience.* Your major purpose is to communicate your ideas as effectively as possible. Keep talking to and watching your listeners as you do in conversation. Here is where your oral practice pays off; it makes it possible for you to concentrate on the thoughts instead of on the words.

FREDERICK WILLIAMS

This student is giving a good talk to an off-campus group, but he should release some of his tension by moving about a bit.

*4. If for any reason your mind goes blank, you are still all right.* First, repeat your last statement. Usually the repetition will put you back on the track of your thought. Second, if you are still lost consult your notes; consult them deliberately and then go ahead. Third, don't be afraid to take the audience into your confidence—as a last resort, grin at them and say, "Well I'm stuck. I had something planned to say at this point but just can't remember it. I guess all of you have been in the same boat at some time." Then repeat your last statement again or jump to your prepared conclusion. Usually you can go on talking conversationally until the thread of your thought returns. When an experienced speaker forgets, he is not disturbed. He is likely to say, "Let's see now, there was something else I wanted to say about this matter . . . Oh yes, it was . . ." You will learn by experience that forgetting is not a serious problem.

## The program in practice

### In class

As you have already seen, the best way to control stage fright is by regular practice. Your public speaking class provides you with the necessary guinea pigs, and with the opportunity to become gradually accustomed to facing an audience. Attend every class meeting, get wholeheartedly into the spirit of it, and carry out each assignment with enthusiasm. If everyone in a class is responsive, friendly, and sympathetic to others' speeches, a group spirit develops. When it does, learning how to speak becomes fun.

NBC

Here is an intercollegiate debate, one of a series televised nationally by NBC. You learn to control stage fright by speaking frequently in situations of gradually increasing difficulty.

## Outside class

You will build confidence and poise better and faster by speaking as often as time permits. As soon as you feel ready, try your wings on other audiences. Perhaps you can give an oral report before another class, or a talk before a campus club or a church group. Going out and searching for speaking opportunities will give you poise.

## The right attitude

With the help of this chapter, you should be able to think through your problem of stage fright. If you are still in doubt, talk it over with your instructor and one or two friends whose opinions you value. As soon as possible visualize your goals and set yourself a program. When these decisions have been made, *let them alone!* Stop thinking about your problems and sensations; just go ahead with your program—keep your mind on that. Do not worry about your every reaction until you become morbid. Worry will not help; thinking about your program will. Once you have embarked upon your journey, don't look back.

## Summary

The conquest of stage fright begins with an understanding that stage fright is a common and normal experience, that beginners tend to exaggerate the seriousness and difficulty of the problem, and that the key to the problem is frequent and regular practice. Stage fright is overcome by setting an attainable goal, planning a systematic program, and putting the program into practice. The speaker should try to control rather than stifle his emotional response to an audience. The program should outline procedures to be followed during the advance speech preparation, immediately before speaking, and while speaking. The procedures should be practiced not only in the speech class but also before as many other groups as possible.

## TOPICAL PREVIEW

# 3

# TAKING PART IN GROUP DISCUSSION

## "Thinking independently together"

Participation in group discussions such as panels in the classroom is an excellent way to get started in the study of public speaking. Such practice not only alleviates stage fright but helps bridge the gap between daily conversations and speeches before larger audiences. Thus small-group discussion provides a living illustration of the fact that public speaking should be viewed as enlarged conversation. Furthermore, group discussion develops a communicative attitude because of the direct and immediate give-and-take among the participants. Finally, group discussion provides a lesson in democratic citizenship, a lesson which was gracefully expressed by Alexander Meikeljohn, "So far as minds are concerned, democracy is the art of thinking independently together."

Group discussion is often defined in terms of what it ought to be, rather than in terms of what it actually is. Thus group discussion ought to be a device by which several persons pool their knowledge. They may, however, merely pool their ignorance. Discussion ought to be a process of cooperative deliberation, but frequently it is neither cooperative nor deliberative. Discussion ought to exemplify the process of reflective thinking, but often it is dominated by highly emotional thinking. Discussion ought to be an unbiased search for the truth, but many times it is a political maneuver to put something across. Discussion ought to be a technique for securing joint agreement on the solution of common problems. It may instead become a process wherein unnecessary antagonisms are bred and avoidable stalemates achieved. Discussion should rise to the level of the best minds in the group, but it may fall to the level of the poorest. These difficulties in group discussion should not be concealed. They should be frankly faced so that the student may learn to do what is efficient and ethical, yet also learn to detect and to counteract what is inefficient or unethical.

Time does not permit giving a short course in group discussion as a part of a beginning class in basic speech. In fact, you may decide to take an entire semester or year of work in discussion and conference leadership later in your college career. Therefore, in this course, group discussion will not be treated in detail or as an end in itself, but will be presented as a stepping stone toward the practice of public speaking. One virtue of this approach is the fact that you participate so frequently in so many different types of group discussion.

Group discussion provides a lesson in democratic citizenship.

## Types of discussion

If group discussions are classified on the basis of the major purposes for which discussions are held, three broad categories emerge: social groups, educational groups, and problem-solving groups.

A social group gathers for the purposes of recreation, enjoyment, and entertainment. You have participated in many discussions of this type: dinner parties, visits with friends, bull sessions, teas, receptions, coffee hours. You have also enjoyed such entertaining discussion programs on TV as "What's My Line?" and similar panels on radio, such as the old-time favorite "Information Please."

The purpose of an educational group is to investigate, to give or get information, and to understand. You have participated in class discussions, study groups, and open forums. You may have attended a public hearing conducted by a Board of Education, or you may have observed the workings of a congressional investigating committee. You may have heard of "group dynamics"

You participate almost daily in social group discussions.

FREDERICK WILLIAMS

**41**

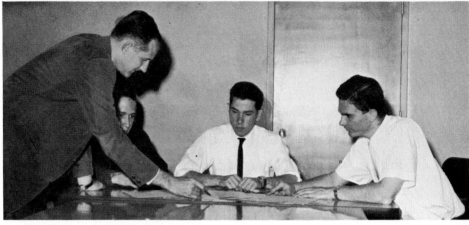

Most of your instructors use group discussion as a teaching-learning method.

or "group therapy" where discussion is used to help people develop better personal attitudes or gain insight into their mental and emotional troubles. Some specific examples of this approach: role playing, psychodrama, sociodrama, play therapy, group counseling. Likewise, you may have read about "brainstorming" where interstimulation and response and free association are used by a discussion group to break up habitual channels of thought in the hope that new, unusual ideas will occasionally pop to the surface. And, of course, you have gotten information about many subjects from TV and radio discussions, such as "Meet the Press" and "Chicago Round Table."

The purpose of a problem-solving group is to make and sometimes to implement group discussions. Examples are plentiful: committees (and there are many kinds), conferences, juries, boards, councils, cabinets, staffs, vestries, legislatures, conventions, congresses, commissions, business meetings of various other organizations.

The three major types of discussion are not mutually exclusive. For instance, an educational discussion can and should be pleasurable; certainly it need not be painful. Likewise, a problem-solving discussion almost inevitably must include an exchange of information, and in addition it can be enjoyable. This overlapping among discussion types and purposes can be used to advantage in a basic speech course because some of the hybrid forms can provide an introduction to the whole field—even when time permits only one practice round.

Your instructor may assign one or two practice projects in discussion, such as a panel or an open forum. A panel is a small-group discussion held in the presence of an audience. The purpose of the panel may be to entertain, to inform, to solve a problem, or a mixture of two or three. An open forum is a type of discussion in which members of the audience may ask questions or make contributions from the floor. The purpose of a forum is almost always to clarify or to amplify the subject. Panel-forums are sometimes presented as a combination of types.

Even if time does not permit a practice project in your speech class, you have many opportunities to join in class discussions there, as well as in almost all of your other classes. You have been exposed to class discussions since your kindergarten days, but perhaps you have not thought much about improving your participation in them. Therefore, you may wish now to review your past experiences, to systematize them, and to understand the basic principles that underlie effective participation in panels, forums, class discussions, or any of the other types.

## Participation in group discussion

### Come prepared

Your first duty begins before you arrive at the meeting. You should think through the discussion problem, trying to get it clearly defined in your mind. You should gather all the information needed to improve your own understanding of the problem—some of this information may be offered at appropriate times later on during the discussion. You should prepare notes of such data, but do not prepare set speeches. You will probably reach some conclusions about the problem, but try to keep them tentative so that you will not join the group with a closed mind.

### Take an active part

Active participation means talking, listening, and thinking. So do not just sit there. When you have an idea express it. If you feel nervous or self-conscious, it is especially important for you to plunge in at the earliest opportunity—you will be surprised at how rapidly your confidence will grow.

CONTRIBUTE FACTS  Having studied the problem in advance, you will have gathered information which should be offered at appropriate times; some of this information no one else will have found. Occasionally you may use notes or documents. "I found some statistics which may help us on this point. Let me read from . . ."

CONTRIBUTE OPINIONS  During your reading you may have written down a few quotations from authorities on the subject. If it is pertinent to a point under discussion, read the quotation; if necessary, identify the source and mention his qualifications.

Express your own personal opinions and judgments; this is both your right and your responsibility. Even a faulty judgment often helps by stimulating the group to find the flaws. In stating your opinions avoid a dogmatic manner. ("This conclusively proves my contention.") Avoid abuse of the first person pronoun. ("I may be wrong, but I'll tell you what I think.")

**ASK QUESTIONS**  There are many types of questions, some of which are especially helpful for group discussion. The examples on page 48 suggest the usefulness of leading questions. However, *mis*leading questions are unethical and you should learn to detect them; for example, be wary of the sly gambit that begins with, "Don't you agree that . . . ?" Following are some worthwhile types of questions:

1. To clarify: "Would you explain what you mean by 'multiple use'?"
2. To test the validity of facts: "How do you know that the amount was 72 per cent?"
3. To test the validity of authorities: "Could you tell us something about Dr. Harold Livingston's qualifications?"

The well-known discussion program "Meet the Press" almost always illustrates the skillful use of leading questions.

4. To test unsupported assertions: "You just said that 'experts agree.' Would you name a few of these experts?"

5. To test the practicality of a proposal: "How would this work?" "How much would this cost?"

6. To test a colleague's logic: "Why?"

## Control your participation

**BE RELEVANT**  Speak to the point and stick to the point. An efficient discussion group follows an outline or agenda in a systematic and orderly fashion. Ideally, the points should be in proper sequence, and each point should be settled before proceeding to the next. An efficient group seldom has to go back and rediscuss an earlier point, or jump ahead to later items. An inefficient group is constantly leaping backward ("If you don't mind, I'd like to go back to a point Bill Lantz made a few minutes ago.") or forward ("As far as I'm concerned, the real solution is already clear. So let's get to the main point. Here's what should be done.").

**BE BRIEF**  Most discussions have time limits; there are several points to be covered, and everyone in the group has a right to be heard. Have something worthwhile to say but say it as briefly as is consistent with clarity. Do not reminisce ("And that reminds me of an incident that happened last summer when I was visiting Boulder Dam"). Or belabor the obvious (an example here would violate the advice). Or give more evidence than needed. Or insist on bringing up the same idea over and over. Or keep talking because you want to show off. Or keep talking because nobody stops you.

**BE COURTEOUS**  Courtesy is the basic rule in conversations and other small-group discussions: give the others a chance to speak. One aggressive individual can hog half or more of a committee's allotted time, and he will reap boredom, irritation, or antagonism. A courteous individual will temper his talking with plenty of careful listening and thinking; he will often go further, helping the chairman to restrain the overtalkative and draw out the reticent ("We haven't heard from George Enell on this question. George, what is your opinion about the . . . ?").

**BE COOPERATIVE**  A discussion participant should abide by the chairman's decisions with good grace. If by chance he is convinced that the chairman is grossly inefficient or unfair, he will object. However, he will state his objections in such fashion as not to stoop to the very tactics he is condemning.

A good participant comes to the meeting with information and ideas, but

Problem-solving discussions are a tool of business and professional groups. Notice the name cards, a useful technique for getting members of a group acquainted.

he does not come with a closed mind. He is not only willing but anxious to hear the other people. He hopes to learn from them. He is willing to modify his views in light of others' views. When disagreements occur, he tries honestly to understand the opposition's evidence and reasoning. He is not willing to compromise his principles but he is willing to recognize that it is often difficult to answer the question, "Is this truly a matter of principle?" He does his best to work out a solution to the common problem which will be mutually agreeable to all the participants. He subscribes to the view that in a democratic society the decision of the majority prevails but the rights of the minority must be protected. He knows from his experience that sometimes you must be a gracious winner, sometimes a gracious loser.

### Leadership of a group discussion

Occasionally you will be appointed or elected to lead a discussion group, and you should welcome such opportunity. The duties of the leader or chairman are different from those of the other participants.

## Advance preparations

The most important job for the leader before the discussion is to study the topic openmindedly and then prepare a chairman's outline. The outline should be adapted to the topic and to the purpose of the group. Usually the topic can be put in the form of a question or problem, and in that case the following stock outline may be helpful.

I. Analysis of the problem
   A. Terms of the problem: Do any need defining or clarifying? Possibly reword the question to "aim" it more directly at the group's goal?
   B. Nature of the problem: How big is it? How serious? How difficult?
   C. Causes of the problem: What are the immediate reasons for discussing it? Are more remote or fundamental causes involved?
II. Finding a solution
   A. Determine the criteria for evaluation.
   B. List suggested solutions: Which ones should be discussed? Are we already agreed on some of them? Do we lack sufficient time to discuss some of them?
   C. Evaluate suggested solutions: What are the arguments pro and con?
   D. Choose the best one or best combination.
III. Putting the solution to work
   A. Determine the necessary steps to put the solution into effect.
   B. Fix responsibility for action on some or all members.

The chairman should also analyze the members of his group. Two important questions are: Who is likely to be overtalkative and who is likely to be a silent member? What are likely to be the areas of agreement or disagreement within the group?

Often the chairman must also check the advance arrangements such as heating, ventilation, needed equipment, and the location of tables and chairs.

## Guiding the discussion

The main duties of the chairman in guiding a discussion may be summarized in the briefest form as follows: Open the program with a brief statement introducing panel members and their topic. Get the discussion started in accordance with the advance plan. Keep the discussion moving by asking questions or by other devices. Give all the members of the panel an equal opportunity to talk. Remain neutral on the topic; act as an impartial moderator during disputes. Guide the discussion in terms of the pre-arranged outline. Watch the time limits, and close with a brief summarizing statement.

For a beginning speech class project the leader's most important duty is to get the members of the group started talking and to keep them talking. This job is made much easier if during the planning stage you make sure that the group has a lively controversial topic. Also during the planning stage do not permit them to prepare canned speeches. During the discussion you want spontaneous give-and-take among all the members. So you will usually try to interrupt lengthy dissertations in order to give more people a chance to speak more often. In order to restrain the overtalkative and to encourage the reticent your most useful technique is to ask leading questions. Here are a few examples.

*To restrain the garrulous:* "Art, I wonder if I might interrupt and get the group to react to that point before you go on with the rest of it?" "In other words what you're driving at is . . . Joan, what do you think of Art's idea?" "Art, I notice that our time limits are growing short. Shall we set a thirty-second limit on everybody's remarks from now on?"

*To encourage the reticent:* "That's a good point. Won't you tell us more about . . . ?" "Edith, I can see that you've been thinking hard the past few minutes. Now what do you think about the . . . ?" "Recently I heard a student say, 'It's better to be Red than dead.' Tony, what's your reaction to that statement?"

Although you want to encourage maximum participation, you do not want your discussion to degenerate into a series of digressions from the topic, and digressions from the digressions. In guarding against this danger in small-group discussions you do not have the protection of the generally accepted codes for conducting legislative groups: codes such as *Robert's Rules of Order.* Therefore, an efficient chairman comes to the meeting equipped with a tentative outline, and he attempts to get the group's approval of it during the first part of the discussion, thus committing them to a general plan and its implied procedures. When difficulties arise later the chairman has the psychological advantage of being able to say directly or indirectly, "You agreed upon a set of rules—they're yours, not mine. I am only your servant whom you authorized to enforce your own rules. Let's not change them in the middle of the game." Of course, the leader should enforce his rules gently (although sometimes firmly); otherwise he may antagonize, frighten, frustrate, or squelch the discussants.

## Summary

Group discussion bridges the gap between daily conversations and speeches before larger audiences; it illustrates the point that public speaking is enlarged conversation. The key to good discussion in a democracy is "thinking independently together." The three main types of discussion groups are the

The success of our negotiators at the United Nations depends on their past experience and training in group discussion.

social, the educational, and the problem-solving. In a beginning speech class group discussion is a means to an end—it is a good way to get started on the road to better public speaking.

The duties of a discussion participant are these: (1) Come prepared. (2) Take an active part by contributing facts, opinions, and questions. (3) Control your participation by being relevant, brief, courteous, and cooperative.

The duties of a discussion leader are these: (1) In advance of the meeting prepare a discussion outline, analyze the group, and check the physical arrangements. (2) During the discussion encourage maximum participation yet hold the discussants to the subject so that remarks will be relevant and the group will progress toward its goal. The two most useful techniques are to ask good leading questions and to hold the participants to a logical thought sequence.

Experience and training in group discussion begin at least as early as the elementary school.

TOPICAL PREVIEW

I Where to begin

II Steps in preparation

    A Audience analysis

    B Choice of subject

        1 The right attitude

        2 Appropriate speech subjects

        3 Testing speech subjects

    C Determination of purpose

    D Collection of materials

    E The speech outline

        1 The beginning, middle, and end

        2 The speech unit

    F Practice of delivery

        1 Place

        2 Practice notes

        3 Wording

        4 Voice

        5 Posture and movement

III Summary

# 4

# PREPARING THE FIRST SPEECHES

## Where to begin

Every speech, whether it be by a freshman addressing his class or by the President of the United States addressing Congress, includes all the fundamentals of speechmaking: communication, thought and emotion, voice, language, bodily action, speaker, audience, and occasion. But no one can master all the fundamentals at once; certainly you cannot before you give your first talk. Recognizing that fact, we will begin with the minimum information necessary to you for the preparation and presentation of your first speeches; but at the same time we will try to give you a perspective on the entire process. The study in expanding detail of that process will continue throughout this book and this course.

## Steps in preparation

The process of preparing a speech may be divided into six steps.

1. Analyze the audience.
2. Choose the subject.
3. Determine the purpose.
4. Collect the materials.
5. Build the outline.
6. Practice the delivery.

In getting started, you should undertake the steps in the order given. As you become more experienced, you will be able to change the order to advantage sometimes (especially the first three steps), and to carry on two or more of the steps simultaneously.

## Audience analysis

Communication requires both a speaker and an audience. Whether or not the speaker communicates anything, how well he communicates, and what he communicates can be decided only by the audience. No other standard of speaking effectiveness will make sense. The verdict of the audience may be wrong, but it is still the verdict. The audience is the speaker's supreme court. Thus Chapter 1 stressed that students of speech should begin early to develop a "you and I" attitude. This attitude requires interest in and knowledge about the members of the audience. Securing information about the audience should be the first step in speech preparation; the application of that information should modify every remaining step.

Your speech class will be your only audience for a while. You should know the name and something about each member of the class. Size up your classmates, individually and collectively. In Appendix A a practice exercise is described by which an informal poll of your speech class may be made. Part I of this poll is entitled "Composition of Audience" and covers common traits and interests. Part II provides for a sampling of "Audience Attitudes on Current Affairs." If the poll is used, each member of the class will fill out the questionnaire anonymously. Totals for each question can then be tabulated and recorded by everyone in the class. Thus all members will have useful data about their "laboratory" audience. This polling method was

FREDERICK WILLIAMS

Here we have an early talk by a beginner; obviously he will have to improve his posture. But more important is the fact that he is learning about audience reactions as he listens thoughtfully to a question from the floor.

developed by Professor W. Charles Redding [1] and indicates an ideal way of gathering information about an audience. In other situations, come as close to this method as circumstances will allow.

As you listen to experienced speakers outside of this class, begin to pay as much attention to the audiences as you pay to the speakers. Then in later chapters we will be ready to broaden and systematize this important matter of audience analysis.

## Choice of subject

**THE RIGHT ATTITUDE**   "What shall I talk about?" may be a troublesome question. You are looking for subjects, not speeches. The root of your trouble may be that, consciously or subconsciously, you are trying to avoid the work of speech preparation. If so, disillusion yourself. There are no ready-made speeches. You are looking for subjects that can be developed into speeches.

Do not try to maintain the ridiculous position that your background is so impoverished that this simple task is impossible. It is impossible for any-one to get as far as college without an interest in something, without any experiences, without any emotions, without any ideas, without any sincere beliefs or convictions. You have a storehouse of subjects; you have only to recognize them.

The finding of subjects is *your* responsibility. You are going to talk about your own experiences or ideas. You are the only person who knows what they are. You must make the choices. Your instructor will be glad to help, but don't expect him to do the job for you.

**APPROPRIATE SPEECH SUBJECTS**   Your trouble may be that you are not sure just what you are looking for. One student, for example, associated "speech" with the speeches he could recall from his elementary and high school studies. They were Patrick Henry's "Give Me Liberty," Lincoln's "Gettysburg Address," Webster's "Reply to Hayne," and a few others. In searching for similar subjects to use in the classroom he was stalled, and no wonder. A few minutes of conversation with his instructor revealed that the student was working part time as a shoe salesman. Why not talk about selling shoes? "You mean *that* would be acceptable for a *speech*?" he asked in astonishment. Well, he worked out a speech with the title "If the Shoe Fits," which proved to be an amusing and provocative discussion of the psychology of salesmanship.

Let us take a few more examples of typical subjects that have been successfully used by speech students. A music major talked on "The Most

[1] W. Charles Redding, "Audience Analysis," *Western Speech*, XI (October 1947), 19–20.

Suitable speech subjects are drawn from your personal experience. Here a student with experience as a shoe salesman is giving a lively talk on the subject "If the Shoe Fits," illustrating his talk with shoes of different styles, ages, and sizes.

R. GRAVES

Important Musical Instrument," which turned out to be the conductor's baton; the student explained what a symphony conductor must be able to do. Another student who liked to play chess gave a talk called "The Royal Pastime," an account of the origins of the game. A history major talked on "Benedict Arnold Was *Not* a Traitor." A young woman discussed the local marriage course, and asked, "Can Marriage Be Taught?" A skin-diving enthusiast described his sport, exhibited the necessary paraphernalia—goggles and flippers—and finally produced an enormous live lobster which he had caught the previous day. "What's Wrong with Our High Schools?" was discussed by a student teacher who thought he knew, and who had a thought-provoking opinion. An advertising major criticized television commercials, using the title "At Laughably Low Prices." A political science major with a talk on "How to Win a Public Opinion Poll" made his class ponder an aspect of democracy. "The Worst Speech I Ever Heard" was vividly described by a student who hoped to do better. Subjects? They are everywhere. You have only to choose. You can compile a list of half a dozen good topics right now, and by the time you have used up that half dozen, a dozen more will have suggested themselves. Nevertheless, you will find lists of additional speech topics at appropriate points in the Appendixes.

TESTING SPEECH SUBJECTS   Once you have a list of possible speech subjects, how can you choose among them? The first speech topic should usually be one where you can draw mostly on your personal experience. There are two main tests: Are you interested in it? Can you interest the audience in it? As you progress in the course you will want to discuss subjects of increasing difficulty, seriousness, and significance. In assessing the comparative merits of future speech subjects, the following seven tests are helpful:

1. Does the subject reflect my personal interests and qualifications?
2. Can I relate the subject to the interests of the audience?
3. Does the subject suggest a clear-cut, specific speech purpose?
4. Is it appropriate to the assigned class project?
5. Can the subject be adequately handled within the time limits?
6. How much information about the subject do I already have?
7. Is additional information available?

## Determination of purpose

Many public speakers, even experienced ones, are, to quote Owen Young, "in the same boat with Christopher Columbus. He didn't know where he was going when he started. When he got there he didn't know where he was, and when he got back he didn't know where he had been." Such speakers are apparently just out for a verbal walk. They may enjoy it, but the audience is not likely to. The audience wants to know where the speaker is going and why he is going there. In other words, they want to know his purpose. If he is to tell them, he must know it first; indeed, he must know it before he plans the first word of his speech because, obviously, if he does not plan his speech to accomplish a definite purpose, he does not plan it for anything.

Whatever the specific purpose of any speech may be, there is an over-all purpose common to all speeches—to get an audience response. For practical use, let us break down that over-all purpose into four general purposes:

| General Purpose | Audience Responses Sought |
| --- | --- |
| To entertain | Favorable attention; enjoyment |
| To inform | Clear understanding; learning |
| To stimulate | Strengthening of a belief |
| To convince | A change of belief |

Sometimes we seek only to influence the audience's thoughts and feelings. At other times we seek, in addition, to produce overt action as a part of the response. For example, in a talk to entertain we may want not only silent appreciation but also laughter and applause; in a talk to inform, not only covert learning, but also overt demonstration (as in answering examination questions correctly); in talks to stimulate or convince, not only belief, but also action (in such form as voting or giving money or signing a petition).

But a general purpose is not enough. Your speech must have a specific purpose. Thus, don't be content to say, "My purpose is to inform." And it doesn't help much to add "about football." Be as specific as possible, such as, "My purpose is to make clear to my audience the differences between the T formation and the single wing."

## Collection of materials

At this stage of preparation, your problem is: What can you say to get the particular audience to make a desired response to a chosen subject? Your next move is to take an inventory of the knowledge you already have about the subject. This may be enough. If you are a member of the football team, for example, it is likely that you already have an extensive knowledge of the T formation and of the single wing. As a rule, however, you will need to supplement your current knowledge by further research.

The three main methods for gathering speech materials are observation, conversation, and reading. If you are qualified to give a talk on some aspect of electronic computers, you should probably draw largely upon your observations of the machines in action. If you choose to speak on student attitudes toward space travel, you might secure your best materials by conducting an informal poll through conversations with various student leaders. On most subjects, however, you should read as widely as possible. On almost any current subject you can readily find a variety of books, magazine articles, or newspaper reports. Be sure to read from more than one source. In many cases you will want to cite your sources during the speech, so be careful to take notes on your exact references as well as on the materials themselves.

## The speech outline

1. THE BEGINNING, MIDDLE, AND END. An elderly preacher, renowned for his sermons, was asked how he made them so effective. "Well," he replied, "first, I tell them what I'm going to say; then I say it; then I tell them what I have said." He had a good basic outline that illustrates the first important principle of outlining: there should be a beginning, a middle, and an end. These three parts have been traditionally called introduction, body (or discussion), and conclusion. In some speeches it is easy to identify the three

divisions; in others, the parts blend together so closely that it is impossible to pick a word or a pause as the dividing line between the introduction and the body. The beginning, the middle, and the end, however, have different functions. For your first speeches, therefore, it is wise to think in terms of the three divisions: introduction (How should I get started?); body (How should I develop my main idea?); conclusion (How should I close?).

**2. THE SPEECH UNIT.** It is usually easier to outline the body first. You begin by thinking about your subject until you can decide on what the main point of the talk will be. Then put that in the form of a short declarative statement. For your first class talk, be sure there is only one main point; and be careful not to make it too broad or ambitious. Then pick one or more items from your available materials that will develop or support your main point. Perhaps the easiest way to select those materials is to speak the main statement aloud and immediately add, "For example, . . ." That is likely to suggest an anecdote or quotation or some facts or figures. *A statement and one or more items of support, together with necessary transition statements, constitute a "speech unit," which is the basis of all speech organization.*

Now, let us illustrate a one-unit speech by thinking through together a simple speech outline. This chapter is being written in a cabin in the California mountains, and the author has just returned from a most pleasant fishing expedition. So fishing is our subject.

We begin with the body of the speech and consider possibilities for our main point. Suppose the audience is a college speech class. If a majority of the class were girls, we might try a central idea such as, "You Should Marry a Fisherman." But let us suppose that three-fourths or more are men. We might try "Fishing Is America's Number One Sport." But that would probably create controversy. We would run up against everybody else's favorite sports—and let us assume that we are not going to try to convince anyone of anything. "Fishing Is My Favorite Sport" has possibilities but seems to emphasize the speaker's interest too much as compared with the audience's. How about "Fishing Is Fun"? We might expect that a majority of the audience is already in general agreement with the idea; so our general purpose would be to stimulate. We might state the specific purpose as: "To reinforce and vitalize the class belief that fishing is fun."

Now we might say aloud: "Fishing is fun. For example, . . ." This immediately suggests today's trip. We might, therefore, develop the main point just by telling the story of today's trip. If it were told in some detail, it might be all the support we would need or have time for. If we wanted or needed more developmental materials, we might review our whole past experience with fishing and choose one or two additional anecdotes. Or we might recall that many famous men have been ardent fishermen and see if we could find a quotation or two from them in which the main idea is developed. Now we can outline the body of the speech:

*Main point:* Fishing is fun.
    *Anecdote one:* My recent fishing trip . . .
    *Anecdote two:* Last year some friends of mine . . .
    *Quotation:* Supreme Court Justice William O. Douglas has said . . .

And there we have a speech unit: statement and supports together with a few obviously necessary transitions. If that is the entire body, we would call this a one-unit speech.

The speech unit is the basis for outlining the body of any speech. For lengthy speeches you enlarge the basic unit by adding to the supporting materials or you increase the number of speech units. But the principle remains unchanged: each unit should consist of a statement, its supports, and transitions. To suggest how this principle applies to longer and more complicated speech outlines let us suppose that you wanted to expand the above outline on "Fishing Is Fun." On reflection you might decide to use a standard design: *before, during,* and *after.* Three main points are immediately suggested, and the body of the speech might be outlined as follows.

*Main point (or central idea):* Fishing is fun.
  I. Planning a fishing trip is fun.
    A. *Visual aid:* Here is a new catalog with color photographs of . . .
    B. *Quotation:* Dr. Merritt B. Jones says . . .
  II. The trip itself is fun.
    A. *Example:* Dr. Forrest Seal of our faculty is a fisherman who . . .
    B. *Anecdote:* My recent fishing trip . . .
  III. Talking about it afterward is fun.
    A. *Anecdote:* The big one that got away . . .

To complete either outline, we would have to decide on an introduction and a conclusion. The simplest and quickest introduction is just to tell the audience what you are going to say. In other words, start off with a statement of your main point in one sentence. Probably a better introduction would be to open with a question, such as "How many of you have ever gone fishing?" or "Do you know how many fishing licenses were sold in this state (or the United States) last year?" Another effective way to begin is with a reference to the previous speaker. Listen to him with a view to finding something that you can mention and tie up with fun or lack of fun. Thus, perhaps: "John Shepherd has just told you about his experiences with malaria. Obviously, that was no fun. This morning I want to discuss something that *is* fun. I want to discuss fishing. And fishing is fun. For example, . . ." The simplest conclusion is to tell the audience what you have said. To illustrate we might conclude: "I think fishing is fun, most of my friends think so, and even famous men like Justice Douglas think so. If you have missed out on this experience, all you have to do is go fishing! Then you will join the rest of us in saying, 'Fishing is fun.'"

Now, to the outline for the body of the speech which we have just given, you have only to add at the top and at the bottom brief write-ups of your planned "Introduction" and "Conclusion." You then have a complete and workable outline for a one-unit speech. It seems like a fairly simple job and it is—provided you follow the process of thought we have just been through.

## Practice of delivery

**1. PLACE** Your object should be to work out a habitual practice routine that will be tailor-made for your temperament. We will describe a possible routine in some detail. Give it a trial, making adjustments as experience reveals the procedures that work best for you.

Suppose you are scheduled to give a five-minute talk on Friday. Complete

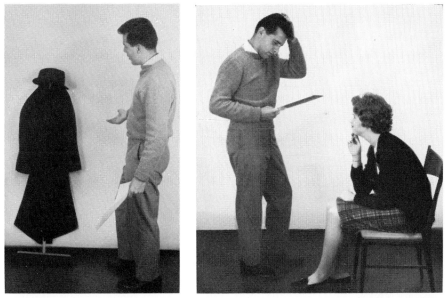

HARBRACE PHOTOS

When you are practicing a talk, imagine that you have an audience. Perhaps you can rig up a dummy to remind you that you are preparing to talk to a real group of people. Or perhaps you can get a friend to be this "audience."

your outline by Wednesday and practice aloud from the outline several times that day. Do the bulk of the practice Thursday. Run through the talk only once on Friday, an hour or two before you are to give it. In general, several shorter practice periods are better than one long period.

When you are ready to begin practice, find a place where you will not be disturbed. Imagine that the audience is seated in front of you. Now you're ready to talk through your outline just as was described in Chapter 2.

**2. PRACTICE NOTES** The outline should be written, preferably typed, and eventually condensed on one or two cards; for cards are easier to handle and not as conspicuous as sheets of paper. The four-by-six size is good, big enough to hold a good many notes yet small enough for easy handling. For a five-minute talk, the outline will usually go on one side of one card, on two at most. You should be able to see the whole outline at a glance so that you will always have the pattern of your ideas clearly before you. Resist the urge to make your notes too detailed.

**3. WORDING** Glance at the first item of your notes, look at your imaginary audience, and begin talking. Talk your way through the outline this first time regardless of difficulties. Refer to the notes as frequently as you wish, but keep your eyes toward the "audience" the rest of the time. Your first problem will be that of language—putting your ideas into words. As you take up each item in the outline, word your thought as you would in conversation. At first your flow of words will probably be hesitant and awkward, but stagger on. If in wording an idea you reach a dead end, go back and approach the idea from a slightly different angle. If you pause while struggling for the right words, don't worry. Just pause. But let the pause alone. Don't give way to the temptation to fill it with "and" or "uh" or other meaningless sounds.

After the first time through, sit down and think about the outline—possibly make a few adjustments in it. Then get up and start again. Time this trial. Eventually, you must develop a sense of speech timing, but it comes only from much practice with the clock. On this second trial, you will find that you are more fluent. Here and there you will find a word or phrase coming out exactly as it was the first time. That is all right, but make no conscious attempt to use the same words as before; avoid word for word memorization. If you stall occasionally while groping for the right word later on when you are giving the talk to the class, the pause can increase your effectiveness, can show your audience that you are thinking and not just reciting like a parrot. The second time through, you should not refer to the notes so frequently. An occasional glance should suffice.

**4. VOICE** As soon as the words begin to flow a little better, you can begin giving some attention to your voice. First, talk loud enough to be heard—just a little louder than in ordinary conversation. Don't shout or strain. Avoid letting your voice die away at the ends of clauses or sentences. Variety of tone is the only other thing to watch in the beginning. Try to avoid speaking at the same rate or in a monotone. In conversation you vary your tone, its pitch and loudness, and you change speed. Try for that conversational variety as you practice.

**5. POSTURE AND MOVEMENT** After several trial runs you will have limbered up your vocabulary, freed yourself from overdependence on the outline, and become accustomed to hearing your voice. You can then consider the third element of your delivery: bodily action. For this part of your practice, a large mirror is helpful.

See to it that your posture is good; look alert and yet at ease. It would be nice if this could be achieved by saying, "just stand naturally." Your habitual posture will feel natural to you, yet your habitual posture may be very bad. Stand in front of the mirror and experiment. Find a way of stand-

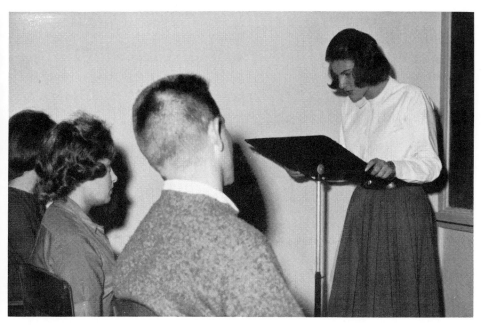

FENWICK ENGLISH

Perhaps this girl is "just standing naturally." Her posture will improve after she has practiced in front of a large mirror.

ing that looks natural and at the same time feels comfortable. If in doubt, check the result later with your instructor. When you get up in front of the audience for the first time or two, you may forget your practiced posture and succumb to the temptation of leaning on the speaking stand for support. Lounging on the stand is, of course, not recommended for habitual use, but it may be all right at first to put yourself at ease. It is better to look slouchy and at ease than to give the impression that rigor mortis has set in.

Next, practice changing your position before the mirror. During a speech it is wise to move about once in a while in order to punctuate thought, help hold the listeners' attention, and reduce nervous tension. Put a chair in front of the mirror and practice moving about the chair. Stand behind it and talk; rest the right hand lightly on the chair back as you move from behind and forward to the left. Then try again with the left hand on the chair as you move forward to the right. Adjust your movements until they look natural to you in the mirror.

Don't worry yet about gestures. Allow your arms to hang loosely at your sides, or rest one hand or arm lightly on the chair. If you should feel the urge to gesture, go ahead; but if you do not feel that urge, ignore gestures entirely for the present.

FREDERICK WILLIAMS

Do you think that this student had practiced enough for this talk? Compare with the next picture.

This picture was taken on the same day in the same class. Do you think that this student had practiced more? Or less?

You will discover that you cannot do everything at once. You need time and practice. When you rehearse give your attention each time to a single problem. How many times should you rehearse a given speech? From three to a dozen. You needn't expect to attain perfection. Progress is enough.

Now let us go back to the speech you were preparing for Friday. Rehearse about four times Wednesday, about six times Thursday, and once Friday morning. Then when you get up to give the talk, *forget all about the delivery details you were practicing!* Keep your mind concentrated only on the thought and the audience. The goal of this type of practicing is to make your delivery mechanisms habitual, so that when you are speaking you have only the ideas and the audience to think about. Eventually your delivery will take care of itself!

**Summary**

The major steps of speech preparation are analyzing the audience, choosing the subject, determining the purpose, gathering the materials, building the outline, and practicing the delivery. All six of these steps will be studied in gradually expanding detail throughout this course. In preparing the first speeches two things are especially useful. First, you should learn to outline a speech unit consisting of a statement and supports. Second, you should begin the habit of practicing aloud from your outline.

# PART TWO

# CONSTRUCTING THE SPEECH

*The outline is the architectural blueprint, the ideas are the bricks, and the words are the mortar of a speech.*

Example of a key-word outline was provided by former President Eisenhower as he prepared to address a large crowd. His own hand-lettered notes were written large so that he could read them with quick glances during the speech.

TOPICAL PREVIEW

I   Importance of speech purpose

II  Avoiding common mistakes

    A   Attempting too much

    B   Attempting too little

    C   Attempting the wrong thing

III Choosing the general purpose

    A   One purpose only

    B   Factors influencing choice

        1   Audience attitudes toward topic

        2   Other factors

IV  Stating the general purpose

V   Making the general purpose specific

    A   Stating the specific purpose

    B   Centering the purpose on the audience

    C   Making the specific purpose concrete

VI  Summary

15785

# 5

## SPEECH PURPOSES

### Importance of speech purpose

The importance of aiming every speech toward a definite goal seems obviously, yet students often prepare and deliver speeches without ever consciously thinking about speech purpose. A typical example was the student who gave a talk advocating that cola drinks and coffee should be forbidden because they contain caffeine, and caffeine is harmful to health. The audience responded to the talk with a mixture of boredom, irritation, and confusion. The instructor questioned the speaker.

"Bill, what was your speech purpose?"

"Well, I wanted to show the dangers of cola drinks and coffee."

"Then your purpose was not to entertain us?"

"No."

"Was it to inform?"

"Well, yes, I think so."

"What did you want us to learn?"

"About those dangers."

"But we already knew about them, Bill. All of us knew that these drinks contain caffeine, and that caffeine is sometimes harmful."

"I suppose you're right."

"Was your purpose to convince?"

"Yes, that's it, to convince."

"Convince us that we should stop drinking coffee?"

"Yes."

"But you didn't say that. You said that these drinks should be forbidden. Did you mean forbidden by law?"

"I thought so."

"But you didn't describe such a law. Is a law pending?"

"I don't know."

"Apparently you hadn't thought about the purpose of your speech until now."

"I guess not."

This example shows that a purposeless speech is usually a futile speech, and that a speaker should always determine in advance the audience response he hopes to get. A well-chosen speech purpose guides a speaker through all the steps of speech preparation and presentation, keeping him steadily on a course, constantly reminding him of his goal. A poorly chosen speech purpose misleads a speaker, dissipating his efforts.

### Avoiding common mistakes

#### Attempting too much

Perhaps the most common error among beginning speakers in choosing a speech purpose is that of attempting to get audience responses that could not possibly be achieved. The error may take any of several forms.

Select a speech subject that can be adequately presented within the time limit. Suppose your general purpose is to inform and your time limit is three minutes. One student actually undertook to explain the Einstein theory in that time! Could you clarify the psychology of learning in three minutes? No. Could you cover "How to Study" in three minutes? No. What could you hope to cover? Something like "The Best Study Method I Have Found"? Probably.

Speakers sometimes attempt subjects that are too broad for a single speech regardless of time. There is no use in trying to cover "The History of Religion" in one talk—that could scarcely be covered in a year's course in college. You would have to plan carefully in order to do justice to "The History of Our University Chapel" in one speech of ordinary length.

Sometimes a speaker exhorts the audience to an action that is beyond its power. There is no use pleading for blood donations from audiences under eighteen or over sixty years of age (the Red Cross would not accept them), or trying to persuade a high school audience to vote for your candidate in the next primaries, or demanding that the PTA fire the principal. Such futilities may seem obvious, but they are not exaggerations. This fact highlights the importance of considering carefully exactly what lies within the

Here the speaker's purpose is to inform. But just how much information can he put across? If he attempts too much, the students will be frustrated; too little, and they will be bored.

power of a given group to perform in reference to your subject. If, for example, you are a member of the executive council of a national society and a disturbing problem has arisen, much time may be wasted by members speaking in favor of actions that a reading of the society's constitution would reveal as beyond the council's legal authority.

Finally, a speaker may attempt more than his status or his own speaking abilities make possible. A speaker who is highly respected by a group can attempt a more difficult purpose than someone who is unknown or disliked. An expert can attempt more than a novice. The trouble is that some beginning speakers lack insight into their own limitations. One student takes a course in psychology and immediately imagines that he can tell other people how to live their lives. Another student makes a hit with one audience and imagines that he is a born speaker. A little bit of knowledge or a little bit of success may therefore be a dangerous thing. Or, to reinforce one platitude with another, fools rush in where angels fear to tread.

## Attempting too little

Sometimes a speaker attempts too little. A speaker should avoid trivial purposes. Of course, triviality is often a matter of opinion. A member of the faculty might consider trivial a talk to convince an audience that dormitory hours for freshmen women should be changed; a freshman woman might rightly entertain an opposite opinion. Nevertheless, endless amounts of time are wasted at all sorts of meetings by speakers whose apparent purposes are not worth achieving. At the salesmen's meeting of a large company one salesman spends thirty minutes advocating a small change in procedure that would have been granted immediately on a simple one-sentence request. In club meetings everywhere hours are wasted by members strenuously trying to convince the group regarding some unimportant refinement of parliamentary procedure.

A speaker may attempt too little because he fails to adjust his purpose to audience knowledge or attitudes. You decide to inform your audience about Abraham Lincoln. But what do you do? You recite briefly the highlights of Lincoln's career with which every listener is already familiar. You should go beyond the audience's existing knowledge, and inform them of some aspect of Lincoln's life that is new to them. Or you are asked to give a classroom talk with the general purpose to convince, and you prove to your listeners that they should drive safely. But all of them would agree with your proposition without your making the speech. You should attempt more —assume that they believe in safe driving and go on from there. Perhaps you could convince them that certain traffic regulations should be changed. In any speech where your purpose includes getting overt action, you attempt too little if you ask the auditors to do something they have already done. For example, a minister worked himself into a lather in a lengthy sermon summoning his audience to join the church, when at least 95 per cent of his congregation were already members.

Finally, a speaker may attempt too little because he is too lazy to attempt more. Information may be minimum, or proofs may be thin, because the speaker did not give enough time to research and thought.

## Attempting the wrong thing

Sometimes a speaker's purpose is inappropriate to the audience or occasion.

A local lawyer was asked to deliver a Memorial Day address at a famous country cemetery. After a few words at the beginning in which he touched upon the day and the honored dead, he launched into a discussion of public policies and ended with a political harangue urging his audience to vote for his party at the next elections. The audience was offended. His speech purpose was inappropriate to the occasion.

A university professor wrote an important scientific book that received a lot of publicity. He was invited to speak before the Kiwanis Club of his city. He read a learned scientific paper. The audience slept. Two days later most of them could not even describe his general topic. His speech purpose was inappropriate to the interests of his audience.

A city official was speaking before a convention of the local medical society. He tried to convince the doctors that they should support a plan to provide complete medical care at public expense. The speech purpose was inappropriate to the doctors' attitudes toward socialized medicine. All the speaker succeeded in doing was to antagonize the doctors, setting their opposition more firmly than before. If he had attempted to inform them about, let us say, the costs of medical care, leaving them with a clear understanding of the problem, he would probably have secured a response consistent with his beliefs and eventual hopes. He might have indirectly helped his cause instead of directly hurting it.

A young woman who was a brilliant student in a university was invited to speak before an influential women's club. She gave a well-documented lecture on the failures of American women to make proper use of the right to vote. Most of the audience were irritated by the speech; some were even insulted. The speech purpose was inappropriate to the attitudes of an audience toward a speaker much younger than themselves. The same speech would probably have been successful if it had been given by a mature woman with a record of achievement in civic affairs.

### Choosing the general purpose

In order to avoid the common mistakes just described, you must determine speech purposes by a careful and systematic method. The first step is to choose one of the four general speech purposes discussed in Chapter 4: to entertain, to inform, to stimulate, to convince. The value of this first step is that it immediately narrows the field for your search. There are thousands of responses that human beings might make; you would waste your time trying to review them all. Therefore you begin by considering four basic types of response suitable for public speaking situations.

### *One purpose only*

The four general speech purposes are closely related, and therefore students often think that two or three or even all four may be successfully accomplished by one talk. For example, a student had just heard a television speech by the Attorney General. "The speech was certainly informative," he said; "it contained plenty of new facts and ideas. But it was entertaining, too: it was cleverly worded and had some humor. It was also stimulating; it reinforced a lot of beliefs. And the speech was convincing; it changed my mind on at least one question. Therefore the speech had all four general purposes." Not at all. A more careful analysis showed that the Attorney General's purpose was who to convince—he would have been satisfied with nothing less. The entertaining, informative, and stimulating elements of his speech were means, not ends.

A single speech should have a single purpose, and everything the speaker says should be a means to that end. Catching and holding audience interest can be an end in itself or can be a means to some other end. Likewise, presenting information may be either an end or a means. The same is true of building new beliefs or reinforcing existing beliefs. When the relationship between ends and means is understood, it is no longer difficult to choose only one general purpose for a speech. For instance, you would not say, "My purpose is to entertain and inform with facts about the Panama Canal." Instead you would choose as your purpose either to entertain or to inform, demoting the other to a supporting role.

### Factors influencing choice

1. AUDIENCE ATTITUDES TOWARD TOPIC  In choosing a general speech purpose the most important factor should be the attitudes of your audience toward your subject. Let us work through a hypothetical case.

If you were to discuss a proposal for a new high school building in a small town, what would be the attitudes toward this proposal by various groups? Favorable attitudes would probably be found in most of the students who would be going to school in the new building, in the teachers, and in the children's parents, especially if they owned but little property. These attitudes might be lukewarm or strong, depending largely on the age and condition of the existing building, the amount of overcrowding, and whether or not nearby towns have newer buildings.

Unfavorable attitudes could be expected from people who pay high taxes but have no children in school, from groups fighting for tax reductions, or from groups advocating other community improvements that would have to compete for funds with the school proposal.

The undecided vote could be subdivided. First, there might be those who are completely neutral, interested but open-minded. Most psychologists, however, agree that it is difficult to know enough about a controversy to be interested in it without forming active opinions about it, and therefore the number of true neutrals would probably be small. Perhaps the school board could be classed as neutral toward the proposed new building.

The second subdivision would include those people who have certain prejudices for and other prejudices against the proposal. Conflicting implies a balance of forces as contrasted with neutral, which implies an absence of forces. Conflicting attitudes might be expected in taxpayers with children in school, and in businessmen wondering if the extra costs of a school building would be offset by the extra income attracted to the community by a school improvement.

People would be indifferent toward the proposal either through lack of personal interest or lack of information. Lack of personal interest would be found among itinerant workers who do not expect to make this town their permanent home. Lack of information might be found among citizens with no children in school and with little property.

With the foregoing probabilities in mind, what should be your general speech purpose? Well, first you have to consider your own honest convictions. Assume that you favor the construction of the new school.

If the attitudes of most of your listeners were also favorable, your purpose should be further to stimulate them to support the proposal for a new building. You would want to reinforce their convictions and secure overt action —get them to vote, or to sign a petition, or to go out among their neighbors and secure more converts.

If the audience were opposed, your purpose would be to inform or convince. If they were strongly opposed, you might decide to shake their convictions with new information, paving the way for future talks which might carry the purpose another step forward. If opposition were not strongly entrenched, you might try to change their beliefs. It is unlikely in any case that you could produce actual overt action. That response should be left to future speakers.

If the audience were undecided, your general purpose would hinge on your analysis of the reasons for that indecision. Probably your purpose would be to convince. If the audience members were uninformed or apathetic, your purpose would become to entertain, to arouse attention and interest. If the attitudes of the audience were mixed, you would have to decide in which proportions. You might have to sacrifice the hope of convincing some of your listeners in order to persuade the remainder.

**2. OTHER FACTORS**  Although audience attitudes toward your topic will usually be of greatest importance in choosing a general speech purpose, other factors will also influence your choice. The nature of the occasion may suggest the most appropriate purpose. An after-dinner speech suggests entertaining; a study club, informing; a ceremonial, stimulating; a debate, convincing. Common traits and interests may indicate the best choice of purpose. If your subject were household accidents, for example, the speech purpose would be influenced by the audience's age, sex, family status, or occupation. Audience attitudes toward you, the speaker, may bear upon the purpose. Thus if you had reason to believe that they would be prejudiced

Here the occasion dictates the speaker's purpose: to stimulate. In other words these people did not gather to be entertained, or to become better educated, or to engage in controversy.

against you because of your age or sex or race, you might decide to entertain or inform rather than attempt to convince. Therefore, taking into account your subject, occasion, audience, and yourself, but paying attention particularly to the probable attitudes toward your topic, you make a choice of general speech purpose.

### Stating the general purpose

You should state your general purpose: to entertain, to inform, to stimulate, to convince, or a synonym for one of the four. Synonyms are useful in giving more exact shades of meaning in some cases.

However, the statement of your general purpose is only the first portion of what will become your full statement of speech purpose. The full statement, as we will presently see, requires the addition of specific details. Therefore the wording of the general purpose should lead naturally into statement of specific details.

Following are some examples of statements of general purposes, showing use of possible synonyms, and suggesting how specific details will be added to complete the statements.

1. *Entertain*
   To entertain my audience with . . .
   To get my audience to pay favorable attention to . . .
   To arouse the interest of my audience in . . .
   To get my audience to laugh about . . .
2. *Inform*
   To inform my audience about . . .
   To get my audience to understand clearly . . .
   To show my audience how to . . .
   To get my andience to learn that . . .
3. *Stimulate*
   To reinforce my audience's belief in . . .
   To inspire my audience with . . .
   To revitalize my audience's attitudes on . . .
   To strengthen my audience's appreciation of . . .
   To release into overt action my audience's existing belief that . . .
4. *Convince*
   To get my audience to believe that . . .
   To get my audience to stop believing that . . .
   To change my audience's attitudes toward . . .
   To persuade my audience to vote (or sign or give money or buy or other specific action) . . .

## Making the general purpose specific

Notice again that all items in the foregoing list are incomplete statements. The final and crucial task is to complete the statement of the general purpose so as to make the purpose specific. You will then have a full statement of your speech purpose—a description of the audience response you hope to get.

The value of a specific speech purpose may be illustrated by comparing speechmaking with traveling. You cannot plan a trip unless you first have a destination or itinerary; likewise, you cannot plan a speech unless you first have a specific goal. You might, of course, start a vacation trip saying, "We haven't planned anything definitely—we're just going to drive north." To say "north" is vague and general; to say "entertain" or "inform" is also vague and general. If a traveler does not have a specific destination, he will just wander aimlessly; so will a speaker.

### Stating the specific purpose

Make your statement of a specific purpose as specific as possible. In the following examples you will see that the first attempt to state your purpose specifically can often be improved by further effort.

*General purpose:* to entertain
*Still too general:* to amuse my audience with a talk about snoring
*Better:* to get my audience to laugh at some anecdotes and at some sounds of people snoring

*General purpose:* to inform
*Still too general:* to explain how to tie the fire underwriters' knot
*Better:* to instruct my listeners so that they will be able to tie the fire underwriters' knot

*General purpose:* to stimulate
*Still too general:* to stimulate my audience regarding the value of a college degree
*Better:* to strengthen my audience's belief in the value of getting a college degree

*General purpose:* to convince
*Still too general:* to convince my audience that certain classes should be dismissed during homecoming week
*Better:* to get my audience to sign a petition requesting dismissal of all classes on Friday and Saturday of homecoming week

### Centering the purpose on the audience

Since the effectiveness of a speech must be measured by audience response, the statement of the speech purpose should always be audience-centered, avoiding the common dangers of being speaker-centered or subject-centered. For example, a student said that his general speech purpose was to inform, and that his specific purpose was "to explain why I believe in going to church regularly." He said he did not care whether anyone agreed with him; he just wanted to explain his ideas. Because the talk was speaker-centered, most of the class members were bored and none seemed to understand either the speaker's intention or his subject matter. However, the speaker thought his speech was effective because he had explained his own views to his own satisfaction. Consider another example. A student said that his general purpose was to convince, and that his specific purpose was "to prove that Alfred Korzybski's non-Aristotelian system of logic is sound." The speaker was obviously wrapped up in his subject, and had obviously spent much time in preparation. However, no one in the class was convinced —the arguments were too abstract and technical. The speaker thought it was an effective speech because, "I did prove the proposition; everything in the speech was true and well supported." The talk was not speaker-centered, but it was subject-centered—the speaker had prepared as though Korzybski were to be the judge, but Korzybski wasn't there.

The distinctions between speaker-centered or subject-centered purposes and audience-centered purposes are often delicate. Consider the following examples.

*Speaker-centered:* to be interesting while discussing statistics
*Subject-centered:* to present interesting statistical information
*Audience-centered:* to get my audience to show interest in the uses of statistics

*Speaker-centered:* to explain my definition of love
*Subject-centered:* to talk about the problem of defining love
*Audience-centered:* to get my audience to understand the differences between psychological and religious definitions of love

*Speaker-centered:* to give an inspirational talk on the benefits I received from membership in the Boy Scouts
*Subject-centered:* to praise the record of the Boy Scouts
*Audience-centered:* to heighten the favorable feeling which my audience holds toward the Boy Scouts

*Speaker-centered:* to defend my reasons for being a Republican
*Subject-centered:* to prove that the recent record of the Republican party is better than that of the Democratic party
*Audience-centered:* to get the members of my audience to decide to vote Republican in the next election

## Making the specific purpose concrete

The statement of speech purpose is for the guidance of the speaker; the purpose may or may not be spoken to the audience during the speech. For example, you certainly would not say to an audience, "My purpose this morn-

Bob Hope entertains. And this picture shows that speech purpose and speech effectiveness are "before and after" descriptions of audience response.

ing is to get you to laugh at some jokes." Nor is it likely that you would ever say, "My purpose is to make you change your minds."

The value of the speech purpose to a speaker is based on the fact that if he knows in advance the audience response he wants, he can aim everything he says toward arousing that response. A speaker is more likely to be successful if he knows what success is. In other words, speech purpose and speech effectiveness are "before and after" descriptions of audience response. Purpose is the response you hope to get; effectiveness is the response you actually get. In successful speeches the desired audience response and the actual audience response correspond.

It is easier to aim a speech at a concrete goal than at an abstract one. It is easier to judge ways and means if you can visualize the desired end, that is, if you can see and hear the desired audience response in imagination. Thus it is helpful when you can say, "I want every member of the class to contribute at least twenty-five cents to this annual drive for the Student Emergency Loan Fund," because you can visualize them digging into their pockets or purses and putting money into envelopes. It is less helpful to say, "I want the class to understand how ice cream was invented," because it is difficult to visualize anyone in the act of understanding.

You will be able to make your statement of purpose more concrete by asking yourself this significant question, "If my speech is completely successful, exactly what will my audience think, feel, or do?" The answer is the response you want to get, and to get that particular response is your speech purpose. In answering the question you should think in terms of observable behaviors.

The observable behaviors of an audience that has been successfully entertained or interested include: sitting quietly, listening attentively, perhaps smiling or laughing, asking questions afterward, or making comments such as, "I enjoyed the talk," or, "That was a fascinating subject."

The observable behaviors of an audience that has been successfully informed include: listening thoughtfully, taking notes, asking pertinent questions, and afterward talking about the subject, passing a quiz, performing an activity learned during the speech, or making comments such as, "I understand it clearly," or "I learned a great deal about the topic."

The observable behaviors of an audience that has been successfully stimulated include: listening eagerly, nodding in agreement, applauding during the speech, sometimes spontaneously saying encouraging things to the speaker ("Give it to 'em, Harry," "Preach it, brother"), or spontaneously replying to rhetorical questions ("Are we downhearted?" "No!"), and afterward cheering, talking about the speech subject, performing overt acts suggested by the speaker, or making comments such as, "I believe it more strongly than ever before," or "It was deeply moving."

The observable behaviors of an audience that has been successfully convinced include: listening intently, nodding or shaking head, making facial expressions consistent with the speaker's argument, and afterward perform-

This rare photograph of an actual trial shows a speaker trying to convince. The lawyer gauges his progress by observing everything the jury does —every frown or smile, every nod or shake of the head, every stretch or yawn.

PHOTO RESEARCHERS

**79**

ing appropriate overt acts such as voting, signing, contributing, or making comments such as, "I agree with you now," or, "That put the problem in a new light."

If you think in terms of observable audience behaviors, you will be more likely to state your purpose specifically and concretely. Sometimes it is wise to supplement your statement of purpose by hypothesizing observable audience responses. For example, you might supplement the purpose to get your audience to believe in the principles of free trade by mentally adding, "If a show of hands were requested at the end of the talk, a majority of the class would vote favorably." An actual show of hands need not be taken. The important thing is to visualize in advance the audience response wanted, and it is possible to visualize a show of hands whereas it is difficult to visualize the behavior of believing.

As we mentioned at the beginning of this section you do not always state your purpose to the audience during a talk. For example, in a public speaking contest your underlying purpose may be to win the first prize; you are aware of this and so is the audience, but you surely would not state it during your speech. Or suppose that you are speaking to an audience that is strongly opposed to the proposition you favor. You might decide that it is impossible in one short talk to swing them completely over to your viewpoint. So your purpose might be to get them to take a step in your direction by undermining one or more of their cherished beliefs. But to say that to them would be a pretty good way to guarantee failure.

In many speeches, however, you should reveal your purpose to the listeners. Sometimes the purpose should be stated specifically, even bluntly:

### To convince

My purpose today is to ask for your support in the coming election.

### To inform

The purpose of this lecture is to prepare you for the final examination in this course. I will explain precisely the type of examination that will be given, the materials that will be covered, and the study methods that you should use.

### To stimulate

The behavior of the student rooting section at last Saturday's game was a disgrace to this school. I speak for the alumni, and I do not intend to mince words—we are ashamed.

## Summary

The purpose of every speech should be to get an intended audience response.

Poorly chosen speech purposes mislead speakers into attempting too much, attempting too little, or attempting the wrong thing.

A single speech should have a single purpose, and everything the speaker says should be a means to that end.

The first step in determining a speech purpose is to choose one of the four general purposes: to entertain, to inform, to stimulate, or to convince. The choice among the four is influenced mostly by audience attitudes toward the topic, but other factors may also influence the decision. The second step is to state the general purpose, using one of the four terms: entertain, inform, stimulate, convince, or a synonym for one of them. The third step is to add to the statement of general purpose so as to describe the desired audience response specifically and concretely. The third step can be accomplished by asking, "If my speech is completely successful, exactly what will my audience think, feel, or do?" The answer is the response you want to get, and the response you want to get is your speech purpose.

TOPICAL PREVIEW

# 6

## SPEECH MATERIALS

---

**You, too, should have a reservoir**

Adlai Stevenson is rightfully rated as one of the outstanding speakers of his time. One reason for his success is that he studies his subjects exhaustively before speaking about them. In 1957 Stevenson introduced and made an award to Albert M. Greenfield, a real estate broker, banker, and philanthropist of Philadelphia. The occasion was the World Brotherhood Dinner of the National Conference of Christians and Jews. Stevenson spoke for approximately twelve minutes. Did Stevenson treat this as a minor and routine assignment, disdain preparation, and make a few off-the-cuff remarks? Quite the contrary, he gathered more materials than he could possibly include in the speech. You, too, should have a reservoir to draw upon when preparing a speech.

Stevenson opened with a *quotation* from Thornton Wilder's play "Our Town." The quotation was unusual—it was simply the address on a letter to a character mentioned in the play. The quotation was apt—it directly illustrated the theme of World Brotherhood. Then Stevenson used the "address" again, slightly abridged, to provide a surprise ending for the talk:

> Ladies and gentlemen, acting for you, I confer the World Brotherhood Award Citation upon Albert M. Greenfield, Sugar Loaf, Chestnut Hill, Philadelphia,

Pennsylvania, United States of America, Continent of North America, the Earth, the Solar System, the Universe, the mind of God.[1]

Stevenson also included three other quotations from such diverse sources as John Donne and the Talmud. As he concluded the talk he apparently used a *visual aid*—he must have presented some sort of certificate or plaque to the guest of honor.

A short *anecdote* was related:

> Mr. Chairman, I have said that there is *no* flaw in the brotherhood title of our honored guest. I advise you now that in 1928 he was a delegate from Pennsylvania to the National Convention of the Republican party. I advise you further that in 1948, 1952 and 1956 he was a Delegate-at-large from Pennsylvania to the National Convention of the Democratic party. This is Brotherhood! And this is also *progress!*

The central idea of Stevenson's talk was that the dangers of nuclear warfare may force mankind to achieve what it has always sought—world brotherhood. He developed this point by means of *explanation.* Some examples:

> A very large part, I suspect, of the maturing of mankind to its present estate has come from adversity, or the threat of adversity. More frontiers of what we call progress have probably been crossed under the pressure of necessity than by the power of reason.

> The significance of what has happened lies not in which nation has first reached into outer space but in the fact that man has now obliterated, for better or for worse, what we used to call time and distance.

> What that "bleep-bleep" is saying is that now the world has no option, that it must turn from narrow nationalism, sectarianism, racialism, that the only conceivable relationship among men is one based on men's full respect—yes, their love, if you please—for each other.

Occasionally Stevenson developed his points by means of vivid *description:*

> . . . a science that has broken down the fences which had before separated the peoples of the world.

> . . . until the hard steel of survival itself has been pulled against our too soft mouths.

> . . . the one realm which knows no boundaries, no capitals, no foreign policy—for there are no foreigners . . .

[1] A. Craig Baird, ed., *Representative American Speeches: 1957–1958,* H. W. Wilson, 1958, pp. 58–63.

If such an experienced speaker as Adlai Stevenson so clearly recognizes the need of a careful search for speech materials, surely student speakers cannot afford to do less.

Several times Stevenson supported his statements by citing specific *instances*. Thus he stated that the honored guest had "taken part in the most extraordinary variety of functions ever to come to my humble attention." Then he gave instances:

> I find that he has lent his name and services (and I suspect frequently something even more tangible) to the United Fund and the Community Chest, to the Philadelphia Symphony and to the Connie Mack Golden Jubilee Committee, to the Chapel of Four Chaplains and to the Army and Navy football games.

Finally *statistics* were employed to support one of Stevenson's points:

> My research, Mr. Chairman, has gone even to statistics. I am in a position to report, what I am sure Mr. Greenfield does not himself know—except perhaps with a kind of numbness—that there is record evidence of his participation, usually as chairman, in sixty-one committees, commissions, campaigns, chambers or celebrations; and of his previous receipt of twenty-nine honorary awards.

Thus this short speech shows that Stevenson spared no effort in securing a supply, even a surplus, of suitable speech materials.

> Mr. Chairman, I have, in the discharge of my appointed duties on this occasion, made what we lawyers (you will pardon this brief "commercial") call a title search.

If such an experienced speaker as Adlai Stevenson so clearly recognizes the need of a careful search for speech materials, surely student speakers cannot afford to do less.

The speech also illustrates the variety of materials from which speeches are constructed. He used (1) speech points and subpoints, sometimes restating them in different words; and he used (2) all seven of the principal forms of support: explanation, description, anecdotes, instances, statistics, quotations, and visual aids. Thus an analysis of Stevenson's talk leads directly into a discussion of the first step in the efficient gathering of materials for speeches.

**What to look for**

*Points and subpoints*

A well-constructed speech consists of one or more speech units. As we saw in an earlier chapter, a speech unit consists of a statement and its supports: the statement of a speech point (or subpoint), together with spoken or written materials that support or develop it. The term "speech point" means a one-sentence summary of an idea. So in gathering speech materials you must first look for ideas about your topic—ideas that can be put into the form of speech points. Some samples:

> Cheating on examinations is (or is not) common on this campus.
> Racial discrimination in this country is crippling our foreign policy.
> The first mark of a scholar is curiosity.
> Faith is fear turned inside out.
> The political power of labor unions is declining.

Sometimes you will come upon a single sentence which suggests the exact point or set of points that you want for your speech. For instance, Bernard De Voto wrote in an article for *Harper's Magazine:* "The professor's function in society is to appraise, increase, and disseminate knowledge." There you have the makings of three points which might become the major framework for a speech. Usually, however, you will come upon a variety of ideas scattered here and there. So you must make choices.

Recall our sample outlines for a talk on "Fishing Is Fun," pages 56–59. There was only one point or central idea. We showed how this topic could be developed as a one-point talk in which the point was supported by one or two anecdotes and a quotation; we also showed how the same topic could be developed into a longer speech with a central idea and three main points, each supported in various ways.

In doing research for a speech you must constantly look for potential main points and subpoints, separately or in sets. Without them you cannot construct an organized speech.

## Supporting materials

FUNCTIONS  The bare statement of your points and subpoints is like a table of contents without the development that makes the book. You must look for materials to support each of your potential points and subpoints. Often your final choice of points will be the ones for which you have found the most adequate supporting materials. To recognize and evaluate supporting materials requires that you understand their functions. *To support (or to develop) means to clarify, reinforce, or prove a point.*

*To clarify* a point is to make the speaker's intended meaning clear to the audience. Suppose your point is, "Our impressions of other people often result from subliminal stimuli." Most of your listeners will not understand "subliminal stimuli." Your first job, perhaps your only job, is to clarify the meaning of your point by explaining the technical terms. More frequently, however, your point itself may require clarification, not because of technical words, but because of words that have more than one possible meaning. An example of this type of point is, "This college should adopt the honor system." What do you mean by "honor system"? Or, "Congressional investigating committees should be curbed." Exactly what committees do you mean? And precisely what do you mean by "curbed"?

*To reinforce* means to strengthen a point with which the audience already agrees. The point that "all of us should vote in campus elections" is clear enough, and most of your classmates would agree that the point is true. Yet a large percentage of students neglects to vote. Therefore the job is to strengthen that existing agreement. Make the point more vivid; dramatize its importance; motivate the students to turn their belief into action. You can readily think of other points that require and deserve reinforcement: "Drive safely," "Give to the Red Cross," "Be loyal to your school."

*To prove* means to demonstrate the probability that a statement is true. If you said, "Jim Jackson is the best qualified of the candidates for student body president," your meaning would be clear enough. If you were addressing a group of Jim Jackson's friends and supporters, you would try to reinforce the point. If the point were to be discussed before an audience who disagreed with you or were undecided, however, proof would be necessary. Any point with which the listeners are not in accord must be proved. On controversial questions, do not expect to demonstrate absolute truth; seek to establish the probability that your point is true. If your point, for example, is that "intercollegiate football is being overemphasized," you cannot show that the statement is absolutely true or absolutely false; you can only undertake to demonstrate the probability of its truth.

You will see that often a point needs to be clarified *and* reinforced, clarified *and* proved, or all three.

With a clear understanding of the functions of supporting materials, you are now prepared to look for, recognize, and evaluate the principal forms of support: explanation, description, anecdotes, instances, quotations, statistics, and audio-visual aids.

FORMS    *Explanation.*    Explanation is most often used to clarify, sometimes to reinforce, occasionally to prove. In a talk where you plan to use a good deal of explanatory material your research should accomplish two purposes: (1) improve your own understanding of the subject; and (2) help you gear your talk to the audience's level of knowledge and experience. Explanation includes definition, analogy, classification, or analysis.

Every beginning speaker should learn to define his terms. He should learn to define not only single words but also phrases or even concepts. There are several ways of classifying types of definitions. One useful classification is this:

> I. Nominal
> II. Formal
> III. Operational
>   A. Denotative
>   B. Connotative

In nominal definition you simply give a synonym such as "IQ means intelligence quotient." In a formal definition (often quoted from an authority) you first name the general class of phenomena and then give the *differentia* or details which distinguish the object or event from other members of the same class. Thus, "IQ is a measurement of intelligence which shows the numerical relationship between an individual's mental age and chronological age." In a denotative operational definition you tell the audience how the object or event acts, occurs, or is produced (often using visual or verbal examples); for example, "IQ is a numerical score which is obtained after giving the Stanford-Binet intelligence test." In a connotative operational definition you reveal individual attitudes toward the term being defined. For instance, "IQ is supposed to be a measure of intelligence but no one really knows whether it is valid; it is an attempt of an inexact science to become exact merely by using or misusing formulas and numbers."

If you plan to use an unfamiliar term, either define it yourself or look for definitions of it, remembering that ordinary dictionary definitions are sel-

**Choose explanatory speech materials that can be presented vividly and clearly.**

dom adequate. Devereux C. Josephs, speaking before the New York State Bar Association, used an unusual term which he defined immediately, briefly, and clearly:

> This will mean more income per capita and an even greater growth in discretionary income, which is the technical term for money in the family budget not dedicated to the necessities of food, housing and clothing.[2]

College students and graduates are often called on to discuss technical subjects for audiences of laymen. In such talks special care must be taken to clarify technical words and concepts. A chemistry major gave a classroom talk on chemical warfare which was over the heads of almost all of his classmates. His reading had been from chemical journals. He would have been wise to have looked for additional materials showing how to translate technical into nontechnical language. For example, in the following quotation notice how Norman Cousins explained a technical term in plain language and with frequent references to common household chemicals and containers:

[2] Edwin Black and Harry P. Kerr, eds., *American Issues*, Harcourt, Brace & World, 1961, p. 21.

The most revolutionary development of all in the field of chemical warfare has the code name in the United States of "GB." It is a nerve gas. It is odorless and invisible. It is easy to disseminate. It can be packaged and delivered by short-range, medium-range, or long-range missiles. It can be spread over wide areas or used in limited situations by aerosol sprays. It can even be used in tiny dispensers of the kind that carry deodorizers.

GB, now being manufactured by the United States Army Chemical Corps, and, so far as is known, by other major powers, acts like a super-insecticide against human beings. Like DDT, its effect is widespread and almost instantaneous. Exposure to GB in gas form is lethal in a matter of seconds. A liquid droplet the size of a pencil dot on the skin will penetrate surface tissue and kill a man within ten to fifteen minutes.[3]

John Adams clarified a legal concept in his first speech in the Boston Massacre trials of 1770, combining definition and classification:

The law divides homicide into three branches; the first is "justifiable," the second, "excusable," and the third, "felonious." Felonious homicide is subdivided into two branches: the first is murder, which is killing with malice aforethought; the second is manslaughter, which is killing a man on a sudden provocation. Here, gentlemen, are four sorts of homicide; and you are to consider whether all the evidence amounts to the first, second, third, or fourth of these heads. . . .

The need for explanation is also vital when using terms that have various popular meanings, especially when we want to establish our own particular meaning. Harry Emerson Fosdick, in a sermon at Riverside Church, clarified his usage of "Christian ethic" by definition, and simultaneously he reinforced his point:

By Christian ethic I mean no mere ordinary, human decency, loving those who love us, but rather the radical, sometimes incredible, demands of Jesus that we love our enemies, that if smitten on one cheek we turn the other also or if compelled to go one mile we go two instead, that we do good to those who hate us and pray for those who despitefully use us. . . .[4]

The same possibility of using one support for two purposes was illustrated by Ernest Earnest when he used analogy both to clarify and to reinforce (for those who agreed) or prove (for those who disagreed):

Two deeply religious men may both desire the kingdom of heaven; one may try to reach it by praying continually, wearing a hair shirt, and refusing to bathe; the other by ministering to the sick. It is quite possible that the second

[3] "CBR vs. Man," *Saturday Review* (July 23, 1960), pp. 9–10.
[4] A. Craig Baird, ed., *Representative American Speeches: 1938–1939*, H. W. Wilson, 1939, p. 223.

man will find very little time to examine his soul or clarify points of theology. He therefore spends less time on his "specialty" than does the ascetic, but he may be more fully obtaining his objective.

The analogy may apply to a liberal education. It is quite possible that extreme specialization is not the best preparation for most professional or intellectual occupations.[5]

The telling use of explanation to clarify and prove was demonstrated by Dwight D. Eisenhower in a press conference when he was first running for President in 1952:

> I have been asked specifically what is my voting record and why should I have ever stated I was a Republican. As you know, I have been in the uniformed service for a long time and there has been little, if any, voting record to speak about until after February, 1948; I left active duty and felt that I had a right to participate as other citizens do in political activity.
>
> Now, at that moment, I did not register as a Republican because I held the belief and the hope that I could remain somewhat aloof from partisan politics because, as you know, I was not fully separated from the Army in the form of retirement or resignation.
>
> But in 1948, I voted the Republican ticket and there were two special elections in New York, one in '49 and then for Governor in '50, and I voted the Republican ticket. That is my entire voting record and to add to the other question—another question that has arisen in connection with it, I have never voted any Democratic ticket. . . .

Analysis means that you take something apart for purposes of explanation; synthesis means that you put the parts back together again. For example, the editors of *Life* supported the point that planning a flight to the moon is an "incredibly difficult undertaking" by analyzing the over-all difficulty in terms of dozens of technical dangers, each one of which could threaten the success of the entire plan. They said in part:

> Even if the vehicle finally leaves its pad with every part working admirably, even if it flies its pioneering trip with each machine doing its precise job, Apollo is still not assured of success. It must still fly through the hazards of space flight. The most fearsome of these will be solar radiation. High-speed nuclei of hydrogen atoms, called protons, come slamming through space from solar flares on the sun. In the worst flares these protons can penetrate any reasonable spaceship wall—with deadly effect on the men inside—or dislodge dangerous showers of X rays from metal surfaces. Another peril comes from meteoroids. Millions of these tiny bits of cosmic debris, each traveling at least 25,000 miles an hour, will hit the craft during its course.[6]

[5] *The American Scholar* (Autumn 1944).
[6] Paul Mandel—courtesy *Life*. Copr. 1962 Time, Inc. (April 27, 1962), p. 82B.

*Description.*    Description is mostly used to clarify, and clarification is especially helpful in talking about persons, places, or objects. For example, if you are giving a talk on Calvin Coolidge, look for photographs and written descriptions of him; you might even secure a firsthand description from someone who had seen Coolidge in person. You would seek the same types of descriptive materials for a talk on the scenic wonders of Alaska or the workings of a deep-freeze unit. However, description is often also used to reinforce a point. For instance, if you wanted to reinforce the point that facial animation is as important for beauty as perfect features, you could describe several people. Description is occasionally used to prove. For example, a man is on trial for drunken driving; the arresting officers and other witnesses testify that the defendant's hair was rumpled, his shirttail was out, his breath smelled of alcohol, and he wobbled when he walked.

The most important advice for using description is to make your descriptions realistic and vivid by appealing to the senses: sight, hearing, smell, touch, and taste. Barry Goldwater appealed to the visual sense when he wrote:

> Conservatives are frequently pictured as fat, stodgy old men, reclining in overstuffed chairs in the restful surroundings of exclusive clubs, concerned only with taxes and the spending of public money.
> Nothing could be a greater distortion of the truth.[7]

It would be difficult to find a more instructive presentation of the proper use of description than Victor Alvin Ketcham's well-known lecture, "The Seven Doors to the Mind and How to Open Them." He appeals to practically all the senses in this description of a lawyer's plea:

> You could see the dim outlines of that little country station as the train pulled in. You could smell the damp of the river fog as it came up around that station and made the darkness mystifying and confusing, particularly to an old person. You could feel the sharp, icy sting of the sleet as the violence of the storm drove it into the face of the frail old lady when she stepped down from the last step of the coach and stood timidly waiting for the train to pull out. You could hear the sharp puff of the locomotive and the creaking of the old wooden coaches (he made it plain that their equipment was old and worn out) as the train pulled out and the lights from the coach windows passed along the station platform and left it in complete darkness because the railroad had not kept the light on the platform in good condition.
> Then the speaker made every person walk, in imagination, with the frail old lady, over the ice-covered, uneven boards of the old station platform. When she fell off the end, it came with a sense of personal physical pain to every

[7] Los Angeles *Times,* September 3, 1961.

The things your classmates read and discuss in their leisure hours are often clues to their interests and may suggest good speech materials.

person present. She fell on her face in a pile of cinders and the taste of old ashes was in the mouth and their acrid smell in the nostrils of every person present.[8]

*Anecdotes.* For beginning speakers probably the most important form of support is the anecdote. It may be defined as a narrative example or brief story with a point. The anecdote is especially well adapted to the practicing of extemporaneous speaking. It is a potent technique for clarifying and reinforcing; it is often an excellent way to initiate a proof. There are many kinds of anecdotes. They may be humorous, serious, or both; they may be true or imaginary; they may be straight narration or take the form of an analogy, a parable, or fable.

In preparing for a particular speech, hunt for anecdotes that will precisely illustrate your points. Fred B. Millett in an address before the American Association of University Professors opened with a series of anecdotes,

[8] Willard Hayes Yeager, *Effective Speaking for Every Occasion,* Prentice-Hall, 1951, pp. 274–75. Reprinted by permission of Victor A. Ketcham, Jr.

each directly illustrating his point that a wave of censorship was sweeping across the country. One of his illustrations was as follows:

> A month or so ago, a most distinguished audience assembled for the private showing of a double-bill of moving pictures. The audience consisted of the Justices of the Supreme Court of the United States. The pictures were an old German movie entitled "M," and a French movie entitled "La Ronde," which had played for two years in the most exclusive cinema in London's West End. In assembling to view these pictures, the Justices were not moved by a common interest in either abnormal psychology or licentious behavior. They were assembled to decide whether or not the sovereign state of Ohio had acted legally in banning "M," and whether the New York State Board of Censors had acted legally in banning "La Ronde" on the grounds that it "would tend to corrupt public morals." [9]

Part of American folklore consists of often-repeated tales, perhaps fictitious, that have a timeless quality and that may be used to illustrate a variety of points on a variety of topics. In his opening remarks when assuming his duties as Chairman of the National Democratic Convention of 1960, LeRoy Collins made the point that the delegates should comport themselves according to the expectations of the millions of Americans who were following the convention on TV. To reinforce this point he used this anecdote:

> Many years ago I heard of a father who one night went to his son's room to see if he were tucked in and asleep. He entered the room very quietly and then realized that his son was on his knees saying his prayers. And he overheard his boy say clearly: "Help me to grow up to be the kind of man my daddy is."
> The father withdrew unnoticed. He went straight to his own room and got down on his own knees and prayed: "Dear God, please help me to be the kind of man my little boy wants me to be.[10]

Sometimes in your research you come across an idea that stimulates you to invent a hypothetical example of your own. The use of a hypothetical case to clarify and reinforce a point was shown by R. W. Jepson in a talk over the British Broadcasting System:

> Now there is one common characteristic about all these people. They are trying to introduce simplicity into matters where it really does not exist in actual life. This world is a complicated and changing world. But they are trying to make it fit into a more or less rigid framework. . . .
> Have you ever come across the man who buttonholes you and poses you

[9] *AAUP Bulletin* (Spring 1954).
[10] New York *Times,* July 13, 1960.

with a question and insists on your answering yes or no? He will say to you: "Now then, you are a free-trader, or aren't you?" And you might reply: "Well, the removal of all restrictions and barriers on international trade would be an ideal thing to my mind. But as things are—" Then he will burst in and say: "Come along now, I asked you a plain question. Give me a plain answer." Once again you will probably stammer out a few "buts." Then he will tell you you are hedging. "Either you are or you aren't," he will say. "Which is it? 'Yes' or 'No'?" You know the kind of person: the real "whole-hogger." [11]

Part of your research includes a review of your own experiences. Philip Murray used an anecdote drawn from his personal experience to help prove a point:

I addressed a great meeting in the city of Homestead just about two weeks ago. Homestead is a great steel center, and there were some 25,000 or 30,000 steelworkers there. At that meeting I endeavored to express in graphic form the real, true meaning of this issue. There was an old man there sixty-seven years of age. Forty-four out of those sixty-seven years had been spent in the service of the United States Steel Corporation. He stood beside me, broken down, no money, in a state of complete poverty. He could not pay his rent, he could not buy his medicine, could not provide himself with clothing or purchase his food—forty-four years of loyal service to that Corporation. I asked him to tell that great crowd of steelworkers what kind of a pension the Steel Corporation was paying him, after forty-four years of service, and he said, "The Steel Corporation, Mr. Murray, is paying me twenty-nine cents a month." Twenty-nine cents a month! His frame broken, in a state of complete destitution—and twenty-nine cents expended on that man, that human being who bears the dignity of a man and the dignity of God! Twenty-nine cents, and right across the hill, in a great modern plant, where the machinery is carefully nursed and protected, the same industry had expended in the year 1948, $146,000,000 to maintain the health and efficiency of its machine—the inanimate machine, a piece of metal.[12]

*Instances.*    As contrasted with the three forms of support just discussed, an instance is undetailed. It is an example, case, or fact, cited briefly. Instances may sometimes be used to clarify, but are usually used to reinforce or prove.

Sometimes you need to look for but one instance to support a point. Robert J. Blakely relied upon a single instance when he said:

One day in Des Moines a mysterious visit was paid to my editor, W. W. Waymack, by David Lilienthal. A week later Waymack was a member of the

[11] Reprinted from *Vital Speeches*, III (December 15, 1937), 135.
[12] A. Craig Baird, ed., *Representative American Speeches: 1949–1950*, H. W. Wilson, 1950, pp. 183–84. Reprinted by permission of the CIO.

Atomic Energy Commission. This illustrates the unpredictable responsibilities which fall to the lot of the citizens of a free society.[13]

If Blakely had elaborated upon this instance, he could have changed it into an anecdote. He wisely refrained, however, because additional details would only have cluttered, not improved, the illustration of his particular point.

A single instance is seldom sufficient to support a point. Generally, several instances are given in rapid sequence, producing a cumulative effect. In gathering materials, therefore, you look for instances which can be put together as a series or cluster. Here is how Clark Mollenhoff supported a point with a series of instances:

> There was testimony that Hoffa instructed a Teamster official to bring him reports from spying on the work of a Michigan grand jury that was studying Teamster-racket connections.
>
> There was testimony that Hoffa had some of his thugs talk to a key witness, and persuade him to leave the state of Michigan.
>
> There was testimony that Hoffa made a threat to kill or injure a Teamster union official who had been brave enough to testify against him.
>
> There was testimony that Hoffa tried to coerce the prosecutors who were taking aggressive action against his union.
>
> There was testimony that when indictments were returned against some of the members of Hoffa's Hoodlum Empire, he arranged to supply them with the best attorneys at union expense. This was when some of the individuals were charged with selling out their own union members.
>
> There was testimony that Hoffa made political contributions to the campaign of a judge who made key rulings on the criminal cases of his Teamster pals.[14]

Sometimes the gist of many pages of reading should be presented as a series of specific instances, each expressed in a sentence or a phrase. Consider this excerpt from a speech by J. William Fulbright before the United States Senate:

> But I ask you now: What show of "reflection and choice" was there in much of the decade of the 1950's when the word "egghead" became a word of abuse; when education was neglected; when intellectual excellence became a cause for suspicion; when the man in public life, or the writer, or the teacher, who dared articulate an original thought risked being accused of subversion? What show of "reflection and choice" was there in this period when the man of dis-tinction was the man who had a station wagon, a·second car plated with chrome,

---

[13] *Representative American Speeches: 1958–1959*, p. 157.
[14] Edwin Black and Harry P. Kerr, eds., *American Issues*, Harcourt, Brace & World, 1961, p. 74.

a swimming pool, a tax-free expense account, and a twenty-one-inch color television set with the thirty-six-inch star on its screen? [15]

Occasionally you will come upon materials which could be used as anecdotes or instances or statistics, depending on the amount of detail that you think should be included. We have already illustrated how an instance can be elaborated into an anecdote. Let us now consider how instances can be condensed to a point where they almost become statistics. Here is a portion of an address by Benjamin F. Fairless before the Baltimore Association of Commerce:

> The United States Census Bureau has recently completed its latest count of more than 400 American industries, and has reported on the degree of so-called "concentration" in each. And remember, I am speaking of entire *industries*—not individual companies.
>
> Now how many of these industries do you think are more highly "concentrated" than the steel industry? Three? . . . Ten? . . . Fifty?
>
> Well, guess again. The Census Bureau's own report on "steel works and rolling mills" shows this industry is not anywhere near the top at all. It is in the great middle, along with the great body of all American industries. In fact, it stands 174th on the list. *So there are 173 entire industries which are more highly concentrated than steel.*
>
> Now what are some of these industries where the "concentration of power" in the hands of the "big four" is so great as to menace our national welfare and to arrest the pursuit of happiness?
>
> You'd never guess.
>
> There is the pretzel industry for one. Honestly, that's right. I mean it.
>
> And there are the candlemakers too.
>
> Then there are straw hats, and streetcars, breakfast foods and chewing tobacco, wallpaper and cigar boxes, lead pencils and pianos. Then we have women's neckwear and boys' underwear. And, oh yes—window shades and garters.
>
> Now if every one of these—plus 159 other industries—is more highly "concentrated" than steel, and if "concentration" is really as wicked as our theorists tell us it is, I can't for the life of me understand why all these high-priced Congressional committees are wasting their time on me.[16]

*Quotations.*    Quotations are, of all forms of support, the most varied. This form, by its nature, can include any of the other forms; that is, instead of giving your own explanation, you can quote someone else's. Likewise you may quote someone else's description, anecdote, or instance. You may quote

[15] A. Craig Baird, ed., *Representative American Speeches: 1958–1959*, H. W. Wilson, 1959, pp. 128–29.
[16] *Representative American Speeches: 1949–1950*, pp. 176–77. Reprinted by permission of Benjamin F. Fairless.

prose or poetry, you may quote from books, plays, speeches, almanacs, newspapers, conversations, and folk proverbs. Quotations are equally useful to clarify, reinforce, or prove.

In preparing to speak on some topics you may want to gather a few apt quotations from well-tried sources with almost universal appeal—the Bible, the Declaration of Independence, Shakespeare, Abraham Lincoln. However, the first requirement of an effective quotation is that it be directly pertinent to your point. Usually, therefore, your topic and your main points should suggest specific, and often specialized, persons or other sources.

You should be alert for quotations that are not only pertinent, but also clearly and eloquently worded. For instance, here is a "quotable quote" from an address by Nelson A. Rockefeller upon his inauguration as forty-ninth governor of New York:

> And we know something else: we know how and why this world is divided and imperiled.
>
> It is divided, essentially, between those who believe in the brotherhood of men under the fatherhood of God—and those who scorn this as a pious myth.
>
> It is divided between those who believe in the dignity of free men—and those who believe in the monstrous supremacy of the totalitarian state.
>
> It is divided between those whose most potent force is their faith in individual freedom—and those whose faith is force itself.
>
> It is divided between those who believe in the essential equality of peoples of all nations and races and creeds—and those whose only creed is their own ruthless race for power.[17]

When a quotation is used for proof, rather than for clarification or reinforcement, the authority of the source becomes of critical significance. The strength of an authority rests in the attitude of your audience. The current TV Western hero would be a stronger authority than Einstein even on the subject of relativity—before an audience of youngsters. For older audiences, you should look for quotations from persons whom the listeners will consider expert, well qualified, and unbiased or unprejudiced. Sometimes the name of your source will suffice to establish authority; at other times part of your research will include looking up the qualifications of persons you wish to quote—consult *Who's Who* or other appropriate references.

Poetry can often be used to bring emotional or aesthetic reinforcement to a point. Joseph Richard Sizoo, in a sermon for a graduating class at George Washington University, climaxed a series of instances with a poetical quotation:

[17] *Representative American Speeches: 1958–1959,* p. 111.

We have changed from sailing ships to jet airliners, from hieroglyphics to electric typewriters, from clay tablets to Oxford editions, from mud huts to penthouses, but to what end? What is the good of a civilization whose art ends in comic strips, whose music ends in rock 'n' roll, whose learning ends in red-back-magazine stories of smutted lives and soiled tempers coated over with psychoanalysis and tossed off as literature, whose science ends in the capacity of self-destruction? Education may rationalize life, government may nationalize life, business may mechanize life, but only religion can spiritualize life. Vachel Lindsey wrote it for us in these words,

> Not that they starve, but starve so drearily,
>   Not that they sow, but that they never reap,
> Not that they serve, but have no Gods to serve,
>   Not that they die, but that they die like sheep.[18]

In preparing for a speech you should gather a generous supply of quotations—more than you can use. If necessary, you should be able to cite a list of different authorities, all supporting the same point. If you are working on a controversial subject, you should collect quotations on *both* sides of the question. Studying "the other side" always helps to clarify your own thinking; quoting the opposition sometimes provides you with a needed opportunity for rebuttal; quoting them may even demonstrate that their argument condemns itself. For example, in September, 1961, President Kennedy made a clear and eloquent statement to the United Nations General Assembly:

It is therefore our intention to challenge the Soviet Union, not to an arms race, but to a peace race—to advance with us step by step, stage by stage, until general and complete disarmament has actually been achieved. We invite them now to go beyond agreement in principle to reach agreement on actual plans.

The program to be presented to this assembly—for general and complete disarmament under effective international control—moves to bridge the gap between those who insist on a gradual approach and those who talk only of the final and total achievement. It would create machinery to keep the peace as it destroys the machines of war.[19]

Next day Soviet Foreign Minister Gromyko replied to the above statement as follows:

No one knows now what armaments and armed forces the states possess. And this is quite normal. The same situation will endure after the implementation of disarmament measures provided for in this or that stage, pending the completion of general and complete disarmament. Therefore the armament of states will continue to be unknown, but with the substantial difference that a considerable part of the armaments will have been liquidated and over this,

[18] *Representative American Speeches: 1958–1959*, p. 167.
[19] Los Angeles *Times*, September 26, 1961.

effective control will be instituted. Upon the implementation of general and complete disarmament there will be established permanent and comprehensive control.[20]

Gromyko's statement might be quoted for the very reason that it is not eloquent; it is not even clear; it is meaningless double-talk.

*Statistics.* Many speeches require the gathering of statistics—a talk on business trends or one on population growth, for instance. To find appropriate statistics you will sometimes go to special sources, such as the stock market reports or census reports. In such cases you may want to copy down long lists of figures which you can study in order to improve your own understanding of a topic, but you must also be able to condense and simplify these large amounts of numerical data before using them in the actual speech. Frequently, however, you will find books, articles, or speeches in which statistics have already been reduced to usable form.

Writing in *Harper's Magazine* under the title, "The Hidden Affair between Big Business and Big Labor," Bernard D. Nossiter clarified and reinforced a point with statistics:

> For example, U. S. Steel last year gave 120 of its executives options on 151,000 shares at $55. This spring, the stock had risen $40 a share above this. Any time a top Steel executive needed cash, he picked up his telephone, told the company treasurer to issue him a few thousand of his optioned shares, and told his broker to sell them at the market price. Thus our executive cleared $40 a share with two telephone calls—and without investing a cent of his own money.[21]

Harold H. Martin used statistics for clarification and proof of a point regarding inequities of our income tax laws:

> A taxpayer with a wife and two children, with $7,000 in income derived exclusively from wages or salary, would pay a tax of $780. A taxpayer in similar circumstances, with $7,000 in income derived from dividends, would pay $609.60. A taxpayer with $7,000 received from the sale of securities giving him a long-term capital gain would pay a tax of $155. A taxpayer whose $7,000 came from interest on state or municipal securities would pay no tax at all.[22]

*Audio-visual supports.* In many talks, especially when the purpose is to inform, some points can be supported best by means of audio-visual aids. For example, a complicated set of statistics might be translated into a chart,

[20] Los Angeles *Times*, September 27, 1961.
[21] *Harper's Magazine* (July 1959).
[22] "What's Wrong with Our Income-Tax Laws?" *The Saturday Evening Post* (July 15, 1961).

or the uses of a tape recorder might be clarified by actually operating one of the machines during the course of the speech. It is sometimes impractical or inappropriate to use audio-visual aids, but they are so often helpful that you will want to give careful thought to them while gathering materials for almost any speech.

The list of audio-visual supports given below will suggest their great variety. Several of the listed techniques are illustrated by the photographs on pages 102 and 103.

PERSONS (Philip Murray's speech, page 95.)

ANIMALS (TV talk on dog training.)

CLOTHING (Talk on fashions illustrated by costumed dolls.)

OBJECTS (Any TV commercial selling any object.)

APPARATUS (Scientist illustrating a laboratory experiment.)

MODELS (Lecture at a planetarium.)

SILENT MOTION PICTURES (Football coach analyzing last week's game. Advantage of silent movies is that you can talk while they are being shown.)

SOUND MOTION PICTURES (Cheerleader analyzing last week's game. Sound as well as sight would be necessary to develop his points.)

FILM STRIPS (Talk on architecture. Still shots would be better than motion pictures.)

SLIDES (Same as film strips.)

LARGE PICTURES (Talk on art with visual aids used on platform.)

SMALL PICTURES (Same talk but with pictures passed around among audience.)

DIAGRAMS, CHARTS, GRAPHS (Talk involving statistics or complex relationships.)

MAPS (Talk in which geography is vital to the development of your ideas.)

MIMEOGRAPHED MATERIALS (Talk to inform, with too many points to be remembered without written outline.)

CHALKBOARD (You have seen too many examples already.)

OVERHEAD PROJECTOR (See picture and accompanying footnote, page 102.)

PHONOGRAPH RECORDS (Talk on music or the reading of poetry.)

PLACARDS (Cartoons are often effective.)

*Combined forms.* This lengthy discussion of supports should not mislead you into the belief that the several forms are always clearly differentiated or that points are usually developed by only one support. In actual practice you will find many excellent supporting materials that combine two or more of the forms here recommended. For example: Woodrow Wil-

By means of this Vu-Graph overhead projector the speaker has flashed a map on the wall behind him and he is pointing to one place on the map with his pencil.[23]

son was once asked to deliver a five-minute talk, but declined on the grounds that it would require a month of preparation.

"In that case," inquired his astonished guest, "how long would it take to prepare a ten-minute talk?"

"Two weeks."

"And how long for a half-hour speech?"

"One week."

[23] Overhead projectors are remarkably versatile. They can be used in a lighted room. The speaker can use prepared materials or he can write or draw while he is speaking. The machine enlarges his writing or drawing, and projects it on the wall or screen behind the speaker. The advantage over a chalkboard is that he can face the audience at all times while writing. The advantage over a slide projector is that the speaker can operate the machine himself and still remain in front of his audience. Overhead projectors may be bought under several commercial names.

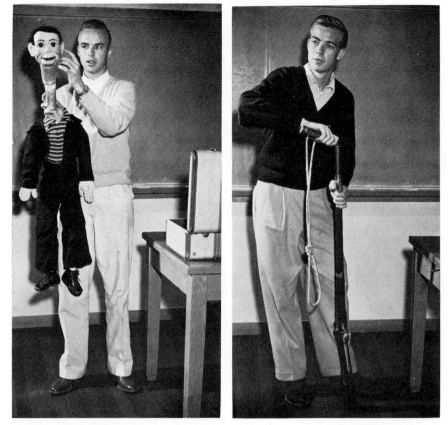

R. GRAVES

The student on the left is giving an ingenious visual-aids talk, using a model as he explains how ventriloquists make their own dummies. At the right is another unusual visual aid used in a talk showing how old-fashioned, muzzle-loading rifles operate.

Choose visual aids that will be clearly visible to the audience. In this picture the visual aid is too small to be seen by the audience comfortably.

FREDERICK WILLIAMS

PRINCETON UNIVERSITY

Here are your three basic methods of research: observation, reading, and conversation.

MONKMEYER

"How long for a one-hour speech?"

"Oh," said Wilson, "I can give that right now."

Now this is an anecdote, of course, but notice that it contains elements of several other forms of support: quotation, instance, explanation, statistics. You will frequently find overlapping among the six verbal forms of support. Some supports cannot be readily classified as one or another of the particular forms. Is this an anecdote or an instance? Is that an explanation or a description? Is this a quotation or a statistic? Such overlapping should not disturb you; regardless of the label, use a support if it clarifies, reinforces, or proves your point.

In actual practice you will normally expect to employ two or more supports for any point. Some of them tend to make especially good sequences. For example, an anecdote is nicely followed by instances; instances blend well into statistics; quotation teams up nicely with any of the others; explanation and description combine naturally with visual aids. Any combination of two or more forms is possible. If you want to prove a point, you might begin with explanation to make sure the audience understands the point. Next you might relate an anecdote to make the point vivid; then give instances to establish that the anecdote was not an exceptional case; next, give statistics to show proportions in terms of a whole population; and finally, quote from authorities to impress the listeners with the fact that qualified experts believe the point to be true. It all depends upon how important you think the point is and how much effort you think is required to clarify, reinforce, or prove it.

## How to find speech materials

There are three principal ways of finding speech materials: observation, conversation, and reading.

### Observation

From your experience as part of an audience, you know that you would much rather listen to a discussion of rattlesnakes by someone who had been bitten by one or who had witnessed the death struggle between a rattler and a king snake than by someone whose knowledge came only from books. As a listener you like materials from firsthand observation.

It should be clear by now that facts gained by direct observation are not merely permissible but vital for good speechmaking. Observation is the basis of all knowledge; it is basic to scientific method. It provides color and vitality in speech materials; it thwarts the tendency toward the bookish or the overly academic. With a little ingenuity, you can gather all sorts of excellent speech materials by observation. Here are three suggestions to get you started.

CASUAL OBSERVATION  Casual observation will provide you with an occasional description or anecdote if you know what to look for. For example, a student found his parked car hemmed in snugly by cars front and rear. After vainly maneuvering to get out, he went to the car in front and tried to open the door. It was locked. Then the frustrated student went berserk. He kicked the offending car furiously, apparently oblivious of the growing circle of astonished spectators. Suddenly he noticed a brick nearby. Grabbing it, he rushed back to the car and beat a window out. Hurling the brick into the car, he reached through the broken window and released the brake. This incident might be used to illustrate any number of points: campus parking problems, auto insurance, crimes of passion, temper tantrums, or emotional control. Probably not a week goes by that you do not witness some incident that would make good speech material.

PLANNED OBSERVATION  For example, if you were gathering materials for a speech on suburban growth, you might supplement your study of zoning maps and building codes by making a planned tour of selected construction areas—frequently using notebook and pencil (and perhaps even a camera).

Planned observations are made not only through the sense of sight but through all the senses. Thus listening is a part of the method. Excellent speech materials of all types may be secured by listening to lectures or plays; to radio or television broadcasts of speeches, news comments, plays, readings; to phonograph recordings; and to sound motion pictures. And so with all the senses. You can collect material for certain speech subjects by your sense of smell, other material by your sense of taste. If you were to speak on the textures of various cloths, you would certainly make planned observations with your sense of touch.

## Conversation

You can also gather good speech materials through conversations. One method is the interview. It is easy to find experts or authorities on many speech topics by scanning a list of the faculty at your institution. Experts may also be found among your local businessmen, politicians, ministers, and labor leaders. Most people are glad to help, even very important people. A university debater made a visit to Washington, D. C., where he was given cordial interviews by three senators, two cabinet officers, and the Vice President of the United States. Don't become a nuisance or waste busy people's time, but don't neglect legitimate opportunities.

Sometimes interviews can provide useful local-color materials. Thus, for a classroom talk on unemployment, one student spent a night at a twenty-five-cent "flophouse," talking with his fellow guests. His speech rated a story in the campus newspaper. Good materials on unemployment might also be gathered by visiting an employment office and chatting with the applicants. There is local color everywhere if you have the eye to see it and the wit to make use of it.

## Reading

Valuable as observation and conversation are, reading must, of necessity, remain the most fruitful source of research materials. Students, however, vary widely in reading ability and library skill. If you read poorly or feel lost in a big library, you should start a program of improvement at once.

**PURPOSEFUL READING**  Much time is saved by knowing what *not* to read. Why spend several hours mechanically plodding through a book only to discover at the end that it is not what you wanted? Learn how to skim a book. Notice the title, author, and date of publication; read the table of contents; scan the index; leaf through the book and read a paragraph here

Each hour invested now in improving your library-research techniques will save you hundreds of hours in the future.

FREDERICK WILLIAMS

and there. You can distinguish between a book likely to contain anecdotes and one likely to contain statistics. You can tell whether a book bears directly or only indirectly on the central idea of your speech. You can tell if it is too old, or poorly written. And if you seriously doubt its value to your search, put it aside, for you have many other choices.

Read slowly and critically when your purpose is to think through the subject. On the other hand, skim through materials when looking only for particular items, such as instances or statistics.

USE OF INDEXES   The next step toward purposeful research is to learn to use the common library indexes. Through them you can get a perspective upon the general types and quantity of material dealing with your subject; if there is a great deal of such material, choose only the most likely references first. We shall list and describe some of these indexes here, but to give them meaning, you will have to go to your library and handle them.

To see what books a given library has that deal with your subject, consult that library's card catalogue. Although used chiefly for books, the card catalogue indexes all materials in a library. Most books have at least three cards in the catalogue, alphabetically listed under the author's name, the title of the book, and the general topic.

To find magazine articles from general and popular periodicals:
  *Readers' Guide to Periodical Literature* (1900–    )
For older articles of the same nature:
  *Poole's Index to Periodical Literature* (1802–1906)
For articles in specialized or technical journals:
  *Agricultural Index*
  *Art Index*
  *Book Review Digest*
  *Dramatic Arts Index*
  *Education Index*
  *Index Medicus*
  *Index to Vital Speeches*
  *Industrial Arts Index*
  *International Index to Periodicals*
  *Psychological Abstracts*
  *The Public Affairs Information Service*
For pamphlets:
  *The Vertical File Service Catalogue*
For government publications:
  *Catalogue of the Public Documents*
  *Monthly Catalogue of the United States Public Documents*

For newspaper materials:
*The New York Times Index*

If you have trouble in finding or using these indexes, ask the librarian for help.

From the foregoing indexes you can secure a long list of references on almost any topic. You must learn to evaluate the references in terms of your needs. The title of an article usually gives the most direct clues, but they are frequently deceiving. If you recognize an author's name, it may help you judge. The dates of publication may be significant. Through experience you will learn what type of material to expect in various leading publications. From the data in the catalogues you can decide which books or magazines are most likely to contain the sort of materials you want.

USE OF GENERAL REFERENCE BOOKS    Every library has general reference books, and many libraries place them conveniently in a section of shelves available for browsing. Spend an afternoon exploring these books. For example, suppose you are preparing a speech and would like to have a few appropriate quotations from famous people. You will find that there are books of quotations, the quotations arranged under headings by topic or by author:

*Bartlett's Familiar Quotations,* Morley and Everett
*Cyclopedia of Practical Quotations,* Hoyt
*Home Book of Quotations,* Stevenson
*A New Dictionary of Quotations,* Mencken

You can sometimes do even better. You can find an appropriate quotation or allusion from a specific important writer by consulting a *concordance* to his works. Concordances to the Bible and the works of Shakespeare are the most commonly useful.

Speech students should be familiar with these four dictionaries:
*Webster's New International Dictionary*
*Funk and Wagnalls New Standard Dictionary*
*Oxford English Dictionary,* Murray
*A Pronouncing Dictionary of American English,* Kenyon and Knott
And two other wordbooks:
*Roget's Thesaurus*
*Webster's Dictionary of Synonyms*
For handy reference to facts and statistics of almost every kind:
*The Statesman's Yearbook*

*The Statistical Abstract of the United States*
*The World Almanac*
For information about people:
*Dictionary of American Biography*
*Webster's Biographical Dictionary*
*Who's Who in America*
And many other specialized *Who's Who* volumes
For historical facts:
*Dictionary of Dates*, Keller
*Encyclopedia of World History*, Langer
For geographical facts:
*Rand-McNally World Atlas*
For social science facts:
*Encyclopaedia of the Social Sciences*
For verbatim record of speeches in Congress, plus miscellaneous material:
*Congressional Record*
For summaries of current controversial questions:
*Congressional Digest*
*Reference Shelf* series
For general factual materials:
*The Encyclopedia Americana*
*The Encyclopaedia Britannica*
*The New International Encyclopedia*
For oddities:
*Famous First Facts*, Kane
*Things Not Generally Known*, Wells

USE OF VARIED SOURCES   Only for rare and special reasons should you ever restrict your research to the reading of a single source or author. For breadth of background, for the stimulus of reading divergent views, and for improvement in the accuracy and originality of your own thought, always read from several sources as you gather materials for your speech. One author may give you the data you need, but it takes several authors to provide you with the points of view you need if your research is to be adequate.

### How to record speech materials

*Note taking for a specific speech*

Develop a system for keeping notes during your research on a topic, and keep all your notes in accordance with that system. Write notes on observations or conversations as soon after the event as possible, while the facts are still fresh in your mind. For notes on reading, do not pause every time you think you have something to write. That will interrupt your thought, and it may be that further on in the text the point is stated even better. Read a logical unit of material such as a section, a chapter, or even an entire short article; then pause and digest the unit in perspective; finally, if anything is worth recording make your notes.

In writing a notation, quote exactly when the materials demand absolute accuracy, when the writer has given a convenient and succinct summary of a main idea, when the writer's name will carry unusual prestige with your audience, or when he has stated a point brilliantly. Summarize in your own words when the foregoing conditions do not hold and when a lengthy block of material can and should be condensed. Note down your own reactions to the materials. Your reactions may or may not be in agreement with what you are reading. Sometimes the best use of an article is that it stimulates you to think of a rebuttal.

The following note-taking procedure is suggested:

1. Use four by six cards.

2. Record only one idea on each card. You may want to file this card later, and one card cannot be filed in two or more places.

3. On the top line write a heading for the card in capital letters. This should resemble the headline for a newspaper story and enable you to tell at a glance what is on the card.

4. On the second line write the source. For printed materials, the identification should be such that you could find the source again quickly. For sources from observation and conversation, put down whatever may have bearing on the use of the data, including the date.

5. Skip a line and then put your notation. Be extremely careful to distinguish among the three types of notations. Thus, if you are quoting directly, be sure to enclose the words in quotation marks. If you omit any words, indicate the omission by three periods separated by spaces (if the omission is at the end of a sentence, use four periods). If you insert any words, surround them with brackets (not parentheses). But never omit or insert words that would change the intent of the writer. When you are summarizing in your own words, do not use quotation marks. Your own remarks should be labeled "Comment."

Your comments may express your attitudes toward the subject matter on the card. Often, however, your comments may deal with the possible use of the materials in a speech. Some examples: "This states my central idea." "Some of these technical terms must be defined." "I could use this item in such a way as to get audience participation. Show of hands maybe?"

These suggestions are illustrated by the specimen card below.

---

"FREUDIAN FEVER"

Ralph Schoenstein, "Merrily We Probe Along," <u>Sat. Eve. Post</u>, Sept. 1, 1962, p. 10.

    "The Great American Game is no longer baseball. It's psychoanalysis. Those who don't play are considered odd. . . . Touched by Freudian fever, people who'd always thought they were happy are suddenly learning how very sick they are. 'You poor fool!' a woman recently exclaimed, regarding me with pity. 'How can you dare tell me you're happy when you haven't even been analyzed!'"

    COMMENT: This quotation might make a good opening for a talk on psychoanalysis.

---

Specimen card of notes.

## *Note taking for future speeches*

In your observation, conversation, and reading, you will continually run across materials likely to be useful to you in future talks for this class or, later on, for speeches in connection with your profession. Thus you may read a striking statement that expresses one of your most profound convictions, or you may find a delightful anecdote that you are sure could be used in many future speeches. If you fail to record these finds, you will soon forget them. The sooner you start a public speaking scrapbook, the better.

The scrapbook may be an actual scrapbook, a loose-leaf notebook, or a card file. Regardless of the form, it should be an expanding and changing record. Eventually, you will want to decide on your own set of categories to file materials, but as a beginning the following are workable:

> Speech subjects and topics
> Ideas for sets of main heads
> Quotable quotes (including poetry)
> Good words and phrases
> Humorous anecdotes
> Serious anecdotes
> Facts and figures

The published example of a speech scrapbook is William Hoffman's *The Public Speaker's Scrapbook* (McGraw-Hill, 1935), which you can find at your library. It will show that a scrapbook must be a personal and individual achievement. You are the only person who can decide when to omit, when to clip and paste, when to add a comment. Start the project now; it is enjoyable, and you may work on it the rest of your life.

## Summary

In preparing for a speech you should gather more materials than you can use in the actual speech. Your listeners should never feel that in one short talk you have exhausted your knowledge of your subject.

Research efficiency is improved when you know what types of materials to look for. Speech materials include points and subpoints, and their supports. "To support" means to clarify, reinforce, or prove a point. A practical list of verbal forms of support comprises explanation, description, anecdotes, instances, quotations, statistics. The verbal forms can be approximately matched by audio-visual aids. All the supporting materials can be used or combined in a wide variety of ways.

Three methods for finding speech materials include observation, conversation, and reading. Skill in library research will be improved if you learn to read with a purpose, use library indexes and general reference books, and read from varied sources.

For the recording of speech materials you should develop a system of taking notes on cards to be used in preparing a specific talk. You will also want to begin the compilation of your public speaker's scrapbook for possible use in future speeches.

TOPICAL PREVIEW

# 7

# SPEECH OUTLINING

### Definition of speech outlining

Speech outlining is a method of putting the ideas of a speech into a condensed written form that indicates the relationships among those ideas by means of alphabetical letters, numerals, and identifications.

Thinking is the core of outlining; the outline itself is only a written record of thought. The making of a written outline assists your thinking process in several ways: (1) It helps clarify thinking by slowing you down and reminding you of idea relationships. (2) It conserves the product of thought by forcing you to record ideas before forgetting them. (3) It provides a way to test the accuracy of your thinking because you (or somebody else) can review it later on.

### The speech unit

If you were to ask a beginning student to give a short one-point talk on "There Is No Use Trying to Please Everybody," you would probably get something like the following:

| | |
|---|---|
| *Salutation* | Mr. Chairman, Fellow Students: |
| *Main point* | I have been asked to give a speech on the subject, "There Is No Use Trying to Please Everybody." |
| *Support* | This is an important and interesting topic. I believe that the point is a true one. After all, human nature is human |

nature. On most questions, some people believe in one side, other people believe the opposite side, and still others believe yet another side. If you cater to one group, you will probably antagonize the others. If you try to reconcile all the contradictory points of view, you will probably be accused of being an appeaser. Furthermore, you cannot appease them all without sacrificing your real principles. And, after all, what is more important than one's principles? They are the real lamps by which our feet should be guided. If we are willing to depart from our principles, we cannot be trusted. Therefore, you might better decide from the start upon your basic principles; chart your course like a mariner who wishes to cross a stormy sea; and take a consistent stand regardless of what other people think. Too many people try to steer their ships in terms of what the neighbors will say. But if we try to be guided by what the neighbors say, we will constantly have to turn the steering wheel because some of our neighbors will say one thing while at the same time another neighbor will say something else.

*Straying* — to the left of the second/third lines
*from*
*point*

*Confused and* — to the left
*confusing*
*metaphor*

*Restating* — So let's face it. If you try to please everybody, you
*Main point* usually end up by pleasing nobody.

The main point is supported mostly by restating the point, and to some extent by a weak explanation. The sequence of sentences is logical only in a loose, free-associational sense. The sample illustrates a typical, ineffective development of an idea.

For contrast, consider another way of developing the same talk.

*Salutation* Mr. Chairman, Fellow Students:

*Main point* There is no use trying to please everybody.

*Transition* Aesop illustrated this point hundreds of years ago when he related the fable of the farmer who made a journey in company with his son and his mule.

*Support* This farmer and his son and the mule started their journey
*(anecdote)* by walking along the public road in single file. Presently they passed a group of neighbors, and the farmer overheard someone say, "Look at those stupid people—walking when one of them might just as well ride the mule." Not wishing to be considered stupid by his neighbors, the farmer mounted the mule, and the journey was continued. Soon they passed another group of travelers, and the farmer was shocked to

hear one of them remark, "There goes an example of a father who likes to pose as a king—he rides in comfort but forces his young son to trudge in the heat and dust." Sensitive to such criticism, the farmer at once changed places with his son. This was all right until they passed another pair of travelers. One of them said to the other, "Just observe that ridiculous picture—a healthy, strapping boy riding the mule while his poor old father must walk." Much chagrined, the farmer thought of another solution; he mounted behind his son and both of them rode. But shortly they encountered another group, and this time the farmer flinched at the criticism, "Seldom will you see worse cruelty—two big strong men riding that exhausted little animal." So the farmer and his son dismounted, secured the mule's feet with a rope over a timber, and began carrying the mule. They were crossing a bridge where the mule, upside down, looked into the water with alarm and began to kick so vigorously that all three members of the party toppled off into the water.

*Transition*      The moral of Aesop's fable is clear.

*Restating*       If you try to please everybody, you usually end up by

*main point*      pleasing nobody.

This talk consists of a single *unit*, the principal parts of which are one main *point* and one *support*. The point is in the form of a *statement* and the support is in the form of an *anecdote*. The point is also in the form of a *restatement* at the end of the unit. Point, support, and restatement are linked together by *transitions*.

This speech contains all the fundamental elements of speech construction. Longer and more complicated speeches involve the following elaborations of these elements:

1. Subpoints (as well as a main point)
2. Several main points (instead of one)
3. Several supports (instead of one)
4. Several forms of support (instead of anecdote only)
5. More numerous, subtler, more complex transitions

## Mechanics of speech outlining

### Detail in an outline

Here is a stack of student speech outlines. They vary in almost all respects, including length. For brevity and stimulation of a reader's imagination, one outline entitled "Wrestling and Rassling" is a masterpiece. Here is the entire outline:

I. Wrestling takes brains.
II. Rassling takes brawn.
III. Last June in Detroit I broke my ankle.

That is condensed, all right. It tells just enough to goad the reader's curiosity—how is that last point related to the others? Such brevity in outlining is not uncommon. A substantial percentage of students think that an outline is simply a listing of three, four, or five main points. But an outline should contain more than main points—there should also be subpoints and supports.

Excessively detailed outlines, however, are as common as very brief ones. Here is just the first point from an outline for a three-minute talk:

I. In my experience last summer as a Y.M.C.A. supervisor for both boys and girls, I found that children do think and have minds of their own.
  A. "My" children were from the ages of nine to twelve.
    1. This is a dangerous age because they are preparing to enter adolescence.

This student has an outline on the lectern in front of him. Thus he can keep his entire speech in perspective, while his notes remain inconspicuous to the audience.

B. The real fun began when we took them to the alligator farm. The attendant guided us through the pens filled with the monsters.
   1. Billy, my most obnoxious and curious charge, disappeared.
   2. Where did I find him but in the position of almost being eaten alive.
   3. Billy was dangling from the fence of the most dangerous bull alligator's pen.
   4. I approached carefully, not wishing to scare Billy or the alligator.
   5. I said, "Billy, you shouldn't be up there. You'll get your arm eaten."
   6. Billy said, "It's my arm. If I want it eaten, I'll have it eaten."
   7. What could I do?
   8. Yes, children do have minds of their own.

The outline continues in similar style for six pages. As you see, it adds up to a script containing all the words of the speech with most of the sentences numbered and indented. Result: Too much detail destroys perspective and defeats one of the main purposes of outlining, which is condensation.

There is no hard and fast rule by which to establish the exact length of an outline. Avoid the extreme brevity of the "rassling" outline and the excessive detail of the "alligator" outline. Be guided by the general principle that an outline should contain all the ideas essential to the speech but not all, or even most, of the words. The application of this principle will become clearer as you study other aspects of outline building.

### The three major divisions

Most speeches should have a beginning (introduction), a middle (body or discussion), and an end (conclusion). Inexperienced speakers will be wise to use introduction, body, and conclusion as the three major divisions for all their speech outlines; variations from this practice should not be tried until the student has had considerable speaking experience. In a speech outline the three major divisions should stand out clearly; they should be capitalized and centered but not numbered. They should not be confused as in the following student outline:

   I. How would you feel if confronted by sudden death?
     A. Illustration
     B. Illustration
  II. Conclusion of point
     A. How
     B. "Fear, fear itself"

Of course, the outline is too brief. A more interesting fault, however, is its confusion as to introduction, body, and conclusion. One might suspect that the rhetorical question (*I*) was planned as an opening designed to arouse attention, but it is not so labeled. And the use of the word *Conclusion* (*II*) is a further hint that the student was trying to follow the proper form. This speech may have had a good plan, but the outline conceals rather than reveals it.

### The central idea

A well-organized talk should have a central idea to which every thought in the speech is clearly related. This central idea should be concisely stated in the outline. The importance of such a statement in clarifying the plan of a speech may be illustrated by another outline.

 I. Opening sentence
 II. Example of the coed
 III. The minister's troubles
 IV. The story of Mark Twain
 V. Closing statement

Another teaser. Apparently the student planned an opening and a conclusion —his Roman numerals *I* and *V*. Therefore *II, III,* and *IV* must be the body of the speech. But what on earth is uniting the coed, the minister, and Mark Twain? To find out, we would have to know the central idea, which the student failed to state.

A statement of the central idea should be the first thing you write after you have written the introduction, body, and conclusion headings. The best place to write it is immediately under the word *Body*. Print a caption, *Central Idea*, at the left margin; write the statement all the way across the page.

### Complete statements

Each statement in an outline should be sufficiently complete to be clear to its intended readers. There are several types of outlines. Most common for speeches are the topical outline, the key-word outline, and the full-sentence outline. Which type should be used depends on the intended purpose and the intended reader.

The first draft of a speech outline is usually intended as a rough sketch of the over-all design. Therefore you jot down the ideas in incomplete sentences. This is called a topical outline.

At the end of the outlining process, you may want to condense the final outline into brief notes on a small card. By that time you have rehearsed the speech a number of times, and you require only a word or phrase to remind you of a given idea. Those brief notes are called a key-word outline.

In key-word outlines (and sometimes in topical outlines, too) you are using a sort of private shorthand—and only you can fully translate it. Consider, for example, the photograph of Dwight D. Eisenhower on page 65. We can actually read his card of notes. At the top is the single word GOVERNORS, printed in capital letters. The meaning was clear to Eisenhower. You and I, however, haven't the slightest notion of what he intended to say about governors. Therefore, when an outline is intended to be read by others, the customary practice is to use complete sentences. This is called the full-sentence outline.

It should be added that, even when outlining a subject for personal use only, writing the sentences in full will often help to clarify your thinking. Furthermore, you will soon forget the meaning of key words and phrases; use complete sentences when you expect to file an outline for possible future reference.

## Principal, coordinate, and subordinate headings

The section of the outline labeled *Body* should show the relationships of principal, coordinate, and subordinate ideas. This rule is probably the most difficult to grasp, and beginners' outlines frequently confuse such relationships badly. For example, here is an outline entitled "A Few First Aid Pointers," reproduced verbatim.

   I. Most of us are unprepared even for the smallest emergencies which might arise when living away from home.
  II. The first thing to do is call a doctor.
 III. I would like to show you a few bandages which could prove handy.
     A. The bandage most often used is in the form of a triangle.
     I. It can easily be improvised.
     II. Will stay on without tape.
     III. May be folded into other forms.
     B. The way to tie these bandages is with a square knot.
     A. When people are active it is easy to trip and injure ankles.
     I. A triangle folded into a cravat makes a wonderful bandage which even allows the victim to walk.
     B. For a sprained arm or wrist there is the "sling."
     I. This is made with a plain triangle.
     C. A very useful bandage is this head bandage.
     I. It may be used to hold compresses for earaches, etc.
     I. Today everyone is beginning to realize the need for first aid training.
     A. It is now a required subject in the city schools.

B. A working knowledge could save many lives in a real emergency.

Note: In order to make demonstration easier I changed the order of bandages to sling, ankle, head.

P.S. I missed the two class meetings last week because of a sprained back.

On first reading, that outline seems to be a hopeless hodgepodge. On further reflection, the student's plan can be roughly discerned. The first three items must have been meant as the introduction, the last three as the conclusion, and the other items as the body of the speech. But the form of the outline does not bring out these relationships.

In comparing two ideas, there are three logical possibilities: The first may be subordinate to the second, or the second to the first, or they may be coordinate. Any idea may be considered subordinate to another idea for any of various possible reasons: It may be a part of the principal idea (the Democractic party has two major parts: the Northern faction, and the Southern faction); or an aspect of it (the motion picture industry may be viewed from three standpoints: the financial, the artistic, and the educational); or an illustration of it (haste makes waste—for instance, . . .); or a proof of it (this proposal should be adopted for two reasons: it is needed, and it will work).

As you think about your subject, mentally juggling ideas this way and that, you should try to arrange those ideas in the form of a descending hierarchy or pyramid. At the peak is the central idea. Under this are a few main points. Under them are subpoints. At the base are facts, figures, quotations, or other forms of support. In a hierarchy of ideas each level is said to be subordinate to the level above it; the ideas within a level are described as coordinate. Putting thoughts into their proper places in a hierarchy is a measure of the accuracy of your reasoning.

*Numerals, letters, and indentations*

Relationships among items in an outline should be shown by a consistent system of numerals, letters, and indentations. In order to indicate clearly the logical relationships in the hierarchy of ideas, you should use a set of symbols corresponding with the several levels of subordinacy. The customary sequence is as follows:

I. Roman numerals
  A. Capital letters
    1. Arabic numerals
      a. Small letters
        (1) Arabic numerals in parentheses
          (a) Small letters in parentheses

When an item in an outline requires more than one line for its statement, misunderstandings of the rules for indentation often occur.

I. Short statements cause no trouble.

    A. But if a longer statement (like this one) is needed, you should *not* return all the way to the left edge of the paper—like this.

    B. Neither should you make it difficult to read the symbol by returning to a point beneath it—like this.

    C. This is the correct way. Notice that the symbol is allowed to stand out clearly.

The following model may help you to visualize all of the suggestions made in the several preceding pages, pertaining to the proper form for a speech outline:

INTRODUCTION

I. _____

II. _____

BODY

*Central idea:* _____

I. _____

    A. _____

    B. _____

       _____

II. _____

    A. _____

        1. _____

        2. _____

        3. _____

           _____

    B. _____

        1. _____

           _____

        2. _____

CONCLUSION

I. _____

II. _____

For an example of the violation of most of our suggestions about the mechanics and form of speech outlining, take another look at the weird

FENWICK ENGLISH

How many errors can you spot in this chalkboard outline? Compare it with the model on the preceding page.

system of captions, letters, numerals, and indentations in the outline, "A
Few First Aid Pointers," pages 121–22. For examples of proper usage, glance
ahead to the sample outlines on pages 138–39, 266, or 416–20.

## A six-step procedure for speech outlining

You cannot build a speech outline from hot air. You must come to the task
with proper tools and materials: You must know your audience, your subject, your purpose, and your outline mechanics.

There is no set procedure for making an outline, but each student should
adopt a method and make it habitual. You may like this well-tried, six-
step method:

1. State the central idea.
2. Choose the main points.
3. Support each main point.
4. Plan the conclusion.
5. Plan the introduction.
6. Test the transitions.

The foregoing procedure should be used flexibly. For example, you may
find it easier to reverse the order of steps four and five. You will also find
that you must work with transitions all through the outlining, especially
during step three. Eventually you will be able to work on two or more steps
simultaneously. In the beginning, however, master the basic sequence.

## Outlining the body of the speech

In building a speech outline, you do not begin at the beginning; that is to say, you do not plan the introduction first. You begin by outlining the body of the speech in three steps: statement of the central idea, selection of the main points, and support for each main point. These are the first three steps in the method described above; they will be discussed in detail here. The remaining three will be discussed in Chapter 8.

### *Stating the central idea*

Many students can state in a word or two their general topic for a speech, but cannot express the central idea. Before you can properly begin the construction of a speech, you must state the central idea clearly and explicitly.

The central idea may be defined as a summary of the subject matter of the whole speech. Usually it can be stated in one sentence. Occasionally two or three sentences are required. Approximate synonyms for the central idea include: the gist of the speech, the principal or key idea, the theme, the thesis or the proposition.

FUNCTION OF THE CENTRAL IDEA   The central idea properly conceived and stated narrows and unifies the subject matter of the speech. Choosing and stating the central idea forces you to think through your subject, and when you think through a subject you are forced to narrow that subject and to provide yourself with a theme around which to unify a body of materials.

A speech without a carefully chosen central idea is a rambling speech—merely a series of loosely related points, connected by transitions such as "and-uh," "my next point is," or "another thing I want to discuss is . . ." The following student outline is typical:

"Target Practice"

A. Purposes of target practice
   1. Harmony of body coordination
   2. Sense of achievement
B. Organizations representing the sport
C. Rules and method
   1. Ten commandments of safety
   2. Common sense
   3. No artificial supports
D. Positions and types of rifles
E. Target pistols versus target rifles

There are a good many things wrong with this outline besides the lack of a central idea. Many of the other weaknesses, however, stem directly from that lack. So let us analyze the outline. It is clear that the only thing that holds the points together is the fact that all of them have something to do with the subject of target practice. The points should be more closely related. It is obvious that there must be dozens, perhaps scores, of ideas on target practice. From all these possibilities, the student has chosen half a dozen. How did he happen to choose them? It would appear that he chose the first ones that came into his mind, probably rejecting those that would require research.

The outline contains several implicit central ideas. In fact, any one of the phrases A through E can be worded as a central idea in complete sentence form. Furthermore, any one of these would be enough for a short talk. For the student to attempt to cover them all means failure to achieve success with any. To put the student's faults in terms of his own topic: he used a shotgun when a rifle was required.

Now if the student had concentrated on one of the central ideas suggested above, he would have narrowed his subject. If he were actually to confine his points to one central idea, he would inevitably have a more unified speech; narrowing the subject automatically brings the points closer together.

CHOOSING AND WORDING THE CENTRAL IDEA   Choosing the central idea first will guide and simplify the remaining steps. It may help if you think of the entire speech as centered on or built around the central idea. Remember, too, that the body of the speech is built specifically to support the central idea. Do not fret over trying to state it perfectly at the time, for you can revise and improve it later.

Word the central idea briefly. Its function, as we have seen, is to keep the speech unified. A lengthy statement is seldom explicit, and your statement should, above all, be explicit. The length of the speech has nothing to do with the length of the statement of the central idea. It takes more words, for example, to state the central idea of Lincoln's "Gettysburg Address" than of Conwell's "Acres of Diamonds." Lincoln's idea might be stated thus: These soldiers died in defense of the great American principle that all men are created equal, and we must dedicate ourselves to the task of justifying their sacrifice. Conwell's idea might be worded: Success and happiness are frequently found right in your own back yard. Lincoln's address took about two minutes to deliver; Conwell's about two hours.

Choose and word the central idea in terms of your specific purpose and of your audience. As you think about your general topic, ask yourself, "What can I say (narrowing subject) to get these persons (audience) to respond in this desired way (purpose)?"

The foregoing question indicates that the central idea, then, is related not merely to the subject, but also to the purpose and to the audience. The nature of these relationships will be traced in the two following sections.

**THE CENTRAL IDEA AND THE SPEECH PURPOSE** One of the greatest difficulties that students experience with the central idea is that they confuse it with the specific purpose. The central idea is stated in terms of the subject matter; specific purpose is stated in terms of the desired audience response. That distinction should be kept clear both in choosing and in wording the two ideas. As we said in the previous section, you choose your central idea as the best way you can think to accomplish your purpose. To return to an earlier analogy, you aim the rifle—your speech—at the target—your speech purpose.

A few examples will illustrate the differences and resemblances among title, subject, purpose, and central idea. Notice in particular that the purposes are in terms of audience response; central ideas, in terms of subject matter.

AUDIENCE   Banquet of young people's church organization
TITLE   "A Crazy War"
SUBJECT   My experience in the army
PURPOSE   To entertain my audience with some of my experiences in the army
CENTRAL IDEA   Some of my experiences in the army were funny, some were exciting, some were sad.

AUDIENCE   High school girls
TITLE   " . . . And Eat It Too"
SUBJECT   Cake baking
PURPOSE   To explain to my audience how to bake a cake
CENTRAL IDEA   Successful cake making requires a knowledge of the proper ingredients, the process of mixing, and the techniques of oven baking.

AUDIENCE   Teachers' convention
TITLE   "Rats in a Maze"
SUBJECT   Importance of thinking
PURPOSE   To reinforce my audience's belief in themselves and their vocation
CENTRAL IDEA   We should cease paying tribute to the business tycoons or athletic heroes, and pay that tribute to our thinkers.

AUDIENCE   College speech class
TITLE   "Inventing Secrets in Order to Keep Them"
SUBJECT   Fraternities and sororities

PURPOSE   To convince my audience that national social fraternities should be abolished by this university.

CENTRAL IDEA   Fraternities on our campus do more harm than good.

**THE CENTRAL IDEA AND THE AUDIENCE**   The choice of central idea should be directly checked against the audience analysis. For example, in choosing and stating a central idea for the target practice speech, how would you state the central idea for an audience of college women, of college men? Despite the dominant role of the central idea in the process of building your outline, it may never be spoken to the audience. The function of the central idea is to help you think more clearly and build a unified outline of that thinking. In delivering the talk you may change the wording or leave out the statement entirely. The statement that clarifies your thinking may or may not be equally effective in influencing the listeners' thinking.

**REVISING THE CENTRAL IDEA**   You develop your central idea throughout the outlining process. You begin by choosing a tentative central idea, and after reasonable deliberation writing it down. As you progress through the subsequent steps of outlining, you are free at any time to go back and revise that idea.

After choosing a central idea, you may decide while outlining that it should be not merely improved but radically changed. You might, for example, have picked the central idea, "Sex education should be taught to all high school students." As you outline, your viewpoint may change and you may decide upon another central idea such as, "Sex education should be taught to all parents." But if you do change the central idea, you immediately change the whole outline; that is, you change the entire speech.

## Choosing the main points

**FUNCTION OF THE MAIN POINTS**   The function of the main points is to support the central idea. This means that if all the main points can be clarified, reinforced, or proved, then the central idea will of necessity be clarified, reinforced, or proved. Let us illustrate.

Your general purpose is to convince the audience that your central idea is true, and let us suppose that your central idea is as follows: Some type of religious education should be included in the public school curriculum. You have evolved the following tentative main points:

 I. The present lack of religious education in public schools has proved detrimental in several ways to the majority of our school children.
 II. The inclusion of religious education in the curriculum would eliminate or alleviate these detrimental effects.

III. A workable plan can be developed that will be fair and satisfactory to all religious denominations.

If you can prove that each of those main points is true, will the three of them suffice to prove that the central idea is true? Probably the answer is yes. Suppose, however, that your set of main points is as follows:

I. The present lack of religious education in public schools has proved detrimental in several ways to the majority of our school children.
II. It has proved detrimental to our schoolteachers.
III. It has proved detrimental to our churches.

How about these points? Do they meet the test? Probably not. Even if you could prove all three to be true, it would not necessarily follow that your central idea is true. The trouble is that all three points aim to establish the belief that something ought to be done, but they do not establish what ought to be done. You should either narrow your specific purpose and your central idea or find a more adequate set of main points.

COORDINATION OF THE MAIN POINTS   Comparatively, main points should be of approximately equal weight or importance. In both the examples above, this test was met. However, analyze the following set:

I. The present lack of religious education in public schools has prevented most of our children from developing a working system of ethics.
II. A system of ethics, common to all denominations, could be taught without unfairness or offense to any denomination.
III. Some parents would save money.

It is obvious that the third point is not of equal weight or importance as compared with the other two. The third point should probably be omitted entirely, or demoted to a subpoint that supports a more important third point.

NUMBER OF MAIN POINTS   As a general rule the number of main points for any speech should be from one to five. The maximum should ordinarily be five because few subjects would be suitable for a single speech when more than five main headings would be logically possible without overlapping. Generally, when you think a subject requires more than five main points, you are thinking in terms of minor rather than main points. The psychological objections to more than five main points are also important. It is almost impossible for the ordinary listener to see more than five points as a related whole, and, further, few listeners are able to remember more than five points. Suppose, for example, that you hear a speech in which the speaker discusses a ten-point program for improving our state government. Could you grasp all ten points as a related program? And how many of the ten points could you name after the speech? Generations of experienced speakers have shown by their speeches that three main points are the most practical, but two, four, or five are also common. If you must have more, supplement the speech with written materials, such as pamphlets, mimeographed handouts, chalkboard lists, or the like.

To sum up, then, it is best to have a set of two to five main points of approximately equal importance, which together will suffice to support your central idea well enough to achieve your specific purpose. How will you find them? A good beginning is to review your central idea in terms of your purpose.

USING THE SPEECH PURPOSE TO FIND THE MAIN POINTS   If your general purpose is to entertain, considerable flexibility in choosing your main points is permissible. Usually all you have to do is support your central idea in the simplest sense: amplify it or illustrate it. Careful logic is needed only in exceptional cases, which will be discussed in Chapter 13. Consider, for instance, speeches by Mort Sahl, Bob Hope, Shelley Berman, Jack Benny. Therefore, to entertain, you ordinarily choose main points that are individually amusing or interesting or likely to get favorable attention. Often they do not have to hold together or be closely related to the main theme (as will also be discussed in Chapter 13).

If your general purpose is to inform, your main points should clarify your theme and help your listeners understand the central idea. Sometimes the central idea should be divided into constituent parts; if listeners understand each of the parts, they will understand the whole. Sometimes the central idea suggests choosing key points; if listeners understand these crucial points, they will understand the process or idea. Other methods may suggest themselves to you.

If your general purpose is to stimulate, your main points should reinforce the central idea. When you read the central idea, say to yourself, "Here is something most of my audience already believe. How can I make them believe it more?" Sometimes this suggests proving the central idea in a way the audience has not previously considered. Sometimes it means bringing them new information, or repeating a familiar pattern with new attention-getting techniques. Whatever your method, you will look for main points of which you can say, "If I can develop these main points, I will reinforce my audience's belief in the central idea."

If your general purpose is to convince, your choice of main points is more restricted. Your central idea is normally in the form of a proposition con-

Sometimes the speaker can help his audience take notes by putting the main points of his outline on the chalkboard as the talk progresses.

cerning which some of your listeners are undecided or opposed. Your job is to prove the truth of the proposition to them. How can you get them to believe it? "Well," you say, "if I can show them that this and this and this are all true, they will have to believe that is true." It sometimes helps to think of the main points as the reasons for believing the central idea.

Thus by reviewing your central idea in terms of your general purpose, you may find a set of main points suited to your needs. However, beginning speakers often draw a blank because they are not sure of what they are looking for. This difficulty can be met by becoming familiar with some of the many stock sets of main heads.

**STOCK SPEECH DESIGNS** There are many logical and psychological speech patterns that have universal value and convenience; they have been used over and over again by speakers and writers down through the centuries. Here is a list of some of these stock designs.

1. Past, present, future (or other time sequence)
2. Local, state, national, international (or other space sequence)
3. Cause, effect
4. Need, desirability, practicality, alternatives
5. Problem-solution
6. Who, what, why, when, how, where
7. Advantages, disadvantages
8. Attention, need, satisfaction, visualization, action
9. Theory, practice
10. Physical, mental, emotional, spiritual
11. Heredity, environment
12. Thinking, feeling, doing
13. Structure, function
14. Political, economic, social
15. Resemblances, differences
16. Background, characteristics, accomplishments
17. Stop, look, listen
18. Symptoms, prevention, cure
19. Extended analogy
20. Partitioning a quotation
21. ABC's (or other letter combination)
22. Spelling a key word

Some of these patterns will be more fully described in the next two sections. A few reflect such fundamental logical or psychological relationships that they will be discussed in detail in later chapters. The list is not exhaustive; as you read it you may be reminded of a few patterns of your own.

*Fitting stock designs to subject matter.* In using the check list to help you choose a set of main points you must, of course, adapt a given basic design to your particular subject matter. First, you may increase or reduce the number of points in a given design. Thus for item 1 (past, present, future) you could use any two of the three; or you could expand the number of points by subdividing past into ancient and medieval. For item 6 (who, what, why, when, how, where) you might choose any number of the six points.

Second, you can change the sequence of any item. Item 3 could be developed from effect to cause, rather than from cause to effect.

Third, you can expand and adapt the wording. Do not say, "My first point is the problem"; state in your own words what the problem is. In phrasing points, you may follow the idea pattern suggested by the key words without necessarily using the words themselves. Sometimes you may use synonyms

—instead of "problem" say "difficulty," "trouble," or "the mess we're in." Sometimes the idea pattern may best be implied rather than stated directly. For example, the "Gettysburg Address" has three main divisions in accordance with item 1 of our list. However, Lincoln did not bluntly say, "First, I shall talk about the past; then about the present; etc." He did it this way:

*Past:* "Fourscore and seven years *ago* . . ."
*Present:* "*Now* we are engaged in a . . ."
*Future:* ". . . dedicated to the great task remaining *before* us . . ."

Having given the foregoing general suggestions for finding main points from one or more stock patterns, we turn now to some examples of exactly how this might be done for specific subjects.

*Use of stock designs.* Check list item 6 (who, what . . .) is one of the most useful, especially when your general purpose is to inform. Many good combinations are possible from among the six possible headings. Thus if you were speaking against a proposed amendment to the state constitution on the grounds that the proposal is being presented to the people under false colors, your main points could be these:

I. *Who* is really behind this measure
II. *What* the proposal actually means
III. *Why* the proposal is being presented

If you are trying to explain a thing or process, the following main ideas serve equally well for an explanation of anything from a washing machine to a philosophy of life.

I. *What* it is
II. *How* it works
III. *Who* can use it

You will notice as you study the items various other useful combinations that can be drawn from the six key words: who, what, why, when, how, where.

Assume that you want to speak in favor of a plan for relieving campus parking congestion. Several of the check list items might be suitable: note in particular items 4, 5, 8, and 18. With item 5 (problem-solution) the simplest design would be to develop just two main points:

I. We have a serious problem of campus parking.
II. Solution *X* will solve that problem.

But perhaps a variation upon the basic design is desirable. Suppose there have been two leading proposals. You might then try:

I. We have a serious problem of campus parking.

II. Solution *Y* is inadequate.

III. Solution *X* will solve the problem.

Other elaborations of the same basic design could be suggested by changing circumstances. Here is another possibility:

I. We have a serious problem of campus parking.

II. Several alternative solutions have been proposed.

III. Each proposal can be tested by certain criteria.

IV. Solution *X* emerges as our best available solution.

By now it is clear how you can use the check list to suggest sets of main points, and to suggest how you can adapt items on the check list to a central idea. The last four items of the list, however, may require additional clarification.

*Extended analogy* means that your main points are derived from an analogy that extends throughout the speech. An analogy is a comparison, more detailed than a simile, showing resemblances between two apparently dissimilar things. Thus if a commencement speaker compares life to a ship's voyage, his main points might develop from:

I. Weighing anchor

II. Steering a straight course

III. Riding out the storms

IV. Coming safely to harbor

*Partitioning* a quotation means that you secure your main points by dividing a quotation into its several parts. Many provocative quotations lend themselves to this treatment. One speaker discussed the subject, "Putting Faith to Work," before a church group. He quoted Admiral Hart, "Dear God, give us strength to accept the things that cannot be changed. Give us courage to change the things that can and should be changed. And give us wisdom to distinguish one from the other." The speaker then used the three sentences in this quotation as the three main points of the talk.

Item 21 (ABC's) of the check list has been used by innumerable popular lecturers. Someone entitling his speech, "The ABC's of Democracy," chooses three key words beginning with *A*, *B*, and *C* respectively, and builds each main point around the key word. He chooses, for example, ability, bravery, and cooperation. Another common variation is to choose a set of key words, all beginning with the same letter. Alan Nichols, dean of American intercollegiate debate directors, sometimes talks on the "Three Cardinal C's of Debate":

I. Courtesy
II. Competency
III. Courage

Closely related to the above items is item 22 (spelling a key word, having each letter of the word stand for a main point). There is an old story, however, about an alumnus who was speaking on "The Meaning of Yale." After a lengthy introductory section he came to his first main point, "Y stands for youthful spirit," and discussed this point for twenty minutes. The second point was, "A stands for achievement." That took twenty minutes more. In the midst of "L stands for loyalty," a bored listener remarked, "I'm glad this isn't the Massachusetts Institute of Technology."

## Wording the main points

In general, the main points should be worded (1) to show that the points are all related to a total pattern, (2) to make points easy to remember, and (3) to motivate the listeners to want to respond in the fashion sought. To accomplish these characteristics the wording of the main points should be concise, parallel in construction (often repeating some of the words), and expressed in terms of the listeners' interests. Consider the following wording from an address by Frederick L. Schuman before the Chicago Council on Foreign Relations:

> The first answer is that appeasement as practiced by the democratic powers in the 1930's in dealing with Fascist totalitarianism was an attempt to appease the unappeasable, to satisfy the insatiable, to reason with the irrational, and to bargain with those whose objective was not bargaining but annihilation.[1]

Restatement is often an effective technique to increase clarity, vividness, or persuasiveness. To achieve emphasis it is sometimes effective to restate a point immediately and in the same words: thus: "My final point is that we have no alternative. I repeat, ladies and gentlemen, we have no alternative."

In addition to immediate restatement, speakers often plan to restate a point again or several times throughout the speech. Occasionally this also may be done in exactly the same words—in the manner of a slogan. You have read Antony's speech from *Julius Caesar* and have relished the repetitions of "Brutus says he was ambitious" and "Brutus is an honorable man."

[1] Harold F. Harding, ed., *The Age of Danger: Major Speeches on American Problems,* Random House, 1952, p. 44. Reprinted by permission of Frederick L. Schuman.

Effective use of both immediate and subsequent restatement is made by Frederick L. Schuman in the address already quoted:

> If Fascist totalitarianism and Communist totalitarianism are alike in these respects, are they sufficiently alike in all respects to warrant our regarding them as identical? More important, can we reasonably conclude from these undeniable similarities that all negotiations with, and all bargains with, Communist totalitarianism in the 1950's are likely to have results comparable to negotiations and bargains with Fascist totalitarianism in the 1930's? In short, are we again in the position of trying to appease the unappeasable, to satisfy the insatiable, to reason with the irrational and to bargain with those whose object is not bargaining but annihilation? [2]

You will want to develop discrimination in choosing when and how to restate your points to avoid monotony. Do not restate every point just for the sake of restating. Even so, the power of restatement is indicated by national advertisers who repeat slogans on television and radio *ad nauseam,* and find repetition effective for their purposes.

## Supporting the main points

You now have a central idea and a set of main points; together they provide you with your over-all speech plan. Of course, they are not a speech; they are only part of the framework, and the main points have yet to be developed. Think about each main point and about your audience. Ask yourself "Will this sentence make my idea and its implications clear to my audience?" If not, what should you do to clarify it? "Will this sentence express something they already believe?" If so, what should you do to give it new life and intensify the belief? If they do not believe, what should you do to make them believe?

In looking for answers to these questions, we return to familiar territory.[3] A main point usually requires two or more subpoints to develop it. The job of choosing subpoints is exactly like the job of choosing main points described in the previous section. Furthermore, subpoints are to a main point what the main points are to the central idea. Subpoints require development by means of explanation, description, anecdotes, instances, quotations, statistics, or audio-visual aids.

Let us apply these principles by doing some outlining. Study the student outline on the next page with the instructor's critical comments in longhand. You will see that many aspects of this outline deserve commendation. The use of numerals, letters, and indentations is satisfactory; the general effect is orderly; the number of main points and subpoints is proper; parallel

[2] *The Age of Danger,* p. 47.
[3] See Chapter 6.

Title and Subject: "Labor Unions"

Body

I. Labor has arrived at a democratic means of dealing with management.

A. Instead of violence, we have negotiation.

B. Instead of mass killing, we have mass strikes.

Supports overlap.
— All seem to support a single point.

II. How do labor unions accomplish their purpose?

Not really a main point

A. Collective bargaining.

B. Not just one man strikes, all the workers strike.

III. Unions have promoted the general welfare.

Not really in sequence with points I and II

A. Workers can afford to educate themselves as well as their children.

B. Keep up demand, which in turn maintains production.

wording has been used for *I.A* and *I.B*. However, the outline can be improved—not made perfect, but improved.

Three major criticisms can be made: (1) The specific purpose and central idea are not clear. (2) There is overlapping among the statements. (3) The subpoints are not supported.

The purpose is not clear—is the student trying to inform or to convince? It would be difficult to summarize the whole outline into a clear-cut statement of central idea. To form a basis for improving the outline, let us suppose the attitudes of the audience are either undecided or unfavorable toward labor unions. The purpose might then be to convince the audience that they should approve of labor unions. Now we want a central idea that will summarize the evidence necessary to support that purpose. A choice might be: Labor unions have promoted the general welfare of the United States.

This brings us to the main points. The student's three main points do not hang together; they fail to form an over-all related pattern. The second main heading is in the form of a question, but questions are transitions, not main points. The subpoints overlap. Notice that *I.A* is to all effects the same as *II.A*; likewise *I.B* and *II.B*. Why not combine *I* and *II* entirely? How do *I* and *II* compare with *III*? The first two deal with labor union methods, while the third deals with labor union results. Therefore two main heads are all we need. Can these two main heads be worded so that they will adequately support the central idea? Here is one possibility:

I. The methods of labor unions have become more peaceful and orderly.
II. The results of labor unions have benefited the whole country.

The two main points are in balance; the wording is fairly satisfactory; and surely if both can be proved the central idea is true.

Now to develop the first main point. We want subpoints that will prove that the point is true. The student's outline suggested two methods employed by the labor unions: strikes and collective bargaining. History suggests that both methods have been used with increasing effectiveness, moderation, and wisdom, and therefore perhaps the following subpoints can be sustained.

A. The method of strikes has become less disruptive.
B. The method of collective bargaining has become stronger.

Now we must support both A and B. To prove that strikes have become less disruptive, we can show that strikes have become less destructive (the student's outline referred to a change from mass killing). We perhaps can also show that strikes are becoming less numerous. Both these points require direct support—instances, statistics, quotations.

Now we want to develop the second main point: results. Results of strikes and collective bargaining are said to promote the general welfare. A support for this point is suggested by the customary divisions of labor, management, and public.

A. Labor has benefited.
B. Management has benefited.
C. The public has benefited.

If all three of these are true, then II is true, but all three points require direct support.

Very well, let us put the whole thing together and see how the outline looks.

BODY

*Central idea:* Labor unions have promoted the general welfare of the United States.

I. The methods of labor unions have become more peaceful and orderly.
  A. Strikes have become less disruptive.
    1. Strikes have become less destructive.
      a. *True anecdote:* Early mass killings
      b. *True anecdote:* Recent orderly procedure

2. Strikes have become less frequent.
   a. Statistics showing decline
   b. Quotation from labor authority
   B. The method of collective bargaining has become stronger.
   1. Collective bargaining has become more widespread.
      a. Quotation *re* early lack of bargaining
      b. Instances of recent successful bargainings
   2. Collective bargaining has become more efficient.
      a. Explanation of how efficiency improves with practice
      b. Description of current practices
II. The results of labor union activities have benefited the whole country.
   A. Labor has benefited.
   1. Statistics on better hours
   2. Statistics on better pay
   3. Description of improved working conditions
   B. Management has benefited.
   1. Quotation on increased productivity of workers
   2. Statistics on increased demand for products through increased buying power of workers
   C. The public has benefited.
   1. Explanation of educational programs of unions
   2. Statistics on higher standard of American living

This revised outline is not a finished product. However, it shows how the student's original outline may be improved. In particular it shows how points and subpoints can be supported in terms of the purpose, the central idea, and the audience.

Let us do some more practice outlining. Get a pencil and some paper so that this time you can take a more active part. Suppose that you are to talk to a college group that is not a speech class. Let us choose as your subject "The Values of Speech Training," since by now you probably have quite a few ideas about it. Your purpose is to convince your audience that every student should have some speech training.

Now what might be an adequate central idea? Think about your audience and your speech purpose, and write down at least one possible central idea. Because the audience is a college group you might think of something like, "Speech training will help broaden and integrate your entire program of college course work." But think again. You are talking to students, not to faculty. Reread the statement carefully. Can you prove that it is probably true? Does it apply to *every* college student? Most students might agree that speech courses would "help," but they might mentally add "only a little bit." So you must look further for a central idea. What are some educational needs common to all students? Well, one universal need is preparation for democratic citizenship. Does that provide a clue? Very well, continue the thought process until you are able to write down a satisfactory central idea.

Next you need a set of main points. Perhaps you have already solved this problem in the course of your thinking about a central idea. If so, write down the gist of the main points. If not, the list of stock designs on page 132 may help you. How about an adaptation of item 14 in that list? Put the key words on paper; let them stimulate your thinking:

   I. Political (This ties up with democracy and citizenship.)
  II. Economic (Almost everybody must be prepared to earn a living.)
 III. Social (We all want to be able to get along with other people.)

In choosing and wording the central idea and the main points you should be influenced at all times by the kind and amount of available supporting material. At the present moment you are trying to outline a talk to convince, and the ultimate task of your supporting materials is to prove your points. Do you have or can you get appropriate instances, statistics, and authorities? What else do you need? Do you need some anecdotes or visual aids to enliven the talk?

Go ahead with your thinking until you have completed a rough outline for the body of this talk. Then turn to Appendix B. Here you will find a sample student outline for a speech on "The Values of Speech Training." As you compare your ideas with his, you may evolve a third plan that will be the best of all.

You will notice, of course, that the outline in the appendix presents not only the body of the speech but also includes the introduction, conclusion, and important transitions. These three steps in speech construction will be discussed in the next chapter.

## Summary

Speech outlining is a method for putting the ideas of a speech into a condensed written form that indicates the relationships among those ideas by means of letters, numerals, and indentations.

Thinking is the core of outlining. The outline itself simply records some of the thinking process. However, an understanding of the mechanics of outlining and a systematic procedure for building an outline will often assist you during the thinking process.

Important suggestions on outline mechanics include the following: (1) In a speech outline the words *Introduction, Body,* and *Conclusion* should be capitalized and centered but not numbered. (2) The central idea of the speech should be written immediately below *Body.* (3) Each statement in an outline should be sufficiently complete to be clear to its intended readers. (4) The section of the outline labeled *Body* should show the relationships of principal, coordinate, and subordinate ideas. (5) Relationships among items in an outline should be shown by a consistent system of numerals, letters, and indentations.

A definite but flexible procedure for building an outline follows: (1) State the central idea. (2) Choose the main points. (3) Support each main point. (4) Plan the conclusion. (5) Plan the introduction. (6) Test the transitions.

The central idea is a brief summary of the subject matter of the whole speech. The central idea should be chosen and worded with both the purpose and the audience in mind. By thus summarizing in advance the subject matter of a proposed speech, the speech materials are narrowed and unified.

An outline should contain from one to five main points. Taken together, the main points should suffice to support the central idea. Main points may simply represent a speaker's idea of the natural divisions of his subject. However, the choice of main points is usually assisted by studying a list of stock designs. The main points should be worded so as to show the total pattern, to make the points easy to remember, and to motivate the listeners.

A main point is usually supported by two or more subpoints, which in turn are supported by explanation, description, anecdotes, and so forth. As usual, the supporting materials should clarify, reinforce, or prove the point to which they are subordinate.

# 8

# CONCLUSIONS, INTRODUCTIONS, AND TRANSITIONS

Your introduction may determine the attitude with which the audience will listen to the rest of your talk, or perhaps whether they will listen at all. Your conclusion may determine what their final attitude will be. Your transitions may determine whether or not the listeners will follow what you say. Usually your first and last words will be the easiest for the audience to remember.

## Planning the conclusion

The purpose of the conclusion is to bring the entire speech into focus on the central idea. In it the speech ideas should be concentrated and brought to a head. All that you have said—points, subpoints, supports—should be pulled together in the conclusion so as to hit with a combined impact.

In order to accomplish its purpose the conclusion must be carefully planned and carefully phrased. Do not assume that, after giving the body of your speech, you can unfailingly improvise an effective conclusion. Effective conclusions rarely arise from inspirations of the moment. Failure to understand the purpose of the speech conclusion or failure to plan properly causes speakers to fade in the homestretch.

## Undesirable conclusions

*1. The abrupt conclusion.* Audiences like to feel that a talk is rounded off at the end. They dislike a speaker who completes his discussion of the last subpoint of his outline and then abruptly sits down. The effect is even worse if he pauses and says, "Well, I guess that's about all I have to say. . . ." A well-planned conclusion may seem abrupt, however, if the speaker has failed to warn his audience that his conclusion is under way. The speaker should let his audience know when he starts his conclusion by implication, by change in mood or manner, or by using a transition such as "in conclusion" or "finally."

*2. The multiple conclusion.* Audiences also dislike speakers who string several conclusions together like sausages. The audience becomes increasingly exasperated as the speaker builds up to what seems to be the final sentence—then goes on to another final thought—and then to another—and another.

*3. The apologetic conclusion.* A speech should end on a positive note. Do not spoil your talk by ending lamely with, "I'm afraid I haven't clarified the electoral college system very well but I just thought that maybe . . ." Or, "I don't want to bore you with further details, but there is one final point that ought . . ."

*4. The tacked on conclusion.* Some speeches have an unfortunate break in logic or psychology between body and conclusion. A conclusion should spring from the body of the speech. A speaker should not think of introduction, body, and conclusion as three separate entities, but as interwoven parts of the whole. The progression from body to conclusion should sound natural and inevitable.

*5. The anticlimactic conclusion.* Some speeches seem to build up to an awful letdown. After a forceful and slashing attack on the evils of some existing situation, the speaker ends by proclaiming that something should be done or that there ought to be a law against it. Then there is the speech that starts strongly and gradually runs out of gas, the conclusion sputtering slowly to a stop.

*6. The indecisive conclusion.* A more subtle weakness exists in the conclusion that leaves a first impression of adequacy but a second impression of doubt in the listeners' minds. Just what *is* the main point of the speech or the exact response expected? The speaker does not know; so the audience does not know either.

## Desirable conclusions

There are three useful ways of concluding a speech: a summary, an emotional appeal, a call for action. They may be used singly or in combination.

The effectiveness of any of the three ways is often enhanced by means of the following devices:

1. Enumeration
2. Restatement
3. Quotation
4. Climactic anecdote
5. Rhetorical question
6. Epigram
7. Prophecy
8. Personal reference

Oscar R. Ewing once brought an entire speech into focus with a summary in the form of a succinct restatement of his central idea:

> What would national health insurance mean to you? It would mean that, when someone asks you, as I ask you, "Can you get all the medical care you and your family really need?" you could answer with confidence and relief, "Yes, under national health insurance I can." [1]

President John F. Kennedy's 1961 Inaugural Address was justly acclaimed by leaders of both major political parties. His conclusion brought the whole speech into focus; it combined emotional appeal with a call for action; restatement and epigrams were effectively used:

> And so, my fellow Americans: ask not what your country can do for you—ask what you can do for your country.
> My fellow citizens of the world: ask not what America will do for you, but what together we can do for the freedom of man.
> Finally, whether you are citizens of America or citizens of the world, ask of us here the same high standards of strength and sacrifice which we will ask of you. With a good conscience our only sure reward, with history the final judge of our deeds, let us go forth to lead the land we love, asking His blessing and His help, but knowing that here on earth God's work must truly be our own.

Clarence Darrow was the most famous defense attorney of the first half of this century. During his long career he took part in many important cases and he delivered many memorable pleas to juries. One of the most dramatic of his courtroom speeches was given in 1912 when Darrow was accused of trying to bribe jurors in a labor case; Darrow spoke in his own defense. After carefully and logically analyzing the evidence in order to show that the charges were a frame-up, he concluded with an emotional plea which put a call for action into the form of a prophecy:

> There are people who would destroy me. There are people who would lift up their hands to crush me down. I have enemies powerful and strong. There are honest men who misunderstand me and doubt me; and still I have lived a

---

[1] Harold F. Harding, ed., *The Age of Danger: Major Speeches on American Problems,* Random House, 1952, p. 355. Reprinted by permission of Oscar R. Ewing.

long time on earth, and I have friends—I have friends in my old home who have gathered around to tell you as best they could of the life I have lived. I have friends who have come to me here to help me in my sore distress. I have friends throughout the length and breadth of the land, and these are the poor and the weak and the helpless, to whose cause I have given voice. If you should convict me, there will be people to applaud the act. But if in your judgment and your wisdom and your humanity, you believe me innocent, and return a verdict of Not Guilty in this case, I know that from thousands and tens of thousands and yea, perhaps millions of the weak and the poor and the helpless throughout the world, will come thanks to this jury for saving my liberty and my name.[2]

The emotional impact of Darrow's plea was reported by Weinberg:

> All through the trial, it was the feeling that jurors number seven and number eleven were against Darrow. But when the accused attorney concluded his speech, the two men were openly weeping, as was everybody else in the courtroom including the judge.[3]

For a final example we go back to a hearing by the Senate Banking and Currency Committee on July 26, 1950. The Korean conflict had just begun, and the Committee was considering a bill for economic mobilization. Bernard Baruch read a prepared statement and later answered questions. There was no doubt that his words were effective and later helped shape the mobilization program. Examine the conclusion of his prepared talk in which he first summarized by enumeration, then called for action with anecdote, epigrams, and a final powerful rhetorical question.

> To sum up my recommendations:
>
> 1. Organize America for all-out mobilization, with a general ceiling over the entire economy to prevent further inflation and an all-embracing system of priorities to strengthen our defenses and minimize dislocations.
>
> 2. The very least that must be done is to amend this priorities legislation to provide for effective price and wage control and rationing authority. To do less is to invite cruel suffering and possible disaster.
>
> 3. Taxes high enough to eliminate profiteering and to cover *all* defense costs. These taxes should take effect for at least half of this year.
>
> 4. Continued rent controls with provision for clearly justifiable increases.
>
> 5. Prompt creation of an over-all mobilizing agency to synchronize all our efforts.
>
> 6. Postpone less essential expenditures. As an aid to that a Capital Issues Committee should be established under the Secretary of the Treasury to review all capital issues, public and private, deferring less essential projects to

[2] Arthur Weinberg, ed., *Attorney for the Damned,* Simon and Schuster, 1957, p. 530.
[3] *Attorney for the Damned,* p. 531.

At the conclusion of any speech, success is judged by some sort of audience response. One of the most common responses is that of voting.

UNITED NATIONS

make sure housing, schools, hospitals and other more essential needs are met first.

7. Strengthen the United Nations by coordinating our efforts with it in common defense of peace.

8. Speedier assistance in the rearming of those nations ready to resist aggression, along with the expansion of our own defense forces.

Nearly three years ago I clipped an item from a newspaper which seems ominously prophetic today. It told of a boast made by a Soviet general. This general boasted that the Western democracies were bound to be defeated by the Soviet Union because they would not make the sacrifices necessary to arm themselves. They prized their standards of living too highly. They would not be willing to accept the discipline to put "guns" over "butter." In Russia, though, this general boasted, the people were inured to hardship. The Soviet government would force the sacrifices to mobilize. A lean and hungry but mobilized Russia would overrun a Western world which couldn't bring itself to mobilize—in time.

That is the test which confronts us—not only this country but all of the free peoples of the world. It is the choice of "peace" or "butter," of mobilizing our strength now, while peace can still be saved, or of clinging to petty wants and petty profits, imperiling our freedom and our civilization.

No outside enemy can defeat us. We *can* defeat ourselves. Gentlemen, yours is the decision. Which shall it be—discomfort or defeat? [4]

The foregoing examples vary greatly in length. Sometimes a whole speech can be focused by a single concluding sentence, but sometimes many sentences are required. However, the conclusion should rarely run more than 5 per cent of the length of a speech.

## Writing out conclusions

After planning a conclusion, a speaker has considerable freedom in the form he uses to outline it. Parts or even all of the conclusion should sometimes be written out, especially when quotations, epigrams, or key words and phrases are to be used. Freedom of form is needed because the job of focusing final attention on the central idea differs from the job of developing the central idea in the body of the speech.

Once you have your conclusion prepared, you are ready to build the final part of the outline—the part you might have supposed should be done first.

### Planning the introduction

By this time you undoubtedly have deduced why we have delayed consideration of the speech introduction. The reason, of course, is obvious. You cannot plan an introduction until you know what you want to introduce.

The opening words of a talk are often the most important. The very fact that they are heard first gives them psychological significance. If you fail to secure the listeners' attention at the beginning of a speech it is hard to arouse it later. And, of course, if you fail to get their interest, it makes little difference what you say. Furthermore, if you should antagonize the listeners at the start of a speech, how can you influence their response later? And if you begin by confusing your audience, you will have difficulty making your subject clear.

## Purposes of the introduction

The purposes of a speech introduction are three: to arouse favorable attention, to promote friendliness and respect, to lead into the subject.

**1. AROUSING FAVORABLE ATTENTION** Once in a while your listeners know beforehand what your subject is to be and arrive eager to hear what you

[4] Reprinted with the permission of Bernard Baruch from A. Craig Baird, ed., *Representative American Speeches: 1950–1951*, H. W. Wilson, 1951, pp. 92–93.

have to say. They lean forward with attention as you mount the platform. But that is only once in a long while. Usually if they lean forward it is because they are tired and want to stretch, or because they are nearsighted. They expect you to make the subject interesting. The listeners' attention is on a variety of other matters: that cute blonde in the third row, that overhead light that keeps flickering, that dental appointment tomorrow, that tight left shoe, and so forth. So you must devise a way to overcome inertia and distractions.

If you walked to the rostrum and fired a shotgun, you would get attention all right. But that attention would probably hurt your subsequent speech rather than help it. You must not only attract attention; you must attract favorable attention.

Getting favorable attention is the first concern of any speaker. Once captured, it must be held during the rest of the talk. In fact, the psychology of attention is so basic to public speaking that we shall not only discuss it in this chapter but later devote an entire chapter to it.

**2. PROMOTING FRIENDLINESS AND RESPECT**   The aim of your opening is higher than merely to get attention; you must also promote good will toward yourself. This takes us back to the audience analysis. Do most of the audience

By mood and manner this speaker is promoting friendliness and respect.

R. GRAVES

already know you? If so, what are their attitudes? With most groups, such as your speech class, you can probably count on a sympathetic or friendly attitude. But do they also respect your ability, knowledge, intelligence, and judgment? Maybe they think a girl speaker charming but dumb; a man speaker a personality boy with nothing behind the façade. The listeners may know you by reputation rather than personally. If so, what attitudes should you expect? How can you capitalize on the good or offset the bad? The audience may comprise mostly complete strangers. If so, how can you get on friendly terms with them and earn respect early in the speech? Whatever their attitudes, you must do or say something early in the speech to reinforce or counteract, whichever is demanded.

**3. LEADING INTO THE SUBJECT** Yet a third aim must be achieved during the beginning of your speech. You must lead into your subject, and just getting into it any way is not sufficient. What is the best way to approach the subject in order to accomplish the speech purpose?

Again audience analysis must be considered. What is their predominant attitude toward your subject? Are they already in favor of it? If they are, you may want to jump into the body of the speech directly. But if they are undecided, you may want to approach your subject more gradually. Are they opposed? If so, you may want to establish a common ground before getting into the body of the speech. If they are indifferent, you may want to approach your subject through its most entertaining aspects.

At this time you also must consider when and how to state your central idea to the audience. On page 126 we discussed the fact that the time, place, and wording of the central idea should first assist your thinking as you plan the outline, and that later adaptations might be made in terms of the audience. Now ask yourself when and in what words the central idea should be stated.

Should the central idea be stated in its normal place, at the beginning of the body of the speech? Usually this is the best place for several reasons: It satisfies the listeners' desire to know what the speech is about; it prepares the listeners for what is to follow; it helps the listeners grasp the speech as a unified whole. However, these reasons are sometimes outweighed by others. If you have a hostile audience, it is best to delay revealing your central idea or purpose until later in the speech. If you tell them the point early they may close their minds at once. Likewise, if your purpose is to entertain or stimulate, it is sometimes wise to build a speech on suspense, delaying the revelation of the point until the very end. On the other hand, there are rare occasions when you may want to state the central idea earlier than usual, perhaps as the first words of the speech, in order to get attention. Weigh the alternatives and decide where to state the central idea.

## Undesirable introductions

*1. The "hem-and-haw" introduction.* Nobody is favorably impressed by the speaker who, from lack of either preparation or of confidence, starts off in a hesitant, faltering manner. "This is—uh—a good time to begin—uh—thinking about—I mean preparing for—the—uh—final examinations. Well—uh—I thought I might sort of discuss them." The opening should be definitely planned. Sometimes it may even be wise to memorize the first sentence or two.

*2. The apologetic introduction.* Start positively. You should be modest, of course, but do not apologize for your presence by either words or manner. "I couldn't think of a topic today so I . . ." "Public speaking is not in my line and I don't know why I was asked to make a speech here." "I'm afraid all of you know more about this subject than I do, and I don't suppose you'd be much interested in . . ."

*3. The trite introduction.* Most audiences are too sophisticated to fall for, "It is a profound pleasure and a high honor to be asked to speak here today." Or the hackneyed flattery: "I'm glad to see so many young people here tonight. Your bright and eager faces remind us that the youth of today are the leaders of tomorrow. And your presence here is high tribute to your parents, whose devotion and self-sacrifice . . ." In general, avoid such phrases as, "it gives me great pleasure," and, "on this auspicious occasion."

*4. The pedantic introduction.* Avoid opening your speech with big words and long sentences: "Speech correction is a process of re-education of the whole individual, not simply the diagnosis and therapy of so-called speech impediments or other purely symptomatic manifestations."

*5. The misleading introduction.* There is always a speaker who thinks he must begin by telling a joke. He is likely to pick one because he thinks it is funny, not because it leads into his subject. Perhaps it goes something like this: "My father used to tell of a man who was about to be hanged, and was asked if he had any last words. 'Well,' he replied, 'all I can say is—this has certainly been a lesson to me.'"

The audience laughs—politely or loudly, depending upon how well the joke was told. But what does the speaker say next? Suppose he says: "I don't know whether this talk will be a lesson to anyone or not. Probably it will be a lesson for me. In any event, I'm going to discuss today why the United States should have a new major political party."

What is your reaction? Irritated, aren't you? The joke was misleading because it did not really lead into the proposed subject. Only a tortured transition made it connect with the subject at all (although a good transition might have saved it). Jokes, however, are not the only type of misleading opening; any other opening device can be similarly misused.

## Desirable introductions

Keeping in mind the foregoing functions of a speech introduction, let us list the most frequently successful ways of opening a talk:

1. Reference to previous speaker or chairman
2. Reference to occasion
3. Honest compliment to audience
4. Appropriate joke or other humor
5. Unison audience reaction: singing, applause, show of hands
6. Statement of central idea or main points
7. Startling statement
8. Quotation
9. Illustrative anecdote
10. Development of common ground
11. Rhetorical question
12. Personal reference
13. Reference to recent event
14. Visual aids
15. Definition of terms.

The introduction may consist of just one of the above ingredients; more often, however, it consists of a combination of two or more. When a combination is attempted, the ingredients should usually be blended rather than simply strung in sequence.

You might assume that the ideal opening would consist of three ingredients: one to get attention, one to promote good will, and the other to lead into the subject. That is a perfectly good possibility. However, a single ingredient may simultaneously accomplish any two or all three of the functions. For example, an illustrative anecdote might be found that would command favorable attention, establish your pleasantness, fairness, cooperativeness, and insight, and at the same time lead naturally and effectively into the body of the speech. Such a multiple-purpose ingredient is not always easy to think of but is worth the try.

Next let us analyze some actual speech openings in light of our previous discussion.

A student majoring in forestry introduced a classroom speech by handing out envelopes in which there were leaves from trees. After everyone had taken the leaves from the envelopes, felt them, and smelled them, he said, "My subject today is 'Poison Oak!'"

He certainly got attention: first, through curiosity aroused by the visual aids; second, through a startling statement. But he continued:

> Before anyone faints, let me state that those leaves you have in your hands are *not* poison oak. In this box [showing the leaves] you can see the real thing.
>
> You will notice that your leaves are quite similar to these, however. And so today I want to explain how you can identify poison oak by its foliage.

He made sure that the initial attention would be favorable, and then led directly into his subject. The introduction also promoted friendliness and respect toward the speaker because his listeners thought the introduction intelligent, clever, and amusing, and because they respected the care and preparation the introduction showed. And so it was an excellent introduction for a one-point classroom talk.

Archibald MacLeish gave the feature address at the inauguration of Margaret Clapp as President of Wellesley College. He began as follows:

> Except for Banquo's ghost, who is present but not expected to talk, I can think of no role less relevant to its occasion than that of the speaker at the inauguration of the president of an institution of learning.
>
> It is not his place to welcome the new president to her post: the young ladies have seen to that.
>
> It is not his function to compliment the trustees on their good taste and sound judgment in her selection: the trustees have never questioned their possession of either quality, and besides they have the proof before them.
>
> It is not his privilege to remind the new incumbent of the superlative merits of her predecessor, of which she is only too anxiously aware, or to reassure her as to her own abundant qualifications to succeed that famous lady: everyone within sight of the platform is already and entirely satisfied on both points.
>
> It is not even his duty to advise the new administration on the educational policy it should pursue—though I would not go so far as to contend that he never offers his willing back to that enticing burden.
>
> His sole function—if it can be called a function—is to expose to an audience concerned, and properly concerned, with something else, his private thoughts —which may or may not merit or survive exposure.
>
> My private thoughts on this occasion can be compressed to one: a lively sense of the astonishing paradox of our presence in this room, for this purpose, in this year of the republic's history.[5]

MacLeish fulfilled all three functions of a speech introduction. He got favorable attention, promoted good will and respect toward himself, and led

---

[5] *Representative American Speeches,* pp. 131–32. Reprinted by permission of the *Atlantic Monthly.*

naturally into his subject. He did these things through a masterly blend of reference to occasion, delightful humor, honest compliments, and a final striking statement of his central idea.

In October 1937 when Thomas E. Dewey was first achieving national prominence as a "Racket Buster," he opened his campaign for district attorney with a radio address. He began his address with these words:

> Tonight I am going to talk about murder—murder in the bakery racket. I am also going to talk about an attempted murder.
>
> Day before yesterday afternoon, on a New York City street, Max Rubin, an important witness in my investigation, was shot in the back. The bullet struck his neck, passed through his head, narrowly missing his brain. Tonight he still lies between life and death in a hospital. Upon the fragile thread of his life hangs evidence of the utmost importance to the people.
>
> For two years I have been prosecuting rackets. Every chieftain of the underworld who has been indicted by my office is in jail or is a fugitive from justice. The criminal underworld is afraid for the first time in twenty years. It has gone into hiding, waiting for the fight against organized crime to blow over.
>
> Today I have become a candidate for district attorney of New York County to see that trouble for the underworld does not blow over. I intend to see that the grip of the underworld is broken in the next four years.[6]

Here we see the effective use of a startling statement, an exciting anecdote, establishment of personal fitness to discuss the topic, and statement of the central idea. By these combined means the speaker got attention, promoted personal respect, and introduced his subject matter.

Speaking before the House of Representatives on a bill involving racial segregation in the armed services, William L. Dawson opened with words which demanded attention, commanded respect, and plunged directly into his subject:

> Mr. Chairman, I was born in the South. I lived there all during the days of my young manhood. When World War I broke out I was above the draft age. I did not have to go, but I believed then as I believe now that it was the duty of every citizen, when the welfare of the nation in which he claims citizenship is at stake, to rally to the call and to give his life if need be, for the preservation of the nation.
>
> I went to war. I was commissioned William L. Dawson, first lieutenant of infantry. I led Americans in battle—black Americans. This mark you see here on my forehead is the result of German mustard gas. This left shoulder of mine is today a slip joint. I cannot raise this left arm any higher than the shoulder unless I lift it with the other hand. That would have been a good joint, hos-

---

[6] Lew Sarett and William Trufant Foster, eds., *Modern Speeches on Basic Issues*, Houghton Mifflin, 1939, pp. 311–12. Reprinted by permission of Thomas E. Dewey.

pitalization would have been available, if I had not been a Negro American. I served in a segregated outfit as a citizen trying to save his country. How long, how long, my confreres and gentlemen from the South, will you divide us Americans on account of color? Give me the test that you would apply to make anyone a full-fledged American, and by the living God, if it means death itself, I will pay it. But, give it to me.[7]

In a short talk the introduction may require but a sentence. As an approximation, one can say that the average length for an introduction should seldom take more than 10 per cent of the total time of the speech. But fluctuations are wide. It is conceivable that under unusual circumstances an introduction should comprise over half the speech. Length should be determined by the three functions of a speech opening. What do you need to do in order to accomplish the three functions?

## Writing out introductions

Writing down the outline of your planned introduction, like writing down the conclusion, is subject to most flexible rules. This is true because the job of getting attention, promoting friendliness and respect, and leading into the subject, is quite different from the job of supporting the central idea. Unlike the body of the speech, for example, the introduction does not necessarily require the use of speech units with strict regard to point and support. So the ideas for the introduction may simply be listed. Likewise, unlike the body, the materials for the introduction need not necessarily be severely condensed; some or all of the introduction may be written verbatim to insure a smooth and positive start.

We now come to the final step in building an outline—and probably the most difficult to handle.

## Testing transitions

### Functions of transitions

Transitions show the logical or psychological relationships among the divisions of your outline. During the construction of a speech outline, attempts to state transitions between points help the speaker test the strength of the structure of the outline. For example, a point, subpoints, and supports in correct outline form look all right on paper. Try rehearsing that section aloud. If you have trouble connecting adjoining items or holding the several items coherently together, that is a hint that something is wrong. Perhaps

[7] *Congressional Record,* April 12, 1951, p. 3765.

one item does not belong, or the sequence should be altered, or the section should be reworded.

During the delivery of the speech the function of your transitions is to show the listeners how each point fits into the scheme of the speech. Sometimes, especially with minor items, the relationships are so plain that the audience is bound to grasp them; stating them only belabors the obvious and bores people. Most of the time, however, speakers err in the opposite direction; they lack enough transitional statements. The relationship among points is clearer to the speaker than to the listeners. In the first place, the speaker can see the points, all labeled and indented, as he reads his outline. The listener can only hear them—he cannot pause to think about the relationship involved or go back and relisten; he must perceive the relationship instantaneously. In the second place, the speaker has been through the mental processes of preparing the speech and may forget that what seems clear to him now was not clear earlier. The listener has no such advantage; he is thinking through the speech for the first and only time. Therefore transition statements should be scattered liberally throughout the speech, constantly telling the audience why B follows A, and C follows B.

Therefore the stating of transitions fulfills two functions: During the building of the outline, it helps to test the speaker's logic; and during the speech delivery, it helps to show the audience what the speaker's logic is.

## Wording of transitions

If you have carried out the process thus far described in this chapter, you have before you what appears to be a completed speech outline. You have an introduction, a body, a conclusion, and a central idea. The body of the outline has its main points, subpoints, and supports. You have made mental transitions throughout the outlining process, for the outlining process is a thinking process. But silently thinking that two points are related is easier than expressing that relationship aloud. The final test of your important transitions is wording them aloud. This task can be broken down into four steps and undertaken in the following order:

1. Getting from introduction to body of speech
2. Getting from body to conclusion
3. Getting from a point to a coordinate point
4. Getting from a point to a support

*1. Transitions between introduction and body.* The transition from introduction to body is usually the most critical transition in the entire speech because it involves your central idea which, as we have seen, is the keystone of the speech. We have also previously pointed out that the important decision is whether or not to state that central idea here, postpone stating it, or state it earlier. The central idea is most commonly placed between the introduction and the body of the speech. In order to set up a hypothesis to illustrate the use of transitions at this place in the outline, let $X$ be the last item of introduction, $Y$ be the central idea, and $Z$ be the first main point of speech body. The first function of the transitions is to get from $X$ to $Y$, and from $Y$ to $Z$. But we may want to accomplish more than this one function. For example, we may want to show the over-all relationships among $X$, $Y$, and $Z$, or we may want to include a preview of all the main points. There are two types of transitions to fulfill the two functions. *Connective* transitions show the relationship between two adjoining points; *perspective* transitions show the relationships among several items.

Both connective and perspective transitions can be achieved in various ways:

1. Connective words and phrases
2. Rhetorical questions
3. Repetitions
4. Perspectives centered about first, second, third
5. Perspectives centered about speaker, audience, occasion

These are not the only ways to effect transitions, but they will suffice most of the time. We will next show how transitions are effected in actual practice.

For illustrative purposes we will set up a hypothetical section of a speech outline. Our hypothetical case will, of course, require the three ingredients $X$, $Y$, and $Z$.

> $X$ (last item of introduction): Anecdote about a friend, Helen Jane, who wasted endless hours, curtailed her recreations, reduced her grades, and almost developed an inferiority complex—all because of slow and inefficient reading habits. Assume the anecdote ends with Helen Jane saying, "And you may be just as inefficient in your reading as I was!"
>
> $Y$ (central idea): Modern psychology has developed scientific methods by which you and I can learn to read better and faster.
>
> $Z$ (first main point of speech body): Make an accurate test of your present reading rate.

The foregoing wording, beginning with the last sentence of $X$, will be retained, as we now apply our five kinds of transitions.

> a. *Connective words and phrases.*
> ". . . And you may be just as inefficient in your reading as I was!"

> *However,* modern psychology has developed scientific methods by
> which you and I can learn to read better and faster.
> *Therefore,* make an accurate test of your present reading rate.

Those two transition words are helpful but leave something to be desired. Perhaps you can think of substitute words or phrases that would be improvements. The main trouble, however, is that connective words and phrases are better adapted to minor transitions. At best in this example, they will only connect X with Y, and then Y with Z. They cannot show interrelations among all three, or give broad perspective, or make the central idea stand out prominently.

> *b. Rhetorical questions.*
> ". . . And you may be just as inefficient in your reading as I was!"
> *I wonder if we are? And, if we are, must we suffer the same tragic consequences as Helen Jane suffered?*
> Modern psychology has developed scientific methods by which you and I can learn to read better and faster.
> *How, then, can I get started? How can I begin to improve?*
> Make an accurate test of your present reading rate.

You will note that this is better, and perhaps good enough. However, rhetorical questions sometimes have to be supplemented by other methods if perspective is desired.

> *c. Repetition.*
> ". . . And you may be just as inefficient in your reading as I was!"
> *Yes, you may be inefficient in your reading but* modern psychology has developed scientific methods by which you and I learn to read better and faster.
> *These scientific methods begin when you* make an accurate test of your present reading rate.

Repetition is similar in the scope of its usefulness to rhetorical questions: more flexible than simple connectives, but still mostly limited to two-point transitions.

> *d. Perspectives—"First, Second, Third."*
> ". . . And you may be just as inefficient in your reading as I was!"
> *Well, in that case we have available a step-by-step solution for the problem.* Modern psychology has developed scientific methods by which you and I can learn to read better and faster.
> *There are four major steps in carrying out these methods. I shall describe all four. Let us begin with the first step—*make an accurate test of your present reading rate.

This speaker is stressing the transition, "However, there are *two* sides to this question." Perfect timing of the gesture is proved by reading his lips.

It can be seen that this type of transition gives broader perspective than the previous types. A particular advantage is that it carries through the entire set of main points. For example, a little later on, you can say, "Having described the first step, we may now proceed to the second step." However, listeners may get a bit tired of "first," "second," and "third." To offset this, you can often use synonyms for these words: *the beginning of the process is, the origin of the inquiry is, the starting point of this series is,* and others.

> e. *Perspectives—"Speaker, Audience, Occasion."*
> ". . . And you may be just as inefficient in your reading as I was!"
> *Helen Jane might have added, "you and thousands of others." And because this problem is so serious, I want to describe for you this morning how modern psychology has developed scientific methods* by which you and I can learn to read better and faster.
> *To make this description vivid, I would like to take you now on an imaginary trip through a reading clinic. So get ready for the clinicians to* make an accurate test of your present reading rate.

Twice in the above passage *I* (the speaker) was related to *you* (the audience) as well as to *this morning* and *now* (the occasion). Synonyms, of course, should often be used for all three terms. This kind of transition provides the broadest perspective and also serves to emphasize the statement of central idea.

*2. Transitions between body and conclusion.* The transition from body to conclusion is usually easier to handle than transition from introduction to body. It can often be done with a word or phrase, although a sentence or several sentences may occasionally be justified.

Among the common words used for transition between body and conclusion are *finally, lastly,* and *summarizing.* Among the common phrases are *in conclusion, last of all, to sum up, to recapitulate,* and *in closing.* Rhetorical questions, such as, "And what are we to conclude from all these facts?" are often useful.

A transition may be stated in figurative language to lend color: "As we have followed this long train of evidence, we have been led inevitably to the lair of the true criminal in the house of juvenile delinquency."

*3. Transitions between coordinate points.* On the main points in the body of the speech rests the fate of your central idea of your speech purpose. You want the audience to grasp those points, and you want the audience to know at any given time which one you are talking about. This means that you should make it clear when you are finishing one main point and starting the next. The same thing is true when you are handling a series of coordinate subpoints.

Most of the ways of transition already treated can be used between coordinate points. Here are some sample possibilities:

Now having described my first reason, I would like to discuss the second.
You have before you the crux of our problem. What is to be our solution?
But all that is past. Let us look at the present.
This brings us to the fourth and final stage.
Before you are the sinister results. Next we must unearth the causes.

We have just visited the East, the South, and the Middle West. Our next stop is in the Far West.

*4. Transitions between point and support.* The speaker must make clear the relationship between each point and its supports. However, the job is fundamentally the same as making major relationships clear, though on a smaller scale. Transitional devices need be less elaborate and more frequent use can be made of repetitions, questions, and connective phrases. Here are some common ones:

| | |
|---|---|
| For example | What does this (term) mean? |
| For instance | Let me explain |
| This is illustrated by | Likewise |

| | |
|---|---|
| Accordingly | Not only . . . but also |
| Therefore | But even more important |
| According to | Now let us turn to |
| On the other hand | Approaching it from another angle |
| As I previously pointed out | What are the proofs? |

Minor transitions are seldom written into the outline. Major transitions or exceptionally difficult ones should be inserted at the proper point in parentheses. To prevent confusion, they may further be labeled "transition" instead of given a letter or numeral.

## Summary

The purpose of the conclusion is to focus the speech. You should avoid multiple conclusions, and conclusions that are abrupt, apologetic, tacked on, anticlimactic, or indecisive. Three useful ways of concluding a speech include summary, emotional appeal, and call for action. Any of the foregoing three ways may be improved by enumeration, restatement, quotation, anecdote, rhetorical question, epigram, prophecy, or personal reference.

The purposes of the introduction are three: to arouse favorable attention, to promote friendliness and respect, and to lead into the subject. You should avoid introductions that hem and haw, and those that are apologetic, trite, pedantic, or misleading. There are many useful ways of opening a talk, such as reference to previous speaker or chairman, appropriate humor, quotation, and rhetorical question.

Transitions show the relationships among the items of your outline. Testing the transitions means testing both your thinking process and your ability to make your thinking process clear to the audience. A good test of transitions is made when you put them into spoken words. You should test the transitions between all major parts of your outline.

# PART THREE

# DELIVERING THE SPEECH

*Speech delivery can be summarized by three "V's"—the visual, the vocal, and the verbal.*

The qualities of effective speech delivery are illustrated equally well by Mrs. Jacqueline Kennedy greeting Venezuelans in their native language and by Prime Minister Harold Macmillan addressing the United Nations.

UPI

## TOPICAL PREVIEW

# 9

# VISUAL COMMUNICATION

### Importance of bodily communication

By this time you have discovered from classroom experience that physical activity while speaking gives you confidence and poise; it relaxes you. However, bodily action in speech serves another and, in the long run, more important function: it communicates thought and emotion. Your next classroom talk will begin before you utter a word. That talk will begin when you rise and walk to the front of the room. The *first* impressions your audience get will be visual ones: your appearance, your dress, how you walk to the platform, and your posture just before speaking. *During* the talk your audience will get visual and auditory impressions. The two sets of impressions will either be supplementary or contradictory; and if they contradict, the visual will usually prevail. The *final* impressions will be visual: after you have said the last word, you will walk back to your seat.

Perhaps you challenge the statement that when there is a conflict, the visual will usually prevail. Just check your own experience. When a young man says to his girl friend, "I think your new hat is beautiful," and at the same time struggles unsuccessfully to repress his merriment, which do you believe, the words or the grin? When a student stands before the class with trembling knees and says, "I'm happy to speak to you this morning," which do you believe, the words or the trembles? Or when another student stands with one foot on the floor and the other on the speaker's stand, or slouches on the stand with one hand to his chin, and says, "I'm enthusiastic about this," which do you believe, the words or the slump? It is not always true that actions speak louder than words, but it generally is.

Thus bodily action is no mere decoration of the speech; it is an integral part of it and is woven into the whole communication fabric. Furthermore, it is one important part where a little of the right kind of practice can produce big dividends in a hurry.

To get those dividends: first make an inventory of your assets and liabilities in regard to appearance and bodily action; second, plan a program for self-improvement; third, put the program into practice, in class and out.

**Personal inventory**

In trying to see yourself as others see you, objectivity is essential. Your instructor, and perhaps others, can help you make an accurate self-appraisal. If you have the chance to study yourself in motion pictures or candid camera shots, you can see yourself more objectively; you certainly can by studying yourself in a mirror.

It will be useful to estimate the stage of the learning process where you now stand. We suggest four stages, arranged in progressive sequence: (1) the distracting stage, (2) the neutral stage, (3) the awkward stage, and (4) the skillful stage. Not all of your appearance and bodily action is likely to fall into just one of the four categories. You may find that you are in the distracting stage on posture, neutral on platform movement, awkward in gesture, and skillful on facial expression; or any other combination. Since all of your qualities are likely to be within one of these categories, let us examine them in some detail.

## The distracting stage

In the distracting stage your appearance and bodily actions actually decrease your effectiveness as a speaker. If you succeed, it is in spite of your appearance and bodily actions. If you are in this stage, you may note the following in the mirror:

DRESS  Careless or sloppy; overdone; inappropriate for the occasion

POSTURE  Weight on one foot, hip thrown out prominently ("coed slouch"); straddle; feet together ("at attention"); teetering; swaying

PLATFORM MOVEMENT  Motionless throughout talk; pacing; jiggling; awkwardness; scraping of feet when walking

BASIC HAND POSITIONS  Hidden behind back; clasped in front of stomach; rammed into pockets; rubbed together; held tensely at sides

GESTURES   Incomplete or incipient; limp; same gesture all the time; too many gestures; fiddling with pencil, notes, jewelry
FACIAL EXPRESSION   None at all; inappropriate to the thought; overdone; mannerisms, such as blinking the eyes or smacking the lips
DIRECTNESS   Eyes notebound; looking at floor, ceiling, out the window; faraway look; eyes constantly shifting

## The neutral stage

In the neutral stage your appearance and bodily movement neither significantly help nor significantly hinder your speaking effectiveness. On the basis of our check list, we might describe the neutral stage as follows:

DRESS   Drab
POSTURE   Not very good but not bad enough to distract
PLATFORM MOVEMENT   Occasional unplanned changes of position
BASIC HAND POSITIONS   Usually with hands lightly clasped behind back or lightly resting on speaking stand
GESTURES   None, or perhaps an occasional movement of head
FACIAL EXPRESSION   A little
DIRECTNESS   Looking at audience about half the time; looking at notes too often

## The awkward stage

You reach the awkward stage when you have begun practicing to improve and are still so conscious of your appearance or bodily actions that your appearance is stiff and your actions jerky.

If you are in this stage, your posture may be right but you neither feel nor look comfortable. If you change platform position, the change seems mechanical rather than spontaneous. If you try to keep your arms relaxed at your sides, you find them straying to some other position, and you will suddenly and guiltily jerk them back. If you practice a certain gesture, you make it jerkily, or overdo it, or time it badly. Sometimes you even look at your own gesture instead of at the audience. If you practice to get more facial animation, you seem at times to be making faces. Such ineptitudes are a part of a natural, and usually necessary, awkward stage. In general, they mean that you have not practiced long enough to integrate a given position, movement, or gesture into an all-in-one-piece habit.

## The skillful stage

In the skillful stage your appearance and bodily action increase your communicative effectiveness. Now in the mirror you see:

R. GRAVES

FENWICK ENGLISH

The distracting stage of bodily communication not only fails to increase but actually decreases effectiveness.

The neutral stage neither helps nor hinders effectiveness.

The awkward stage occurs when the student is beginning to learn gestures. At first the gestures are likely to appear wooden and mechanical.

FENWICK ENGLISH

The skillful stage is here illustrated by Charles De Gaulle. His gesture is spontaneous, appropriate, and expressive.

DRESS   Neat; well groomed; attractive

POSTURE   Alert and yet at ease

PLATFORM MOVEMENT   Inconspicuous; helps punctuate thought; adapted to situation, occasion, and speech content

BASIC HAND POSITIONS   Usually hanging relaxed at the sides; occasionally lightly clasped behind back, one at side with other bent at elbow, one or both resting lightly on speaking stand

GESTURES   Spontaneous in number and variety; habitual in execution; appropriate to occasion, content, and speaker's personality; expressive

FACIAL EXPRESSION   Animated; communicative

DIRECTNESS   Looking at audience most of time; looking at all the audience; actually seeing the audience

## A planned program

Do not suppose, however, that there is only one correct way of doing everything in the skillful stage. Your program should be tailor-made for you only, and should differ from that of everyone else in the class. Do not look for a cut and dried formula. You may develop a gesture that is highly effective

In these two photographs you can study approximately the same gesture—hands on hips—used by both a woman and a man. The gesture seems appropriate for the man, unladylike and distracting for the woman. Gestures should be personalized.

when you use it, but that might appear ludicrous if any of your classmates tried it. If you study six excellent public speakers, you will find six entirely different behavior patterns. They will all be different, yet all effective. This is certainly fortunate—what a dreary world it would be if all speakers looked, stood, moved, and gestured alike!

In manner as well as appearance men and women should be different on the platform. For example, most men can occasionally clench a fist and even pound the table for emphasis; but what woman can use these gestures effectively? In general, women's gestures should be graceful and subtle. At one of the national political conventions, viewed by millions on television, a prominent woman speaker harshly reprimanded the delegates for noisiness and poor attention. This restored order but briefly. She then refused the help of the chairman and insisted on wielding the oversized gavel herself in a manner which, as one newspaperman put it, "resembled a railroad workman driving a spike." She would have been far more effective had she been gracious rather than hard-boiled, and had she asked the chairman to handle the gavel rather than pound it herself. As a woman, she could probably have restored order by an appeal to the gallantry of the delegates. On the platform, as elsewhere, feminine appeal has power.

Dress should be appropriate to the occasion and therefore inconspicuous so as not to distract from the speech itself. Most students will dress according to the prevailing campus style, and for men this may pose a problem.

Campus fashions for men are always casual, and often appear careless or sloppy in any off-campus gathering. Even in the classroom the current mode becomes distracting when carried to extreme, and it is bad manners, and will detract from his speech, if a man appears before the class needing either a shave or a haircut. If a student extends his hand and reveals dirty fingernails, his audience is bound to be repelled. We should evaluate ourselves strictly on habits of neatness and cleanliness.

Most coeds are usually more careful of their grooming than most men, and their campus dress is seldom as sloppy as men's dress. Sometimes, however, women students will overdress for a classroom speech, wearing too much jewelry, too brilliant fingernail polish, or clothes that are too formal. If a girl loads her wrist with bracelets, their clanking when she gestures will kill the gesture and take attention away from what she is saying.

Perhaps a word should be added for both sexes about physical appearance. If you will think over a list of your favorite public speakers, it will be clear that good looks matter little, that ease and naturalness are much more important than a peaches-and-cream complexion, that animation is far more valuable than perfect features, that a direct and friendly manner is worth more on the platform than the finest figure.

Next let us consider planning the improvement of posture and basic hand positions. Check yourself with a large mirror; do not assume a special pose, but stand as you habitually do. Start talking aloud as though you were before the class. Is the general effect satisfactory? If so, you can forget about posture, arms, and hands. If not, make a note to work out better habits.

Continue your practice speech before the mirror. Try changing position and observe how you walk. Do you need more practice on moving about? Try a few gestures. Do the gestures feel natural? Do they look all right? Perhaps your walking and gesturing should be let alone; perhaps one or both should be noted as requiring some work.

Finally, check your habitual facial animation and directness before the mirror. Does your facial expression help express your changing thoughts and moods? And what has been your experience when speaking before the class —do you usually maintain eye contact with members of the audience? Do you look at your notes too often? Again you must decide whether or not to add to your proposed program.

In making the foregoing evaluations, do not be hypercritical. At the same time do not be complacent; try to be honest and objective. If in doubt, consult your instructor.

In planning your program, it is wise to recognize that you cannot do everything at once. Lay out the program in sequence, planning to master one thing and make it habitual before going ahead to the next one.

Dress should be appropriate and inconspicuous. Here the chairman of the entertainment committee reports to a women's club. Would you pay attention to the hat or to the fact that the recent card party grossed $116?

### A program for practice

You now have before you a concrete program for improving your appearance and bodily actions. You should even have an approximate time schedule for the semester for getting the job done. You are wondering now how to get it done.

The job divides itself into two major parts: (1) practicing in private to establish a set of skillful mechanical habits; (2) using those habits spontaneously while giving a speech. Practice produces habit, and habit makes it possible for the speaker to produce easily and naturally the gesture his inner impulse requires.

The establishment of mechanical habits is the basis for spontaneity on the platform. If a speaker feels the urge to gesture, but has no particular habits of gesture, he is likely to saw the air meaninglessly or merely twitch the hands. If that same speaker has developed a set of habitual gestures, he will gesture skillfully and unconsciously at the proper moment.

### *Skillful habits*

Making or breaking action habits in speech is practically the same as in any other mechanical skill—driving a golf ball, fingering a flute, riding a bicycle. One is tempted to say that the three big rules are practice, more practice, and still more practice. But more is involved: As in golf, you must practice the right things and in the right way.

**1. POSTURE** To improve your habitual posture, you should begin by standing in front of a large mirror and experimenting. The object is to find a posture that looks natural, alert, and yet at ease. The exact positions of the feet, trunk, shoulders, arms, and head depend on height, weight, and build. Work out a trial posture and check it with your instructor. Once you have determined your own best posture, practice it frequently and with exactness in front of a mirror. Practice it throughout the day—sit right and stand right wherever you are. Your speech class is only a convenient checking-up point in this schedule. At first, the new posture may feel unnatural and awkward because it differs from your old posture. If you stick to your guns, gradually you will find that you can maintain the new posture with less and less attention. There comes a time when you are pleasantly surprised to discover that you have been maintaining the proper posture for the past half hour or longer *without having consciously thought about it.* When this happens, your job is done. The new posture has become a habit. The tables have been turned—now the *old* way feels unnatural or awkward!

**2. PLATFORM MOVEMENTS** Practice walking about the platform before a mirror. Experiment. Try moving forward, backward, to the left, and to the right. Try moving a short distance and a longer distance. Start with the foot that is already closer to the point to which you plan to go; when moving to the left, start with the left foot; when moving to the right, start with the right foot. Study the angle of the feet—are you turning the toes in, or splaying them out? What length of stride looks best? Talk, and try to synchronize your movements with what you say. Move sidewise to indicate transition to a new idea, forward to emphasize a point, backward to begin a new one. In such fashion, decide on the most effective set of movements. Then practice them as often as possible alone.

The same procedure applies to your basic hand and arm positions. Let your arms hang relaxed at your sides. Do not get the elbows too tight to the body. At first, your hands may seem like two huge hams, hanging conspicuously. Eventually the new position becomes comfortable and natural.

**3. CONVENTIONAL GESTURES** Gestures should be worked out one at a time. Your program should provide for developing a wide repertory, giving you eventually maximum variety. There are, however, seven gestures that have acquired almost universal meanings. These are often called the conventional gestures, and they afford a good starting list for practice.

FENWICK ENGLISH

R. GRAVES

The beginning student at the left is making a commendable effort to stress a point by using the conventional gesture of the clenched fist. But the gesture is awkward.

The varsity debater at the right uses the same gesture in a practice debate. He shows the results of training. Compare these two pictures carefully.

*a. Giving and receiving.* This gesture is accomplished by extending either or both hands with fingers separated and palms toward the audience. You can produce the gesture by handing an imaginary cake of soap to somebody, or by extending your hand as though to receive a packet of matches. As you practice it, use first one hand, then the other, then both together. Do not clamp the elbows into your sides. Keep the thumbs well out.

*b. Rejecting.* The hand or hands are extended, usually with a sweeping motion, palms turned down and away from the speaker. You can approximate the effect by preventing an imaginary kitten from leaping into your lap.

*c. Nodding and shaking head.* Try these common gestures with varying degrees of vigor. Be careful in nodding the head to avoid bowing the trunk.

*d. Dividing.* Extend the hand, with fingers closed, and make a chopping motion or move the hand from side to side. You will approximate the gesture if you bring your hand down on a table and say, "On this side put the books; on that side, the papers."

*e. Pointing.* In public speaking it is not impolite to point the index finger to locate or identify something. Thus you point as you say, "That chart pictures the problem."

*f. Clenching fist.* This gesture is most useful when reinforcing an idea, to indicate power or determination. The gesture usually looks best if the row of knuckles is parallel with the speaker's shoulder, and the wrist slightly bent. The gesture is appropriate when exclaiming, for example, "We will *never* give up!"

*g. Restraining.* The hand is extended at about shoulder height, palm facing outward and downward. This is the gesture you use when saying, for example, "Now, take it easy. Just wait a minute. We're coming to that."

You should be able to use any of these gestures in several effective ways. Perhaps one or two are not suited to your style and should be avoided entirely. The job is for you to work out as many of them as possible until you can use them effectively. Then practice your way of making them until the execution becomes routine. Most can be practiced in conversation. All can be practiced in speech class.

After the conventional gestures have been mastered, you can experiment to create others that will become standard in your own speaking although perhaps rare in the speaking of other people.

**4. CHARACTERISTICS OF EFFECTIVE GESTURES** There are certain criteria by which to judge and perfect any set of gestures. Observe your own and practice to acquire the desirable characteristics.

*a. Strength.* Unless you are ridiculing or showing what not to do, avoid flabby or listless gestures. Every gesture requires decisiveness or vigor to make it look real and alive. The exact amount of vigor required must be determined by experiment, in terms of the mood felt and the thought spoken.

*b. Carry-through.* The importance of carry-through is well illustrated in sports—pitching a baseball, putting the shot, stroking a tennis ball. Each gesture should be made completely and wholeheartedly. Some gestures are made with the hand only, some with the hand and the arm, but vigorous gestures are made with the whole body. If you are going to point to a flag on the side of the platform, do not make a weak, halfhearted motion with the hand and wrist; it is *you* who are pointing, not just your finger; the whole body should point to that flag.

*c. Proper timing.* If your gestures fall just a little behind the words to be emphasized, the effect is awkward or even humorous. The effect is almost as bad when the gesture comes noticeably too soon. The gesture should be made at the precise time the stressed word is spoken, or just slightly before. Acquiring the knack of precise timing requires much practice. Invent short statements, appropriate to each gesture, and practice to get your words and movements coordinated.

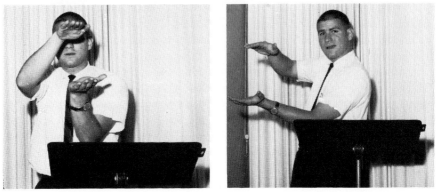

The wrong way and the right way. Either way can become habitual; practice must be guided.

**5. HANDLING NOTES** The question is often asked, "Is it permissible to use notes?" Yes. But don't overdo it, and learn to use notes skillfully. During the semester, both in practicing alone and in speaking before the class, develop a definite habit system with regard to notes. For example, put your notes on cards, as already recommended, and develop a personal system for writing them so that you can tell where you are at a glance. When you are on the platform, it should not be necessary to study your notes as though you were seeing them for the first time.

When you are introduced, come to the platform with the notes in your pocket or carry them inconspicuously in your hand. During your opening remarks, take the cards from your pocket and place them on the stand in a casual way so the audience will scarcely know you have done it.

Develop the knack of glancing at the notes when changing your position around the speakers' stand. Experienced speakers can do this many times during a speech; yet the audience never realizes that there are any notes at all.

In introducing an important quotation, or statistics, or a list of facts, utilize your notes deliberately and conspicuously. This technique makes the materials stand out from the rest of the speech, makes them seem more important, and gives the audience the feeling that absolute accuracy is guaranteed.

For most short talks, however, it is more effective to use no notes. You will not need them if you have a proper outline and have rehearsed adequately. However, if it will give you confidence, you can carry them in your pocket as insurance against an emergency. If you need the notes, take them out unhurriedly as though you had planned to all the time.

**6. HANDLING VISUAL AIDS** You must also develop habits for the effective handling of visual aids. This requires advance planning and practice in just when to introduce them, how to handle them, how long to display them, and how to dispose of them. For example, suppose you were going to use a chart, such as the type pictured just below. You would not display the chart at the very beginning of your talk unless you planned to discuss it immediately. Usually you do not allow the audience to see the chart until you come to the point which the chart illustrates. Then you must be sure that the chart is clearly visible to the entire group. If it is large enough, you might hang it on the wall; otherwise, you might hold it up close to the front row, or even walk from one edge of the audience to another, giving everyone a chance for a close look. If the chart is hanging on the wall, avoid the temptation to turn your back on the audience and address your remarks to the chart, and avoid the danger of putting yourself between the chart and the audience. Usually it is best to stand to one side of the chart and use a pointer. When you have completed your references to a visual aid, you should usually remove it from view; otherwise it may distract from your discussion of subsequent points.

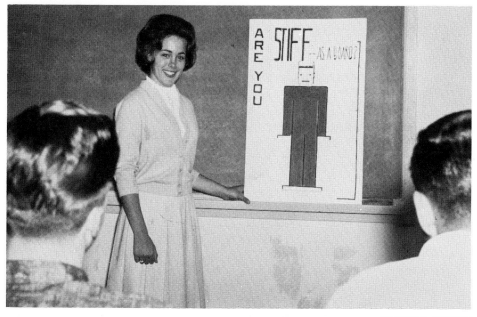

Should the placard be displayed throughout the talk? Or should it be removed when she has completed her direct references to it?

These posters were gathered during a recent tour of the Soviet Union and they caught the attention of the entire class. In the right-hand picture, however, the speaker blots his audience's view by standing in the way.

In a sense, of course, you are your own principal visual aid; you cannot expect a chart or an object to do all your work for you. Generally the effectiveness of the audio-visual support will be largely determined by your words and movements in relation to it. Charles F. Brannan used a visual aid when he addressed the National Farm Institute:

At my request a bushel of corn has been placed on the platform. If you will assume that this bushel of corn is the first extra bushel beyond our assumed domestic need, beyond export requirements, and beyond even the safe reserves required to protect the nation against crop failure or other emergency, then it is a symbol of our major national farm problem. It is the extra bushel. It is the bushel for which . . .[1]

Obviously, the effectiveness of Secretary Brannan's visual support depended largely on his platform positions in relation to the bushel of corn, his gestures toward it, the emphasis he gave to key words such as *"this bushel."*

## Spontaneity of gesture and movement

As we pointed out earlier in this chapter, skillful mechanical habits should be the servants of your thoughts and feelings. The urge to stand alertly, the urge to move about or gesture, the urge to smile or frown, the urge to look your listener in the eye—all should arise from your thoughts and feelings. Spontaneity comes from within. You will find that the spontaneous impulse to use bodily action comes naturally to you. Just follow the impulse.

If at first you find it difficult to let yourself go, here are three suggestions to help to get you started:

1. In planning the content of a speech, provide some ideas that will *require* you to move about or use your hands. For example, include something that requires writing on the blackboard, handling a book, or demonstrating a visual aid.

2. Provide a few spots where you are to describe something that involves size, height, shape, position, or movement. Any one of them will strongly suggest the use of descriptive gestures. Thus the table was "this wide," the youngster was "so tall," the urn was "shaped like this," the two groups were lined up with "one of them over there" and the other "here."

3. Provide yourself with a chance to mimic some person. Act out his mannerisms, imitate his gestures. He walked with a peculiar limp "like this"; he had a habit of twirling a fountain pen in his fingers "like this."

In using any of the foregoing suggestions, never try to remember particular gestures that you may have used during practice, but do remind yourself that you are going to use some movements or gestures. Once you break the ice, the release of inner impulses into bodily communication will come easily. Eventually all your bodily actions while speaking will be in response to your thought and feeling, and the actions will be carried through

[1] A. Craig Baird, ed., *Representative American Speeches: 1949–1950*, H. W. Wilson, 1950, pp. 204–05. Reprinted by permission of Charles F. Brannan.

skillfully and automatically. Thus you are in the midst of a speech; you are not consciously thinking of your delivery at all, but you feel an urge to emphasize a point and simultaneously you do it by some means, often involving bodily movement. You do *not* think, "Now I shall raise my right arm, clench my fist, and shake it on such-and-such word"; rather you *feel* that what you are about to say should be made emphatic, and so you do clench your fist, and you do it exactly in the way that you have made habitual by privately practicing. Then clenched fist and strong statement blend into each other so naturally that neither you nor your audience is aware of the gesture as such.

When you have restudied the above advice and put it into classroom practice, you will resolve the apparent paradox that spontaneity of bodily action during a talk is based upon previous private practice of the mechanics of gestures. Turn back to the pictures on page 174. In the left-hand picture the student is giving a classroom talk and he is trying to emphasize an idea by a clenched-fist gesture, but you must agree that the gesture is not as effective as it could be. The gesture was spontaneous—he was scarcely conscious of using it. But he had not established effective habits by previous practice: notice that the wrist is straight, the fist is vertical, the thumb is awkwardly positioned, and the total effect lacks strength.

In the right-hand picture the student's gesture is also spontaneous—he wants to stress an idea but he is scarcely conscious of the gesture itself. In his freshman year this student's gestures were no more effective than those of the beginner in the left-hand photograph, but the debater practiced until his chosen method of using the clenched-fist gesture had become automatic. Note the slightly bent wrist, the horizontal position of the fist, and the placement of the thumb—all of these details had been worked out in front of a mirror and had been practiced until a habit system was established.

The two pictures illustrate that mechanical practice does not prevent or replace spontaneity. Such practice encourages you to greater freedom of bodily action, and it makes spontaneous gestures more effective.

### Summary

Bodily communication includes dress and grooming, posture, platform movements, gestures, facial expression, and eye contact with the audience. The visible elements of speech are not mere decorations but are integral parts of effective communication.

Take a personal inventory of your use of the visible means of communication, plan a program for self-improvement, and put your program into practice.

In taking personal inventory you should consider four stages of the learning process: the distracting stage, the neutral stage, the awkward stage, and the skillful stage.

Your program should be tailor-made for you, and should differ from that of everyone else in the class.

Putting your program into practice may be divided into two main jobs: (1) practicing in private to establish a set of skillful mechanical habits; (2) using those habits spontaneously while giving a speech.

TOPICAL PREVIEW

# 10

# VOCAL COMMUNICATION

**"Mend your speech a little"**     (*King Lear*)

Charles Laughton is justly regarded as one of the foremost actors and public readers of his generation.[1] But what about his voice? You will probably agree that nature did not bless Laughton with a particularly good voice. Probably half of your friends have better natural voices than Laughton. He has made the most of what he has. Making the most of the voice you have will be the theme of this chapter.

In this text and this course the emphasis must of necessity be on voice improvement, not on speech correction. If your instructor suspects you have an organic defect in your vocal mechanism, he will recommend medical advice and the help of a speech pathologist. If you have vocal defects symptomatic of fundamental emotional or mental disturbances, he will refer you to a speech or psychology clinic. If you have long-standing habits of faulty production of certain sounds, or if you have a marked foreign dialect, he will refer you to a speech clinic. If you need work on changing your basic pitch or vocal quality, he will refer you to an expert tutor. In short, voice deficiencies that require long periods of treatment with individual guidance throughout cannot be handled in this course. Here you will have plenty to do learning how to make freer and better use of the voice you already have.

[1] Hear one of his phonograph albums, such as *The Story-Teller* (Capitol, TBO 1650) or *Charles Laughton Reading from the Bible* (Decca, DL 8031).

Voice improvement requires five steps: (1) studying the basic process of voice production, (2) making a personal inventory, (3) determining your potential, (4) planning a program, and (5) practicing the program.

## Voice production

The speech process is so complicated that even experts are uncertain about many of the details. Had nature devised a mechanism solely for the production of speech, a much simpler instrument could have sufficed. As it is, all the organs used in speech also serve other, and often more primary. biological functions. As Gray and Wise have said:

> Indeed, the opportunities for maladjustment of so many reflex arcs governing so many muscles performing so intricate a process, are so infinitely numerous that the marvel is not that we sometimes speak faultily but that we speak at all. The vital, life-sustaining functions of breathing and taking food are more comprehensible, because the reflex arcs connected with them are natively established; but the function of speech, being in a sense overlaid or superimposed upon the musculature of these primitive functions and being forced to use borrowed mechanisms, represent acquired or learned adjustments, adaptations, and coordinations nothing short of miraculous.[2]

You will realize, therefore, that the story of voice production must here be simplified and confined to essential details. With that thought in mind, we may conveniently divide speaking into four major processes: (1) respiration, (2) phonation, (3) resonation, and (4) articulation. The following discussion will be clearer if you refer to the accompanying diagrams frequently.

### Respiration

The *torso* (trunk of the body) contains two major cavities: the upper, called the *thorax* (chest cavity), and the lower, called the *abdomen*. The two are separated by a sheet of muscle and tendon called the *diaphragm*, which thus becomes the floor for the thorax and the ceiling for the abdomen. The thorax contains the *lungs* and heart; the abdomen contains the stomach, intestines, liver, and kidneys. The walls of the thorax consist of muscles and bones. The bones are the *ribs*, *vertebrae* (backbone), *scapulae* (shoulder blades), and *clavicles* (collarbones). The walls of the abdomen, to a much larger degree than those of the thorax, are composed of muscle tissue.

The lungs are cone-shaped and sponge-like. They contain practically no muscle tissue, and their role in breathing is passive except for the elasticity

---

[2] Giles Wilkeson Gray and Claude Merton Wise, *The Bases of Speech*, Harper, 1959, p. 234.

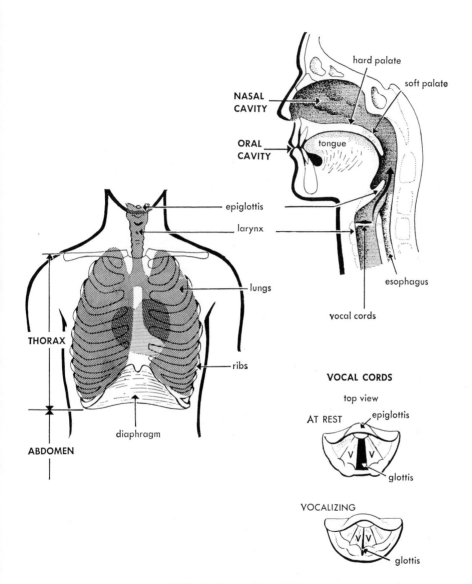

hard palate

soft palate

**NASAL CAVITY**

**ORAL CAVITY**

tongue

epiglottis

larynx

esophagus

lungs

vocal cords

**THORAX**

ribs

diaphragm

**ABDOMEN**

**VOCAL CORDS**

top view

AT REST

epiglottis

V V

glottis

VOCALIZING

V V

glottis

**THE SPEECH ORGANS**

of the tissue. In other words, the lungs do not expand and contract themselves during breathing. Instead, they are acted upon. It is as though you took a large sponge in your hands and squeezed, forcing the air out. Then if you relaxed your fingers, the elasticity would bring the sponge back into shape, and air would be sucked into the cells.

The lungs are acted upon by three major sets of muscles: the diaphragm, the rib muscles, and the abdominal muscles. Their action is to squeeze the lungs by pulling in the sides and lifting the floor of the thorax during *exhalation,* and by putting the process into reverse during *inhalation.* When the abdominal muscles are contracted, the abdominal organs are pressed inward and upward, thus decreasing the volume of the thoracic cavity. When the abdominal muscles are relaxed, the opposite effect occurs. The movements of the rib cage are controlled by both the rib muscles and the abdominal muscles. The action is like that of an old-fashioned bellows. You can approximate the effect of this action by placing the tips of your fingers together about a foot in front of your nose, with elbows down; then, keeping your fingers in the same position, move the elbows up and down. You will soon see how this action expands and contracts the space between your arms, especially at the lower end of the cone.

When the lungs are squeezed, the air is forced from the air sacs out through a tributary system of air vessels, the last of which are the *bronchial tubes* (anyone who has suffered the discomforts of bronchitis knows about them), which lead directly into the *trachea* (wind pipe). Thence the column of air escapes through the mouth or nose.

The beginning student should remember that frequent inhalations are better than fewer very deep inhalations. In exhalation the speaker should learn to control the abdominal muscles. He should be able to start or stop the exhalation at will, suddenly or gradually, strongly or gently. Finally, he should learn to control his breathing with the torso muscles rather than with the muscles of the neck and jaw.

## Phonation

At the upper end of the trachea, the *larynx* (voice box or Adam's apple) is suspended by muscles which can move the larynx upward and downward. The larynx is constructed of a number of cartilages. Inside, attached to the cartilages, are the *vocal cords,* which are not in the least like cords or strings but rather like folds, or curtains, or lips. The vocal cords consist of bands of relatively thick muscle tissue, bordered along the inside edges by a thin white membrane. The opening between the vocal cords is called the *glottis.*

When the voice is used, compressed air from the lungs strikes the vocal cords; the cords are set into vibration; the vibration of the cords sets the surrounding air to vibrating; and the air in vibration is the sound. (The action by which this is done may be compared with that of the lips when one is playing a trumpet.) The vibrations thus produced may be measured in two ways. The amplitude of the sound waves is a measure of the loudness or intensity of the sound. The frequency (or number of waves per second) is a measure of the pitch.

Going up and down the scale in pitch is a function primarily of the vocal cords. However, the individual muscles that move the cords closer together or farther apart are not subject to conscious control. They can be controlled only as a group, and indirectly. You hear the pitch of your own voice, and wishing to change it, you unconsciously change the position of the cords. Thus development of nice discriminations in pitch is more a matter of ear training than of vocal-cord training. Loudness or intensity is partly a function of the vocal cords and partly a function of breathing. When you exhale air forcefully, you cause the vocal cords to vibrate at larger amplitudes that produce louder sounds.

Many people when speaking in public suffer tension in the muscles of the neck and throat. This results in voice fatigue, strain, and other undesirable effects. The goal is to have a relaxed and "open" throat.

## Resonation

If the process of voice production could be confined to respiration and phonation only, the effect would be somewhat comparable to playing the mouthpiece removed from a horn—you could produce sound and vary its duration and pitch, and to a limited extent vary its loudness, but it would be a thin and squeaky sound. The process by which sounds are amplified and modified is called resonation.

The first group of organs used for voice resonation are cavities, the most important of which are the *pharynx* (throat), the *oral cavity* (mouth), and the *nasal cavities* (nose). Sound waves are amplified by being reflected from the surfaces of the cavities, roughly in the manner of a megaphone. At the same time the sounds are modified by changing the shape and size of the throat and mouth, and by permitting or preventing the escape of air through the nasal cavities. These changes produce the different vowel sounds.

Resonation also involves the tissues of the upper part of the body, especially the bones of the head and chest, which amplify and modify tones by acting as sounding boards. However, the effects of these sounding-board tissues are of much less importance than the effects of the cavities.

The total process of resonation not only amplifies the voice and gives vowels their different sounds, but also provides the richness, or mellow-

You learned to talk when you were a child, but would you reveal good or poor speech habits if you were observed by experts through this one-way glass?

ness, usually termed voice quality. Because the bodily structures of human beings are all different and because individuals differ in making the innumerable small adjustments of the many organs during speech, no two voices are ever exactly alike. The term *quality* is used to describe that characteristic which distinguishes one voice from another when both voices are approximately alike in the pitch, duration, and loudness of vowel sounds.

Practical application of the preceding discussion to your own speaking voice indicates that three main aspects are involved in resonation: loudness, production of vowel sounds, and vocal quality. Faulty resonation accounts for such difficulties as a weak or thin voice, errors in vowel sounds, or such unpleasant voice qualities as nasality or stridency.

## Articulation

Speaking requires one more process. You must further modify sounds to produce the consonants, and you must join vowel and consonantal sounds together (or separate them) to produce complete utterances. These tasks are performed chiefly by the *lips, tongue, teeth, hard palate, velum* (soft palate), and *jaw*. In general, the consonants are produced by blocking the column of vibrating air in various ways. For example, you may completely block the flow of air with your lips for a moment and then release it, creating a small explosion which becomes *p* or *b*. Or you may partially block the stream of air by placing the lower lip close to the upper teeth, and the friction that results by forcing the air through this narrow opening becomes *f* or *v*. The practical application of this final process to your own speaking determines the clearness and accuracy of your articulation and pronunciation.

## Voice and articulation inventory

With the facts of the preceding section in mind, you will be better prepared to evaluate your own voice. You will need further assistance, however, which your instructor will provide. He will give you a systematic appraisal; in doing so he may use some kind of printed or mimeographed form. One useful voice and articulation criticism form is presented on page 403 of the Appendix. Regardless of what form sheet is used, your instructor will record his impressions of your voice as compared with certain standard criteria. The criteria may be stated in various ways, but they can usually be classified into four major categories: audibility, accuracy, meaningfulness, and pleasantness.

### *Audibility*

Audibility is a matter of degree. It may be that your natural voice is so soft that your listeners must constantly strain to hear you. Or your audibility may be spotty; listeners may be able to catch most of what you say, but be forced to guess at the gaps in terms of the context. Or perhaps your voice is audible during the first and middle parts of statements but trails away or dies out on the endings. You may be audible in some situations but not in others—you may or may not adjust effectively to size of room or

Be audible, but not too loud. Most people dislike being bellowed at— they may even hold their ears.

STANDARD OIL

audience, to acoustics, to competing noises. Even under difficult conditions, you should remember that too loud a voice is often as objectionable as too soft a voice—most people dislike being bellowed at.

## Accuracy

There are two kinds of vocal accuracy: accuracy of articulation and accuracy of pronunciation. If your listeners do not know whether you said "none" or "one," your articulation is inaccurate; if you say something that sounds like "known" for "none," your pronunciation is inaccurate. The first is a problem of distinctness; the second of correctness. In practice the two problems often overlap.

Articulation is the process of forming, joining, and separating speech sounds. You should carry out this process with enough accuracy to be easily understood and yet not sound overprecise. In evaluating your own speaking habits, you may find that you already speak with reasonable distinctness, adequate for most of your needs. More likely, however, you can stand improvement.

Pronunciation involves the sounds you make and the syllables you accent, rather than how distinctly you make them. As you know, standards for pronunciation vary among regions of the country, and you probably use the accent of the region in which you grew up. In the United States there are three major accents: general American, Eastern, and Southern, with local versions within each of the three. Furthermore, the preferred pronunciation of many words is in constant flux. Any rule for choosing an over-all standard, therefore, must be flexible. Normally, that pronunciation is best that attracts the least attention. This usually means avoiding localisms, avoiding imitations of an accent different from your accustomed one, and adopting the current pronunciations used by educated people of the region in which you live.

Perhaps the most common faults of articulation and pronunciation are due to general slovenliness or "lip laziness." Ask yourself how often during face-to-face or telephone conversations your listeners ask you to repeat what you have just said. It is but small exaggeration to report that college students will say,

> Lives of great men all remind us
> We can make our lives sublime,

with such laziness of the articulators as to sound like,

> Liza greatmun awe remindus
> Weaken maycar liza blime.

Sometimes the articulatory fault lies in one or more specific consonant sounds. Those which give the most trouble are *s, r, ng, th, l, z, sh, j,* and *ch.*

You may habitually make one or more of the following five types of errors in pronunciation:

1. *Sound substitutions:* tremenjous for tremendous; jist for just.
2. *Sound reversals:* childern for children; calvary for cavalry.
3. *Sound additions:* athuletes for athletes; warsh for wash.
4. *Sound omissions:* pitcher for picture; pome for poem.
5. *Misplaced stress:* compar'able for com'parable; superflu'ous for super'- fluous.

All of us, of course, make occasional mistakes in trying to pronounce controversial or unfamiliar words, such as "camellia" or "culinary." Such mistakes should be distinguished from those due to sloppiness and carelessness, such as "git," "ketch," "strenth," "jist," "kin," "exscape," "instid," "liberry," and "wunst." As already mentioned, it is equally undesirable to go to the other extreme and become so precise as to sound affected.

## Meaningfulness

At this point in your inventory, the question arises: How much meaning do you convey with your voice? Suppose for example, that in the transcript of a trial one of the witnesses answered, "Oh, yes." How would you know what meaning the witness intended to convey without having heard him say it? "Oh, yes," can be spoken in many different ways, each with a different meaning; you can even make it mean "no." In other words, variations in loudness, inflection, pitch, and rate produce meaningfulness in a speaking voice. So the question may be restated: Are you using all the variety your voice is capable of? And is your voice capable of a sufficient range of variety—that is, is it flexible?

Variety is most needed in rate, loudness, and pitch. If you lack such variety the result is monotony, probably the most common fault of beginning speakers. Monotony of rate is characterized by an unchanging beat, monotony of loudness by sameness, and monotony of pitch by the repetition of the same note or pattern of notes.

## Pleasantness

It is difficult to get a reliable judgment of the pleasantness or unpleasantness of your own voice from friends and relatives; they are so accustomed to it that their reaction to it is different from that of strangers. However, you will find it instructive to secure reactions from your classmates to see how

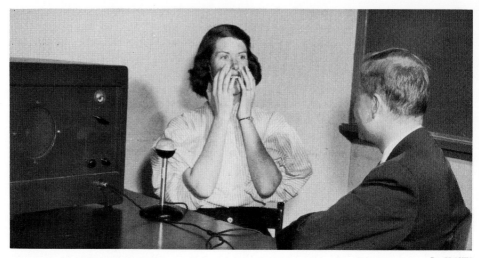

"That's not *me!*" is the usual exclamation on first hearing your own voice from a recorder. For the first time you hear yourself as others hear you.

much agreement they show in trying to describe your vocal quality. Do they tend to use adjectives with a pleasant connotation, such as mellow, resonant, soft, musical, interesting, or forceful? Or do they use adjectives with an unpleasant connotation, such as nasal, breathy, harsh, strident, fuzzy, grating, whining, or thin?

Suppose that you have now secured ratings of your audibility, accuracy, meaningfulness, and pleasantness from your classmates and instructor. These evaluations will not help you unless you can hear yourself as they do. To hear yourself objectively some type of voice recorder is almost indispensable. In recording your voice it is wise to try several kinds of speaking: conversation, an extemporaneous speech, reading from prose and poetry. It is also helpful to record in cooperation with somebody else—to provide for side-by-side comparisons and contrasts. The first time you hear your own voice played back, you will probably exclaim in confusion, "That's not me!" Your confusion will result from the fact that it is physically impossible for you to hear yourself during ordinary speech as others hear you. They hear only one set of vibrations, the external, while you hear these plus the internal vibrations. So you have to get used to this new voice. There is the advantage that you can rather easily listen to your recorded speech as though it were the voice of a third person coming in on the radio, and appraise it objectively. If you tuned in on that voice, would you stay tuned, or turn the dial?

## Determination of potential vocal ability

Once you have evaluated your voice, you must try to imagine its future potential. It will be difficult for you to imagine the full possibilities until you learn to listen critically to conversations, speeches, radio, television, and especially to phonograph recordings.

Listen to the best two or three conversationalists you know, paying critical attention to the ways they use their voices. On what points are they strongest? Who are the two or three best speakers in your class? Next time they speak, listen attentively to their voices. What are their strongest points? Attend a meeting where an effective speaker is taking part. How about his audibility, accuracy, meaningfulness, pleasantness of voice? Listen to radio and television. Choose several speakers who are acknowledged as good. Listen to their voices. Notice details of their articulation and pronunciation, their variations in quality, pitch, rate, and loudness. Are these speakers effective in spite of, or because of, voice and articulation?

Phonograph recordings have the advantage that they can be replayed for careful listening and can be compared almost directly with recordings of your own voice. Allowances must be made, however, in terms of each speaker's purpose as compared with your own purposes. A good idea of your own potential can be secured by speaking a given piece, recording it, playing it back, then playing the same piece as spoken by a professional on a phonograph record. The immediate contrast between what you were able to put into the reading and what the professional put into it will reveal vocal possibilities that will surprise you.

Discover what can be done with the human voice by critically analyzing phonograph recordings of experienced speakers and professional actors.

FENWICK ENGLISH

Many excellent spoken recordings have been released in recent years and may be found at your listening library or record shop. A challenging example of vocal variety is provided by Orson Welles' *No Man Is an Island* (Decca, DL 9060). Welles reads eight selections from famous speeches, Pericles to Zola. The differences among these readings are so marked that you can easily imagine that you have listened to eight different men.

A few phonograph records of speaking voices were produced in the early years of the industry; in recent times, however, the number, variety, and availability of spoken records have increased many-fold. A new dimension has been added to literature, drama, and history as well as to the field of speech. The voices of great teachers, readers, and actors can be heard and studied in your own living room; authentic sounds of history in the making can also be heard there. In your speech course you should become well acquainted with this new kind of literature, and simultaneously you will be rewarded with many ideas about what can be done with the speaking voice. You will be better able to set goals for your own voice improvement when you can literally hear those goals. You do not have to develop the voice of a Charlton Heston or an Ingrid Bergman. Even if you could, it might not be worth your time. Exercise discretion and build a practical program for yourself, setting your goals in a proper perspective.

**The program in practice**

*Audibility exercises*

If your voice is always audible, you need read this section only for an understanding of how the voice functions. If your voice is weak, do not be unduly alarmed. So much speaking is done through radio, television, or public address systems that a weak voice is not an insurmountable handicap. But if you do not speak audibly, you should find the principal cause, then practice to eliminate it.

1. The cause may possibly be faulty breathing. Some years ago this was considered almost the only cause. Recent research, however, casts much doubt on the matter. Some people, in fact, use less breath on loud sounds than on quiet ones. If your instructor finds that a fundamental change in breathing habits is indicated, however, many exercises are needed, with guided practice over a relatively long period of time. You will need a clinician to do the guiding.

2. The cause may be simply a lack of energy, coupled with a failure to realize that you have fallen into the habit of speaking inaudibly. The obvious advice to speak louder is the principal treatment. To break the habit you

must deliberately and systematically practice talking louder. Practice in daily conversations, using a friend as a checker; in your class talks use your instructor as critic. Remember that breaking this habit, like breaking other habits, will take time and constant reminders.

3. The cause may be a failure to adapt your voice to groups or rooms of different sizes. If so, find an unused classroom and ask a friend to be your audience.

a. Stand at the front of the room with your friend only two feet away. Talk for a while, asking your friend to check for appropriate loudness.

b. Have your friend sit in one of the front rows. Repeat the foregoing.

c. Have your friend move several rows further away and repeat.

d. Have him go to the back row and repeat again.

Be careful that you do not simply raise the pitch, becoming shrill; be careful also that you do not become *too* loud. Now this whole procedure can be best practiced in class talks or in any other audience situation by remembering the rule: *Talk to the back row.* To check on yourself, have someone sit in the back row with instructions to signal if you speak too soft or too loud.

4. The cause may be the habit of dropping or swallowing the endings of sentences. If your voice is adequately loud on the first and middle parts of sentences, you can easily hold up the end, too. Practice the same procedure as in item 2 above, but concentrate on sentence endings.

5. You may not open your mouth wide enough. Find out whether or not you do by sitting alone with a small mirror in your lap and talking in your normal way. Occasionally, glance at the mirror, catching yourself off guard, and watch for the amount of space between your upper and lower teeth, and for the amount of variation in this space on different sounds. You may be surprised at the small amount of space and of jaw movement. To eliminate this fault, exaggerate your jaw movements while reading aloud or talking. Ask your instructor to indicate the right amount and then get the feel of it. You will find at first that the right amount will feel as though it is too much; but before long it will feel perfectly natural. Attention to articulation exercises, soon to be discussed, is also helpful in solving this problem.

6. Inaudibility may be caused by habitually speaking below your natural key. Men sometimes get into this habit because they think a lower pitch sounds more masculine; women sometimes think a low, husky voice is glamorous. Get a competent critic to assist you, and then practice reading a passage several times, raising the over-all pitch level slightly for each reading until you have established the best combination of pitch and

audibility. Practice at this pitch level in conversations as well as in class speeches.

7. Remember that some people's voices are naturally soft or light. Those people should not try for additional loudness by strain and struggle. Sometimes it is better to let the loudness alone and compensate for lack of it by developing exceptionally clear articulation. Your attendance at plays has doubtless demonstrated that even a whisper, properly articulated, can be heard throughout a large theater.

## Articulation exercises

There are approximately fifteen vowel sounds, nine diphthongs, and twenty-five consonant sounds in the English language. We say approximately because some people do not make fine discriminations between vowels, and actually use fewer sounds than other people do. We stress sounds because there is a vast difference between them and written symbols. For example, many people think there are just five vowel sounds corresponding to the five symbols *a, e, i, o,* and *u.* A moment's reflection will show that the one symbol *a* represents several different sounds. One way of studying the relationships between the written and the oral is to use the phonetic alphabet—a system of written symbols in which there is a one-to-one relationship between symbols and sounds. Obviously the twenty-six letters of the ordinary alphabet had to be supplemented by the invention of additional symbols.

If you are told you are producing a certain sound inaccurately but cannot hear the fault, or cannot correct it even when trying, you should consult with your instructor.

FREDERICK WILLIAMS

Following is a list of the principal sounds used in the United States from the International Phonetic Alphabet (IPA). In each item notice (1) the usual written symbol, (2) the phonetic symbol in brackets, and (3) a sample word.

CONSONANTS

1. p, [p], papa
2. b, [b], baby
3. k, [k], kick
4. g, [g], gag
5. t, [t], tat
6. d, [d], dad
7. l, [l], lull
8. r, [r], rare
9. m, [m], mum
10. n, [n], none
11. ng, [ŋ], ringing
12. y, [j], yes
13. wh, [hw], what
14. w, [w], wow
15. th, [ð], this
16. th, [θ], think
17. h, [h], hah
18. f, [f], fife
19. v, [v], vivid
20. j, [dʒ], Georgia
21. ch, [tʃ], church
22. zh, [ʒ], measure
23. sh, [ʃ], shush
24. z, [z], zeals
25. s, [s], sass

VOWELS

26. oo, [u], rule
27. oo, [ʊ], wool
28. o, [ɔ], law
29. a, [ɑ], calm
30. a, [æ], cat
31. e, [ɛ], pet
32. i, [ɪ], pit
33. ee, [i], see
34. a, [ə], above
35. u, [ʌ], up

DIPHTHONGS

36. a, [eɪ], date
37. o, [oʊ], crow
38. u, [ju], you
39. ou, [aʊ], out
40. i, [aɪ], pipe
41. oi, [ɔɪ], oil

If you are told you are producing a certain sound inaccurately but cannot hear the fault, or cannot correct it even when trying, you should consult with your instructor. At the same time, you may consult a book in which every sound is separately considered, its production described in detail, and special exercises suggested. Two such books are: Grant Fairbanks, *Voice and Articulation Drillbook*, Harper, 1960; John A. Grasham and Glenn G. Gooder, *Improving Your Speech*, Harcourt, Brace & World, 1960.

Articulatory errors that you can hear, when they are called to your attention, and that you can correct, when you try, are the kind that will be handled as a part of this course. They are the most common, and are due to carelessness, lack of attention or effort, "lip laziness," imitation of poor models, or talking too fast. The result may be either a general slovenliness or merely an indistinctness on certain sounds.

1. The best exercise for general slovenliness of articulation is whispering. This excellent exercise can be practiced in many ways. For example, get the cooperation of a friend and find an unoccupied room. Have the friend sit about fifteen feet away. Then converse with him entirely in a whisper. Do not allow any voice to creep into the whisper—just use the breath. Keep

trying until your friend can understand you. You will soon discover the purpose of this exercise: when you try to communicate by whispers, you are forced to pay attention to the formation of all sounds, and to put more energy into forming them; thus you get the feel of what you should be doing during ordinary talking. An added advantage of the whispering exercise is that it can easily be transferred from practice sessions to your actual class speeches —during a speech you can deliberately reduce your loudness to a point where your voice becomes a semi-whisper.

2. If your trouble is with specific sounds, and you can hear the errors, the following exercise can be recommended. Make a list of the sounds that are troublesome and then make a list of words and phrases that include these sounds. Look for words where the sound is the initial one, other words where the sound occurs within the word (the medial position), and still other words in which the sound is the final or terminal one. Show this list to your instructor for verification. Now sit down alone somewhere and practice, preferably with a voice recorder. A hand mirror, especially of the magnifying type, will also be of assistance. Begin practicing the list, producing the sounds the wrong way and the right way in alternation. Study and compare with three purposes in mind: first, watch the positions of the jaw, lips, and tongue; second, listen to the difference in the sounds; third, feel (with your eyes shut) the differences in the positions of the jaw, lips, tongue, and soft palate. When you get the proper sound associated with the proper feel, your problem is half solved. Now you must transfer this practice into ordinary speech. This can be done by conscious effort, possibly with the aid of a critic at first. Your aim is to make the sound the correct way often enough to start the formation of a new habit.

3. Inaccuracy may lie not so much in the production of specific sounds as in joining and separating them during conversation. Thus, you may be guilty of the following:

"Whirl ut gitcha?"

"I'm gonna gitcha drink."

"You dint gimme whatcha promised."

"Chowt! Yawlmos gotcher self run over!"

In working on such slovenly speech habits, use a combination of exercises 1 and 2 described above; but do not overdo them. Avoid sounding over-precise and pedantic. Notice that many adjoining sounds are normally blended or assimilated. For example, read the following sentence slowly and precisely, "He was satisfied because he had done the assignment." Now read it at your normal rate, stressing the words "satisfied" and "done." Notice the natural blending and assimilation of some of the first and last sounds of adjoining words. Thus your goal is to produce separate sounds clearly enough to be distinct, but at the same time not to sound like a school child reciting a piece.

4. For careless and sloppy mispronunciation of common words, like "jist," "git," "kin," "whur," and "ketch," no special exercises are needed. Probably, when reading aloud for others or simply being careful, you pronounce such words perfectly well. The task, therefore, is to introduce new habits into your daily talking. This, curiously enough, is not easy. Take one or two words to begin with and resolve to practice them all week. Approach this practice both positively and negatively.

The positive approach is to remind yourself every hour to introduce these words into conversations. When you are talking with someone about the next game, deliberately say, "I *just* hope that Bill Banowsky *gets* a chance to *catch* a couple of passes." Or, "I *just* can't wait to *get* to the game." And so on. These words are so common that it is easy to put them into your talking without distorting the flow of thought. You must, however, use them frequently and correctly in actual speech.

The negative approach is to stop yourself, go back and repeat the word, "That *jis'* gives me . . . I mean, that *just*. . . ." This method can be reinforced by a helper, such as your roommate. Make a bargain with him that every time he catches you mispronouncing the words being practiced, you pay a fine—and he gets the money!

As soon as you have formed new habits on the two or three chosen words, you are ready to choose two or three more. Even if you correct your pronunciation of only a few common words, you will be rewarded by a noticeable rise in the whole cultural level of your speech.

## Exercises for meaningfulness

1. ANALYSIS OF VOCAL MONOTONY Suppose your inventory lists your voice as monotonous. Perhaps the rate or loudness of your speech does not vary, or your pitch is a monotone. These faults can rarely be ascribed to organic defects; the cause is more likely to be emotional. Perhaps you are tied up by stage fright; or maybe you simply have not learned to relax. Or the faults may be a manifestation of your whole personality—to put it brutally, maybe your voice is uninteresting only because you haven't taken the trouble to make yourself an interesting person. Maybe you have not learned to sense the full meanings of what you read or think about; maybe your voice is not flexible enough to express the meanings you intend; or perhaps you simply have never tried.

Regardless of its cause, monotony is a voice problem especially well adapted to treatment in this course. If you follow the other suggestions in this text, *every class speech you give should mark an improvement in*

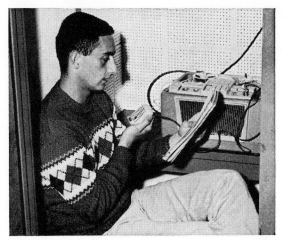

Many schools have language laboratories with special equipment to facilitate individual voice practice.

*meaningfulness.* Our entire subject involves the communication of meanings. And everything you learn and apply—audience awareness, good choice of subject, definite speaking purpose, efficient research, clear organization, rehearsal of language and bodily action, emotional adjustment—all contribute toward meaningful talking.

**2. SENSITIVITY TO MEANING** Often the first job in learning to communicate meanings is to become more sensitive to them. A good way to start is to restudy some old familiar literature—things you learned in childhood and have heard so often that they now have almost no meaning for you. The game is to give them a meaning, or a new meaning, or several meanings. Read over Lincoln's "Gettysburg Address," which you probably know by heart, and think about it. Can you detect Lincoln's basic organizational plan? Can you read the speech so that the implications as well as the actual statements become significant? How many different meanings can you draw from that famous closing phrase, ". . . that government of the people, by the people, and for the people shall not perish from the earth"? Stress different words; each stress will suggest a new meaning. Then practice in the same way on such pieces as the Pledge of Allegiance or the Twenty-third Psalm.

**3. DEVELOPING VOCAL VARIETY** *a. Rate.* The simplest way to achieve more vocal variety is by learning to change pace. Learn deliberately to slow down or speed up your rate, depending on the thought and mood of the content. A slow rate helps convey the suggestion of thoughtfulness, deliberation, or sadness. A fast rate is appropriate for joy, excitement, and descriptions of things in motion.

You probably think of rate as number of words per minute. But rate can be altered in either of two ways: you can change the duration of a given sound, or you can change the length and number of pauses. You will need practice to sense the difference between the two ways.

A completely mechanical exercise to make you aware of rate changes, both in duration and pauses, is counting, or reciting the alphabet at different rates. Thus:

> O-o-o-one,     Tw-o-o-o,     T-h-r-r-e-e-e-e-e
> O-o-o-one,     Tw-o-o-o,     T-h-r-r-e-e-e-e
> One,     Two,     Three
> One,     Two,     Three
> OneTwoThree     (And other variations)

Next, choose literary passages that vary widely in mood and thought, and that obviously demand different reading rates. For a slow rate, try The Lord's Prayer; for a fast rate, Lanier's "Song of the Chattahoochee." Count the words and time yourself to become aware of how much you are varying your rate of reading. Slow them down or speed them up by changes in both duration and pauses.

*b. Phrasing.* Pauses are oral punctuation, which differs radically from the written variety. In general, the two main purposes of pauses are to enhance your meaning and to permit you to breathe. The principal rules can be listed:

1. Pause at logical places.
2. Pause frequently.
3. Adjust length of pauses to the meaning.
4. Inhale often, and inhale during meaningful pauses.

Practice these rules by reading passages aloud, marking them for different possible phrasings. In marking them, a single diagonal ( / ) can indicate a pause of ordinary duration, while a double diagonal ( // ) can indicate a longer or dramatic pause.

Following is an example of too many pauses, most of them at illogical points, and several of them too long:

The first // reason / we worry // is this: We // worry because we / like to. / Yes, that's // what I / said: because we like // to.

A better phrasing for the same sentences would be:

The first reason we worry / is this: / We worry because we like to. / Yes, / that's what I said: / because we like to.

Another acceptable phrasing, more dramatically done.

The first reason we worry / is this: // We worry because we like to. // Yes, / that's what I said: // because we like to.

You can invent or find many other passages of varying lengths, which you can practice and mark in a similar fashion. You will become aware of the crucial effect of any pause upon the meaningfulness of a statement. You will note particularly how a dramatic pause emphasizes the word immediately before or after that pause.

While practicing the relation of pauses to meaning, you can also study your breathing. Synchronize your breathing with meaningful pauses. Ordinarily, this does not present much of a problem because the number of pauses required for proper meaningfulness far outnumbers the times it is necessary to inhale. Just remember that there is no advantage in taking very deep breaths. If you learn to pause often enough for proper meaning, and if you inhale as often as you want to during such pauses, you will have no difficulty. The chief virtue of practice is to verify that fact.

*c. Loudness.* It is easy to produce variety by experimenting with various degrees of loudness. Try going from a whisper to a roar and from a roar to a whisper. Try a gradual crescendo or diminuendo; then try stressing a word or phrase by suddenly increasing or decreasing its loudness. Again, a good mechanical exercise is counting aloud, trying out the variations of loudness just described. Also, find some selections of various types that suggest opportunities for loudness variation. Let yourself go when reading them—don't be afraid to shout.

*d. Pitch.* The subtlest but best road to variety is by varying your pitch. This can be done gradually (a glide) or suddenly (a step). A rise in pitch usually conveys a question: Is that you? A drop in pitch usually suggests finality: This is the end. A combined rise and fall indicates doubt: I am not sure. Possible pitch variations are infinite.

Here is a good mechanical exercise to develop flexibility and range. Start counting at your lowest comfortable pitch level; gradually move up the scale until you hit the highest pitch possible without cracking; then go back down the scale gradually until you reach your lowest note again. The same exercise can be done by talking up and down the musical scale. You can speak do, re, mi, etc., as a singer sings them. In these exercises, you can ascertain your range by finding your lowest and highest notes on a piano. Talking the scale while playing the notes on the piano is also a helpful exercise. Finally, find selections that call for obvious pitch differences. For example, the remarks of a child would require high pitch; those of a ghost, very low pitch. Try for extremes just to see what your voice can do.

*e. Combined variations.* A final suggestion for practice in vocal variety is to compose or to find materials in which changes in rate, loudness, and pitch can be practiced all together. An excellent example is Edgar Allan Poe's "The Bells." The ideas, emotions, and choice of words all combine to make this poem a challenging voice exercise. Stanza 1 describes sleigh bells and calls for a rapid rate, little loudness, mostly high pitch, and an over-all tinkling effect. Stanza 2 describes wedding bells and calls for a medium rate, medium loudness, varied pitch, and a resonant or mellow effect. Stanza 3 describes fire bells and calls for a very fast rate, extreme loudness, mostly high pitch, and a harsh or strident general effect. Stanza 4 describes funeral bells and calls for a very slow rate, medium loudness, mostly low pitch, and a ghostlike or hollow effect. At the end of each stanza you will find the word "bells" repeated many times. These repetitions provide an opportunity to imitate the kinds of bells described by the poet. There is sufficient thought and emotion in the poem to permit penetration into the mood of each stanza and communication of the mood of each.

## Summary

The goal in this course is not to change your voice, but to make the most of what you have. Voice improvement requires five steps: (1) understanding how the speaking voice is produced, (2) making a voice and articulation inventory, (3) determining your potential, (4) planning a program, and (5) practicing the program.

To understand how the speaking voice is produced, you must understand the processes of respiration, phonation, resonation, and articulation.

In making a personal voice and articulation inventory, you must evaluate your speaking in terms of acceptable standards. An acceptable speaking voice is audible, accurate, meaningful, and pleasant.

You can help determine your vocal potential by listening critically to conversations, platform speeches, radio, television, and phonograph records.

A personal program for voice improvement should first include a list of faults that can be rather quickly eliminated. The ultimate goal should be fitted to your future proposed vocation.

There are many exercises for voice improvement that can be practiced with or without your instructor's help. Practice sessions are often most successful when a recording machine is used. The purpose of all voice and articulation exercises is to make your speaking more communicative.

# 11

# VERBAL COMMUNICATION

**What's in a name?**

When a football coach is planning a new play he usually gets a pencil and paper and starts drawing diagrams. He represents each player by an *x* or an *o*, and shows their movements by arrows. The convenience of this method of planning is at once apparent: instead of moving 200-pound players from here to there on the gridiron, the coach moves symbols—letters that stand for the players—on a sheet of paper. While drawing the diagrams the coach murmurs to himself, "So we put the left end there and the tackle there. No, wait a minute. That won't do. The tackle goes here." Thus he manipulates mental symbols, language symbols, to test the play in thought before trying it in an actual game.

Next day the coach shows his squad the new play. Again he presents a diagram, this time on a chalkboard. Again he accompanies the drawing with language symbols, this time spoken aloud. In addition to thinking, the coach is now communicating by both written and spoken symbols.

The foregoing example illustrates the three most common forms of language symbols: the mental (from electrochemical impulses), the written (by light waves), and the spoken (by sound waves). Consider the concept symbolized by the word *football*. You can think it, read it, write it, hear it, or say it. Whichever you do, the word itself is a symbol, and the symbol stands for the same thing, whether it is thought, read, written, heard, or said.

But how does it happen that a certain word becomes the symbol for a particular object or event? A word acquires a meaning through agreement and repeated usage. To recall an old joke, pigs are not called pigs because they are such dirty creatures, nor was the name assigned by editors of a dictionary. A number of English-speaking people began to refer to this animal by the symbol *pig*, and proceeded to use the word with that intended meaning or denotation. Other people agreed upon other symbols: the French agreed upon *cochon;* the German, *schwein;* the Italian, *porco;* the Spanish, *cochino.* Dictionaries record such agreements after they are in widespread use.

In the original denotation, *pig* would be reported in the dictionary as "a young swine, or a swine of any age." However, a word may gain more than its original denotation as people associate it with other concepts within their personal experience. To an extent this new meaning is connotative, as when the greed and filth of a pig are associated with some other animal or perhaps with a human. But when this association becomes widespread the connotative meaning actually becomes one of denotation and eventually is reported as such in the dictionary. In this manner words may gain literally dozens of denotative meanings. The dictionary, for example, further reports that pig can mean "a person or animal likened to a pig," "crock," "hot water bottle," or "a metal casting."

Now we come to a basic but often overlooked fact—agreements about word meanings are only approximations. The same word can never mean exactly the same thing to any two people. For example, the words *Los Angeles* are commonly accepted to symbolize a large city in California. But what about the full and exact meaning? A New England student's experience with the symbol *Los Angeles* comes from talk he has heard, books he has read, and movies he has seen; therefore the name may suggest to him all-year tans (from swimming pools in every back yard), Disneyland, and glamorous movie stars dining in plush restaurants. But to a student who has lived in Los Angeles most of his life, the associations would be more likely to include smog, endless miles of suburbs, and traffic which sometimes races madly, sometimes inches maddeningly, on the freeways.

Exact communication in either speech or writing is impossible, even in science and mathematics. Scientific vocabularies are created in an effort to approach complete accuracy, but even technical terms have different meanings for different scientists. For example, the leukemia specialist's associations with the word *leukemia* are different from those of a general practitioner who may never have treated a case.

Spoken ideas are not transferred directly into the listener's mind, but must be translated by the listener. Thus the speaker tries to find words that will

The power of words! Ben-Gurion's words have helped to shape a new nation, and have influenced millions of people in all parts of the world.

arouse thoughts and feelings similar to those he is trying to communicate. The arousal of thoughts and feelings and the active role of listeners are charmingly illustrated by the story of the minister who always said the right thing upon first seeing a new baby. Proud parents remarked that the minister noticed the things that made their baby different from, and better than, any other baby in the town. When a friend complimented him upon his tact, the minister confessed that he always said the same thing. "Well," he would declare beamingly, "This *is* a baby!"

You will see that the advice to make your language clear is easier to give and accept than to put into practice. Nevertheless, the job of communicating is not a hopeless one. An understanding of the nature of our language, its limitations, its confusions, and its dangers, is the first major step toward improving your own word accuracy. Do not suppose that the meaning of a word is self-evident, or that a word has only one meaning, or that the same word means the same thing to different people.

## Words as symbols

A word is only a symbol for something, yet we constantly behave as though the word were the thing itself. For example, when someone vividly describes cutting a lemon and biting into a slice, your mouth may water as though you were biting into an actual lemon. People can be made to laugh, weep, tremble, or become violently ill—all by means of words alone. So many people react so violently to the number thirteen that in some office buildings and hotels the floor above the twelfth is called fourteen to avoid having a "thirteenth floor." A label—*socialistic, communistic*—can defeat a proposed new law. "Sticks and stones may break my bones, but names will never hurt me!" simply isn't true. Names are words, and words are symbols. And wars are fought for symbols. Said Byron:

Religion—freedom—vengeance—what you will,
A word's enough to raise mankind to kill.

When we have learned to treat words only as symbols, realizing that the meaning is not in the word but in us, we will be less gullible as listeners and more accurate as speakers.

We must learn to look beyond the symbols to the things symbolized. Shall we support a proposed policy because it is called "the American way"? Precisely what do the proponents mean by the American way? Exactly what is the proposal? Does the proposal *actually* correspond with our definition of the American way? Such questions will help get at the meaning beyond the symbols. When preparing your own speeches remember that your words should be firmly rooted in meaning, for beautiful words won't clarify ideas that aren't there. Begin with an analysis of your ideas to clarify what you want to say—what facts or opinions, what thoughts or feelings. Then only are you ready to consider possible choices of symbols.

Help your listener do his share of the job. You cannot explain anything to your listener; he explains it to himself. You cannot tell him a story; he tells himself the story. You cannot talk him into your point of view; he talks himself into it. Your job is to use words that will arouse in the listener a process of thought or feeling; once begun, the listener will carry the process through to a conclusion. You hope you have stimulated him so that his eventual conclusion will agree with your own; but you cannot do his thinking for him, nor should you want to. It is similar to shopping for clothing. We resent high-pressure sales talks; we want to examine the clothing and sell it to ourselves. If the clothing is good, the salesman needn't worry. Likewise, in speaking, if the ideas are sound we should need only to present them; the listener will sell himself.

How can you improve the accuracy of communication through language? Employ the suggestions we have just discussed: (1) treat words only as symbols; (2) look beyond the symbols to the things symbolized; and (3) help the listener do his share of the job.

You can easily take stock of your present ability to arouse thought in your listeners. Soon after your next class speech ask several classmates to give a brief summary of your talk. You may be surprised at the results. Perhaps you will find yourself silently exclaiming, "But I didn't say *that!*" Or, "Is that all you got out of it?" Or, "But you missed the whole point." However, you may get a summary that carries your point further or states it better than you did! Whatever the result, this sort of checking will teach you that your goal is to get across the gist of your main point.

## Characteristics of effective language

### Clarity

Always remember your "ignorant" audience. You have thought about or experienced the ideas to be presented in your speech; your listeners will be ignorant of what you intend to say. Your first task, therefore, is to choose words that will make your ideas as clear as possible to them. You do not expect them to get exactly the same meaning from your words as you get, but you do expect them to understand your main ideas. You can reduce the possibility of misinterpretation among your hearers by stating your points carefully, restating them in different words, and supporting them. You may then approach the goal suggested by Quintilian, "Not that language may be understood, but that it cannot be misunderstood."

1. MEANINGFUL WORDS  To say, "Use meaningful words," may strike you as unnecessary advice. "I do use meaningful words," you insist. Yes, but in addition, what percentage of *meaningless* words do you use? Have you any pet words or phrases which you constantly inject into your speaking? Here are some common examples:

| | |
|---|---|
| well | more or less |
| see? | like |
| I mean | in other words |
| see what I mean? | really |
| and-uh | in my opinion |
| now-uh | it seems to me |

The exasperation this habit produces can be sensed by supposing that Lincoln had said at Gettysburg, "Fourscore and seven years ago—see?—our fathers brought forth on this continent—see?—a new nation—get what I mean?" Your instructor will tell you if you have such language mannerisms. Pet words and phrases can be eliminated if you practice listening for them and heading them off.

The overuse of trite expressions will also boost your percentage of meaningless words. Old familiar sayings can be packed with meaning if used in proper contexts, but constant reliance upon hackneyed terms should be avoided. Listen for them when you practice your speech. Better just say *white* rather than *white as snow; I was lucky* rather than *I had a stroke of luck; last* or *final* rather than *last but not least.*

Most beginning speakers can improve their oral styles by reducing their use of adverbs and adjectives. When you use a modifier in practice speech or in writing, try striking out the word—you will be surprised how often the omission improves clarity and interest. Perhaps the worst offender is the word *very.* You may find yourself relying upon *very* every time you want added emphasis, but usually you get the opposite effect. Winston Churchill has provided many memorable examples of word economy. Read aloud his tribute to the Royal Air Force, "Never in the field of human conflict was so much owed by so many to so few." Now try adding modifiers and see what happens! For example, "Never in the [broad and vast] field of human [military] conflict was so [very] much [legitimately] owed by so [very] many to so [very] few." Inserting *any* of the bracketed words reduces the punch.

Mark Twain reported about one modifier-filled paragraph (in "A Double-Barrelled Detective Story"): "It was a joke . . . not a vestige of sense in any detail of it." The whole incident was fictitious, yet he alleged to fool nearly everyone who read the paragraph. Haven't you often listened to people who talk on and on saying nothing? In the following passage search for the meaning. Look for the facts; evaluate the thought:

> If you want my opinion and you can take it or leave it for whatever it is worth, I'd say that I, for one, would like to give a vote of thanks to the state of Wisconsin for having the good sense and the sound judgment with reference to the real underlying problems which confront this whole country today—the good judgment, I say, to elect to the United States Senate a man who is unafraid to undertake a task for which men, and women, too, have been persecuted in the past, just the same as they are today, and will be tomorrow.

Words should symbolize facts and reasoning; a surplus of empty words can reflect a shortage of ideas.

**2. SIMPLE WORDS** The genius of great speakers lies not in their ability to use long words or unusual words, but in their ability to put simple words together in meaning-packed combinations. Lincoln said, "You can fool all of the people some of the time, and some of the people all of the time, but you can't fool all of the people all of the time." Note that Lincoln said *fool,* not *mislead* or *deceive*, and certainly not *victimize* or *outmaneuver*. He said *all*, not *the totality, the aggregate,* or *one hundred per cent.* He said *people,* not *populace, multitude,* or *general public.* All of Lincoln's speeches are models of simplicity. The "Gettysburg Address" has 265 words; of these, 195 are one-syllable words. Try to imagine him saying:

> Eight and seven-tenths decades ago the pioneer workingmen in this continental area implemented a new group based on an ideology of free boundaries and initial conditions of equality.

For effective usage listen again to Winston Churchill:

> I have nothing to offer but blood, toil, tears and sweat.

> We shall fight on the beaches, we shall fight on the landing grounds, we shall fight in the fields and in the streets, we shall fight in the hills; we shall never surrender.

> If the British Empire and its Commonwealth last for a thousand years, men will still say, "This was their finest hour."

Franklin D. Roosevelt had the knack of choosing simple and precise words and combining them into unforgettable phrases: "the forgotten man," "a new deal for the American people," "the great arsenal of democracy," "December 7, 1941—a date which will live in infamy."

Or study the simplicity of Franklin Roosevelt's language:

The only thing we have to fear is fear itself.

The test of our progress is not whether we add more to the abundance of those who have much; it is whether we provide enough for those who have too little.

More than an end to war, we want an end to the beginnings of all wars.

Don't be misled into using big words and stilted phrases; don't be "overwhelmed by the magnitude of the occasion."

Take a few lines from a speech full of big words, and see if you can state the same thoughts in short plain words. Make a game of it; word games are fun. You take the first big word in the speech and ask what it means; then you look for a small word that means the same thing. You may need a bit of time to get just the right word at first, but the time is well spent. You will soon find that a real need for big words is rare. In fact, you can spoil a speech with high-flown prose—the "grand style" long since went out of date. As a rule short words give a thought more punch. So chop the big words out of the speech and watch how well short words fill the gaps. Of course, short words will not do the job all of the time—you may want to say, "All of the words in the last ten lines have but one—*syllable!*"

**3. PRECISE WORDS**  Some of us are so word-lazy we expect too much from a few overworked expressions. For example, *cute* may be used to describe anything from a baby to a house; *beautiful* may be expected to communicate our feelings about a sunset, girl friend, golf shot, rug, painting, song, or race horse. What word could replace *cute* or *beautiful* in each of these instances? What word would be precise?

You cannot increase your working vocabulary without effort. You should study your dictionary and a wordbook such as *Roget's Thesaurus*. This type of study provides you with alternatives for expressing almost any meaning. For example, there are probably over 200 variations on the word *said,* of which these are a few:

| | |
|---|---|
| replied | asked |
| thought aloud | implored |
| drawled | denied |
| added | shouted |
| agreed | protested |
| bellowed | snorted |
| went on | murmured |
| declared | muttered |

Rudolf Flesch believes that the "lack of well-used verbs is the main trouble with modern English writing." We might say the same for speaking.

It is necessary, therefore, not only to develop a list of alternative words, but also to be able to choose the precise one. A nice choice among several shadings of meaning can help clarify your idea. A wrong choice can be ridiculous—for instance, that by the chairman introducing one of the first women to be elected to the United States Senate. Intending to say that the speaker was justly famous, the chairman blurted, "I now present one of the most *notorious* women in this nation."

You can find words that come close to expressing not only the thing itself, but also your degrees of approval or disapproval. An exercise in such nuances is the "I, you, he" game. Here are some examples:

I am thrifty; you are stingy; he's a miser.
I am slender; you are thin; she is skinny.
I'm a statesman; you're a politician; he's a rabble-rouser.
I agree; you must admit; he's forced to confess.
I'm well read; you're studious; he's a bookworm.
I'm in love; you're infatuated; she's boy crazy.
I'm a liberal; you're a radical; he's a communist.

Try inventing some yourself, noticing the insinuation of approval or disapproval.

Another technique for getting precision in meaning is to define important terms for your audience. Most of the commonly accepted meanings of words are listed in a good general dictionary, but sometimes a dictionary definition of a word or phrase is inadequate. You must then compose your own definition or seek one in the appropriate literature. For example, Justice Oliver Wendell Holmes defined a difficult concept in these words:

If there is any principle of the Constitution that more imperatively calls for attachment than any other it is the principle of free thought—not free thought for those who agree with us but freedom for the thought that we hate.

4. CORRECT USAGE   You have been practicing language usage most of your life; you began studying it during your elementary school years. By this time you should have an adequate awareness of ordinary grammatical usages, but you have probably acquired a few bad habits. In this course, therefore, attention will be confined to eliminating habitual errors. A single habitual mistake (such as saying *them* for *those*) not only detracts from your meaning, but also stamps you as uneducated and lowers you in the esteem of your listeners.

Check yourself against this list:

| WRONG | POSSIBLE CORRECTION |
|---|---|
| them books | those books |
| this here (that there) book | this (that) book |
| disregardless | regardless, irrespective |
| in regards to | in regard to, concerning |
| anywheres, everywheres | anywhere, everywhere |
| between you and I | between you and me |
| him and me did | he and I did |
| us men can | we men can, we can |
| it could of | it could have, it could've, it might have, could it have |
| leave us go | let's go |
| he lies the paper down | he lays (he puts) the paper down |
| where are you at? | where are you? |
| where you going to? | where are you going? |
| he sets here | he sits here |
| cooperate together | cooperate, work together |
| consensus of opinion | consensus |
| if you'd of said so | if you'd said so |
| they had ought to say it | they ought to say it, they should say it |
| that will learn him | that will teach him |
| providing you agree | provided that you agree, if you agree |
| I suspicion that | I suspect that, I suppose that |
| you can't only (hardly, scarcely) do | you can only (hardly, scarcely) do, you can't do just |
| erase it off of the board | erase it |

Are any of these errors habits with you? If so, start work now to eliminate them.

Some common expressions are acceptable in certain situations but not in others. Here is a list:

| SOMETIMES ACCEPTABLE | USUALLY PREFERRED |
|---|---|
| kind of a, sort of a | kind of, sort of |
| I will | I shall |
| this data is | these data are, this datum is |
| different than | different from |
| these kind, those sort | this kind, that sort |
| less pages | fewer pages |

| SOMETIMES ACCEPTABLE | USUALLY PREFERRED |
|---|---|
| he laid down to nap | he lay down to nap, he napped |
| sit it on the desk | set (put, place) it on the desk |
| I expect you found it | I suppose you found it |
| try and be there | try to be there |
| choose between the three | choose between the two, choose among the three (or more) |
| between each inning | between the innings |
| the reason is because | the reason is that |
| it looks like we'll win | it looks as if we'll win, we'll probably win |
| he is dark complected | he is dark complexioned, he has a dark complexion |
| which do you like best, *a* or *b*? | which do you like better, *a* or *b*?, which do you like best, *a*, *b*, or *c*? |
| it's me | it is I |

When you practice your speech you should decide whether a generally correct form will be correct in that speech situation.

In finding and correcting your own weaknesses in grammatical usages an English handbook is essential. Some standard references are H. W. Fowler, *A Dictionary of Modern English Usage* (Oxford); Porter Perrin, *Writer's Guide and Index to English* (Scott, Foresman); and John C. Hodges, *Harbrace College Handbook* (Harcourt, Brace & World).

## Interest

Anything that makes language clear is also likely to make it interesting. Language that is sparklingly clear will catch attention. However, language may be adequately clear, yet dull. Clarity is basic but not enough; on it you must build interest. Concrete words, vivid words, and varied sentence structures help make your language interesting.

1. CONCRETE WORDS Abstractions are necessary and desirable in speech because they are often the quickest way of saying something. Usually your points and subpoints will be stated in abstract words. To say that a plan has all the strengths while avoiding the weaknesses of the present system is highly abstract. We do not know what the plan is, what the present system is, or the strengths and weaknesses of either. But most of a speech is spent in supporting the points and subpoints, and supports should be worded concretely. The substance of almost any good 5,000-word speech can be told in less than fifty words; the other 4,950 words are devoted almost entirely

to concrete details. Abstract statements can summarize or generalize your ideas, but concrete details are necessary to relate your ideas to your listeners' experience. You want to guide the listeners' thinking, but it takes only a little abstraction to put an audience to sleep.

There are degrees of abstractness or concreteness. Thus the word *all* is highly abstract—you cannot visualize *all*, nor feel it, nor taste it, nor hear it. *All living things* is only slightly less abstract. By degrees we can become concrete: *all animals, all cats, all Persian cats, several Persian cats, six Persian cats, a yellow Persian cat.* And perhaps finally: "The yellow Persian cat crouched behind the peach tree and fixed unblinking eyes on the sparrow."

Practice using specific and concrete words. Consider "automobile." Was it a Ford sedan, a Rambler convertible, or a Chevrolet coupé? Was it a truck, a station wagon, or a racer? You say, "He drove it down the street." Can you be more specific? Did the car creep, roar, race, rattle, or whiz? Was it a street, road, alley, lane, or freeway? "The hot rod shot through the alley like a bullet through the bore of a rifle."

**2. FIGURATIVE WORDS**   When Winston Churchill wanted to refer to the fact that America had just entered World War II, he did not prosaically state, "The United States has declared war." He used figurative words: "The United States . . . has drawn the sword for Freedom, and cast away the scabbard."

Figures of speech are based on the principle of showing resemblances between apparently dissimilar things. A simile is a comparison, generally introduced by *like, as,* or *as if*. A metaphor is the calling of one thing by the name of another. For example, Shelley's "Ode to the West Wind" opens with a metaphor in the first line, and introduces a simile in the third line:

> O Wild West Wind, thou breath of Autumn's being,
> Thou from whose unseen presence the leaves dead
> Are driven, like ghosts from an enchanter fleeing,

Figures of speech make language vivid and colorful. In 1931, on his ninetieth birthday, Justice Oliver Wendell Holmes in a radio address used this figurative analogy:

> The riders in a race do not stop short when they reach the goal. There is a little finishing canter before coming to a standstill. There is time to hear the kind voice of friends and say to oneself, "The work is done." But just as one says that, the answer comes, "The race is over, but the work never is done while the power to work remains." The canter that brings you to a standstill need not be only coming to rest. It cannot be, while you still live. For to live is to function. That is all there is in living.

Truman, Goldwater, Rockefeller, Murrow. All four of these speakers are effective yet they have been chosen because they represent distinctly different language styles. Go to your library and secure typical samples from speeches by these men.

WIDE WORLD

UPI

Daniel Webster gave us many examples of figurative language:

> Knowledge, in truth, is the great sun in the firmament. Life and power are scattered with all its beams.

> He smote the rock of the national resources, and abundant streams of revenue gushed forth. He touched the dead corpse of Public Credit, and it sprung upon its feet.

In his famous speech at the Democratic National Convention of 1896, William Jennings Bryan used vivid figures of speech, such as:

> The humblest citizen of all the land, when clad in the armor of a righteous cause, is stronger than all the hosts of Error.

> You shall not press down upon the brow of labor this crown of thorns, you shall not crucify mankind upon a cross of gold.

Figurative language can, of course, be overdone or poorly done. Mixed metaphors can be ludicrous: "The American space avalanche has racked up a tidal wave of achievements." But when used with discretion, figures of speech are (to use a metaphor) the salt and pepper in the food for thought that you offer your listeners. For example, Norman Topping used the following vivid sentence in addressing a university gathering, "Without a faculty devoted to excellence, a university's buildings would echo with questions unanswered and with answers never questioned." [2]

**3. SENTENCE VARIETY** The interest value of your language is also heightened by sentence variety. You should use long sentences and short ones; loose sentences (in which the sentence is grammatically complete before the end) and periodic ones (in which the sentence is not grammatically complete until the end). You should use rhetorical questions often, dialogue, exclamations, and imperatives occasionally, and incomplete sentences rarely.

Let us analyze sentence variety in a passage from Winston Churchill's address to Congress on December 26, 1941. The passage begins with a lengthy sentence of loose construction, in which the main clause and essential meaning occur at the beginning of the sentence. The second sentence is also long but is periodic, for the main clause and the meaning are not complete until the end of the sentence. Then to give contrast to the two long sentences, Churchill has a brief simple statement, "They have certainly embarked upon a very considerable undertaking." Then come two long periodic sentences, holding us in suspense and building toward a magnificent climax. The brief sentence that follows hits like a hammer, and might be classified either as a rhetorical question or an exclamation: "What kind of

[2] Reprinted by special permission of Norman Topping.

people do they think we are?" The climax of the passage comes with the powerful rhetorical question, "Is it possible . . . ?"

We know that for many years past the policy of Japan has been dominated by secret societies of subaltern and junior officers of the Army and Navy who have enforced their will upon successive Japanese cabinets and parliaments by the assassination of any Japanese statesman who opposed or who did not sufficiently further their aggressive policy. It may be that these societies, dazzled and dizzy with their own schemes of aggression and the prospect of early victories, have forced their country, against its better judgment, into war. They have certainly embarked upon a very considerable undertaking; for, after the outrages they have committed upon us at Pearl Harbor, in the Pacific islands, in the Philippines, in Malaya, and the Dutch East Indies, they must now know that the stakes for which they have decided to play are mortal. When we consider the resources of the United States and the British Empire, compared to those of Japan, when we remember those of China, which has so long and valiantly withstood invasion, and when also we observe the Russian menace which hangs over Japan, it becomes still more difficult to reconcile Japanese action with prudence, or even with sanity. What kind of people do they think

Study Winston Churchill's speeches as models of the oral use of language. Listen to some of his recorded speeches (for example, Columbia album KL 5066).

WIDE WORLD

we are? Is it possible they do not realize that we shall never cease to persevere against them until they have been taught a lesson which they and the world will never forget?

## Appropriateness

Your words may be both clear and interesting, yet your speech will fail if they are inappropriate. Slang sometimes raises the issue of appropriateness, as do other words in poor taste occasionally used in class talks.

In many public speeches slang can be appropriately used. Words such as *stooge* or *jeep* in the proper place can be strong, accurate, and simple. The danger, especially among college students, is that slang expressions may be overworked or used when only formal language is appropriate. In a speech, for example, it is monotonous, irritating, and noncommunicative to describe a girl friend, football game, sandwich, and motion picture all as "fantabulous" or whatever the current word fad may be. When you do use slang, do not apologize by saying, "If you'll pardon a colloquial expression . . ."

Perhaps it is unnecessary to warn you that many often-used words are taboo in public speaking. If you use a crude or vulgar phrase, your audience will be shocked and antagonized. If you use a forbidden word accidentally and innocently, the audience may forgive you, but a single word can sometimes ruin a reputation.

Just because something has been published does not mean that it can be quoted in a speech. For example, a speech student quoted a joke from the novel *The Hucksters* in class, and nearly caused several members to drop the course. "But I only quoted from a best seller," he explained. "What's wrong with that?" The answer is that books are read in private; speeches are heard in public.

### Language and the occasion

Speech delivery may be classified into four types; extemporaneous, impromptu, reading from manuscript, and memorized. In the long run you will want to master all four styles. In this text and this course, however, emphasis will be placed on the extemporaneous speech because it is the most widely useful, and because it is basic to the proper practice of the other three. It develops the fluency needed for impromptu talks and the communicativeness needed for speaking either from manuscript or from memory.

## Extemporaneous speeches

In Chapter 4 we presented a method of practicing aloud for an extemporaneous (that is, non-memorized) talk. We assume that you have been using that method in preparing your class talks up to now. You have discovered that you can get your ideas worded without memorization, though perhaps clumsily. By repeatedly talking through each speech outline, (1) you clarify your thinking, (2) you choose words listeners will like, and (3) you gain fluency.

When you first talk through an outline, you are likely to find that you take too much time, that you are wordy and rambling. Why is it that on this first run-through your statement of point is usually confused, and even your telling of a simple story is hard to follow? Because your thinking is confused and hard to follow. Why is it that your choice of words gets better after several trials? Because your thinking has improved. In short, as you rehearse ideas extemporaneously, you literally think aloud; and as you word ideas differently, you are clarifying your thoughts. When you praise a class-mate for being able to think on his feet, what are you praising? Not his ability to stand before the group and silently ponder! You are praising his ability to talk without having memorized the words.

"Rusk is a master of words, who uses them with precision for clarification, for insistence, for inspiration, or for deliberate opacity," wrote Theodore H. White in *Life* (June 8, 1962).

Although wordiness is the most common difficulty, a groping for words is sometimes encountered. Thus, after stating your idea, "In choosing anecdotes for a speech, be sure that each has but one apparent point," you can think of no more to say. What is the trouble? Again, it is your thinking. You have an idea but you have not thought it through; you have not developed it. So practice aloud. Try stating the thought in different ways. Presently the implications of your idea begin to take shape; by talking about it, you clarify your thinking.

In practicing your talks aloud, you have undoubtedly noticed that you can listen to yourself even when concentrating on the thought to be expressed. More than that, you can listen for one thing at a time, even while all the other necessary speech activities are proceeding. You are analyzing your thought and thus clarifying it, but more is needed: you must also choose words that will communicate your thinking to the prospective listeners. The words that best clarify your own thinking may or may not be the right words for the audience. Therefore you should practice with your prospective audience consciously in mind, varying your choice of words from trial to trial to suit your listeners.

Do not imagine that at this time you are expected to produce polished and memorable phrases. Churchill's prose took years to develop. Your present goal is to learn to use words that are direct, personal, concrete, and immediately clear to your audience.

To show that effective extemporaneous language need not be exalted, consider an excerpt from the verbatim transcription of a talk, given without notes, before a convention of the Chamber of Commerce of the United States by Clarence B. Randall, President of the Inland Steel Company.

> You're perfectly certain that the proposed tax bill is wrong. Do you know why?
>
> Supposing somebody walked up and said, "All right, wise guy, you write the tax bill!"
>
> Can you write a tax bill for the United States? I don't mean in detail.
>
> Have you got an idea of where the revenue should come from to support our debt?
>
> We've got the debt; there's no doubt about that. You think it ought to be paid off. Have you got a clear idea of where the money should come from?
>
> Well, you know you shouldn't pay it, but are you clear as to who should pay it? Is it fair to yell about controls and false economy in high places if you haven't thought through, yourself, what is the sound tax basis?
>
> You start talking to your employees—they'll ask you some questions on that. No good talking to them until you've got an answer.
>
> I don't care whether you've got the right answer or not, as long as it's your

answer; as long as it's held with integrity; as long as you can talk about it with your voice down and be pleasant.[3]

This is not elegant language. It illustrates that effective extemporaneous phraseology need not be fancy or oratorical. Study the quotation again and note some of the characteristics. Most of the sentences are short, but they are varied in structure. There are rhetorical questions, dialogue, repetitions, and even an incomplete sentence. All words are simple and familiar without being trite. Adjectives and adverbs are conspicuously few; verbs and nouns do most of the work. There are many contractions, and other conversational informalities include a "well," and the frequent use of "got." There are a few colloquial words: "supposing," "yell," "no good talking"; a touch of slang, "wise guy"; and an occasional awkward combination, such as "come from to." But the total effect with the use of "I," "we," and "you" is that of direct communication.

Furthermore, the experienced speaker will be able to sprinkle his speech with an occasional neat, vivid, or brilliant expression. For example, at another time in the speech just cited, Randall said:

> If you ask me, in one sentence, to express the present American foreign policy, I would say, we propose to fight half of the world; feed the other half; and have business as usual at home. And that can't be done.[4]

## Impromptu speeches

An impromptu speech is one given without previous specific preparation. It should not be confused with the extemporaneous, which, as we have seen, is carefully prepared in thought and flexibly prepared in language.

Most daily conversations, interviews, and group discussions are impromptu and do not trouble us greatly. However, occasionally you may attend a meeting and be called upon unexpectedly to "say a few words." The possibility of such emergencies worries most students.

You can often anticipate situations in which you might be called upon, and so be prepared. In fact, many a brilliant impromptu talk has been carefully planned in such fashion.

If you are caught, search for an idea, not for words. If you can think of a point and supports, the language will take care of itself. An appropriate main point is likely to be given to you ready-made by the previous speaker or the nature of the occasion. The first step is to think of one or more sup-

[3] A. Craig Baird, ed., *Representative American Speeches: 1951–1952*, H. W. Wilson, 1952, p. 118. Reprinted by permission of Clarence B. Randall and the *Atlantic Monthly*.
[4] *Representative American Speeches*, p. 117.

ports quickly. The best bet usually is to try for an anecdote, because words flow most easily when you are narrating a story. Another good technique is to look about quickly for something that can be adapted as a visual aid: a glass of water, a salt shaker, or a newspaper.

Generally the easiest way to start is by reference to the situation or to something just said. Weave this reference into the statement of your main point. Support it with an anecdote and visual aid, or other form of support if you have thought of any. Then restate your main point and sit down.

This formula is based on the assumption that you have been applying the extemporaneous method of speech practice, through which you become accustomed to constructing speech units, acquire a supply of generally useful supports, and develop fluency. These are the skills that come to your rescue.

## Written speeches

There are circumstances where reading from manuscript is appropriate or required, as in the case where the speaker's words may reflect the official policy of a business or even a nation. Properly done, the manuscript speech has the advantage of precision of thought and language. But if improperly done, the manuscript speech can be especially dull and uncommunicative. There are two special considerations in this style of speaking. First, the written language must lend itself to oral style. Second, the speaker must follow the written page while maintaining a communicative bond with the audience.

When given the opportunity to prepare a manuscript speech, beginners often make the mistake of composing an essay rather than a speech. Speech is a transitory thing. Listeners cannot go back and "reread" (that is, "re-listen to") something they missed or did not understand. Materials delivered orally have to be immediately understood as they are delivered; otherwise they are lost. In a sense, oral language must have "instant intelligibility." The best approach in writing your first manuscript speeches is to "talk out" the sentences and passages as you translate your thoughts into language. Some speech writers actually compose initial drafts of manuscript speeches by dictating their ideas to a tape recorder. When the first written version is composed from the recording, the materials usually maintain a degree of their oral quality.

Many manuscript speeches, however, are composed by someone other than the speaker—perhaps a great speech of the past, or a speech composed by a regular speechwriter. Many times works of prose and poetry are a good subject for oral interpretation. In any of these cases, the speaker's main task is to deliver the materials in a meaningful manner to an audience. Since

Reading from manuscript is frequently appropriate or required. These situations vary from storytelling for children to the reading of an annual report at a stockholders' meeting.

the rise of radio and television, there has been an increased awareness of the problems of communicative reading. Many colleges and universities offer full length courses in the subject. At first, reading from manuscript may seem to be a comparatively easy task—that is, until you try it. In too many cases, manuscript readers are only *readers,* not speakers. Think about the

**225**

characteristics of visual and vocal communication discussed in Chapters 9 and 10. Much of the effectiveness of oral communication comes from its special dimensions of voice and action. If these are not used to good advantage, oral communication loses many of its special qualities. This is the main problem in reading from manuscript. Speakers become so attached to their manuscripts that they forget these special assets of oral communication, and in the process they lose their communicative bond with the audience. The object in communicative reading or the oral interpretation of literature is to give the listener more meaning than he could gain by reading the materials silently.

If the work is not your own manuscript, the first step is to insure that you thoroughly understand every aspect of the materials. Try not only to get the main ideas, but also, in the case of a speech, to interpret the author's speech purpose. Be prepared to think in terms of this purpose as you deliver the materials.

The next step is to practice reading the manuscript aloud. When possible it is helpful to type the manuscript with triple spaces between the lines. Become thoroughly familiar with it. You can invent your own system for marking words to be emphasized and places to pause. Practice delivering the material until you are able to look up frequently from the manuscript at your audience. On key words and phrases it is especially desirable to look away from your manuscript and at your audience. Think the thoughts as you read. If there is no need to remain completely within the manuscript, there is nothing wrong with delivering a portion of it extemporaneously. Introductions, transitions, anecdotes, and conclusions lend themselves well to this treatment. The objective is to get something of the extemporaneous spirit into your whole mood and manner.

When you are not reading your own manuscripts, you can benefit by reading aloud from the great speeches of the past and from other types of literature. Oral interpretation of literature is especially helpful in gaining a good sense of meaningfulness in vocal communication. The practice will not only improve your delivery and add to your storehouse of speech ideas, but will measurably increase your vocabulary. In experimental research, James Young found that students experience the largest vocabulary gain in oral reading when compared with silent reading or simply hearing the material.[5] Therefore, if you want to build your vocabulary, read aloud regularly from good literature. Practice reading naturally, conversationally, meaningfully, and for fun.

[5] James Douglas Young, "An Experimental Comparison of Vocabulary Growth by Means of Oral Reading, Silent Reading, and Listening," unpublished doctoral dissertation, University of Southern California, 1951.

## Memorized speeches

In a beginning speech class the best advice on the memorization of speeches is: Avoid it.

## Summary

Words are symbols, and are the chief tools of thought and of communication. We must constantly look beyond the symbol, however, to find its meaning; and we must constantly remember that ideas are not transferred to our listeners, but aroused in them.

Effective language should be clear, interesting, and appropriate. Clarity is enhanced by using meaningful words, simple words, precise words, and correct English usage. Interest value is enhanced by using concrete words, figurative words, and variety in sentence structure. Appropriateness is guarded by using slang with discrimination, and by remembering that the use of a word in conversation or print does not make it appropriate for a public speech.

From the standpoint of language, there are four types of speech preparation and delivery: extemporaneous, impromptu, written, and memorized. In this course, the extemporaneous will be emphasized because it is the most widely useful, and because it is basic to the other three.

# PART FOUR

# SECURING AUDIENCE RESPONSES

*The fundamental purpose of all speeches is to secure audience response. Audiences vary and so do the desired responses.*

Imagine the differences in securing responses from the audiences shown on these two pages.

## TOPICAL PREVIEW

# 12

## AUDIENCE ANALYSIS

### "Things are different"

A college debate team and its coach were invited to present an open forum program before a steelworkers' union. Four of the students gave prepared speeches; half a dozen other students joined the audience.

There were about a hundred union members, all big burly fellows, some with handlebar mustaches, all dressed in their Sunday best. During the speeches the audience was extraordinarily attentive; some of the men leaned forward in their chairs or nodded their heads vigorously from time to time. When the forum period came, however, the students in the audience were forced to do most of the talking.

After the meeting the coach told the union president that the response during the forum had been disappointingly small. "I'm surprised to hear you say that," said the president, "it was the best I've ever heard them do —when English was being spoken. Of course, when our *Polish* organizer is in charge, things are different!"

This anecdote illustrates that what the speaker intends to transmit may not coincide at all with what the listener receives. Apparently the students did communicate something—but something completely different from what they intended. The intended program became a shambles at the decoding stage. It made little difference whether the students had spent hours of research on the subject, gathered imposing quantities of data, indulged in brilliant reasoning, or clothed ideas in rich and accurate language—all these were canceled by the single fact that these steelworkers did not understand much English.

Again we see the crucial importance of bridging the gap between the speaker and his listeners. But we go further than that. What the audience perceives is always the measure of a speaker's effectiveness. Whether or not the speaker communicates anything, how well he communicates, and what he communicates can be decided only by the audience. No other standard of speaking effectiveness will make sense. The verdict of the audience may be immediate or delayed; the verdict may be wrong; but it is still the verdict. The audience is the speaker's supreme court.

Scarcely ever can you afford the luxury of preparing a speech entirely in terms of yourself. You must also prepare in terms of your specific audience and the available means of bridging the gap between you and them. Therefore, the usual first step in efficient speech preparation is getting acquainted in advance with your prospective listeners.

### Necessary audience information

"Getting acquainted in advance with your prospective listeners" means gathering information about them which is likely to be useful in planning your speech. More specifically, you will want information regarding:

1. The nature of the occasion
2. Common traits and interests
3. Attitudes toward your topic
4. Attitudes toward you

Each of these four major headings may be subdivided into detailed questions. You will then have a check list to stimulate and guide your inquiries about any group.

### The occasion

1. *Date and hour*
   Anything unusual about the date—holiday, anniversary, or such?
   Anything unusual about the hour?
   Time limits for your speech?
2. *Attendance*
   Size of audience?
   Is attendance required or voluntary?
3. *Place of meeting*
   Outdoors or indoors?
   Shape and size of room or auditorium?

What kind of seating arrangements?
Speaker's platform?
Lectern or table?
Any stage props—water pitcher, flag, map, gavel, chalkboard?
Any room decorations?
What kind of lighting?
Heating and ventilation?
Any acoustical problems—dead spots, echoes, public address system, competing noises?
Are there facilities for showing slides or motion pictures?

4. *Type of meeting*
Regular or special?
Who is sponsoring the meeting?
What is the purpose of the meeting?
What is likely to be the general atmosphere, or mood, or tone?

5. *Type of program*
Who planned the program?
Is there a printed program?
What will precede and follow your talk—other speakers, music, refreshments, an open forum?

## Common traits and interests

1. *Age:* children, adolescents, young adults, middle-aged adults, old people, mixed.
2. *Sex:* all men, mostly men, all women, mostly women, approximately equal
3. *Race:* Negro, white, minority group, foreign born, mixed; language problems
4. *Family status:* single, married, parents, children
5. *Economic status:* wealthy, well-to-do, middle bracket, poor, destitute, mixed
6. *Educational status:* grammar school, high school, college, mixed
7. *Community:* farm, small town, small city, big city, mixed
8. *Occupation:* big business, small business, professional, trade, housewives, students, retired, etc.
9. *Religion:* Protestants, Catholics, Jews, other denominations, freethinkers; regular members, occasional attendance, seldom or never attend; mixtures
10. *Politics:* Republican—liberal or conservative; Democrat—liberal or conservative; independent; radical; third party; mixed
11. *Memberships:* lodges, fraternities or sororities, clubs, labor unions

Religious meetings vary greatly. Here a preacher invites all those who want to have an experience in the Lord to come to the altar.

Here another group has gathered for religious worship. But just think of the differences there will be in the content and delivery of this sermon.

12. *Entertainments:* favorite radio-TV programs, movies, dancing, athletic events, hobbies, games
13. *Sources of information:* books, magazines, newspapers, lectures, acknowledged authorities

## Attitudes toward your topic

1. *Favorable*, strongly or moderately
2. *Opposed*, strongly or moderately
3. *Undecided*, passively neutral or actively conflicting
4. *Indifferent*, uninformed or simply uninterested

## Attitudes toward you

1. In what respects are you like or unlike most of your audience (see list of traits and interests above: age, sex, race, etc.)?
2. Will the audience know about these resemblances and differences?
3. What are your personal reasons for speaking here?
4. Will the audience know these reasons?
5. How many in the audience are personally acquainted with you?
6. Will most of the audience be favorably inclined toward you personally or will they be prejudiced against you?
   a. Will your appearance be a help or handicap?
   b. Will your voice be a help or handicap?
   c. Will your personality and usual speaking style be helps or handicaps?
   d. Will your reputation, rank, or title be a help or handicap?

You will not need to know all the foregoing details about every audience in order to prepare adequately. For any one audience, however, particular items will be important. The value of the check list is to help you spot the significant items for any particular audience.

Usually the most significant facts to know about the occasion are the size of the audience and the type of meeting. Is it a group of a dozen or of a thousand? Is it an informal get-together or a solemn ceremonial?

Usually the most significant facts to know about the audience are their age and sex. Is it a group of children or retired oldsters? Is it a men's club or a women's club?

Usually the most significant things to know about their attitudes toward your topic are whether they are already interested, and, if your topic is controversial, whether they are in general for or against your position.

Usually the most significant thing to know about their attitudes toward you is whether they will have any reason to react in advance either favorably or unfavorably.

## How to gather information about an audience

### Observation

Observation and inquiry are the basic methods for getting advance information about your audience. You will frequently find that you can figure out the answers quickly and easily because of previous knowledge of the group. When you speak before audiences with which you are familiar, such as your club or fraternity, or any group you have addressed previously, you should have on hand most of the information you need. Let us imagine, however, that you are asked to speak for the first time at a meeting of the Interfraternity Mothers' Club. You can get most of the information you need simply by analyzing the nature of the club. The audience will be all women; you can guess their average age; and you know their family status. Obviously you would need only a little supplementary information—about the date, hour, place, and size of your audience—most of which you could probably get from the person who invited you to speak.

It is unlikely that you will ever be asked to speak before a group completely outside of your previous experience. However, the less you know about a given group, the more important it becomes to study it in advance. The task is usually easier than it appears.

## Inquiry

The first thing to do, as we have just seen, is to question whoever invites you to speak. Then consider ways of getting additional information. If it is an organized group, try to attend one of its meetings and take notes from direct observation, supplementing them by chatting with the members. If direct observation is impossible, you must depend on inquiry. If you have friends who are members of the group or who have spoken before the group, call on them. It is usually proper to request information from the officers of the group whether you know them personally or not. Whatever the circumstances, you can either interview in person, or telephone, or write letters.

Sometimes you can secure audience information from publications. Most large organizations publish their own newspapers or magazines; small organizations often send out mimeographed newsletters or the like. For example, suppose you were going to speak to a group of people connected with the Santa Fe Railway. This company publishes monthly the *Santa Fe Magazine,* and a recent copy of the magazine would be a mine of information about the specialized activities and interests of employees of Santa Fe.

Useful information about many audiences can be gathered by studying public-opinion polls. These surveys are now published regularly and cover a wide variety of topics. Often they are reported in terms of particular segments of the population. Thus on a given question the poll may contrast the views of businessmen and labor, men and women, or Democrats and Republicans.

Politicians adjust their behavior to the occasion and the environment. The Congressmen in the top picture are hearing the discussion of a bill; the same Congressmen may be among the crowd at a nominating convention below.

## Use of audience analysis data

Having gathered some information about your audience, you next naturally ask, "What do I do with it?" The answer is that you use it to adapt your material and presentation to the audience. Note that you are adapting to the audience, not surrendering to it. You need not and should not compromise your conscience.

You have seen in previous chapters that all the steps in speech preparation should be influenced by your knowledge of your prospective audience. For example, you will recall from pages 72–73 that the most important criterion in determining speech purpose is the attitude of listeners toward your topic. At all times during your speech preparation you should try to put yourself in your listeners' place, seeing and hearing the future speech through their eyes and ears. You should pay special attention to five specific methods of audience adaptation: finding common ground, slanting the subject, selecting supports, modifying the language, and adjusting vocal and visual delivery.

## Finding common ground

You begin by trying to find common ground. You look for areas of likeness or agreement which already exist or can be established between you and your audience with regard to your speech purpose. Ideally you want to create feelings of mutual identification with regard to both you and your speech purpose. Consider the following illustration.

During a Presidential campaign the two major candidates were invited to speak to student convocations on the campus of a large university. The first candidate arrived to find an audience of some 5,000 students and faculty. Placards were waving and students led small cheering sections prior to the speech. During the open forum period a student leader posed the question, "How, sir, can a student best prepare himself for political life and public office?" The candidate replied that he favored a broad preparation in the humanities rather than a specialization in political science. The answer elicited a mixed response: there was a clearly audible but confused murmur of many subdued voices. The probable reason for this reaction was that the university had a nationally famous political science department and equally famous schools of international relations and of public administration.

Two weeks later the second candidate spoke to approximately the same audience. He climaxed his first few sentences with the admission, "But perhaps I am not properly qualified—I majored in political science." Order was restored after at least two minutes of applause.

Let us analyze this example. Obviously the second candidate had secured a report of the earlier meeting and had taken the time from a strenuous schedule to study the report so that he could establish common ground with this particular audience. One might well say that the prolonged applause showed appreciation of the subtle compliment from the candidate. A deeper analysis would show that the candidate identified himself with the special traits and interests of this audience. But even more important, he simultaneously got his audience to identify themselves with him. He was off to a strong start. This initial mutual identification was on a purely personal level, but it eased his remaining task, which was to establish common ground regarding his speech subject and purpose. How, then, does a speaker interrelate these two areas of common ground, the "person to person" with the "idea to idea"? Consider another example.

On radio and television the problem of finding common ground becomes acute; anyone may tune in. In an effort to make his speech palatable for everyone, the speaker may become insipid. On the other hand, he may prepare for a particular segment of the potential listening audience, and say to himself about the others, "Good riddance. Let 'em turn the dial." The ability to find common ground, even on radio, was one of Franklin Roosevelt's achievements. Notice his audience adaptation in the following opening of an address on December 29, 1940; you can hardly fail to see how careful he was to include everyone and to make everyone feel included.

My Friends: This is not a fireside chat on war. It is a talk on national security; because the nub of the whole purpose of your President is to keep you now, and your children later, and your grandchildren much later, out of a last-ditch war for the preservation of American independence and all of the things that American independence means to you and to me and to ours.

Tonight, in the presence of a world crisis, my mind goes back eight years ago to a night in the midst of a domestic crisis. It was a time when the wheels of American industry were grinding to a full stop, when the whole banking system of our country had ceased to function.

I well remember that while I sat in my study in the White House, preparing to talk with the people of the United States, I had before my eyes the picture of all those Americans with whom I was talking. I saw the workmen in the mills, the mines, the factories; the girl behind the counter, the small shopkeeper; the farmer doing his spring plowing; the widows and the old men wondering about their life's savings.

I tried to convey to the great mass of American people what the banking crisis meant to them in their daily lives. Tonight, I want to do the same thing, with the same people, in this new crisis which faces America. We met the issue of 1933 with courage and realism. We face this new crisis—this new threat to the security of our nation—with the same courage and realism.

This example, like the previous one, illustrates speaker-audience identification. The Roosevelt example, however, goes beyond person-to-person identification. It shows how a speaker can get his listeners to identify themselves with his subject and purpose. Even a vast, heterogeneous radio or television audience can be led to feel that a speaker speaks *for them*—all of them.

Suppose you were talking to a group of women, as Mrs. Richard M. Nixon is doing here. Would you discuss sports, business, or finance?

Suppose you were talking to a group of men, as Senator Kerr is. Would you discuss social affairs, fashions, or home furnishings? The composition of your audience should determine your choice of subject.

### Slanting the subject

Perhaps you have an audience composed of all men or all women. This fact should influence your general approach. Experienced speakers have found that men tend to be most interested in such matters as business, sports, money, politics, and news events. Women are more interested in persons, clothes, social affairs, health, and the home. It is a good rule of thumb that women are more interested in people than men are. In mixed audiences women are more likely to adapt to the men's intersts than vice versa.

As an example, suppose you were making an appeal for funds for community playgrounds. For a men's group you might well stress the dollars and cents needed and the savings that would result by lessening juvenile delinquency; you might describe plans to equip and operate a baseball league for children. For a women's group you might give vivid descriptions of actual needy children and of unfortunate home conditions. For a mixed group you might use all the foregoing types of material, emphasizing the men's interests somewhat more than the women's.

Assume that you want to uphold the advantages of small colleges over large universities. You could prepare the talk without any particular audience in mind; that, however, would be a mistake because the speech would then consist entirely of ideas that *you* think are important. Your ideas about small and large colleges would be persuasive only if you happened to share a similar background and viewpoint with most of your auditors. But the arguments that convince you will not necessarily be the best arguments for someone else. What attitudes will most of your listeners have toward the topic? Perhaps the majority already favor small colleges, or perhaps the majority favor large universities. The whole slant of your subject should be drastically influenced by your knowledge of the audience's attitudes toward your topic.

To see how audience slanting works when applied to an actual speech, study a portion of Admiral Forrest Sherman's address to midshipmen at the United States Naval Academy in 1949. Notice how the speaker puts himself in his listeners' place and approaches his whole subject from the midshipmen's point of view.

> The uppermost thought in the mind of every man here, at one time or another, has been: "What are my chances for a successful career in the Navy?"
>
> I make no exceptions, when I say "every man here." Some of us wrestled with that question 30 years ago. So must it have been with the officers and midshipmen of 1899, of 1866, and even of 1815.
>
> I must say to you at the outset, that the young men in the Navy today face a greater challenge, and are confronted by greater opportunities than any of their predecessors in the indispensable service whose uniform we wear.
>
> Times have changed since the days of the frigate, but the necessity for a Navy is as vital to the Nation as it was in the time of Stephen Decatur. That necessity will endure as long as humanity survives on continents separated by oceans. And as long as the necessity exists, just so long will the Navy offer its officers an honorable career, a career of opportunity limited only by the ability and determination of the young man who enters it. I need not tell you that it is not an easy life; that the material rewards are often not adequate to the sacrifices, toil, and devotion to duty required. You took that all into consideration when you accepted your midshipman's warrant.
>
> It seems to me that midshipmen at the Naval Academy are in many ways better fitted to view the future of the United States Navy with complete objectivity than are older officers in mid-career, or nearing the end of their service. There are reasons why, at this time, I should be seeking your advice, instead of offering advice to you. Midshipmen are, in many ways, closer to the glorious history of our service, to its traditions, and to its ideals, than we who have grown gray wearing the Navy's blue and gold. You are certainly less marked by events of recent years which tend to obscure the broad view of the future —and also of the past from which the future must be appraised.[1]

[1] Willard Hayes Yeager, *Effective Speaking for Every Occasion*, Prentice-Hall, 1951, p. 291.

## Selecting supports

Another common method of audience adaptation is through the selection of supporting materials. For any one point there are likely to be several explanations, any one of which adequately develops the point. The type of audience may help you choose the explanation to employ: Pick the one that would be most likely to connect with the listeners' experience. The same principle applies to all the other forms of support. Take quotations, for instance: assuming you had a choice, Henry Ford would be a better person to quote for a businessmen's meeting than Goethe; the reverse would be true of a literary club meeting. John F. Kennedy would be a better authority to quote to a Democratic audience than Barry Goldwater.

James Conant, while president of Harvard, used the following anecdote in an address before the American Chemical Society to support his point that the recent growth of the chemical profession "has been one of the amazing social phenomena of our times."

> When this country entered World War I it so happened that a leading professor of chemistry was a relative of the then Secretary of War. Taking advantage of that fact he called on him in the first week after war was declared to offer on behalf of the American chemists the services of the profession to aid in the war effort. The Secretary said he would look into the matter and asked his caller to return a day later. When he did so the Secretary of War thanked him once again for his offer of assistance, asked him to transmit the thanks to his fellow chemists, but said it would be unnecessary to accept the proffered assistance because on looking into the matter he found the War Department had a chemist.[2]

Dr. John A. Schindler, a physician, spoke before a Farm and Home Week audience about illnesses resulting from mental and emotional causes. Dr. Schindler discussed three types of poorly adjusted people. He illustrated his characterization of the first group, "grumpy" people, with the following anecdote.

> I have a friend who illustrates that group. He has a farm, a beautiful farm, and a couple of years ago in our country we had a wonderful crop of oats. I drove past his farm one week early in July and I saw this field of oats and I thought to myself, "This ought to make Sam happy." Now, I had inquired among his relatives and friends as to whether they had ever heard Sam say a happy, pleasant word. None of them ever had, excepting his wife, who thought that he had the first year they were married, but that was so long ago that she wasn't sure. So I drove into Sam's yard and saw Sam, and I said, "Sam, that's a wonderful field of oats," and Sam came back with this, "Yes, but the wind

[2] A. Craig Baird, ed., *Representative American Speeches: 1951–1952*, H. W. Wilson, 1952, pp. 138–39. Reprinted by permission of James B. Conant.

will blow it down before I get it cut." But I watched this field. He got it cut all right, he got it threshed, and I know he got a good price for it—'twas the year before last.

Well, I saw him one day and I thought, "Now I've got Sam where he just can't get out of this!" So I said, "Sam, how did the oats turn out?" And he said, "Oh, it was a good crop, and I guess the price was all right, but you know a crop of oats like that sure takes a lot out of the soil." Some time later in October —it was a beautiful October—on a nice, warm afternoon, I saw him on the street and I said, "Sam, it's a wonderful day, isn't it?" I said it real enthusiastically, to try to make it contagious. But not Sam, he didn't catch. He just said, "Yes, but when we get it, we'll get it hard." [3]

Both the foregoing anecdotes are good ones; both support a point. But Conant's was chosen because it would appeal particularly to chemists; Schindler's because it would strike a responsive chord among farmers. If the speakers and audiences had been reversed, Conant could have illustrated the recent sudden increase in the importance of chemistry by telling an anecdote about a farmer, perhaps showing the recent improvements in insecticides. Schindler could have illustrated that some people always see the darkest side of things by telling the story of an overpessimistic chemist. Thus we can see how supports can be adapted to a particular audience.

## Modifying the language

It is important to modify the language in terms of the audience. Let us consider other parts of the speech by Dr. Schindler from which we have just quoted an anecdote. Here was a physician addressing a Farm and Home Week audience on a medical subject. He could have put the entire talk in medical terminology, but he never forgot that he was addressing laymen and referred only briefly to technical terms: "The name that it used to go by is psychoneurosis. The name that it has now is *psychosomatic illness.*" Most of the time Dr. Schindler used words like "cares, difficulties, and troubles," and those three words were made even more effective when he said, "Now the thing that brings on this illness is this layer of c.d.t." He used *c.d.t.* to stand for cares, difficulties, and troubles; thus tying in with the common farm and home term *DDT.* After discussing causes, Dr. Schindler discussed cures, but he did not say "proper therapeutic measures"; he discussed "how to get over it." His first suggestion for curing the disease was, "Stop looking for a knock in your human motor." In all probability if Dr. Schindler were discussing the same subject before a medical convention, his choice of words would be strikingly different.

[3] William Hayes Yeager, *Effective Speaking for Every Occasion,* Prentice-Hall, 1951, pp. 238–39. Reprinted by permission of Dr. John A. Schindler.

Information about your audience not only helps you decide what to say, it also warns you of what not to say. Information about race, religion, and politics is especially valuable in saving you from giving offense.

From time to time we witness or read about a speaker who has been cut off television or radio while telling a joke of questionable propriety. It is remarkable that experienced and well-known speakers should fail to learn that a story that is appropriate for one occasion may be improper for another occasion.

A slip of the tongue can wreck the effectiveness of an otherwise excellent speech. In groups of mixed religions it is usually wise to avoid reference to any specific denomination or to any controversial religious belief; religion should be brought into the talk only when absolutely necessary for the development of the subject, and references should be planned so as to touch upon beliefs common to all the denominations in the audience. If you are preparing to talk before a group of one faith, it is obviously wise to become familiar with its special customs and beliefs. For audiences with strong religious convictions, many appropriate speech materials are available: Biblical allusions and stories, quotations from church publications and from outstanding religious leaders, religious poems and hymns.

Politics is another touchy subject. Shortly after the 1952 election, a speaker at a businessmen's luncheon referred with sincere satisfaction to the fact that the people had finally corrected their mistakes of twenty years. Most of the audience were Republicans, but the speaker immediately alienated the 25 per cent who were Democrats.

Sometimes it is impossible to avoid antagonizing some members of the audience. However, avoid unnecessary antagonisms. For example, always avoid words such as *frog, squarehead, nigger, kike,* and *wop.* Avoid sarcasm, cynicism, and ridicule. Derogatory epithets are not vigorous English, just bad taste. And avoid talking down to your audience; it is usually better to say, "as we all know," than, "let me explain this to you."

## Adjusting vocal and visual delivery

In planning your vocal and visual delivery audience data will help.

The size of your audience should suggest a variety of possible adaptations. If it is a small group you might well plan a direct conversational approach, informal but lively. You might increase your effectiveness by bringing the audience into the speech through some form of group discussion. You certainly would plan to avoid a formal style.

Many factors determined through audience analysis can help you in planning and practicing bodily action. Thus for small intimate groups the lift of an eyebrow can be an effective gesture; for a somewhat larger audience a

An informal audience situation suggests an informal speech delivery, but this does not mean that the delivery should be *too* informal.

FENWICK ENGLISH

shrug of the shoulders might be a better choice. For a large crowd in an auditorium, however, the foregoing gestures might not be visible beyond the first few rows of seats—therefore a sweep of the hands and arms might be required if you want to communicate by gesture.

Likewise, aspects of your vocal delivery such as loudness and rate should be adjusted to such audience data as size of group, type of meeting place, general mood or atmosphere of the occasion, presence or absence of some type of public address equipment.

### The unexpected

Sometimes, of course, it is impossible to get advance information about an audience; or the information you do get turns out to be wrong. For example, a speaker traveled to a nearby town to discuss "Television and Your Child" before a parent-teacher association. Much of his material was for parents only, but when he arrived at the meeting he found that over one third of his auditors were between the ages of two and nine! It was not until later that the speaker discovered that there was an important bowling tournament that night, that all the fathers had gone to the tournament, and that the mothers had had to bring their children to the PTA meeting or else stay home. No one could have foreseen the situation. Confronted with the unexpected, the speaker could only make some last minute changes and revise his speech as he went along.

Audience analysis is a ticklish business; audience data are usually incomplete and often misleading. Should we, therefore, discard audience analysis entirely? Not at all.

There are several reasons for this statement. In the first place, the alternative is weak. If you do not plan, you depend on chance. This means that if your speech happens to suit your audience, it is only by accident. Because so many variables are involved, the probability of success by accident is small. As baseball managers say, it is better to "play the percentages." In the second place, when you have analyzed your audience and make a mistake, you have a better chance of spotting the error early in the speech and salvaging something by impromptu alterations. If you have not analyzed your audience and make a mistake, you can scarcely have any insight into the situation at all, and the mistake is likely to become a complete disaster. In the third place, you cannot learn from your accidental mistakes since you do not even know what goes wrong or why; every time, however, that you try to analyze an audience and misjudge, you learn a lesson and eliminate future mistakes. Finally, if you proceed by the method of chance you never get any better. The planner improves with practice. Even experienced speakers will occasionally misjudge an audience, but such misevaluations are rare.

In general, then, analyze every audience in advance and plan your speech accordingly. You will make mistakes, yes, but they will be beneficial mistakes. Such miscalculations in the future will not throw you off balance because you will have developed the healthy attitude of expecting the unexpected.


**Summary**

Audience response is always the test of speaking effectiveness. You can increase your chances of securing favorable audience response by analyzing each audience in advance. There are three main problems: what to look for, how to gather it, and how to use it.

Advance information about an audience is gathered from observation and inquiry.

The principal types of needed data include the nature of the occasion, common traits and interests, attitudes toward your topic, and attitudes toward you.

In general every detail of speech preparation should be adapted to the audience. More specifically, adaptation means finding common ground, slanting the subject, selecting the supports, modifying the language, and adjusting vocal and visual delivery.

Despite advance analysis and planning, the audience may not turn out as expected. Therefore it is wise to expect the unexpected, and to make adjustments when needed just before or during the delivery of a talk.

Adapting to your audience does not mean surrendering to it. In general audience adaptation means the establishment of a feeling of speaker-audience identification. This means, of course, that the speaker should identify himself with his listeners. More important, however, are the audience attitudes. The listeners should have a sense of identification with the speaker: The people who comprise the audience should have a feeling that the speaker and his ideas are of the people, by the people, and for the people. You must become not a speaker, but a spokesman. You cannot achieve this goal by accident. That is why you must learn how to analyze your audience, and to adapt to it.

TOPICAL PREVIEW

# 13

# GAINING AUDIENCE ATTENTION

### Attention!

When the sergeant bellows, "Ten-hut!" the private snaps to attention, freezes in position, and listens for the next command. When the radio or television announcer says, "Your attention please; we interrupt this program to bring you a special news bulletin," you sit up in your chair, lean forward a bit, forget other matters for the moment, readying yourself to hear the bulletin. When the quarterback barks a signal in a football game, each player becomes a picture of attention. His posture proclaims his concentration on the ball and the opposing players. He neither hears the great roar from the crowd nor sees the hundreds of objects and movements actually within his vision. These examples indicate that attention involves observable postural adjustments and inner adjustments, by which a person heightens his response to a given stimulus while reducing his response to competing stimuli.

Elwood Kretsinger invented an electronic device, popularly dubbed the wiggle meter, by which the physical movements of an audience can be measured and recorded.[1] Experiments with the wiggle meter have shown that when an audience is listening to nonhumorous speech materials the amount of movement in the audience varies inversely with the amount of

[1] Elwood A. Kretsinger, "An Experimental Study of Gross Bodily Movement as an Index to Audience Interest," *Speech Monographs*, Vol. XIX (November 1952).

Dr. Elwood Kretsinger points out the restlessness of an audience in another room as recorded by his "wiggle meter." This machine opens up new possibilities for measuring audience attention.

attention or interest. When the average person listens to interesting materials, he sits quietly. When bored, he writhes, looks around the room, confers with his neighbors, yawns, stretches, or fidgets.

Not only can we measure the physical manifestations of attention, but we also know something about attention as a mental phenomenon. Are you aware at this instant of the number at the bottom of this page? Probably not. Nevertheless, it has been in your field of vision as long as the page has. Furthermore, you cannot, even if you try, keep your attention centered on that number for very long. You attend to the number a while; then your attention shifts to something else; then you return to the number again until your attention again wanders. As the physics majors put it: Attention is AC rather than DC; that is, attention fluctuates.

Getting attention is a means to an end in any type of communication. The successful speaker must not only catch attention at the beginning of his speech, but he must also attempt to maintain it throughout his talk. If your purpose is to entertain, the attention step is both a means and an end. But in speeches to inform, stimulate, or convince, attention is a necessary preparatory step to understanding, to a reinforcement of attitudes, or to a change of attitudes.

## What makes a speech dull?

A teacher of speech must, by reason of his profession, listen to an extraordinary number of speeches. One teacher kept tabs and discovered that he had heard approximately 2,500 speeches one particular year—most of them by beginners, of course. Only a few speeches were genuinely interesting; most were so-so; many were so abysmally boring that only grim determination prevented the teacher from falling asleep. You have heard many boring speeches, too. What makes speeches dull?

When listening to a national political convention, our attention begins to lag when the speaker launches into his "I give you a man who . . ." and inevitably concludes with ". . . the next President of the United States. . . ." But politicians have no monopoly on the use of these hackneyed ideas and phrases:

"It is a pleasure and a privilege . . ."
"I am reminded of a story."
"There is just one thought I want to leave with you today."
"So let's get down to brass tacks."
". . . and stay on the beam . . ."
"Let's show our metal."
"And never say die."
"This is no panacea."
"But just plain common sense . . ."
"So let's put our shoulders to the wheel."
". . . and give it all we've got."

Each of us is bound to use some trite materials like the foregoing. Used in a new context, however, a platitude can be interesting; used only occasionally, trite words or ideas may do little harm, but used throughout a speech, triteness will bore an audience into complete inattention.

Too frequent use of abstract words is also likely to produce a dull speech. The speech employing too many abstract words usually deals only with theory. Its points and subpoints are likely to be supported almost entirely by explanations, lacking instances, anecdotes, and descriptions. Examples of speech so abstract as to be not merely dull but almost meaningless are found even in high places. An official of the National Production Authority in a talk on material allocations said:

**251**

We are peaking our program philosophically but it is naive to assume the allotment program is an equity program unless the allotments are so abysmally low that they permit the agency to relax and allow market determination as a percentage of base period sidetracking military return with adjustments. This is based on use levels proportionately and is in the market test sense. We now have a quantitative framework with marginal qualitative allocations to formalize the procedure for further refining and implementing of our objectives.[2]

Then there is the pedantic speech, an exercise in minutiae. College professors are sometimes guilty of this when they maintain that if they have something to say it is up to the student, however bored he may be, to get it. Legal language, which attempts to account for every loophole, is frequently boring and pedantic. Read this portion of a legal decision, being sure to pay careful attention:

We hold that paragraph number 3, in its language and in its coordinate contextual position and relationship, was of such ambiguity or doubtfulness, on what the parties had intended it to connote, and to provide safeguard for between them, as not to be required facially to be viewed as having had a meaningless significance, such as appellants contended, and that a court was accordingly entitled to seek light and explanation from the extrinsic manifesta-

[2] Los Angeles *Times*, April 13, 1951.

Perhaps the speaker has just said, "and that reminds me of another humorous story."

tions of intentions . . . etc. (etc. for 129 more words until the end of the first sentence).[3]

Some speeches are dull because the speaker's ideas seem to stand still; they do not march. Other speeches are dull because the personality of the speaker is colorless. Still others kill audience interest because of the speaker's monotonous voice. Likewise, dullness can result from monotony of bodily action; the speaker who paces steadily back and forth on the platform will hypnotize his listeners into a coma just as readily as the speaker who stands like a post. Finally, speeches may be dull because they are too long. Mark Twain is credited with a story about an overlong sermon. At the end of twenty minutes he was so favorably impressed he decided to put in five dollars when the offering was taken. Twenty minutes later, he decided that two dollars would suffice. After another twenty minutes, the proposed contribution shrank to one dollar. When eventually the sermon ended, Mark Twain awoke from a doze and placed a dime on the plate.

### What makes a speech interesting?

## Adaptation of material to the audience

An artist, a farmer, and a realtor stood looking at a hillside. What did they see?

"See those lights and shadows!" exclaimed the artist.

"Hm. Looks like the topsoil's washed away," murmured the farmer.

"That'll subdivide into fifty lots," said the realtor. "Wonder what's the owner's price?"

All three were looking at the same hill but each paid attention to a different aspect, each in terms of his personal interests.

Naturally this same phenomenon is true of an audience. That presentation of idea or choice of words will be most interesting which most nearly corresponds with audience interests. Thus presentation of ideas and language should be modified in light of the audience analysis in order to get and hold attention. This principle, of course, always applies.

## Factors of attention

Experimental research and practical speaking experience show that there are several factors of attention that influence the intensity of a listener's interest. These include:

1. Significance
2. Humor

[3] *The New Yorker* (December 15, 1956), p. 164.

3. Uniqueness or familiarity
4. Problems
5. Concreteness
6. Antagonism
7. Variation

**1. SIGNIFICANCE** In general, a detail is considered significant by your listener when it affects *him*. His attention to your talk may be lagging—mention his name, or any of his special interests, and his attention will snap back to your speech immediately. But what are his interests? For any audience, most of those interests will be variations on a few basic themes. The basic needs and wants of human beings have been classified by many scholars in several fields of study. A list for the public speaker was provided by A. E. Phillips in his *Effective Speaking* (Newton, 1938), a pioneering work, first published in 1908, which has had great influence on modern speech education. Phillips listed seven impelling motives of human behavior: self-preservation, property, power, reputation, affections, sentiments, and tastes. How can you apply this list to the preparation of an actual talk?

Consider the first basic interest: self-preservation. Whatever affects the health or safety of your listener is likely to capture his attention. The chemistry major who talked on the dangers of certain widely advertised drug compounds made the dangers real, and he got attention, as did the

When you tell an anecdote, live it!

Casey Stengel, famous for his storytelling ability, suggests how it's done.

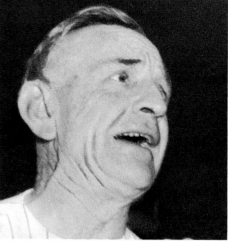

LIFE PHOTO BY MARK KAUFFMAN                    WIDE WORLD

student who advocated regular checkups on vital automobile parts. A pre-medical student got attention by discussing his classmates' chances of becoming victims in a current polio epidemic. A talk on draft regulations and one on military training were tied into the motive of self-preservation by their application to a college audience. A speech on civilian defense, on the Pure Food and Drug Act, on household accidents, or on the local water supply can be made to appeal to the instinct of self-preservation.

Any of the other impelling motives can be similarly treated. Your listener will pay attention if you can show him how to make money, get elected, be applauded, make friends, feel patriotic, or indulge a favorite hobby.

**2. HUMOR** The most widely used method of getting audience attention is humor. Psychologists have offered many theories as to what makes things funny. Most of the theories assume that humor is based on *incongruity* coupled with *a sense of well-being*. A sense of humor, therefore, is some-times defined approximately as a sense of proportion.

Incongruity means that some element of a situation is inharmonious, out of step, unexpected. Thus, in planning how to use a given bit of humor ask yourself, "What is incongruous here?" Then plan how to present the material to emphasize the incongruity, and possibly to exploit the unexpected.

For telling humorous anecdotes, special study should be given to the question of timing. Jack Benny can hold a pause longer and more effectively than most speakers; he can also make certain remarks funny by the very

He waits expressively for the laughter to subside.    Now he takes another swing at the story.

LIFE PHOTO BY MARK KAUFFMAN                                      WIDE WORLD

speed with which he tosses them out. The proper placement and duration of a pause can make or break the success of most oral humor. The incongruity and unexpectedness are usually heightened by a pause just before the punch line. Also, when you get a laugh from your audience, wait until the laughter subsides somewhat before going on with your talk.

Facial expression and attention to inflection of key words are two other delivery techniques of special importance. Some famous humorists use a dead-pan or slightly surprised expression when the audience laughs; others prefer laughing with the audience, although neither as loud nor as long. Just the right inflection of a key word or phrase sometimes makes the joke. It has been said that Jack Benny can get more genuine laughs from a single "Well?" than other humorists from a whole program.

A speaker must be extremely wary of using humor based on race, religion, or sex; a joke, even if sidesplitting, does not get favorable attention if it is even slightly offensive. Neither should he use humor that is unrelated to the speech subject, because the object of speech humor is not simply to get the listeners' attention, but to get their favorable attention, and to get it focused on an idea. Just telling a funny story is not enough; the audience's appreciation of humor is doubled when they recognize its pertinence to the point being discussed.

Some writers warn against using old jokes, but even old jokes have their value. If the humor is relevant and well told, familiarity apparently does not diminish the listeners' enjoyment. As a matter of fact, it is hard to conceive of a truly new joke. Adlai Stevenson made good use of this old joke during a campaign talk in Albuquerque:

> Somebody has been asking me how I was feeling and it reminded me of a story of a man who was shot in the back by Indians in an attack on a wagon train out in this country in the early days. Some time later some troopers came along and found the poor man unconscious with three arrows between his shoulder blades. They revived him with whisky, and when he could whisper they asked if it hurt awfully, and he said, "It sure does, especially when I laugh." [4]

The effectiveness of the story lies both in the way Stevenson told it and in the fact that it makes a point. When you have a good anecdote, do not drag it in by the heels. Plan the transition into it carefully. Stevenson should have avoided the hackneyed "I am reminded of the story of a . . ." Word the transitions with originality. If you begin with an anecdote, do not introduce it with either praise or apology. In other words, *do not* start off like this, "Mr. Chairman, Ladies and Gentlemen: The other day I ran across what I thought was a pretty good story; at any rate, I hope you will think so. . . ."

[4] New York *Times*, September 12, 1952.

Instead, start by going right into the story: "Ten years ago in a small town in Indiana . . ."

Once the anecdote is under way, *live it:* show how the characters felt; tell it with animation. Use dialogue and act it out when appropriate, but avoid using dialect with which you are not familiar. Decide in advance whether or not the anecdote should be related briefly, building up quickly and getting the point across before the audience has time to do more than get the general effect; or whether to build up slowly, giving them a chance to savor all the details. Plan it and tell it so as to build up to the climax. Do not backtrack; never use an unnecessary detail or elaborate any detail unless elaboration is necessary. If names, places, or times are part of the anecdote, make them specific and believable. For example, avoid calling all child characters "Little Johnny"; use some specific name such as "George" or "Ernest" or "Conrad." Plan your story so as to avoid anticlimax; a good suggestion is to plan the ending first and then build up to it. If the anecdote is properly told, its point should be clear to the audience. If you do state the point of the anecdote, state it only for emphasis.

Some students report, often with justification, that they cannot tell a joke without killing it. However, there are probably types of humor that they can present effectively, and they should seek them. In fact, all speakers are wise to experiment with a variety of kinds and styles of humor. In addition to anecdotes, there are puns, paradox, satire, understatement, overstatement, limericks, irony, and ridicule. Franklin D. Roosevelt could use ridicule effectively:

> These Republican leaders have not been content with attacks on me, or on my wife, or on my sons—no, not content with that, they now include my little dog, Fala. Well, of course, I don't resent attacks and my family don't resent attacks, but Fala does resent them. You know, Fala's Scotch and, being a Scottie, as soon as he learned that the Republican fiction writers concocted a story that I had left him behind on an Aleutian island and had sent a destroyer back to find him—at a cost to the taxpayers of two or three or twenty million dollars—his Scotch soul was furious. He has not been the same dog since. I am accustomed to hearing malicious falsehoods about myself—such as that old, worm-eaten chestnut that I have represented myself as indispensable. But I think I have a right to resent, to object to libelous statements about my dog.[5]

Limericks or other humorous verse can sometimes be woven in effectively, especially if wording or meter provide unexpected effects. Satire, irony, and ridicule must be used with discretion. It is almost always safe to make fun of yourself. For example, "The chairman said that my colleague and I were noted for our wit. The implication is unfortunately just. There

[5] New York *Times,* September 24, 1944.

are two of us; and two half-wits add up to one wit." Other persons can be teased provided the teasing is done with obvious good nature. Will Rogers backed Ogden Mills for Congress because he owned a silk hat and because "he is the only candidate for Congress who can go into a Fifth Avenue home without delivering something." Finally, you can make fun of other persons or things when you are sure the audience is opposed to those persons or things. For example, see how Governor Dewey treated the Democrats' "New Deal":

> But even the experts can't advise how to do business under the New Deal, because they can't understand the laws themselves. I have here a dozen examples. Just listen to this little gem for Section 23 (P) of the present tax laws about contributions to employees' pension plans. It says "they shall not be deductible under Subsection (A) but shall be deductible, if deductible under Subsection (A) without regard to this subsection, but only to the following extent. . . ." From here on it gets technical! [6]

A final suggestion: Test your proposed humor aloud; some humor reads well but tells poorly, or vice versa. For speech purposes, humor should usually provide opportunities for verbal play, vocal play, meaningful pauses, facial expressions, pantomime, or other oral devices.

**3. UNIQUENESS OR FAMILIARITY**   People are attracted by the unique. They are interested by things unusually big or small, heavy or light, expensive or cheap. A speaker discussing the advantages of microfilming business papers got attention when he said, "A stack of papers twice as high as this building when microfilmed can be stored in a single drawer of an ordinary filing cabinet." A striking statement gets attention—"Yesterday I held a million dollars of United States currency in my hands!" Travel talks about strange sights or strange customs get and hold attention. Unusual personal experiences arouse interest. If you have faced an aroused grizzly bear, you may be sure the experience will serve you well in a speech. Odd facts of all sorts interest people.

But don't go overboard. Anything too unusual defeats its purpose. A physical education instructor, giving a talk before a high school, decided to get attention by casually undressing himself during the first part of the talk. Once it was revealed that he had a gym suit under his regular clothes, he proceeded to do some calisthenics. The shock of his "strip tease" had been so great, however, that it blotted out everything else in the speech.

Anything completely removed from the listeners' previous experience is meaningless. For example, suppose you were a chess enthusiast and wanted to explain an unusual move to people who did not play chess. If you said,

[6] New York *Times,* October 4, 1944.

"So I moved the queen's bishop to king's rook three as a gambit!" it would be as though you had spoken to them in a strange language. The unusual, therefore, has meaning only if the speaker relates it to the familiar.

In the right context, the familar belief or sentiment can capture attention. If you eloquently utter a truth deeply felt by your audience, they will pay attention.

Here we have a speaker's dilemma: if his materials are too unusual they become bizarre, meaningless, or distracting; if too familiar, they become trite. Triteness is an elusive quality. We have heard the parables of Jesus dozens of times, yet we do not consider them trite. One kind of material might seem trite in a sociology lecture; the same material in a sermon might seem almost startling. A patriotic speech given during peacetime might seem a series of tiresome platitudes; the same speech given during a war crisis might bring the audience to its feet cheering. Triteness, then, is a matter of judgment and context. To define it would require qualifications, such as: Triteness is saying the same old thing, in the same old way, by the wrong speaker, at the wrong time, before the wrong audience. The solution for the dilemma is to find a good combination of the unusual and the familiar. Two practical formulas are to give an old idea a novel twist and to present a new idea in familiar terms.

4. PROBLEMS   A powerful way to capture attention is by posing a problem for the audience to solve with you. If the following story catches and holds your attention, you will have an illustration of how suspense and curiosity operate.

> A loud-talking and inquisitive American businessman was riding a train when an Englishman with only one leg entered the car using a crutch.
> "I see you were in the war," remarked the businessman after a brief pause.
> "No, I was not in the service."
> "These traffic accidents get worse every year."
> "No, sir, I was never in a wreck of any kind."
> "Surgical operation, maybe?"
> "No."
> So the American finally asked point-blank how he had lost the leg.
> "I will tell you only on one condition," replied the Englishman, "that you will promise not to ask another question."
> "I promise."
> The Englishman nodded pleasantly.
> "It was *bit* off," he said.

You can often organize your whole speech in terms of a problem solution. If you can begin by presenting the problem vividly, in terms of your listeners'

DON MOHR STUDIO

Infrared ray photographs can be taken in the dark. Dr. John Robson undertook to measure audience interest by taking these infrared ray photographs of an unsuspecting theater audience. Each photo was taken during a different one-act play. According to ratings by more than one hundred graduate students, the middle picture reveals the least audience attention of the three, and the bottom the most.

experience, and in such a way that it appears difficult to solve, you will have attention. Your audience will be waiting to see if you can solve it or exactly how you will solve it. If you handle your materials skillfully, the audience will try to beat you to the solution. The audience competes with you just as the reader of a detective story competes with the author.

A speaker gave a series of talks on techniques for dealing with people before groups of factory foremen and supervisors. The following sequence worked best:

1. Relate in detail an actual case.
2. Ask, "If you had been that supervisor, what would you have done?"
3. Analyze the elements of the problem.
4. Reject several possible but inferior solutions.
5. Present the recommended solution.

For example, the speaker would begin by relating the case of Joe who had been with his company for over a year and had been considered a good worker. Occasionally, however, Joe was surly for no apparent reason. One morning he arrived late, walked into his department, threw his coat on the floor, and went to his machine to start working. The supervisor came over and said, "Joe, you're supposed to hang your coat on the hooks. You know that." Then in front of all the other workmen, Joe said loudly, "If you want it hung up, hang it up yourself." The speaker would ask, "If you were that supervisor, what would you do?" The audience might suggest various answers, such as:

Hang up the coat yourself.
Command Joe to hang it up.
Ask another worker to hang it up.
Tell Joe he is fired.
Ask Joe to come to your office for a talk.
Call for the superintendent.
Pretend the whole incident is a joke.

By the time several possible solutions were written on a chalkboard, the case would be dramatized into a puzzle, and the attention of the audience would be aroused by the desire to find out what the correct solution should be.

**5. CONCRETENESS** Ideas as well as language can be either concrete or abstract or a mixture. In fact, you can express a concrete idea in abstract words, or vice versa. Just now we are primarily concerned with concrete ideas. "Cooperation" is an abstract idea. Let us present "cooperation" concretely.

It is said that, to enter the final vault in the United States mint, one guard must turn a key on one side of the great steel door while another guard turns another key from the opposing side. Thus the key to cooperation is plural. It always takes two to cooperate.

Ideas are presented concretely by an appeal to the listeners' senses. Cooperation is an abstraction; you cannot visualize an abstraction, cannot see it, hear it, feel it, or smell it. However, you can visualize the opening of the vaults in the mint. By analogy you can associate an abstract idea with a more attention-getting concrete idea.

Concrete ideas often include the visualization of movement, and movement gets attention. Newspaper offices often have big plate glass windows through which one can see the giant printing presses. When the presses are still, nobody does more than glance at them absentmindedly. But when the presses are operating, it is difficult to pass the place without stopping for a look. The same irresistible urge collects crowds of sidewalk superintendents to watch the excavating for a new business building. Our attention is attracted by movement or activity. The speaker should try to put some of his ideas in the form of illustrations in which movement can be visualized. When presented in such form, the idea itself seems to move.

**6. ANTAGONISM** A dogfight draws a crowd. A conflict gets attention. A speaker can also introduce the element of conflict into his talk.

Describe a conflict—a football game, a prize fight, a race, a military battle. Mental conflicts may be equally interesting—the conflict between good and evil, perhaps, as in the story of Dr. Jekyll and Mr. Hyde. Attack policies or ideas. The most attention-getting moments of a campaign speech are likely to be when the speaker is lambasting the opposition. Deliberately antagonize an audience. A speaker was asked, for example, to discuss Americanism before a meeting of the American Legion. His speech could have been banal, but he began by stating that he proposed to give the arguments in favor of Communism. He did so amid increasing tension. When he suddenly changed his mood and manner and said, "Now we're going to answer those arguments," the Legion cheered madly and followed the rest of the speech with blow-by-blow relish.

**7. VARIATION** A speech should be planned to provide variety in its details, both of content and delivery. The serious should alternate with the humorous; the humor should be of different types; the unusual and the familiar should be combined; and the rate of delivery, the pitch, and the volume should vary. As was pointed out early in this chapter, human attention constantly fluctuates. During a talk you must catch the listeners' attention again and again. Variety does that for you.

Variety of detail does not mean that the over-all effect must become disorganized. Hold a dime in your palm and try to concentrate your attention on it. You can pay attention to the whole dime only briefly—your attention fluctuates. You find yourself attending to details: the date, the motto, portions of the Presidential face. Your attention has fluctuated, but all within the pattern of a dime. The same thing happens during a speech. Audience attention also fluctuates, but if the speaker is skillful he provides diversity within unity; he controls the fluctuations, leading his audience from item to item, holding them from start to finish.

### Attention-getting in the speech to entertain

When your purpose is to entertain, favorable attention becomes the end itself and not just a means. Interest is not only the first requirement but almost the only one.

The most common speech given primarily to entertain is the after-dinner speech. However, this type of talk can be appropriate at any meeting, especially at social gatherings where good fellowship and recreation prevail. Many clubs have the custom of holding occasional meetings for entertainment only, or of devoting part of every meeting to fun alone. But banquets provide the most common occasion for talks to entertain.

Humor is the trade-mark of most entertaining talks, but there are many exceptions. Tales of adventure, travel, or mystery can be highly entertaining without relying on humor. In a predominantly humorous speech, humor is often enhanced by having an underlying theme of serious thought or sentiment. The great comedian Charlie Chaplin is a master of emotional rebound —making us laugh the harder by alternating the humorous and the sentimental. Talks to entertain, however, should make use of all the factors of attention, not of humor alone.

## Delivery

Variety is the keynote for entertaining talks. Entertaining talks usually provide opportunity for voice and language variety by way of mimicry, exaggeration, dialogue, dialect, and special sound effects.

A variety of bodily actions can be used: unusual facial expressions, impressions, impersonations, pantomimes, incongruous postures or gestures. Use of visual aids is sometimes helpful.

The total effect of the speaker's personality should be friendly, direct, lively, and good natured. The prevailing tone should be optimistic. Variety of delivery, however, does not mean that the speaker should be constantly in motion. A speaker can be downright dramatic by standing motionless—if

UNIVERSITY OF SOUTHERN CALIFORNIA

A conflict gets attention. People pay attention to intercollegiate football games as long as the issue is in doubt. They want to know "who won?"

The nationally televised CBS series "College Bowl" also captured the attention of millions because of the element of intellectual conflict and the desire to know who won.

M. BERGES  JEROME LEVY  JAMES ZURER  JOE RISHEL    BOB COPAKEN  F. SORENSEN    RICH OLCOTT  JAY GOODMA

HOBART & WILLIAM SMITH          BELOIT COLLEGE

CBS

his motionlessness contrasts with previous action or corresponds with the thought being expressed. Likewise, attention may be gained by silence or by a quiet voice. You can build down to a climax as well as build up to one. You do not have to be funny or lively to be entertaining; you can be serious and deeply moving, yet hold the listeners spellbound.

## Organization

Sometimes all that is required is to string together a series of stories on a thread of free association. Monologues by popular TV comedians, such as Bob Hope or Shelley Berman, provide ready examples.

**1. SIMPLE THEME WITH ILLUSTRATIONS** A step beyond the string-of-beads plan for a speech is the simple theme with illustrations. However, the theme with illustrations is still extremely loose in organization, and the logic need not be tight. The speaker chooses a central idea (as recommended in Chapter 7) and lists a few main points, but his emphasis is on finding a way to weave in attention-getting supporting materials. The organization usually consists of one or more loosely constructed speech units. In humorous talks logic may even be reversed—a point may be "proved" by obviously false logic.

Consider an example of a simple theme with illustrations. One student decided to give a classroom talk about the humorous side of his army experiences. He might simply have chosen five minutes' worth of his funniest experiences and strung them out like beads. Instead, he chose a simple theme: Getting into the army and getting into college are very much the same. He picked three main points:

1. They have similar entrance requirements.
2. Both develop the skill of standing in line.
3. Both involve about a ton of paper work.

He developed the first main point by anecdotes about the physical examinations and a comparison of a school board with a draft board. This framework provided an ample opportunity for using many attention-getting devices.

**2. REGULAR OUTLINE WITH STRESS ON ATTENTION** The third type of organization for speeches to entertain may be called the regular speech outline with special emphasis on the factors of attention. By regular we mean the process covered in Chapter 7. Here is an outline for a talk to entertain entitled "How to Worry Successfully."

I. Most of the things we worry about are absurd, and we know it.
   *Anecdote:* The horse in the bathtub
II. Worrying does no good, and we know it.
   *Explanation:* How to worry about the hydrogen bomb
      *Transition:* Nevertheless, we go right on worrying. And since we insist on doing it . . .

*Central idea:* My thesis today is: Let's make a good job of it. Let's have the biggest and best collection of worries in town!
*Transition:* I can help you achieve all this. I shall present a specific and practical program. And the first step in this program is . . .

I. Try to live in the future.
   A. Worry is always about the future.
      1. *Explanation:* The past doesn't exist; the present is a fleeting moment; only the future can actually be worried about.
      2. *Quotation:* Mark Twain, "I'm an old man and have known many troubles—most of which never happened."
   B. Worry always takes place in the imagination.
      1. *Explanation:* It's all mental and about the future.
      2. *Anecdote:* The elderly couple who made and lost a fortune by imaginary speculation on the stock market.
II. Enjoy your worrying.
   A. *Explanation:* Main cause—people worry because they want to.
   B. *Instance:* Girl who worries after lovers' quarrel—more fun when he comes back.
   C. *Instance:* Mother who worries to get attention and control the family: "You know how I worry."
   D. *Instance:* Lady who brags, "I'm the best little worrier you ever saw."
III. Avoid making decisions.
   A. *Description:* Man afraid to decide for fear decision will be wrong.
   B. *Anecdote:* Mule who starved to death between two haystacks.
      *Transition:* By this time you should clearly understand how to worry successfully.

*Summary:* You must try to live in the future—not just plan for it but live in it. You must learn to enjoy your worries—revel in them, boast about them, feel sorry for yourself. You must avoid making decisions—and if you do make one, go back and reconsider. Follow this program and you, too, can have bigger and better worries. But if you fail to follow it, you'll scarcely be able to worry at all.

In analyzing the outline you will notice that all seven of the factors of attention described in this chapter have been employed.

*a. Significance.* The subject of worry is vital to almost all adult audiences even though they may not admit it. They came to enjoy the talk but have a sneaking hunch that maybe it will actually help them.

*b. Humor.* The speech is liberally sprinkled with humor of several types. There is incongruity all the way through.

*c. Uniqueness and familiarity.* This is the principal attention-getter. The entire speech illustrates the use of an old idea with a novel twist.

*d. Problems.* Curiosity is aroused when the title is first announced. After the central idea is stated suspense is maintained by not revealing in advance all the steps in the program—the listener is encouraged to wonder what the next point will be. As the talk progresses, the audience discovers the reverse logic being used; most of them begin the game of translating it into positive terms.

*e. Concreteness.* There is little theorizing. All the explanations are kept brief and are illustrated by anecdote or instance. Notice, for example, the definition of worry in connection with the anecdote of the mule between the haystacks.

*f. Antagonism.* Worry is defined as an unresolved inner conflict, and the element of struggle is developed in several supports, especially the anecdote about the old couple buying imaginary stocks and bonds.

*g. Variation.* All the factors of attention are used, and all the forms of support, except statistics.

## Attention-getting in other speeches

Getting attention is a means to an end in speeches to inform, stimulate, or convince. The better you control the audience's attention, the better your chances of getting information across, reinforcing existing beliefs, or building new beliefs. According to some psychologists, beliefs and attitudes are shaped by whatever dominates our attention most often and most fully.

In speaking to inform, stimulate, or convince, make your supports do double duty. When you choose an anecdote, instance, or quotation, give it a double test. (1) Does it clarify, reinforce, or prove your point? (2) Does it contain one or more of the factors for catching attention? Remember especially the principle of diversity within unity. Plan the framework of your ideas and then fill out the details with a variety of forms of support and delivery.

Thus in speeches to inform, stimulate, or convince, attention plays a supporting role. However, the role is vital—you cannot inform, stimulate, or convince your audience if they are not paying attention. Capturing and holding interest is a prerequisite to any further audience response.

The role of attention in speeches to inform, stimulate, or convince can become more concrete if you apply what has been discussed in this chapter to some appropriate contemporary address. In October 1962, for example, the attention of almost all of the adult population of the United States was captured and held by President Kennedy's speech announcing a "quarantine" of Cuba. A small portion of this speech is quoted below. Why did this catch attention? Do not limit your answer to the obvious "Well, it was a national emergency." Analyze more specifically.

> Nevertheless, American citizens have become adjusted to living daily on the bull's-eye of Soviet missiles located inside the U.S.S.R. or in submarines.
>
> In that sense, missiles in Cuba add to an already clear and present danger—although, it should be noted, the nations of Latin America have never previously been subjected to a potential nuclear threat.
>
> But this secret, swift and extraordinary buildup of Communist missiles—in an area well-known to have a special and historical relationship to the United States and the nations of the Western Hemisphere, in violation of Soviet assurances, and in defiance of American and hemispheric policy—this sudden, clandestine decision to station strategic weapons for the first time outside of Soviet soil—is a deliberately provocative and unjustified change in the status quo which cannot be accepted by this country, if our courage and our commitments are ever to be trusted again by either friend or foe.
>
> .  .  .
>
> Finally, I want to say a few words to the captive people of Cuba, to whom this speech is being directly carried by special radio facilities. I speak to you as a friend, as one who knows of your deep attachment to your fatherland, as one who shares your aspiration for liberty and justice for all.
>
> And I have watched with deep sorrow how your nationalist revolution was betrayed—and how your fatherland fell under foreign domination. Now your leaders are no longer Cuban leaders inspired by Cuban ideals. They are puppets and agents of an international conspiracy which has turned Cuba against your friends and neighbors in the Americas—and turned it into the first Latin American country to become a target for nuclear war—the first Latin American country to have these weapons on its soil.
>
> These new weapons are not in your interest. They contribute nothing to your peace and well-being. They can only undermine it. But this country has no wish to cause you to suffer or to impose any system upon you. We know your lives and land are being used as pawns by those who deny you freedom.[7]

[7] Los Angeles *Times* (October 23, 1962).

## Summary

In speeches to inform, stimulate, and convince, catching and holding audience attention is the first requirement; in speeches to entertain it is almost the only requirement because dullness defeats everything else a speaker attempts to do.

Speeches are dull when language and ideas are trite, abstract, or pedantic; when the sequence of ideas doesn't march; when the speaker's personality is colorless; when voice and bodily movement are monotonous; or when speeches are too long. Speeches are interesting when they are adapted to the audience, and when they apply the factors of attention, such as significance, humor, uniqueness or familiarity, problems, concreteness, antagonism, and variation.

Speeches to entertain should include a maximum variety of delivery and appropriate speech organization, as well as constant use of the attention-controlling factors. The organization of entertaining speeches may be simply a string-of-beads plan, or a simple theme with illustrations, or a regular outline with stress on the attention values.

TOPICAL PREVIEW

# 14

# GAINING AUDIENCE UNDERSTANDING

## Information, please!

You cannot inform your audience that two plus two equals four—they already know that. To inform implies that the information given is new to them. You cannot inform your audience that "the framble issifies and solarates twice a week"—that is new to them but they would not understand it. You cannot inform your audience merely by reading a long list of statistics. The data may be new and understood at the moment they are given, but you have not informed unless the listener can remember either the statistics or what the statistics were supposed to show.

Three convenient tests of the success of a speech to inform are: (1) How much information was new to the audience? (2) How much information did they understand? (3) How much information will they remember? Let us apply these tests to some common types of informative speaking.

## Occasions for informative speaking

Here is a representative list of speaking situations where the purpose is predominantly to inform:

> Class lectures
> Student recitations or class reports
> Adult education lectures
> Announcements

There are many occasions for informative speaking. Here an elementary school teacher conducts a language lesson.

> Instructions or directions
> Book or play reviews
> Committee reports
> Chalk talks
> Industrial training lectures
> Scientific reports
> Demonstration talks

You have been on the receiving end of many such talks, especially class lectures. You have doubtless complained about some of them. It is a sad truth that college lectures are often notable only as models of what every speaker should avoid. Listed here are some common complaints about informative speeches.

### Common complaints about informative speeches

*It was dry.* "That man can dive deeper and come up drier than anyone I've ever heard."

*It was over the listeners' heads.* "It was too deep for me. Half the time I didn't even know what he was talking about."

*It had too many facts.* "After ten minutes I surrendered. How does he expect us to remember all those facts?"

*It was too technical.* "You should have heard the two-dollar words. What'd he think we were? Experts?"

*It was too theoretical.* "He's the *vaguest* guy. He never said anything you could get hold of."

*He talked too fast.* "What a machine gun! I was trying to take notes. Every time I wrote down a point, I missed the next one."

*He read too much.* "Honest, it got so all I could do was count the pages."

*He was too aloof,* or *colorless,* or *passive.* "First I wondered if he was mad about something. Pretty soon I wondered if he was human. Finally I wondered if he was alive."

Another occasion for informative speaking. A distinguished scientist reports to a convention of his colleagues.

273

### The plan of the informative speech

The frequency of such complaints can be cut down if the informative speech is properly planned in advance. The recommended six-step procedures for preparing and outlining should be followed, but additional suggestions regarding some of the steps will be helpful in preparing and delivering an informative speech.

## Audience interest in the subject

In planning a talk to inform, the analysis of the audience usually centers on their probable attitudes toward the topic. A good way to begin the analysis is to find out if they are already interested in the topic, for you should know to what extent the topic is likely to carry itself and to what extent you must hunt for special methods to make it interesting. For example, it would be safe to suppose that women would be interested in hearing a talk on current fashions, as it would be just as safe to suppose that men would not be interested. But how about a talk on the history of the World Series? You know the answer.

## Audience knowledge of the subject

You have to estimate in advance what your listeners already know about your topic. It is crucial to success that this estimate be approximately accurate. If you underestimate the audience's background, they will consider your information old hat; if you overestimate, they will not be able to understand you. Suppose, for example, you planned to talk about the slide rule. Imagine a class comprising mostly liberal arts majors, and then imagine a class of engineering students. An explanation of the slide rule that would be simple enough for the first group would be boring to the second, and if the talk presented information new to the engineers, it would be meaningless to the liberal arts students.

The danger of overestimating the amount of new material to include is greater than the danger of underestimating it. The speaker must avoid the temptation to show off his knowledge. He must remember that it takes more words to present a fact in speech than it does in writing. He must not be misled into thinking that college lectures are standards for informative speaking. Whether or not notes will be taken is of particular importance in determining the amount of material to be given. If note taking is appropriate or required, as in a classroom lecture, much more information can be included. If note taking is inappropriate or an unaccustomed task, as in most non-classroom speeches, the amount of factual material must be reduced accordingly.

## Audience prejudices toward the subject

On some topics, even though your purpose is to inform, allowance must be made for audience prejudices for or against that topic. If the newspapers, for instance, have been headlining the heroic battle of a captain to save his storm-battered ship, audiences would be favorably inclined toward the captain, eager to learn more facts about him. On the other hand, prejudice against a subject such as communism may be so strong that there may be emotional resistance against even an impartial history or explanation. Therefore the speaker cannot suppose that a fact is a fact to all audiences. Evolution, for example, is not accepted as a fact by fundamentalists. The speaker must anticipate whether the listeners' attitudes will be receptive, resistant, conflicting, or apathetic toward even unbiased facts.

## Use of learning aids

When you undertake to build the outline of an informative talk, you should modify the six steps in outlining (central idea, main points, supports, conclusion, introduction, transitions) in terms of what we may call aids to learning. The following aids to learning are of special importance.

**1. AUDIENCE ATTENTION** Psychological research has demonstrated that the more interestingly the information is presented, the more easily it will be learned. This takes us back to the preceding chapter where we discussed audience attention both as an end in itself and as a means to an end. When the end is to inform, the factors of interest become the means to that end.

Some informative speakers seem to take the attitude that they are casting pearls before swine. "It's my job to give this important information," they say, "and it's the listeners' job to get it. If they're too stupid or lazy to get it, so much the worse for them. I refuse to sugar-coat my profound learning." Surely anyone who professes to teach must assume greater responsibility than that; for the speaker has an obligation not merely to his subject but to his audience as well. Therefore the materials should be reasonably interesting as well as accurate. Soundness need not be sacrificed. If the speaker is willing to work hard, accuracy, clarity, and interest can be combined.

The speaker should introduce his subject with materials that contain one or more of the factors of attention. Then he should outline the proposed subject matter, and look it over with an awareness of the tendency of human attention to fluctuate. He should counteract this tendency by choosing a few critical spots, well spaced throughout the speech, where he should insert other attention-getting materials.

**2. AUDIENCE MOTIVATION** The problem of catching and holding attention is closely allied to what is probably the most important aspect of informative speaking, stimulating the audience's wish to be informed. Experienced teachers often suspect that they do not so much teach as motivate their students to learn. The success of any informative talk depends on the speaker's ability to arouse his audience's wish for the information he is giving them.

In delivering an informative talk, do not simply introduce the subject and proceed to develop the main points. As early as possible in your speech try to establish in the audience a want or need to know more about your subject. Then, from time to time during the remainder of the talk, use techniques that will revive this want. There are many ways to do this.

*a. Penalty.* The importance of motivation as an aid to learning is epitomized by the Air Force practice in teaching the men how to pack a parachute: Each man must pack his own! This example illustrates the technique of motivation by the threat of penalty. If you can show that failure to learn what you present will result in a penalty, you have provided motivation to learn. There are many ways to appeal to penalty motivation. For instance, say or imply, "If you don't learn this . . .

> "You will flunk this course.
> "You will be out of date in your conversation.
> "You will endanger your health.
> "You will lose money.
> "You will disappoint your friends or relatives.
> "People will make fun of you."

*b. Reward.* Reward is usually a better type of motivation than penalty because most people respond more willingly to promises than threats. Suppose you are an art student and want to give a talk on color combinations. You might motivate the listeners to learn about the subject if you put your central idea something like this, "Knowledge of color combinations will make you better dressed and better looking." The variety of possible rewards for learning is suggested by the following list. Say or imply, "If you learn about this . . .

> "You will improve your grade in this course.
> "You will win a prize.
> "You may save your life or someone else's.
> "You will make more money.
> "You will become a leader.
> "You will be more popular.
> "You will be healthier.
> "You will increase your enjoyments."

Promise of reward and threat of penalty can often be combined. The traditional schoolroom device for providing motivation is the grading system.

If you learn, you are rewarded by higher grades and honors; if you do not learn, you are penalized with lower grades and failure to be promoted. A fundamental complaint about the grading system is that it is artificial, extraneous to the materials to be learned. Nevertheless, the grading system has increased learning for most students. Psychologists have found that a student's learning has been increased merely by telling him whether he is right or wrong when he is answering a list of questions. Most of us would probably agree, however, that motivation is more desirable when it is an integral part of the subject matter to be learned. A talk on some aspect of traffic laws, driving, or care of an automobile can readily be motivated, for example, with promises of both rewards and penalties.

Motivation to learn about the duties of the United Nations Security Council could not so easily be provided by punishments and rewards. But there are other means of motivation.

*c. Curiosity.* Another way of motivating an audience to learn is by arousing and satisfying curiosity. When a topic is skillfully presented, the audience may be attracted simply to learn for learning's sake. One of the best ways to arouse curiosity is by introducing a question or series of questions into the early part of the talk. For example, a science major opened a classroom talk with these words:

> How hot is the sun? How heavy is it? What are sunspots? How old is the sun? Does the sun really burn? These are some of the questions people have asked me many times. We will answer these questions today.

As we mentioned earlier, you may have to contend with prejudice or resistance to learning. One way of handling this problem is by a tactful and indirect approach. For example, suppose you wanted to explain the nature of communism. You might say, "One of the major purposes of the extensive investigations by the several un-American activities committees is to reveal the nature of communism. These committees have unearthed some interesting evidence. . . ." Then by means of an explanation of the committees' work you could discuss the nature of communism, probably with audience approbation instead of antagonism. A stronger strategy is to turn the motivation around. To refer to the previous example, an informative talk on communism could be motivated by saying, "Ignorance of the Russian system is dangerous to our democratic survival; knowledge of their system will help us defeat them." You might go on to say, "We will study communism as doctors study cancer: not because we admire the disease or because we want to catch it, but because we know that a disease cannot be prevented or cured without understanding what it is, and how it is caused." In this fashion you might persuade your hearers to want to study communism, even though they are prejudiced against it, by arousing their curiosity as to what it really is.

**3. PRESENTATION OF THE UNKNOWN IN TERMS OF THE KNOWN** We learn by experience. Some learning is by direct sensory experience. You learn about colors by seeing them; you learn something about bells by hearing them; you learn one thing about electricity by touching a live wire. On the other hand, some learning is by vicarious experience. You learn about the War between the States by reading history books, by looking at Brady's famed photographs, by hearing stories passed down in your family from an ancestor soldier. Taken together, direct and vicarious experiences constitute your personal stock of information.

New information is given meaning in terms of the information we already have. We use the known to reveal the unknown. For example, if you mentioned the null hypothesis to an audience with little background in statistics, you would receive only blank stares. The audience would never have experienced the phrase before. Suppose you tried to explain the hypothesis by saying, "The null hypothesis assumes that the differences between two sets of data have occurred by chance." Again, no learning would occur, for the audience would understand the individual words, but the total would still be meaningless to them. But if you began by explaining chance in terms of flipping a coin, learning would commence, for you would have established a relationship with the audience's experience. You could further explain and demonstrate with an actual coin that the chances of getting heads twice in two flips are only one out of three, and so on. Furthermore, the chances of flipping ten heads consecutively are mathematically remote. You could have each of two members of the audience flip a coin ten times and record the results. Then you could explain that the best guess would be five heads and five tails by each participant, and that neither set of results should be very far from that guess. In this fashion you could continue your speech with a better hope of clarifying the null hypothesis to the audience.

If you want to explain the energy and heat of the sun to an audience of laymen, there is no use in talking about $3.8 \times 10^{33}$ ergs per second unless you can first relate ergs and powers of ten to the past experiences of the audience. Nor would true learning result from telling them that the sun's surface is probably 6,000 degrees centigrade in temperature. To make the extreme temperature meaningful, state how much hotter 6,000 degrees is than a red-hot stove or the heat required to melt steel. But to state that the sun is too hot to burn would give you no familiar basis to work from; therefore you could not relate that amazing statement to a layman's past experience.

The need to relate information to the listeners' own experience is not confined to technical subjects; it applies to all new materials. The point was wonderfully illustrated by a little boy in Sunday school when the teacher was trying to explain that Moses was "filled with the spirit of the Lord." She asked if the children knew what this meant. Kenneth thought he knew: "He was like Charlie Updale. Charlie's our cheer leader. He's full of school spirit!" The Sunday school teacher may well have noticed that Kenneth's learning justified the teaching methods of Jesus, who so often put his moral principles into parables, saying that the principle "may be likened unto . . ." He presented the unknown in terms of the known.

**4. DEMONSTRATION** Telling is often not enough to insure learning. If someone were to try to tell you with words alone how to tie a dry fly, the process would probably sound like one of the most complex invented by man. However, if he supplemented the telling by showing you the actual materials and demonstrating the process, you would realize that the task is simple.

Armed services training programs and psychological research have highlighted the fact that for certain types of materials the learning process can be tremendously accelerated by use of visual aids or demonstration. Of course, visual aids are effective in talks where the purpose is to entertain, stimulate, or convince. Their most important value, however, is in their contribution to informative talks. It is wise, therefore, to review your outline from the standpoint of the possible use of visual aids. To refresh your memory for details of such possibilities, review pages 100–03. Remember, how-

Speech alone is often not enough. Here TV reporter Carol Reed explains the weather with the aid of a chalkboard map.

Dr. Boris Morkovin and Mrs. Lucelia Moore clarify their points to a group of hard-of-hearing students, using both audio and visual aids.

ever, that visual aids should be appropriate to the subject—they should not be used just for the sake of using them.

### Organization of the informative speech

Suppose you were going to memorize these two word lists:

| | |
|---|---|
| bumper | spygt |
| headlights | goober |
| hood | bixet |
| motor | rokotinget |
| windshield | wuzzi |
| wheel | jafe |
| seats | taba geetis |
| brake | loors |

There are the same number of words and letters in both lists. Nevertheless, you can readily see that it would be much easier to learn the left list than the right. The reason is that the left list is a meaningful group—all the words have meaning because they are parts of a car; the right list has only nonsense words with no unifying theme or principle.

We have all had the experience of studying a problem or a set of materials or a sequence, of reaching a stalemate, and then suddenly of finding that the whole thing clicks into place. This suggests another useful method in planning a speech to inform. Present a meaningful group of details and at the proper moment reveal the principle that relates those details to one another and makes them a pattern. The moment the listener grasps this unifying principle the details all seem to fall into their proper places and the listener has learned.

**1. INTRODUCTION** Since the most frequent criticism of informative talks is that they are too dry, the speaker should open with an attention-getting idea in order to head off an initial response of resignation to boredom. If possible choose an opening attention-getter that also leads into the subject.

The attitude of the audience toward the speaker is also important. If the listeners get the idea that the speaker is poorly qualified to speak on the subject, resistance to learning is created. It may be necessary directly or indirectly to establish your right to speak on the chosen subject.

In leading into the topic, the question of motivation should be carefully considered. At the earliest feasible time you should try to show why the audience wants or needs the information about to be given. Usually this material can best be included in the introduction; sometimes it becomes part of the speech body.

For some subjects, especially technical ones, learning requires that one or more terms be defined before getting into the body of the material. Definitions are a commonly used technique for leading into the subject.

In talks to inform, more than in other types, it is wise to give a preview of the main points. A preview provides the audience with a framework or pattern which, as we have just seen, helps them understand the details. The preview usually comes as part of the transition between introduction and body.

**2. BODY** When a central idea for the informative talk has been chosen, two principles of learning should be held in mind. First, can you present the idea so that the audience will be eager to learn about it? Second, can you develop the idea so that it will take on an easily seen and easily remembered pattern? Choose your main points to form that pattern and phrase them so that the pattern is evident. Parallel phrasing will help, and so will careful progress from the known to the unknown, or a plain arrangement in time or space.

If you will refer back to the list of stock designs on page 132, you will find that the following item numbers are often adaptable to informative speeches:

Even in talks to convince it is necessary to inform. This intercollegiate debater is giving information as a means of proving her arguments.

1, 2, 3, 6, 9, 11, 12, 13, 15, and 19. Of these the time-sequence and space-sequence items are especially useful. The time sequence can provide designs of considerable variety. You can present your points as past, present, future, or subdivisions within one of the three. You can use units of time of any appropriate dimension, ranging from seconds to eons. You can describe a process by time stages from beginning to end, or present historical or biographical materials in chronological order. Your points can move either forward or backward in time.

The space sequence is even more flexible. Depending on the subject matter, you can have your points move from east to west, north to south, outside to inside, left to right, top to bottom, front to rear, corner to corner, clockwise around a circle, zone to zone, city to city, or nation to nation. You can explain the plan of a new campus building by a sequence of points moving from basement to top floor; or describe a battle by moving from one flank to the other along the battle line. The clarity of a space sequence can frequently be increased by maps or diagrams.

The transitions within the speech body are especially important in talks to inform. Transitions indicate how the details belong to the over-all pattern and tell the listener just where you are in the progress of your talk. To be safe, make your transitions obvious; a liberal use of numerals often helps. For example, "Having described the engineering and the tooling, we now come to the third stage in aircraft manufacture, the fabrication of parts." If you do not have a clear transition, you may be talking about fabrication while half the audience thinks you are still talking about tooling.

## Role of information in other speeches

Thus far in this chapter we have centered on the problem of preparing primarily informative speeches. But when other purposes are foremost, giving information becomes a means rather than the end itself.

It is a truism that in trying to convince people of something, it is always necessary to give information in order to prove the arguments. In trying to reinforce attitudes, it is necessary to introduce new facts or opinions as part of the reinforcement process. Even in talks to entertain, as we saw in the last chapter, new materials are essential in getting and holding attention.

Thus presenting new information is a basic process in all public speaking. The suggestions in this chapter apply to the whole talk when the purpose is to inform; they apply to the informational parts of every other type of speech.

## Summary

Three tests of the effectiveness of a speech to inform are: How much information was new to the audience, how much was understood, and how much was remembered?

Effectiveness can be increased and common complaints about speeches to inform can be decreased if the speaker plans, not only in terms of the subject, but also in terms of the audience and of psychological aids to learning.

In adapting an informative talk to an audience, the speaker should consider the listeners' interest, knowledge, and prejudice in relation to the subject matter.

In planning a speech to inform, five aids to learning should be remembered. (1) Learning is aided when materials are presented in attention-getting ways. (2) Learning is aided when the learner is properly motivated. Motivation means that the listener is made to want to learn, usually through threat of penalty, promise of reward, or arousal of intellectual curiosity. (3) Learning is aided when the unknown is presented in terms of the known. (4) Learning is aided when telling is supplemented by showing and demonstrating. (5) Learning is aided when materials are presented in meaningful patterns.

# 15

# REINFORCING AUDIENCE ATTITUDES

### Definition of attitude

Let us review the structure of a good speech outline. At the bottom of the pyramid are the supports which clarify, reinforce, or prove the points or subpoints to which those supports are subordinate. In addition, every support helps arouse attention. Next the points and subpoints clarify, reinforce, or prove, and help attract attention to the central idea. Finally, the central idea accomplishes the over-all speech purpose: to catch and hold favorable attention (entertain), to clarify (inform), to reinforce audience attitudes (stimulate), or to prove (convince). In this chapter we shall study more intensively than heretofore the basic process of reinforcing attitudes.

An attitude may be defined as a predisposition to respond to a given stimulus in one way rather than another. Let us illustrate.

When the starter for a hundred yard dash says, "Ready, on your marks," each runner becomes a picture of a man with an attitude. An observable attitude is revealed by his crouched position, the straight-ahead direction of his eyes, his facial expression, and his whipcord muscular tensions. In addition there are internal responses of his muscles, nerve tissues, and glands that we cannot see. All these behaviors express a readiness to respond to a given stimulus, the sound of the starter's gun. When the gun barks, the runner will respond by springing forward and running rapidly down a marked lane until he crosses the finish line. Theoretically he might respond to the sound of the gun in any of a thousand different ways. For example, he might stand upright and exclaim, "What the devil was that?" But he will actually respond by running down the track and not otherwise. He has a predisposition to respond in one way rather than in another.

But what about ordinary attitudes toward innumerable personal or social problems? The kind of attitudes with which speakers have to deal? A friend inquires, "What's Paul's attitude toward gambling?" You reply, "He's bitterly opposed." Reflection will reveal that Paul's attitude is the same in all fundamental respects as that of the runner. Paul has a predisposition to respond to a given stimulus. What stimulus? Probably almost anything that pertains to gambling: the sight of playing cards or dice, a newspaper story, somebody's remarks about the odds on a prize fight. Such a stimulus will touch off a characteristic response in Paul. He will sense antagonistic thoughts and emotions welling up; he may frown, walk away, give a bit of a sermon on the evils of gambling, write a letter to his newspaper or congressman. He will respond in some such accustomed way rather than by paying no attention, being amused, praising the practice of gambling, or asking for more dope on the fourth at Santa Anita. Paul's response is thus predetermined by his attitude.

Assume that you have an audience of people with attitudes similar to Paul's, that you approve of their attitudes, and that you want to give a speech to reinforce their attitudes. You should begin by choosing a central idea adapted to the purpose, audience, and subject.

UPI

The definition of an attitude is illustrated by dashmen at the start of a race. They "get set," ready to go at the sound of the starter's gun.

## Outlining the speech to reinforce attitudes

### *The central idea*

Usually the central idea in speeches to reinforce attitudes is a strong statement of praise or condemnation. If you and your audience are opposed to gambling, your central idea might be a statement praising a law or proposed law to limit some type of gambling, or praising the anti-gambling program of the audience, or condemning the laxity of law enforcement against gambling in a particular community, or condemning the operations of a nearby race track. Just what you would praise or condemn would depend on the audience and occasion.

Let us take another example. What is your attitude toward Walter P. Reuther, leader of the United Auto Workers union? If you admire him and are to speak to an audience of union members, your central idea might be, "Walter P. Reuther has contributed mightily to the industrial progress of America." But if you detest him and are to speak before members of management, your central idea might be almost the reverse. If your ideas and those of your audience are different, your speech purpose will not be to reinforce attitudes. Reinforcement is appropriate only when speaker and audience are like-minded.

### *Main points and subpoints*

The basic speech design, of course, comprises the points and subpoints of an outline, and should be logically held together. Furthermore, the logic should relate the design to the central idea. In speeches to inform or convince we think of this logic as carrying the audience along toward comprehension or conviction. When we want to reinforce a belief, however, the reasoning comes after the fact; we do not try to instruct or prove, but to justify. Therefore the logic in speeches to stimulate is a form of rationalization. This fact suggests two possible methods.

The first method is to restate for the audience the reasons that led them to their belief. The second is to give them a new set of reasons for the same old belief. In giving the old reasons, it is usually best to state them in vivid though familiar words. They should strike a cherished and familiar chord; the listeners should nod and say to themselves, "That's right," or even break into spontaneous applause. In giving new reasons, a good method is to give the familiar a novel twist; the listener's reaction should be, "Say! That's good. I must remember that."

Giving old ideas a novel twist is illustrated by Bruce Barton's oft-quoted speech, "Which Knew Not Joseph." This speech was delivered before an audience of public-relations executives, and the opening point was as follows:

There are two stories—and neither is new—which I desire to tell you, because they have a direct application to everyone's business. The first concerns a member of my profession, an advertising man, who was in the employ of a circus. It was his function to precede the circus into various communities, distribute tickets to the editor, put up on the barns pictures of the bearded lady and the man-eating snakes, and finally to get in touch with the proprietor of some store and persuade him to purchase the space on either side of the elephant for his advertisement in the parade.

Coming one day to a crossroads town, our friend found that there was only one store. The proprietor did not receive him enthusiastically. "Why should I advertise?" he demanded. "I have been here for twenty years. There isn't a man, woman or child around these parts that doesn't know where I am and what I sell." The advertising man answered very promptly (because in our business if we hesitate we are lost), and he said to the proprietor, pointing across the street, "What is that building over there?" The proprietor answered, "That is the Methodist Episcopal Church." The advertising man said, "How long has that been there?" The proprietor said, "Oh, I don't know; seventy-five years probably." "And *yet,*" exclaimed the advertising man, *"they ring the church bell every Sunday morning."* [1]

Thus Barton took the old idea of the necessity of repeating advertisements, and gave it an unusual slant by comparing it humorously with the ringing of the church bell. Apply this principle of combining the familiar with the novel to our list of stock designs, page 132; you will note that several of them will probably be especially effective for talks to reinforce attitudes, for example, numbers 6, 16, 17, 19, 20, 21, 22.

The phrasing of points in talks to reinforce demands care. The words should be colorful, impressive, and impelling. The audience expects you to tell them what they want to hear but to say it better than they can; to tell them, in Alexander Pope's words, "What oft was thought, but ne'er so well exprest." This fact partly explains the long life of most of our universal quotations, such as sayings of Ben Franklin or memorable passages from Lincoln. It is often effective to include superlatives: the first or last, the best or worst, the greatest or least, the only, the impossible.

## Supports

When the supports are used to reinforce a point they do not have to clarify or prove the point, but only illustrate it, elaborate it, strengthen it, make it more real. Therefore supports should be chosen and worded so as to revive memories and traditions, touch upon aspirations and ideals, or appeal to the sentiments. Supports should be worded vividly and colorfully. Presentation

[1] Homer D. Lindgren, ed., *Modern Speeches,* F. S. Crofts, 1926, pp. 406–07. Reprinted by permission of Bruce Barton.

The speaker at this labor union convention has just called for a show of hands. He had reinforced an attitude in which they already agreed; otherwise he would scarcely have gotten a unanimous response.

Here is a meeting of representatives from management. What would have been the probable response of this audience to the speech given to the labor union? How many hands would have been raised?

can often be dramatic and forceful; too much restraint in wording and delivery may diminish the effectiveness of supports to reinforce existing beliefs.

The anecdote is the most fruitful source of support to reinforce attitudes. A story of the suffering and heroism of a crippled child, for example, will reinforce the layman's attitude toward the March of Dimes more than any scientific exposition or significant table of statistics.

Russell Conwell's lecture "Acres of Diamonds" is one of the most famous American speeches with the purpose to reinforce attitudes; the supports are mostly anecdotes. Here is an example of one of Conwell's stories:

> There was a man living in Pennsylvania, not unlike some Pennsylvanians you have seen, who owned a farm, and he did with that farm just what I should do with a farm if I owned one in Pennsylvania—he sold it. But before he sold it he decided to secure employment collecting coal oil for his cousin, who was in the business in Canada, where they first discovered oil on this continent. They dipped it from the running streams at that early time. So this Pennsylvania farmer wrote to his cousin asking for employment.

> . . .

> His cousin answered, "All right, come on."
> So he sold his farm, according to the county record, for $833. . . . He had scarcely gone from that place before the man who purchased the spot went out to arrange for the watering of the cattle. He found the previous owner had gone out years before and put a plank across the brook back of the barn, edgewise into the surface of the water just a few inches. The purpose of that plank at that sharp angle across the brook was to throw over to the other bank a dreadful-looking scum through which the cattle would not put their noses. But with that plank there to throw it over to one side, the cattle would drink below, and thus that man who had gone to Canada had been himself damming back for twenty-three years a flood of coal oil which the state geologists of Pennsylvania declared to us . . . four years ago . . . to be worth to our state a thousand millions of dollars. The man who owned that territory on which the city of Titusville now stands, and those Pleasantville valleys . . . sold the whole of it for $833.[2]

The second most fruitful source for reinforcing supports is quotations. When the purpose is to stimulate, quote well-tried authorities, acknowledged leaders, and heroes—the Bible, Washington, and Lincoln among others. Look also for appropriate quotations from poetry and drama, Kipling and Shakespeare, for instance.

Cumulated instances are often effective in reinforcing attitudes. They gain

[2] Russell H. Conwell, *Acres of Diamonds*, Harper, 1915, pp. 10–12.

power when comparison or contrast is utilized. Wendell Phillips was a master of this technique, and in his eulogy of Daniel O'Connell he said:

I remember the solemnity of Webster, the grace of Everett, the rhetoric of Choate; I know the eloquence that lay hid in the iron logic of Calhoun; I have melted beneath the magnetism of Sergeant S. Prentiss of Mississippi, who wielded a power few men ever had . . . But I think all of them together never surpassed, and no one of them ever equalled O'Connell.

Explanation, statistics, and visual aids can be used effectively when the main purpose is to reinforce, but they are not so frequently useful as the other forms of support. Explanations should be succinct. Statistics should be simplified and clearly appropriate to the purpose. A college speaker made appropriate use of statistics in a talk condemning our public schools for failure to teach responsible citizenship. He composed a questionnaire, which he administered to a large number of high school students. Questions included items such as, "Who is the representative in Congress from your district?" Simple percentages showing the pupils' ignorance on this and other questions were cited to reinforce an idea that his audience already believed. Visual aids can occasionally be utilized. For example, in a talk to reinforce attitudes toward safe driving, the speaker might show enlarged photographs of a few gruesome smashups.

Returning to more typical materials in speeches to stimulate, consider a classic of American speeches, Senator George Graham Vest's brief "Tribute to the Dog." Notice how Senator Vest reinforced the favorable attitude that most people have about dogs.

The one absolutely unselfish friend that man can have in this selfish world, the one that never deserts him, the one that never proves ungrateful or treacherous is his dog. A man's dog stands by him in prosperity and in poverty, in health and sickness. He will sleep on the cold ground, where the wintry winds blow and the snow drives fiercely, if only he may be near his master's side. He will kiss the hand that has no food to offer; he will lick the wounds and sores that come in encounters with the roughness of the world. He guards the sleep of his pauper master as if he were a prince. When all other friends desert, he remains. When riches take wings, and reputation falls to pieces, he is as constant in his love as the sun in its journey through the heavens.

If fortune drives the master forth an outcast in the world, friendless and homeless, the faithful dog asks no higher privilege than that of accompanying him, to guard him against danger, to fight against his enemies. And when the last scene of all comes, and death takes his master in its embrace and his body is laid away in the cold ground, no matter if all other friends pursue their way, there by the graveside will the noble dog be found, his head between his paws, his eyes sad, but open in alert watchfulness, faithful and true even in death.[3]

[3] Lewis Copeland, ed., *The World's Great Speeches*, Garden City, 1942, p. 651.

## Occasions for talks to reinforce attitudes

There are numerous speaking occasions where it is appropriate and desirable to reinforce attitudes:

| | |
|---|---|
| Keynote speeches for conventions | Reunions |
| Commencement addresses | Good-will talks |
| Eulogies | Political party rallies |
| Commemorations | Sermons |

Pep talks as at salesmen's meetings, football rallies

There are also speeches for special occasions where the purpose is almost always to reinforce attitudes. They are called special simply because the situations require variations from the standard speech designs. Basic types of speeches for special occasions include:

| | |
|---|---|
| Speeches of introduction | Responses |
| Welcomes | Presentations |
| Farewells | Acceptances |

These Los Angeles State College commencement exercises in the Hollywood Bowl provide a typical example of an occasion for speeches to reinforce attitudes.

# Introductions

In introducing a speaker your over-all job is to set the right tone, direct favorable attention toward the speaker, and increase the audience's desire to hear him. This should be accomplished with a minimum of words. The better known the speaker, the shorter the introduction. For example, there is the oft-quoted speech of introduction by Shailer Mathews for Woodrow Wilson: "Ladies and gentlemen: the President."

You should have more information about your speaker than you will actually use in the introduction; you should be in a position to choose from available details those that will best impress the audience and relate the speaker to the occasion. It is worthwhile to consult the speaker beforehand in order to determine the best approach. For example, a speech teacher was asked by two fraternities to speak at their initiation banquets, which were held a week apart. At the first of the banquets the toastmaster introduced him as a professor of speech. The effect of his introduction was to prepare the minds of the audience for a classroom lecture or for a professional orator, and to direct their attention toward the expected finesse of gesture, voice, and language rather than toward the ideas to be discussed. Thus warned, the speaker tactfully advised the toastmaster prior to the second banquet. As a result he was introduced as a member of the faculty who had been active for many years in fraternity work. The second introduction produced favorable and appropriate attention.

Naturally in building favorable attention you say only complimentary things about the speaker. But do not overcompliment or fawn on the speaker, and do not put him on the spot with too much praise. You have doubtless heard introductions that gave the speaker a build-up that no human could live up to.

It is your duty to announce the speaker's topic, but resist the temptation to make a speech about it yourself. On too many occasions the chairman has made a longer speech about the speaker's subject than the speaker himself had prepared. Of course, it is usually desirable to comment briefly on the significance of the topic or to express curiosity about it, but do not try to steal the speaker's thunder.

Speeches of introduction often comprise a wooden listing of vital statistics or professional accomplishments, which the audience may scarcely bother to hear. Try to humanize your remarks and present the speaker as a real person. Give the listener the impression that he is meeting the speaker on an individual and friendly basis.

Sometimes the design of your remarks will require mentioning the speaker's name early. Generally, however, it is more effective to build to a climax by saving the name until the very end of the introduction. When you do give the name, be sure to articulate it with special care.

As you mention the speaker's name in closing your introduction, turn toward him and smile. Step back from the speaker's stand or the center of the stage but remain standing until the speaker has reached his place. It is often wise to lead the applause as he is approaching the stand. Avoid sitting directly behind the speaker during his talk. If possible, place your chair far to one side of the platform or sit in the front row with the rest of the audience. If you must remain in plain view on the platform, discipline yourself to look attentive and appreciative during the speech. Avoid distracting movements and facial expressions.

When the speaker has finished and is returning to his chair, you should lead the applause as you walk back to the rostrum. Sometimes a brief, sincere expression of the audience's appreciation is in order, but usually the chairman's approval can best be expressed by facial expression and general manner.

A different procedure is required when you have to introduce a succeeding speaker. Then you may properly refer to one of the previous speaker's ideas as a transition into your introduction of the next speaker or topic. When several speakers are to be introduced, it becomes the chairman's duty to weld them together into a unified program rather than to give the impression of a series of unrelated speeches.

## Welcomes

The general effect of a speech of welcome should be to make the visiting person or group feel wanted and at home. The welcomer's mood and manner should be cordial, cheerful, and sincere. Tact, taste, and ingenuity are essential. The welcoming talk should be brief—one or two minutes will usually suffice.

1. **INTRODUCTION**  The opening should touch at once on the welcoming theme. The welcome may take the form of a direct statement or may be presented in the form of a quotation or short anecdote. If you are representing a group in extending the welcome, be sure to say so: "On behalf of the university . . ."; or, "I know that I speak for every member of this audience when I say . . ."

2. **BODY**  You have three things to talk about in the body of the welcoming speech: the person or organization being welcomed, the hosts, and the occasion. You should praise all three by describing the achievements of the guests, giving useful information about the hosts, and enhancing the importance of the occasion.

3. CONCLUSION  Restate the welcome in the conclusion. If the guests are gathered for a conference or a convention, predict or wish them success in their deliberations.

## Presentations

There are two principal types of presentations: gifts and awards. The presentation of a gift usually represents a special occasion, such as the presentation of a gift to a retiring employee, or to a colleague whom you are honoring, or to an elderly couple on their golden wedding anniversary. The presentation of awards is usually an annual event such as a competition. The formality of the talk should be regulated by the occasion and the talk should be brief: one to five minutes.

1. INTRODUCTION  The introduction may be confined to a single sentence of greeting, or to a statement of the speaker's purpose. For some awards a brief review of the history or nature of the award may be needed.

2. BODY  In the body of a speech of presentation you may have to talk about the recipient and the gift or award, and sometimes the occasion or the losers. Which of these to emphasize most depends on the situation. In presenting a gift to a colleague in celebration of his twenty-five years of service, for instance, almost the entire talk should be devoted to the recipient—his achievements, abilities, and character. However, in presenting the prizes to winners of an intercollegiate debate tournament, little need be said about the winners; most of the remarks should center upon the awards and the occasion, with suitable praise for the losers.

In praising the winner or recipient, do not overdo your praise—the poor fellow has to respond. If the occasion permits, the compliments to the recipient should be tempered with humor. In discussing the gift or award, do not neglect to consider its possible symbolic value.

3. CONCLUSION  The entire talk should be planned so that the actual presentation of the gift will come as a natural climax. The final words may be those of congratulation.

## Responses

In responding to introductions, welcomes, or presentations the keynote is tact, for the situation in itself creates a difficult dilemma. If the speaker pooh-poohs the praise in the introduction as inaccurate, undeserved, or overdone, he will be insulting the chairman and possibly the whole audience. If he seriously accepts the praise as no more than his just deserts, he brands him-

In presentation talks a natural climax is usually provided by the giving of the award.

self as an egotist. If he attempts to compromise between these extremes, he is in danger of sounding coy or ludicrous. Therefore ways and means must be found to respond with tact, modesty, and gratitude.

**1. INTRODUCTION** Almost always the first sentence must express the sincere personal feelings of the speaker about the praise or the award. These may be feelings of happiness, embarrassment, or confusion. The emotional content rather than the exact wording is the important thing.

Sometimes it is appropriate to relieve the situation with a quick humorous thrust, as when Harry Emerson Fosdick said, "Flattery won't hurt you if you don't inhale," or when Ernest Holmes suddenly broke the tension by referring to the introduction with a twinkle, "Of course all of it was true."

The person who has received an award or who has been welcomed as a guest may be expected to give a full-length speech. If so, his response to the chairman may become the introduction of the speech proper. There are two speeches, of which the response is the first.

**2. BODY** In a response, the most successful plan usually is to reply to praise with praise. You can praise the person, or the organization, or the spirit of the welcome; or you can praise the gift or award, indicating its merit and appropriateness; or with grace you can frequently share the credit for winning the award by praise of your colleagues and co-workers.

**3. CONCLUSION** Restate your appreciation of the honor conferred. This is one speech where you can meaningfully make your last words, "I thank you."

### Role of reinforcing attitudes in other speeches

In this chapter we have been concerned with talks in which the predominant purpose is to stimulate—to reinforce existing attitudes. However, reinforcing attitudes is a basic speech method and should inhere in any talk, no matter what the purpose. When reinforcing attitudes is not an end in itself, it is usually a means to the other speech purposes.

Let us illustrate how reinforcing attitudes is a basic means in talks to entertain, inform, and convince. When the main purpose is to entertain, the reinforcement of existing attitudes or beliefs may be an excellent technique for arousing or holding favorable attention—you will recall that the familiar is one of the factors of getting attention. In talks to inform you will also recall that one basic means is to clarify the new in comparison with the known. Thus the reinforcement of what the listeners already know is frequently a useful technique for adding to their knowledge. The next chapter will show that in attempting to build or change attitudes, one of the fundamental devices is the reinforcement of existing attitudes before relating them to the new attitude that the speaker wants to build. Once again it is a matter of distinguishing between ends and means. Reinforcing attitudes may often be an end in itself. When it is not, it becomes a means rather than an end.

### Summary

An attitude is a predisposition to respond to a given stimulus in a given way. A speaker often has to reinforce existing audience attitudes.

The central idea in speeches to reinforce attitudes is usually a statement of a belief that you and all or most of your audience accept, and that you will usually develop by praising or condemning. The main points and subpoints should be chosen, not to instruct or prove, but to justify the central idea. The most useful forms of support in talks to reinforce attitudes are usually anecdotes and quotations. Supports should revive memories and traditions, touch upon aspirations or ideals, or make a sentimental appeal.

Ordinary speaking occasions where reinforcement of attitudes is appropriate are numerous, and they include keynote speeches, commencement addresses, reunions, and pep talks.

Special speaking occasions where reinforcement of attitudes is appropriate include introductions, welcomes, farewells, responses, presentations, and acceptances. In speeches for special occasions a few variations from standard speech designs are needed.

When the general purpose is to stimulate, the reinforcing of attitudes is an end in itself; when the purpose is to entertain, inform, or convince, the reinforcing of attitudes is a means to the end.

TOPICAL PREVIEW

# 16

# BUILDING AUDIENCE ATTITUDES

### Democracy in action

On the evening of September 26, 1960, more than 70,000,000 Americans, the largest political audience ever known, gathered before television sets and viewed a unique program. John F. Kennedy and Richard M. Nixon met in face-to-face debate. This was the first time in the history of American Presidential campaigns that the leading candidates publicly confronted one another in a direct exchange of their opposing views. Three other Nixon-Kennedy debates were televised during the next few weeks.

The real winner of the debates was democracy. Many Democrats and Republicans were intrigued into hearing both candidates instead of only one; independent voters were given a chance to make side-by-side comparisons of the men and the issues. Both candidates had the courage to put themselves on the spot under pressure, knowing that a single serious slip of the tongue could cost a million votes. Both candidates were calm and restrained despite constant urging from extreme partisans that they "take off their gloves," "quit sparring," or "slug it out" like prize fighters. Both candidates showed quick intelligence, detailed knowledge on dozens of public questions, and speaking competence. These debates could occur only in a democracy, never in a dictatorship.

The effects of the Nixon-Kennedy debates on the outcome of the 1960 election were estimated by many veteran political analysts and by experi-

**The real winner of the Kennedy-Nixon debates was democracy.**

enced public opinion pollsters. The consensus was that the four debates significantly influenced election results in Kennedy's favor. Elmo Roper, respected for his accuracy in measuring public opinion, reported that some 4,000,000 voters made up their minds on the basis of the debates alone; that about 1,000,000 of them voted for Nixon while almost 3,000,000 voted for Kennedy. On the Monday following the election Kennedy said, "It was TV more than anything else that turned the tide."

Nixon and Kennedy were confronted, not only by each other but also by an audience of enormous size and complexity: millions of Democrats and Republicans whose party loyalties ranged from enthusiastic to lukewarm, and millions of independent voters whose minds were not made up. Each man did a remarkably good job in the face of so many pressures and problems. Each man wanted to reinforce the attitudes of those who already believed in him. But a more important speech purpose was to convince—to convince the independent voters and even some of the members of the opposing party. Apparently Kennedy succeeded to a greater extent than Nixon did. Why?

There were, of course, many important factors influencing the results of these debates. From a public speaking standpoint one explanatory factor seemed to be reasonably clear. Kennedy usually focused on the audience; he seemed to be more concerned with presenting a positive program of his own than with criticizing his opponent's program; more concerned with making a favorable personal impression than with forcing his opponent to make a bad one. Nixon often seemed to focus on Kennedy more than on the audience; he spent more time refuting his opponent's proposals than in building up his own. In his opening statement in the first debate Kennedy stressed the theme that "it is time America started moving again." He indicated the main areas and directions in which we should move. Mostly by implication he criticized the Republican administration of the previous eight years—to advocate that we start moving *again* implies that we have not been moving recently. In his reply Nixon opened by agreeing with Kennedy's goals and saying that their only difference was regarding means. This committed him to a defensive position throughout the entire series of debates. Thus the over-all effect was that most of the time Kennedy held the initiative while Nixon was saying in effect, "Yes, but we can do it better." Even in defending the progress made by the previous administration Nixon provided only an anticlimax by agreeing that still more progress needed to be made, thus reminding the audience of Kennedy's theme of "start moving again." On the whole, then, Kennedy usually addressed himself to the audience while Nixon too often addressed himself to Kennedy.

### The meaning of "convince"

To convince means to build an audience attitude.

In the Presidential television debates Nixon and Kennedy argued with each other but neither man imagined that he could convince the other, and neither of them sought to convince the independent voters by arguing against them. Yet in your everyday life you have frequently known people who think that to convince means to have an argument with somebody. And having an argument seems to mean proving that the other fellow's ideas are silly. "I tried to get him to listen to reason," for instance, implies that you are reasonable while he is not. No wonder so many attempts to convince end with one contestant angrily declaring, "I don't care what you say, I still believe I'm right!"

Many people think that the speaker alone is active in convincing and the listener is merely a passive recipient. But check your own experience as a listener. Have you ever said, "My mind was changed for me"? Probably not, but you have said, "I changed my mind." Have you ever changed your mind on an important issue after listening to a persuasive speech? If so, which of the following statements comes closest to expressing your feelings after the speech?

> He convinced me that . . .
> After hearing him I was convinced that . . .
> After thinking it over I became convinced that . . .

The chances are that you "became" convinced. It is even accurate to say, as we have previously seen, that a speaker never convinces anybody—the listener must convince himself. The speaker provides a stimulus, but nothing happens unless the listener responds. The speaker can set the conviction process in motion, but the listener must carry the process through.

## Logic versus psychology

The ordinary American listener is often accused of responding mostly to so-called appeals to emotion. Perhaps we contrast emotional appeals with appeals to reason, but to do so is misleading.

Many people believe that speeches or sections of speeches are either logical or emotional, and that as you increase the proportion of one, you decrease the proportion of the other. Furthermore, many people believe that they can readily tell whether a speech is logical or emotional. The foregoing popular beliefs were tested experimentally by Randall Ruechelle.[1] He asked a large number of listeners and readers to evaluate many speeches, rating the speeches in terms of degrees of logical and emotional appeal. The agreement among the judgments was scarcely greater than would have occurred if the respondents had flipped coins. It is fair to say that the concept of appeals to reason vs. appeals to emotion is practically useless in studying public speaking.

However, the widespread confusion between logic and emotion should not obscure the fact that an important distinction should be made between logic and psychology. Every speech can be evaluated by the question, "Is it logically sound?" as it can also be evaluated by asking, "Is it psychologically sound?" The logical test is used impersonally to judge the speaker's reasoning. The psychological test is used personally to estimate audience response. Both of these ways of judging a speech can be applied to the same materials.

Perhaps the relationship between logic and psychology may be clarified by comparing a speech to a glass of orange juice. The food values of the orange juice are like the logical values of the speech. Food values such as vitamins, calories, and minerals are impersonal; they remain the same even

---

[1] Randall C. Ruechelle, "An Experimental Study of Audience Recognition of Emotional and Intellectual Appeals in Persuasion," *Speech Monographs*, Vol. XXV (March 1958).

though nobody drinks the orange juice. Chemical tests will reveal their presence. However, if someone drinks the orange juice, he evaluates it by its flavor. Reaction to flavor is a personal thing, and may vary among different people. Better flavor does not imply lower food value, for a certain brand of orange juice might be low on both, another brand high on one and low on the other, and a third high on both. The flavor of the drink, then, resembles the psychological values of the speech. Likewise, the logical and psychological soundness of a speech cannot be considered simply on an either-or basis. Orange juice commits no sin by having a pleasing flavor; neither does a speech. Buyers of orange juice should be concerned with both food value and flavor; they want an orange juice that is both nutritious and flavorful. The speech audience asks whether the thought in a speech is logically sound and whether the speech affects them personally. When a speech is successful, the audience should answer yes to both questions.

Especially when the speech purpose is to build audience attitudes the materials in the speech should be evaluated both logically and psychologically. This double test should be applied to the introduction, body, and conclusion, as well as to the central idea, main points, subpoints, supports, and transitions. The entire speech should be logically and psychologically valid.

**Logical validity**

None of your listeners will change his mind if he thinks your ideas are illogical. You may go through a sophisticated stage of life, during which you think that people are irrational, that they would not recognize good logic if they heard it, and that they can be moved only by emotion. If you do think this way, you had better not let your listeners know that you do! Your listeners, like you, think they make their decisions on logical grounds. Be sure that your ideas will withstand the impersonal tests of logic.

In a talk to convince, the central idea is usually stated in the form of a proposition. The main points, subpoints, and supports should all prove the proposition. Logical support of a proposition can be considered under two headings: evidence and reasoning.

## Evidence

Evidence is anything known to be true. Reasoning is the process of drawing inferences from evidence. Therefore you begin with evidence and end with a conclusion. Reasoning is the process by which you get from the one to the other. For example, the house next door has been vacant and for sale. You observe one day that the realtor's sign has been removed, and that a stranger is mowing and watering the lawn. A neighbor tells you she saw the same stranger looking at the property last week. Now you have three pieces of evidence. First, you infer that the probable reason for the removal of the sign is that the house is no longer for sale. Second, you infer that the probable cause of the stranger's visit last week was to view the property for the purpose of deciding to buy. Third, you infer that his care of the lawn probably means he is getting ready to move in. You reach the conclusion that the stranger has bought the house.

The conclusion reached in the illustration may seem obvious and inevitable. But suppose the realtor's sign had not been removed at all, but had merely been shifted from the lawn to the porch, where you could not see it. Suppose the neighbor had been mistaken and had seen someone else visit the house last week. And suppose the stranger was a gardener who had been hired to keep the lawn attractive pending a sale. It is clear therefore that the soundness of your conclusion depends on the truth of the evidence and the validity of your inferences.

**1. KINDS OF EVIDENCE** Evidence may be classified in several ways. One useful way is to distinguish between facts and opinions. Facts can be defined as objects or events directly verifiable by the senses; that is, you must directly observe them. An opinion, on the other hand, is a fact that is reported by language. The key difference, therefore, lies in the human element. Whenever a direct observation becomes a report of something, some degree of interpretation necessarily takes place; hence it is always to some degree an opinion.[2]

Factual evidence is uncommon in public speeches; it is mostly confined to visual aids. If you show the audience an oil painting, you are presenting factual evidence; if you describe it for them, you are presenting testimonial evidence. Avoiding unnecessary subtleties, however, we can include as facts the recalling of matters that the listener has directly experienced in his past. If you say that the city hall is white and the listener has himself seen the city hall, it is sensible to consider the evidence as fact, even though it is only a statement and the actual city hall is not in the immediate view of the audience.

All evidence, however, has its hazards, even direct sensory evidence. The magician presents direct sensory evidence, yet the whole audience is fooled. Several witnesses see the same accident, yet give contradictory testimony in

---

[2] There are, of course, many definitions of these terms as, for example, the legal, philosophical, or psychological. However, the present definition is basic to human communication; for further discussion see: F. S. C. Northrop, *The Logic of Sciences and the Humanities* (Macmillan, 1949), pp. 39 ff.

court. Probably the chief reason for differences is that we tend to observe what we expect or want rather than what *is*. A professor, for example, noticed a student walking down the hall in the direction of his office. He quietly fell in step just behind her. Reaching the office door, the student knocked. "Come in," said the professor. She opened the door and was nonplused to find an empty room. She had heard what she expected to hear.

Most evidence in speeches is opinion, that is, testimonial evidence, either the testimony of the speaker or of someone quoted by the speaker. Of course, all testimonial evidence should be traceable to someone's actual observation. However, there is bound to be some difference between an observed fact and a reported fact, as the report of anything observed will be colored by the observer. Two people might observe a goldfish swimming in a bowl. The observed facts would be the same, but their two reports of what they saw would be different. And if the goldfish were also able to submit a report . . .

The hazards of testimonial evidence are greater than those of factual evidence because people differ not only in what they perceive, but even more in what they remember and in the ways they narrate it. The unreliability of memories was known even before Freud came along with his theories of how we tend to forget the unpleasant. The confusion that often results when several people try to tell about the same idea was discussed in Chapter 11 in connection with the difficulties of language.

In fact, the hazards of evidence are theoretically so numerous and so great that it is somewhat surprising to find how well people get along in actual practice. We get along because, consciously or unconsciously, most of us apply a few tests to the validity or truth of the evidence we hear. When a speaker undertakes to influence other people's attitudes, it is his obligation to test the truth of his proposed evidence systematically and rigorously. It is also to his advantage to do so.

**2. TESTS OF AUTHORITY** Since most public speaking evidence is testimonial, the qualifications of the authorities used in a speech become of critical importance. An authority is the person or persons responsible for the truth of a given piece of evidence. Sometimes a speaker himself is the authority; frequently, however, a speaker quotes somebody else. The qualifications of authorities can be tested by applying these three questions:

1. Is the authority competent?
2. Is the authority biased?
3. Is the evidence of the authority consistent?

*a. Competence.* The competence of an authority must, of course, be evaluated in the light of the particular evidence for which he is responsible.

Walter Cronkite, one of our most respected TV journalists, often gives extemporaneous, on-the-spot accounts of significant public events. He is respected because the people believe him to be competent, unbiased, and consistent.

CBS

For example, we should immediately ask if this particular evidence requires an expert. If you were giving a speech on cancer research, for example, and you wanted to introduce evidence on the efficacy of radiology treatments, a layman's opinion would not be competent, nor even the testimony of a general practitioner. The authority should be a specialist. In the same speech, however, if you wanted to introduce evidence showing the devastating effects of cancer on a victim's relatives, the testimony of an unskilled laborer impoverished by his wife's illness would be competent.

In a speech on cancer research, if you are a college student, you have to rely on other authorities for most of your evidence. It would be unnecessary and impractical, however, for you to document every fact and opinion in the talk. You, the speaker, can be responsible for the truth of some of your evidence. In general, you can be responsible for evidence that conforms closely with general public knowledge and human experience. For example, you might say, "More than 220,000 people die of cancer each year in the United States," or, "Cancer strikes on an average in one of every two homes." Probably most listeners would consider you competent to report such evidence without explaining the exact source of the figures, for it is widely known that cancer takes a staggering toll.

*b. Bias.* The question of bias is the second test of an authority. You can usually classify available authorities as probably biased in favor of or against your subject, or as probably unbiased. An authority who is prejudiced in favor of your proposal should be used with caution. It is better for you to eliminate a dubious authority than to have your audience reject him. The probability of truth is increased not only when an authority is unbiased, but also when an authority testifies *against* his apparent prejudices. For example, suppose you were discussing the proposition, "Should Musicians Be Unionized?" The national president of the American Federation of Musicians would quite naturally be biased in favor of unionization. To quote him on that side of the question would carry little weight. However, if an accurate quotation from him against some aspect of unionization could be found, the qualification of the authority would be high. Meanwhile, evidence from the United States Bureau of Labor Statistics would probably be considered an unbiased source.

*c. Consistency.* The third test is consistency. Is the authority consistent with himself? Is he consistent with other authorities? Is he consistent with ordinary human experience? If a senator's statement of yesterday contradicts a statement he made last year, or contradicts his voting record on relevant bills, his qualifications as an authority are impaired. When a fact or opinion seems to contradict common knowledge, the authority must be scrutinized carefully—if you do not do it, your audience will.

On most controversial subjects, however, well-known leaders and even unbiased experts are likely to contradict one another. In a sense that is what makes a subject controversial. When authorities disagree, the issue must be settled by weighing comparative probabilities and making choices. Of two sets of evidence, which is more extensive, more pertinent, more reliable? In answering such questions, both the speaker and the listeners will be assisted by applying the tests of competency, bias, and consistency.

## Reasoning

The logical validity of a proposition involves the speaker's reasoning as well as his evidence. The ability to reason accurately from the evidence is probably the most important single characteristic of an effective speaker.

Psychologists are not unanimous in their definitions of reasoning. One definition is that reasoning is mental experiment in which symbols are substituted for real objects or events. An example from Galileo is often cited to illustrate the definition. In Galileo's day it was thought that a heavier object would fall faster than a lighter one. Galileo reflected that if two bricks of equal size and weight were dropped side by side, they should fall at the same velocity. If they were attached together, doubling their weight, should the two bricks fall twice as fast? Galileo reasoned no. Then he experimented by dropping objects from the tower of Pisa, and found that attached bricks fell at the same velocity as separate ones. His mental experiments were verified.

Reasoning has also been described as the detection of relationships. In the example of Galileo the reasoning could be called a symbolic comparison of probable relationships between weight and velocity.

**1. INDUCTIVE REASONING** Inductive reasoning is usually defined as the thought process in which reasoning moves from the specific to the general. If the evidence indicates that this case, this case, and this case are true, you reason that in consequence a general principle is true. However, the validity of inductive reasoning requires checking. For example, since Washington, Adams, Jefferson, Madison, and every other President of the United States were all men, you can reason inductively that all our Presidents have been men. However, you cannot conclude that American Presidents must be men or that all of them in the future will be men. If many municipally owned electrical companies charge lower rates than many privately owned companies, you can reason inductively that municipally owned companies on the average charge lower rates than privately owned companies. But can you conclude that all municipally owned plants are cheaper than all privately owned ones? Or that cheapness of rates is not offset by differences in quality of service, or taxes?

**2. DEDUCTIVE REASONING** Deductive reasoning is defined as the thought process in which reasoning moves from the general to the specific. If one general principle is true of certain instances, the general principle must apply to similar instances. Aristotle invented the syllogism to express and to test the deductive type of reasoning. A syllogism contains three terms: the major premise, the minor premise, and the conclusion. A standard example:

> All men are mortal (major premise).
> Socrates is a man (minor premise).
> Therefore, Socrates is mortal (conclusion).

For two thousand years the syllogism dominated logic, but in recent years it has been subjected to criticism. In light of modern criticism of the syllogism it seems fair to say that a mastery of the syllogism is unnecessary for beginning students of speech. Instead, in practice two tests can be applied. First, if you introduce a general principle, is it actually true or accepted as true? Second, is your specific case relevant to the general principle? The answers to both questions are matters of common sense.

**3. REASONING BY ANALOGY** Analogy is a thought process in which reasoning moves from the specific to the specific, or from the general to the general, by comparing or contrasting two items or concepts. The conclusion depends on whether the resemblances outweigh the differences, or the reverse. There are two types of analogies. First there is the literal analogy. You compare the municipal services, say, of city *X*, which adopted a city manager plan of government, with those of city *Y*, which did not. This may be used as a proof, the validity of which will depend on whether *X* and *Y* are sufficiently similar in all relevant respects. Second, there is the figurative analogy. A student speaker condemned modern advertising on the ground that it reveals only one side of the story, and illustrated his point by holding up a wooden box, which he praised in advertising lingo. Having "sold" the box, the speaker turned it around so that the audience could see that the back of the box had been crushed. Another student who spoke immediately afterward, gave a rebuttal: "Advertisers must sell more than one piece of merchandise. Suppose you had bought this box. After finding the broken side, would you ever buy another one? Not from *this* advertiser!" Thus the second student turned the analogy around by pointing out a difference that the first speaker had failed to see. Figurative analogies are almost always open to such attacks and should usually be used only to illustrate, not to prove.

**4. CAUSAL REASONING** Causal reasoning is similar to analogy in that the thought process moves from the specific to the specific, or from the general to the general. You reason from cause to effect when you say, "If this law is passed, taxes will rise." You reason from effect to cause when you say, "Where there's smoke, there's fire." Probably the most common abuse of causal reasoning is the fallacy known as *post hoc, ergo propter hoc* (after this, therefore because of this). Just because one thing follows another does not necessarily mean that the first causes the second. Superstitions, for example, illustrate the *post hoc* error: A black cat crosses your path and an hour later you break your wrist watch; *ergo*, the black cat was the cause of your bad luck.

The foregoing kinds of reasoning can be used by the student either while planning the structure of a speech or while testing the validity of the first draft of the outline. In planning or testing the logic of a speech, pay particular attention to the transitions. Transitions show relationships and, as we have seen, relationships are the heart of reasoning.

## Psychological validity

Your evidence and reasoning may be sound, yet you may put your audience to sleep, or antagonize them. To build a new audience attitude you must relate your evidence and reasoning to the listeners' drives, motives, or existing attitudes.

Mild emotions, such as moods and feelings, are always with us—they are part of being alive. Occasionally our moods or feelings flare up into anger, fear, grief, or joy. If emotions do not become too intense, they may reinforce our beliefs and actions. But intense emotions disorganize our behavior, and are likely to boomerang against a speaker who plays upon them. For example, during World War II a speaker appealing for blood donations illustrated his talk with films showing closeups (with sound) of rough surgery being performed near a battle front. The films aroused intense emotions. Some members of the audience turned their eyes and held their ears, some were nauseated, two or three fainted. The result was that these intense emotions prevented many of the listeners from giving blood.

Intense audience emotions are difficult to arouse, unnecessary, undesirable, and sometimes disastrous in speeches to build attitudes. Milder emotions are usually helpful, but should be considered by-products by a speaker. Ordinary audience emotions will take care of themselves if the speaker can relate his proposal to drives, motives, and existing attitudes.

## Drives

Drives set people in motion. Consider the hunger drive. When you need food, the internal stimuli of hunger drive you to action. If you were hungry in a completely strange environment, you would be driven to indulge in random exploratory activity until food was found.

There are, however, only a few drives. Psychologists have not agreed on the exact number, but following is a generally accepted list of basic drives: hunger, thirst, sex, fatigue, sleepiness, exploration, visceral tensions (as of bladder or bowels), and internal reactions to pain, heat, and cold. Drives are about the same for everyone. They are a common denominator of human behavior.

We learn through drives to satisfy our most basic needs, because drives determine the direction of hundreds of attitudes and habits. For example, imagine that somehow all your drives were suddenly reversed. Instead of approaching food, you would avoid it; instead of avoiding hot objects, you would seize them; and instead of withdrawing from approaching traffic, you would step in front of it. What would happen? You would soon be dead.

In times of distress or disaster, demagogues and other public speakers can appeal directly to drives, since when in distress we drop our civilized trappings and react more obviously in direct response to our drives. Witness, for example, the lying, fighting, and cheating in connection with food rationing during World War II; or the stampedes that occur in buildings that catch on fire; or the riots in communities stricken by famine or drought.

In normal times, however, the influence of drives is only indirectly observable, and appeals to drives should be made only indirectly by public speakers. For instance, members of an ordinary audience are seldom starving through an inability to secure food, so a direct appeal to the hunger drive by a speaker would usually be absurd. However, a speech favoring a new irrigation dam might indirectly appeal to audience drives because of the promise of avoiding future possible food shortages or flood disasters. Therefore an understanding of our biological drives is important to the speaker, because drives are the foundation upon which we build, through learning, a vast structure of motives and attitudes.

## Motives

Motives may be described as learned responses by which drives are likely to be satisfied. Making money, for example, is a motive. We learn during childhood that money can be used to satisfy the hunger drive, among others. Therefore, we work eight hours a day, motivated mainly by the desire to make money.

STANDARD OIL

This is an annual stockholders' meeting, Standard Oil Company (N. J.). The speaker is trying to build attitudes. What motives should he stress for this audience?

Motives are learned, but people vary in their learning capacities and opportunities. Because motives are learned and because each drive may be satisfied in many different ways, each individual acquires numerous motives. Because people are different and their environments are different, motives vary from one person to another and from one social grouping to another. Despite the fact that motives vary greatly among individuals, a basic list of motives common in our society follows.

1. To make money
2. To be healthy
3. To avoid danger
4. To be attractive to the opposite sex
5. To get married
6. To beget and rear children
7. To care for one's parents
8. To have friends and companions
9. To enjoy physical comforts
10. To gain social approval
11. To conform to customs and traditions
12. To have personal freedom
13. To maintain self-respect
14. To have a clear conscience and peace of mind
15. To satisfy curiosity
16. To have adventures
17. To compete successfully against other people
18. To help other people
19. To have a worthwhile religion
20. To achieve ideals

The foregoing list or a similar one is essential in planning a talk to build attitudes. Decide upon the attitude you want to encourage in your listeners, and ask yourself, "Will my proposal make or save money for my audience? Will it keep them healthy? Will it protect them from danger?" And proceed to work through the list of motives. Unless the answer is "yes" on one or more of these questions, you might as well not give the talk.

The use of the list of motives just given requires judgment on the speaker's part. The list does not include all possible motives, and some of the motives listed overlap or fuse. Furthermore, one motive may move one person but not another. In planning a talk, however, the speaker must consider how to relate his proposition, his points, and his supports to motives existing in his particular audience on this particular subject at this particular time and occasion.

## Attitudes

Having considered motives, you should make the next step in planning and testing the psychological strength of your speech to relate your proposal to particular audience attitudes. Three types of attitudes should be studied: attitudes toward your topic, toward related topics, and toward you.

**1. ATTITUDES TOWARD THE TOPIC** When your purpose is to build new audience attitudes, it is important to estimate the probable attitudes toward your topic before the speech is given. Ideally you would give your audience an attitude test when preparing your speech, and each member would mark a ballot such as this:

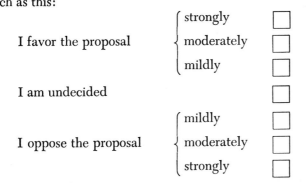

I favor the proposal
- strongly ☐
- moderately ☐
- mildly ☐

I am undecided ☐

I oppose the proposal
- mildly ☐
- moderately ☐
- strongly ☐

Of course, a direct administration of ballots to a prospective audience is seldom practical. Sometimes, however, you can estimate the attitudes by sounding out several representative members of the audience beforehand. If direct inquiry is impractical, estimate the probable distribution of attitudes from indirect evidence, such as common traits and interests. Who are these people: Catholics, Republicans, Boy Scouts, war veterans, college students, Negroes, home owners, Rotarians, unionists, farmers, or members of the Benevolent and Protective Order of Elks? A good guess can be made of the attitudes of almost any group on almost any speech proposal.[3]

Having estimated existing audience attitudes toward your proposal, if you and some of the audience are at odds, consider how to change their attitudes. Ideally you would supplement your pre-speech attitude test with a post-speech test using a ballot such as this:

I favor the proposal
- more than before ☐
- about the same ☐
- less than before ☐

[3] See Chapter 12.

| | | |
|---|---|---|
| I am undecided | | ☐ |
| | less than before | ☐ |
| I oppose the proposal | about the same | ☐ |
| | more than before | ☐ |

Let us reiterate that pre- and post-tests need not actually be given in order to apply the principle. You can imagine that the ballots were given. The advantage of ballots, real or imaginary, is that you can see them or visualize them, and by making the principle specific and concrete you can understand the process of building attitudes. By contrast, you may have only a vague abstract idea if you think in general of the process of building attitudes, because there are usually no observable behaviors when a person is changing his mind or being convinced. As we have shown, then, when your purpose is to convince, you first state your purpose in terms of building attitudes, and then visualize that purpose in terms of shifts of opinion.

**2. ATTITUDES TOWARD RELATED TOPICS**  The audience's attitudes toward related topics are as important as their attitudes toward your particular pro-

In talks to convince delivery should emphasize sincerity, friendliness, tact, and thoughtfulness. Madame Pandit exemplifies these qualities.

WIDE WORLD

posal. New attitudes are never built in a vacuum; they are built upon or added to old attitudes. Suppose your listener already holds beliefs A, B, and C. You try to get him to agree that if (or since) A, B, and C are true, therefore D (proposed new belief) must also be true. Or likewise, if (or since) A, B, and C are not true, therefore (negatively) D must be true.

The role of attitudes toward related topics is especially crucial when the attitude toward your proposal is undecided. On important controversial questions, "undecided" almost always means "conflicting," for the listener has one or more related attitudes predisposing him in favor of your proposition and one or more pulling him in another direction, in a sort of internal tug of war. For example, according to the leading pollsters on the eve of the Presidential election of 1960 a segment of American voters was still undecided. For most of them this did not mean that they were neutral, nor that they were apathetic. It meant that they were torn between conflicting attitudes. Some disliked Nixon but thought highly of Eisenhower's administration. Some were enthusiastic about Kennedy but feared he was too young. Some liked both candidates but were fearful of the men surrounding both. Some favored the foreign policies of one of the parties but disliked its domestic policies. Thus you can see that indecision is likely to be an active, dynamic and even painful state. Furthermore, it is not enough merely to say,

But compare this photograph with the one on the opposite page.

UPI

"He is undecided because of a conflict in his attitudes." The additional question is, "*what* attitudes?" If you can figure those out, you are well on your way to planning the best psychological approach.

When, however, your audience consists mainly of opposed, rather than undecided, listeners, your vital need becomes finding an opening wedge. Related attitudes can provide that wedge. Your listener, for example, may strongly oppose socialized medicine and vehemently denounce mixing politics with medical care. But wait a moment! What are his attitudes toward the work of the Public Health Service? Toward county nurses? Toward the nearby state hospital? Toward the city's department of sanitation? These and other agencies provide samples of government-controlled medical care. Since he is likely to approve of some of these, you can use that approval as an opening wedge against his initial resistance to your argument.

**3. ATTITUDES TOWARD THE SPEAKER**  The check list (on page 235) of possible attitudes toward a speaker is of particular importance when his purpose is to convince. In a nutshell the issue is: Will you as a person arouse approval or resistance in your listeners? Approval may be defined as an attitude of a listener that predisposes him to accept almost anything the speaker says. Resistance is the predisposition to reject. A speaker's prestige actually derives from an attitude within the listener.

The speaker provides the stimulus that sets the audience attitudes into operation. The stimulus may be any known aspect of the speaker: his physique, voice, dress, reputation, age, sex, or race. Approval or resistance involves a dynamic relationship between listener and speaker. For example, your age may be a source of approval with a younger audience, or a source of resistance with an older group. If you are a college student twenty years old, you may be looked up to as an authority by high school students of fifteen, but you may be regarded as a young whippersnapper by businessmen of fifty. Increase or decrease the speaker's age, or the audience's age, and the attitudes of approval or resistance will probably vary accordingly.

### Outlining the speech to build attitudes

Planning and testing your speech in terms of logical and psychological validity does not mean that you should abandon the six-step procedure for outlining.[4] In speeches to build attitudes, however, as you follow the six steps, you should test your outline in two ways: (1) *Analyze* the points, supports, and transitions from the standpoints of evidence and reasoning; and (2) *adapt* the points, supports, and transitions to the drives, motives, and

[4] See Chapters 7 and 8.

existing attitudes of the particular audience. During the remainder of this chapter we shall see how the principles of logical and psychological validity can be applied to speech outlining.

## The design

You begin the organization of your speech by choosing the central idea and main points. Two approaches to the choice of central idea and main points in speeches to convince will be called the direct and indirect approaches. The *direct* approach may be characterized as follows:

1. You state the attitude you favor early in the talk.
2. You preview your reasons.
3. You prove your contentions forthrightly by evidence and reasoning.
4. You rely on support featuring expert authorities and statistics.
5. Your delivery is straight from the shoulder and forceful.

The *indirect* approach has been described by Benjamin Franklin:

The way to convince another is to state your case moderately and accurately. Then scratch your head, or shake it a little and say that is the way it seems to you, but that of course you may be mistaken about it; which causes your listener to receive what you have to say, and as like as not, turn about and try to convince you of it, since you are in doubt. But if you go at him in a tone of positiveness and arrogance you only make an opponent of him.

Contrast the indirect approach with the direct. Which is better? It depends on your audience and your subject. In some circumstances the direct approach may be received as arrogant, as Franklin suggests, but under other circumstances the indirect approach may be condemned as pussyfooting or appeasement.

It is well to follow the rule that to argue directly with an opponent not only fails to convince him, but usually antagonizes him. However, you may be willing to antagonize your opponents in order to influence third parties. That is, the direct approach may be preferable when most of your listeners are undecided, while only a few are opposed. You sacrifice a few votes in order to gain many.

On the whole, however, the indirect approach recommended by Benjamin Franklin is more frequently useful than direct argument. The indirect approach is suggested for speeches in which you are talking to people whose attitudes you seek to change. Indirect arguments for such audiences is your only hope. Check your own experience against this assertion. Can you recollect any "knock-'em-down and drag-'em-out" argument with anybody in which you actually conceded that you were wrong and shifted over to your opponent's point of view? More likely you got angry and defended your original position, right or wrong.

Between these two extremes are many choices, combining in varying degrees the direct and indirect approaches. A study of the transcripts of the Kennedy-Nixon debates of 1960 shows a combination of approaches. Because of the debate situation they were forced to use direct arguments with each other, but when they addressed the voter public both Kennedy and Nixon tended to use more moderate appeals. Both candidates realized the risk in antagonizing undecided voters.

1. THE DESIGN FOR DIRECT ARGUMENT One useful method for building a direct argument is by applying an appropriate stock speech design. As suggested in Chapter 7, a stock speech design is a pattern of points that is applicable to many different subjects. A direct argument either for or against many proposals can often be adapted from a stock design that has four key words: need, desirability, practicality, and alternatives. This design implies a comparison between the speaker's proposal and the *status quo*—the existing system or attitude. One way of elaborating this design is as follows:

I. Is there a need for a change?
   A. Are there existing or threatened evils?
   B. Are these evils due to the present system?
II. Is the proposed change desirable?
   A. Will it eliminate or alleviate the evils?
   B. Will it provide additional advantages?
   C. Will it avoid new or greater evils?
III. Is the proposal practical?
   A. Can it be satisfactorily financed and administered?
   B. Will it satisfy interest groups involved?
   C. Have similar systems succeeded in the past?
IV. Is the proposal better than possible alternatives?
   A. Is it more desirable?
   B. Is it more practical?

The foregoing design can help you build a direct argument that is both logically and psychologically sound. The first step in using the design is to apply logical analysis to the proposal. If you are proposing that the United States should adopt a policy of free trade, you begin by analyzing the present tariff policy or *status quo*, asking yourself if there is a need for a change from the present policy. You jot down a list of evils or dangers resulting from the tariff policy. These are your potential subpoints under "need." The analysis is of the subject matter without reference to any particular audience.

Using the stock design to guide your thinking, you continue to analyze tariffs and free trade until you have gone through the entire list of questions. The list protects you against the danger of overlooking any important logical points. In fact, you are likely to conclude your analysis by finding that you have listed too many points and subpoints for a single speech.

The second step in using the stock design is to adapt it psychologically to your particular audience. From the list of possible points and subpoints just compiled, choose some and word them in terms of audience drives, motives, and existing attitudes. For instance, you would hardly say to an audience, "The lack of adequate traffic supervision on our main highway has introduced many existing and threatened evils." You would translate the point into audience language, and "existing evils" would become, "At least one auto accident has occurred on our main highway since we began our meeting an hour ago." And "threatened evils" would become, "When you next take your family for a drive on our main highway, you may become one of the twenty-five people a day who . . ."

In the foregoing fashion you plan a design that meets the impersonal tests of logic, and you then translate it into points and language that will be interesting, clear, and impelling. Review these points early in your speech so your listeners will be able to see the whole pattern and feel that it is a logical one. They can then follow you step by step as you develop each argument.

**2. THE DESIGN FOR INDIRECT ARGUMENT**    One of the most useful stock designs for an indirect argument is that of problem-solution. One way of elaborating this design is as follows:

I. Analysis of problem
   A. Is there a serious problem?
   B. What is the nature of the problem?
   C. What are its causes?
   D. What are the obstacles to its solution?
II. Finding a solution
   A. What are the possible solutions?
   B. By what criteria should solutions be evaluated?
   C. How do the several possible solutions compare in terms of these criteria?
   D. What should be the final choice?

Notice that this design applies regardless of whether you plan to speak for or against a given proposal, and that you can use the design in the same way described for direct argument—that is, analyze and adapt. Analyze in terms of subject matter; then translate into terms of audience motivation.

The problem-solution design leads to a speech outline that will give you at least a fighting chance to change an opponent's mind. You begin with what John Dewey has called "a felt need," which occurs when some drive or motive has been thwarted. You help the listener analyze this thwarting and help him to review the ways of satisfying his thwarted drives. Then you suggest criteria drawn from his existing knowledge and beliefs, and help him apply these criteria to two or more of the possible solutions. If you are successful, the listener will himself have built a new attitude that will replace his former one.

## Supports

After choosing main points and subpoints in accordance with the designs suggested for direct and indirect argument, supports for the points must be found.

The bare statement of a point is rarely enough to insure that all the listeners will understand clearly and accurately. They may read in a meaning different from what you intend. Therefore it is sometimes necessary to clarify a point as a preliminary to proving it.

As it has already been pointed out, an indispensable technique in attitude-building is the establishment of relationships between old and proposed new attitudes. It is often wise to reinforce an existing attitude before going on to relate it to the new proposal.

However, the characteristic role of the supports in talks to convince is to prove. You can employ explanation, description, and anecdotes to prove, but more frequently you need instances, statistics, and quotations. Logically, those supports are chosen that best fit this formula: If these supports are true, therefore, the point must be true. Psychologically, those supports are chosen that relate most closely to the listeners' existing knowledge and beliefs.

Suppose, for example, that you are planning a talk favoring national health insurance and that one of your main points is that our present system of medical care is financially unfair. You might begin the support with a brief explanation to clarify the phrase "present system of medical care." Then you might give a description of a person's reactions to the receipt of a devastating doctor bill, in order to reinforce the audience's unfavorable attitude toward anything that is unfair. Next you might relate an anecdote that would reinforce the distaste for anything unfair, and in addition begin the proof by establishing at least one case of unfairness in paying the doctor bills. "But this is not an *exceptional* case," you would say by way of introducing a series of brief instances that are definitely intended as proof of unfairness. "In fact," you continue, "this sort of unfairness is typical of our whole nation. Just look at these statistics that were recently compiled by such-and-such highly reliable agency." The statistics, of course, are also cited as proof. "Finally," you say, "let me quote Dr. Richard Ek," and you establish Dr. Richard Ek as qualified and unbiased, quoting him as saying that the present system is financially unfair. The quotation concludes your proof.

If the anecdote, the instances, the statistics, and the quotation are all true, it follows that the point must be true. However, some listeners may not be convinced of the soundness of your argument, for supports prove the point *only for the listeners who think so.*

What makes them think so? Relationship to their own previous experiences. That is why anecdotes are so often accepted as proof. Logically, an anecdote is poor proof. But it is easier to relate anecdotes than statistics, for example, to the listeners' past experience. Choose your proofs logically but also choose them psychologically. Look for supports that will be "true" to the listeners' experience.

For an example of an effective attempt to tie a point of view to the listeners' experience, study the following opening of an address by Oscar Ewing, a Federal Security Administrator who was in favor of national health insurance. This speech, on a problem that has continued in the public eye for many years, was broadcast over a national hookup to a large and heterogeneous audience.

Good evening. I want to talk to you tonight, not about the nation's health, but about your own health. Suppose that tomorrow morning, you should become suddenly ill—seriously ill. Suppose you found that you needed an operation, with special medical care, and all kinds of x-rays and drugs. Suppose you had to stop working for some months while you went through your operation and your convalescence. Suppose the doctor's bill, the hospital bill, and bills for special laboratory services and medicines, added up to hundreds of dollars—maybe even thousands. Would you be able to afford it?

If you are like most other people in this country, I can tell you the answer just as quickly as you would tell it to me if I were sitting there in the room beside you. The answer, for most of us, is one word: No.

Most of us are neither very rich nor very poor. People who are very rich don't need to worry about their medical bills, any more than they need to worry about whatever other bills they run up. On the other hand, people who are very poor do generally get medical treatment in the United States, because we have charity care which does make doctors and hospitals available to the real needy. But, if you are like the majority of Americans, you are somewhere between those two extremes. You've got a job. You've got your self-respect. And you like to stand on your own two feet. But you're not made of money; and when sickness strikes, when you wake up one morning with acute appendicitis, or when your old folks get sick, or when your child comes home from school restless and feverish, you have two worries—your first worry is that they should get the best treatment in town; and your second worry is how you're going to pay for it.

If you have ever been lying in a hospital bed after an operation worrying about where the money to pay the bills would come from, you know what I mean. If you have had to go to a loan company and borrow money to pay a hospital bill, you know what I mean. If you have ever received a note from your child's school, telling you that your little boy or your little girl needs adenoids or tonsils out, and wondered how you'd pay for it, you know what I mean. If your wife has noticed a lump in her breast, but puts off going to the doctor because of the cost, you'll know—and she'll know—what I mean.[5]

Notice that Mr. Ewing's hypothetical anecdote and descriptions provided excellent probability that many listeners would find similarities to their own personal experiences. Also notice that in less than three minutes Mr. Ewing touched on at least seven motives. Can you spot them?

### The introduction

The importance of the opening portion of a talk to build attitudes is illustrated by your own experiences in listening to other people. Suppose you are opposed to national health insurance and a public speaker is trying to persuade you to change your mind. His chances for success are likely to be made or broken within the first minutes of his talk. If the opening is dull, your mind will wander to other matters and he will be defeated by competing stimuli. If you feel a personal dislike for the speaker, you will actively resist accepting his ideas—"I wouldn't like him even if he was good." If you decide that the speaker is poorly informed or biased on the subject of health insurance, you set up a mental barrier against what he is about to say. If the opening words are, "I intend to speak tonight in favor of socialized medicine," the speaker puts you on guard, in the position of being his opponent, and you immediately set out to find rebuttals to all his coming arguments.

On the other hand, if the opening is interesting, if the speaker is likable and has prestige, and if he begins with some aspect of the subject with which you can agree, then he may be able to get you to change your attitude toward his proposal. For an example of an effective introduction in a talk to build attitudes we may refer back to Mr. Oscar Ewing's remarks just quoted. All three functions of a good opening were fulfilled.

Study especially how he led into his subject. Mr. Ewing was defending the unpopular side of a controversial question, so he sought to begin on common ground—a most important fact to remember about introductions to talks

[5] Harold F. Harding, ed., *The Age of Danger: Major Speeches on American Problems,* Random House, 1952, pp. 350–51. Reprinted by permission of Oscar Ewing.

to convince.[6] Mr. Ewing did not mention the words "national health insurance" nor directly touch on anything with which most listeners could disagree. Could you raise several hundreds or even thousands of dollars right now? Of course you couldn't. If you were sick, would you worry about the doctor bill? Of course you would. Do you want to protect the health of your children, that of the old folks, and of your wife? Of course you do.

## The conclusion

The most common way of closing an attitude-building talk is a summary, followed by a restatement of the belief you have tried to establish. However, you may be trying not only to build an attitude, but also to release the attitude. If so, additional processes and techniques must be considered. These additional considerations may influence the whole structure of the speech; they drastically influence the speech conclusion.

### Summary

To convince means to build audience attitudes. Fundamentally, listeners must always build their own attitudes; however, a speaker can provide the audience with reasons and motives for building an attitude.

In a speech to build attitudes the materials should be evaluated from both the logical and the psychological points of view. The logical is in terms of the subject matter; the psychological is in terms of audience response. Each speech or part of a speech should be judged from both points of view, not from the either-or point of view.

Logical validity involves evidence and reasoning. Evidence is anything which can be found to be true by the senses; reasoning is the process of drawing inferences from evidence. The major types of evidence are facts and opinions. The major types of reasoning are inductive, deductive, causal, and reasoning by analogy.

Psychological validity involves drives, motives, and existing audience attitudes. The speaker should avoid confusing *emotion* with *motivation*. Existing attitudes include attitudes toward your topic, toward related topics, and toward you.

In outlining talks to build attitudes there are two basic designs, the indirect and the direct. The indirect design is usually better when talking with persons whose attitudes are opposed to yours. The direct design is usually better when arguing before persons whose attitudes are neutral or undecided. A basic suggestion is to look for common ground.

[6] For a discussion of the common-ground principle see Chapter 12.

TOPICAL PREVIEW

# 17

## RELEASING AUDIENCE ATTITUDES

### "Let's all sing!"

In 1928 a psychology student attended a revival meeting led by Aimee Semple McPherson, a world-famous woman evangelist who founded her own church and attracted many thousands of converts. The psychology student went to study crowd behavior, and later wrote a paper detailing his observations.

One had to go early to get a seat, although the auditorium accommodated several thousand persons. While the congregation waited for the services to begin, they were entertained by music from a pipe organ, orchestra, choir, and male quartet. The quartet sang a number making fun of the devil, which had the crowd laughing heartily. Time passed swiftly.

Then came Aimee Semple McPherson. A spotlight followed her from the side entrance as she walked smiling to the center of the stage—a strikingly handsome woman, tall, well proportioned, and with auburn hair. She wore a long, flowing white gown. Her first words were, "Let's all sing!"

All sang. She led them. Most of the songs were lively. In one song she had all the men whistle the chorus; in another she had the whole audience clap hands to emphasize the tempo. In between the hymns she talked *with* —not *at*—the people. "How many of you folks are visiting here in California?" she asked. "Stand up so we can welcome you." Many people stood and smiled while others applauded. She asked other questions to be answered by raising hands or standing. One that probably had special significance for the corps of ushers and other assistants was, "How many of you are visiting our church for the first time? Stand up and let us welcome you here!" After a while it seemed natural and easy to raise hands, or stand up, or participate in other active ways.

Then came the sermon. She had a husky, appealing voice and a dramatic manner. The sermon was sprinkled with vivid illustrations. She stressed again and again that you must repent and be saved. She stressed the dangers of waiting too long—you might be stricken by an auto accident on your way home this very night!

Then came the conclusion. "All those who love Jesus," she commanded, "stand up." Everybody stood. Then she said something the psychology student did not quite comprehend. He was thinking about it when most of the congregation suddenly sat down—apparently the regular members had understood the statement. Those left standing were prospective converts and she was now pleading directly with the prospects to come to the altar. The stu-

Aimee Semple McPherson, evangelist, was a master of the art of releasing audience attitudes. Her techniques to stimulate an audience and to get response from them are well worth studying.

WIDE WORLD

dent sat down. Meanwhile, many people were making their way down the aisles. The congregation began to sing some old revival hymns, such as "Almost Persuaded."

Aimee Semple McPherson concentrated on the group kneeling at the rail. Many people repented that night; many rose from their knees rejoicing; many joined the church. The meeting illustrated with almost brutal simplicity the mechanics of releasing audience attitudes.

## Releasing attitudes

Let us think of attitudes in terms of stimulus and response. Any act by a speaker or listener can be described as a stimulus or response or both. Generally, however, the voice, language, and bodily actions of a speaker are considered stimuli, while the thoughts, emotions, and overt acts of the listeners are considered responses. As we have seen, communication is a two-way process, and stimuli and responses are reciprocal. Thus the speaker tells a joke (stimulus), and the audience laughs (response). But the audience laughter is also a stimulus. It stimulates the speaker, and members of the audience, by laughing, stimulate one another.

As we have recently learned, some stimuli are internal (hunger), and others are external (sight of food). Stimuli are also classed as directly sensory (sound of crashing thunder), and as symbolic (sound of spoken words).

Responses may also be classified as internal or external, directly sensory or symbolic. In addition, responses may be described as preparatory (watering of mouth) or consummatory (eating food). Applying this classification to attitudes, you will see that your attitude toward Russia is predominantly internal, symbolic, and preparatory. By contrast, the act of casting a vote in an election is external, directly sensory, and consummatory.

An attitude is a response; your attitude toward Russia is a response to various stimuli. An attitude is also a predisposition to further response; your attitude toward Russia will influence the way you vote on certain issues. Furthermore, the attitude itself may be considered a preparatory response; what you do as a result of an attitude may be called the consummatory response. Diagrammatically the sequence is like this:

A. *Stimulus*

↓

B. *Preparatory response*

↕

C. *Stimulus*

↓

D. *Consummatory response*

Let us put the foregoing sequence into the form of a concrete illustration. To eliminate subtleties suppose we utilize a common type of radio-TV program.

A. *Stimulus:* Pleasant sights and sounds, such as dancing and music, together with words of praise for the name of a product

B. *Preparatory response:* A favorable attitude toward the product—a predisposition to respond to a stimulus in one way rather than another, in other words, a predisposition to buy the product

C. *Stimulus:* "Go to your telephone *now* and call Richmond 4-2311. We will send you a Deluxe vacuum cleaner absolutely *free* for ten days. And if you are among the first twenty-five to call we will . . ."

D. *Consummatory response:* You call Richmond 4-2311.

## Relation to speech purposes

Some writers consider the release of attitudes as a fifth major speech purpose: to actuate. However, the arousal of overt actions as a response to a speech may be a part of the purpose in any talk: laughter or applause (to entertain); actual performance of a manual skill or passing a written examination (to inform); voting, signing, or buying (to convince or stimulate). In fact, it would be difficult to imagine any release of attitudes in a speech that was not preceded by entertaining, informing, convincing, or stimulating. The release of attitudes, therefore, may more readily be studied as a *part* of any of the four basic speech types.

## Immediate versus delayed release

Sometimes a speaker is trying to release an attitude immediately, as by calling for a vote at the conclusion of a speech at a club meeting. However, an immediate response may not be practical. If it is not, the speaker may try to release the attitude at a specific future time. For example, he may say, "And so next Tuesday when you go to your polling place be sure to vote for Sarracino for councilman"; or, "Go to your Red Cross blood-donor station tomorrow." That speaker is trying to get what we may call a delayed release.

## Techniques for releasing attitudes

### Reinforcement

Very seldom does a speaker try to release an attitude in his very first words. You have doubtless attended a meeting where most of the audience sat in the rear of the room, leaving the front rows vacant. The chairman may have decided to ask the audience to move forward. If the chairman simply walked to the rostrum and bluntly said, "Will the people in the back of the room please fill those front rows?" he may or may not have got results. His chances for success would have been increased if he had preceded his request with a few remarks reinforcing the attitude that it would be better for all concerned if the audience sat nearer the speaker.

The first step then in releasing an attitude is to get the audience in the right mood. A listener has hundreds of attitudes but he can be aware of them only one at a time. The speaker must focus the listener's attention on the proper attitude before trying to release it.

## Clarity

It is frustrating to hear a speech that gets us into a mood for action only to have the speaker conclude weakly that "something ought to be done," or "let us all firmly resolve." It is also confusing to have the speaker call for an action that we do not clearly understand; we want to act but don't know exactly what to do. Therefore, another technique for releasing attitudes is to make the audience understand exactly what they are expected to do.

One method of accomplishing this step is to describe what they are to do in concrete terms; tell them specifically when and how they are to act. Make the picture unmistakably clear. Examples:

> The ushers will pass among you with pledge slips. We ask *everyone* to take one of these slips. Take one whether or not you are able to contribute, etc.

> The wording of this resolution is complex. Do not allow that complexity to confuse the issue. When this resolution is put, vote *No*.

> When you go to the polling place next Tuesday, you will receive your ballot. In the privacy of a curtained booth, you will cast your vote. Look for Proposition Four—and mark that proposition *Yes*. I repeat—*Yes* on *Four*.

## Stimulus

When you know that a listener has formed an attitude, when you are sure he knows what action is expected of him, and when you sense that he is in the mood to act, then is the time to provide the releasing stimulus. Timing is often of critical importance, but there is no formula to tell you when. An innocent remark at the wrong moment can wreck a perfect buildup. Suppose you are giving what you hope is the final pep talk to a prospective pledge for your fraternity. You feel sure that he has a favorable attitude toward your house; he knows what is expected of him to become a pledge; you are trying to create the right mood. Just as you have arrived at the psychological moment, in strolls an insensitive brother who yawns and says to your prospect, "Well, didjuh git registered today?" The magic moment is ruined.

A releasing stimulus can theoretically be anything—the howl of sirens for an air raid drill, for example. In public speaking situations, of course, a stimulus is usually verbal. Ask the audience to do something; suggest that they do it; predict they will do it; command them to do it. For example:

> And so, with deep confidence, I call upon the citizens of the state of Arkansas to assist in bringing to an immediate end all interference with the law and its processes.
> DWIGHT D. EISENHOWER

> I hope you will vote for the Price amendment.
> WILLIAM L. DAWSON

> Give us the tools, and we will finish the job.
> WINSTON CHURCHILL

> No organization ever had a greater opportunity to do a greater service for America. No organization was ever better suited or better equipped to do the job. I know the Legion. I know what a tremendous force for good it can be. Now go to it.
> HARRY S. TRUMAN

## Response

If you can get your listener to start the action you desire, he will usually go ahead with the remaining steps. It is something like opening a jar of olives— if you can get the first one out, the rest come easily. The same principle also applies when dealing with a group—if you can get one or two people to respond to your stimulus, the others are likely to follow the lead.

In releasing attitudes, therefore, it is a good rule to make the first step easy. Notice how Aimee Semple McPherson made it easy for people to raise their hands or stand up. Notice how advertisers say, "Just visit our great display of secondhand cars tonight. We don't ask you to buy—just come and look at them." Notice how political workers offer to provide transportation of voters to the polls.

Before a group, the speaker can sometimes provide the impetus for action himself. Opening a Liberty Bond Drive in World War I, for example, Woodrow Wilson publicly bought a fifty-dollar bond and challenged the people to match it.

If your cause is just, and if your speech has been well received, you can be certain that at least a few members of the audience will respond immediately and enthusiastically. If a few contribute, you can be sure that others will also. The sight and sound of others responding is a powerful stimulus in releasing attitudes.

Of course, no speaker can rightfully or safely call for an immediate and public response from his listeners unless he is sure that the requested action is reasonable and morally right. On the other hand, a speaker neglects his duty if he permits a worthy cause to die because of inertia. People like to build strong attitudes, based on evidence, reasoning, and decent motives, and they welcome the leader who will show them how to turn their beliefs into worthwhile actions.

## Summary

Sometimes a speaker's job is to build an audience attitude, or to reinforce one. Occasionally the speaker is expected also to release an attitude into overt action. He may want to secure either an immediate response or a delayed response. For either the methods are the same.

There are four ways of increasing your effectiveness in the releasing of audience attitudes: (1) Reinforce the attitude to be released. (2) Be sure the expected response is clearly understood. (3) Provide the releasing stimulus. (4) Make sure of a prompt response by one or more members of the audience.

# PART FIVE

# DEVELOPING A PHILOSOPHY OF SPEECH

*Principles of responsible speechmaking are as old as civilization and as new as tomorrow.*

The success of any forum, ancient or modern, is always dependent upon the ability of men to speak knowledgeably, responsibly, and communicatively.

PHOTO RESEARCHERS

TOPICAL PREVIEW

I The speaker

II The nature of personality

III As others see you

    A First impressions

    B Lasting impressions

    C General versus detailed impressions

    D Seeing yourself as others see you

IV As you see yourself

    A Misevaluations

    B Insights

V Personality pattern

VI Improving a personality pattern

    A Adding details

    B Omitting details

    C Changing details

    D Consistency of details

VII Summary

# 18

## THE SPEAKER'S PERSONALITY

---

### The speaker

It is impossible to dissociate the speech from the speaker. What you say, how you say it, and what you are so fuse together that they can be separated only in imagination for purposes of study. Therefore we are interested not only in the speaking a person does, but equally in the person himself.

The close and reciprocal relationship between speaking and the person who speaks is illustrated by the derivation of the word *person*, the root word of *personality*. *Person* derives from the Latin *per* meaning through, and *sonare* meaning to speak. Originally the word applied to the masks worn by actors; inside each mask was a megaphone for the actor to speak through. Modern psychologists still stress this relationship: Speech is an important part of personality, and personality is an important part of speech.

Speaking is done by the whole person or personality. When about to give a class talk, you do not simply put on your mouth, carry it to the platform, and say, "All right, mouth, you're on your own now." Your mouth does not speak, you speak.

But no two persons are alike; the average man is but a statistic. When two persons memorize and deliver the same speech, the effects are always different. Therefore we must consider different-personalities-speaking. Naturally you will focus upon the most important one—you.

## The nature of personality

What does the word *personality* mean to you? How do you use the term? In daily conversations you commonly make such remarks as:

"What a magnetic personality!"

"He sure has lots of personality."

"She has everything—beauty, brains, and personality."

"His trouble is he has no personality."

"Her personality leaves me cold."

Therefore you judge the other fellow's personality by his effect on you; and, of course, he judges your personality by your effect on him. According to this view, then, personality is what other people think you are. Psychologists express this definition as your social stimulus value.

The above viewpoint is a popular one, but it has been justly criticized as superficial. Is personality something you can turn on or off like an electric light? If so, the flashing smile, the ready compliment, and the "charm school" manner are all you need to improve your personality. Most of us, however, would agree that personality goes beyond the surface. Should other people be the sole judges of your personality? Other people may be deceived; in fact, some of them must be wrong, since some like you and some dislike you. Furthermore, you say you admire a person who chooses to be himself despite what other people think. According to this view, then, personality is what you think you are. Psychologists express this definition as your conscious responses to yourself and your environment.

However, objections can be raised against this analysis too. True, other people's impressions of you may vary, but your idea of yourself varies also. On one day and in one situation you may sincerely think of yourself as interesting, sophisticated, and quite able to control your own destiny; on another day in another situation your honest opinion of yourself may be the opposite. Also some of your behaviors are rooted beneath the level of consciousness, as the psychoanalysts have often demonstrated. Therefore personality is not just what others think, nor just what you think, but what you actually are. In an effort to express this last definition, most psychologists now define personality as the patterned, organized total of an individual's physical, intellectual, and emotional characteristics.

Thus in a sense there are three "you's": what others think you are, what you think you are, and what you actually are. All three of you have enrolled in this speech class. What can speech training do for any one of you? Certainly, speech training cannot be expected to change your basic personality. However, speech training can help you to improve your personality in two ways. First, you can learn to evaluate yourself more objectively. Second, you can learn to reveal your attractive qualities more effectively to other people. One unusual feature of a speech course is that it is perfectly all right to practice being an effective person.

## As others see you

You are walking down the street and you meet a friend who introduces you to his companion. You acknowledge the introduction in the customary way and pause to chat for a few moments. You talk about the weather or other conventional topics. Then you resume your walk. Now you encounter another friend who also introduces you to his companion. You respond again to the introduction; you again chat about the weather. You have now made two new acquaintances in almost exactly the same way. It is perfectly possible that your reaction to one might be, "There's a person I'd like to know better"; and to the other, "I don't like that fellow." You might, of course, have practically no response—you wouldn't recognize the second fellow if you met him again the next day.

### First impressions

How is it that you can have such strong and diverse reactions? Upon what do you base judgment? Well, you may be influenced by the feel of a hand-shake. Otherwise, all you have to go on is another person's appearance and voice! You may be impressed by his physique, dress, posture, directness of eyes, facial expression, or gestures. You may be impressed by the loudness or pitch of his voice or his rate of speaking, by his articulation or pronunciation. Upon such limited impressions you first react to other people, and they to you.

Suppose you check your own first impressions of an individual against the first impressions he has made on others. You may be surprised to discover that while you strongly dislike the individual, all your friends like him, which probably indicates that you have some prejudice, peculiar to yourself, that has been touched off by something in that particular individual's appearance or voice. Such reactions are usually unconscious. Perhaps, as a child, you disliked someone who happened to have prominent ears, and now you dislike anyone with prominent ears without realizing why.

Most of the time, however, your first impressions of any individual are much the same as the first impressions others have. There are many characteristics of voice and appearance upon which there is widespread agreement. For example, most of us respond favorably to a person with an attractive and spontaneous smile, unfavorably to one whose smile seems forced, sickly, or overdone.

## Lasting impressions

We have been talking about first impressions. First impressions may be lasting ones, or they may change when you come to know the person in question. What are these additional bases for judgment? The most important is what he talks about. From this we judge his intelligence, background, range of interests, and knowledge. We also judge him by the friends he has, his reputation, or anything else that indicates what other people think of him. We judge him by what he does and how he does it, whether or not he is a good dancer, swimmer, tennis player, or bridge partner. Such specific criteria, however, are often simply extensions of the general criteria mentioned above.

From the foregoing analysis of the bases on which we judge and are judged by others in daily life, it is easy to see why public speaking can be viewed as personality in action. We reveal and judge personality in public speaking

Speech is personality in action. You form your first impressions of a speaker's personality by his physique, dress, posture, directness of eyes, facial expression, and gestures. Discuss the personality of Edward Steichen, famous photographer, as revealed in these candids.

exactly as we do in other social situations. The difference is that usually in public speaking the process is condensed and intensified.

When we meet a public speaker for the first time, we form first impressions based on his appearance and voice. We form strong visual impressions before he utters his first word and we react to his voice and articulation before becoming consciously aware of the ideas he is trying to communicate. These first impressions may either be strengthened or modified as he continues to speak.

Later impressions are based on what he talks about, what other listeners think about him, and sometimes his non-speaking behaviors. (For example, how does he behave while sitting on the platform after his speech?)

## General versus detailed impressions

When you meet somebody, whether at a street corner or at a public lecture, you receive an indefinite number of stimuli. If they were broken down into

the minutest detail, the number of such stimuli would be too great for you to describe. Of necessity you must condense them into general impressions. Your general impressions may reflect the combined impact of innumerable details, each of which carries about the same weight as any of the others; however, sometimes your whole general impression is influenced by one or two details that seem to you to stand out. You do not stop to analyze the relative effects of details; you simply form general impressions. In public speaking as in all other social intercourse it is the general impression that counts.

Hardly any of your future listeners, in class or elsewhere, will be speech experts. They will not systematically analyze the several aspects of the content of your speech or its delivery. For example, in a recent political campaign, following an important nationwide address by one of the candidates, a TV station conducted man-on-the-street interviews asking, "What did you think of the speech?" Nobody responded by criticizing the speaker's posture, facial expression, gestures, voice, articulation, organization of points, forms of support, or vocabulary. Instead, everybody criticized in general terms. Those who were favorably impressed called the speech "moving," "sincere," "straightforward," "powerful," and the like. Those who were unfavorably impressed called the speech "corny," "evasive," "weak," or "inadequate." These responses illustrate the type of briefly stated general impressions with which your future listeners will give their judgments of you.

### Seeing yourself as others see you

To get an actual sampling of your impressions on others, a class project is suggested in the Appendix, page 413. Here a ballot is recommended by which every member of the group can record his general reactions to the personality of every other member.

The ballot provides first for a rating of the total effectiveness of the speech and speaker, ranging on a five-step scale from "almost completely effective" to "almost completely ineffective."

Next there is a list of general impressions, some of which are likely to be applicable to every speaker. This list is constructed to demonstrate a useful personality concept, namely, that desirable characteristics shade off into undesirable ones in either direction: too much as well as too little. You must remember that the human tendency to overdo a good thing may turn your greatest strength into your greatest weakness. For example, there was a student who as a freshman had a most appealing smile. By the time he was a sophomore he had become aware of its appeal, and with his awareness, the appeal vanished. One term there was a student in a speech class who was considerably older than his classmates. He was proud of his poise and assurance on the platform. The classmates considered the poise and assurance intolerable condescension. Some of the varieties of "too little and too much" were demonstrated recently by a talk given by one of the writer's advanced students. She chose several of the traits in the following list, and showed right and wrong ways of expressing each. That she was able to give her audience many different general impressions is suggested by the candid shots on pages 342–43.

Study the list and use it to analyze the personalities of some of your acquaintances and friends—or enemies.

| *Too little* | *About right* | *Too much* |
| --- | --- | --- |
| aloof | friendly | fawning |
| colorless | animated | showing off |
| insincere | sincere | fanatical |
| nervous | confident | arrogant |
| ill at ease | poised | condescending |
| tactless | courteous | oily |
| listless | alert | tense |
| weak | forceful | bombastic |
| grim | humorous | clownish |
| poorly informed | knows the subject | displays his knowledge |
| fumbling | fluent | gushy |
| passive | enthusiastic | boisterous |
| evasive | direct | fixed stare |
| empty-headed | thoughtful | ponderous |
| dogmatic | open-minded | vacillating |
| banal | original | eccentric |

The ballot also provides for the recording of additional impressions not covered by the foregoing list.

If your class undertakes this project, you will have a set of ballots reflecting your social stimulus value for your classmates. To a considerable extent you will be able to see yourself as others see you.

**As you see yourself**

*Misevaluations*

There is the possibility that you may tend to overevaluate yourself. Do you go on the defensive every time you hear a negative criticism? Do you refuse to believe such criticisms, dismissing them as mistakes or evidence of jealousies of the listeners? Do you rationalize them, always finding excuses

Too little.               Too much.

or favorable explanations? More subtly, do you admit one or two minor faults in order to prove your objectivity and thus justify your rejection of the more serious criticisms?

Then, on the other hand, there is the possibility that you tend to under-value yourself. Do you feel generally inferior? Do you accept every negative criticism as simply another proof of the fact that you are not much good? Do you refuse all compliments as undeserved? Do you think you are being truly honest with yourself, truly objective in dismissing compliments and accepting criticism? The chances are that you are nothing of the sort.

## Insights

Between these two extremes lies the possibility that you can look at yourself with considerable insight. You know that you have your good points and your weak ones. You can accept praise without becoming either swell-headed or coy, and accept blame without becoming either despondent or defensive. You recognize, both intellectually and emotionally, that to plan your own improvement you must understand yourself accurately and objectively. For the moment let us assume that you are able to maintain this attitude as you analyze the class ballots after you have made a speech.

First ask yourself: "Is this a representative cross section of my social

These camera shots show an advanced speech student demonstrating to a class some differences in personality.

**About right.**

stimulus value? How does the class poll compare with all other information I have regarding the impressions I make on other people? Is there anything unusual in my relations with this group as contrasted with other groups?"

Your second question: "Is the general trend of the ballots favorable or unfavorable?" The ballots are not identical. However, you can readily find items about which there is agreement by several listeners, perhaps even by a majority. Look for such "clusters." You can also strike an average of the rating-scale judgments of the total effectiveness of the speech.[1]

Your third question: "Do I agree with the trends?" Do you think you have been undervalued? Overvalued? Or do you think the listeners have checked the wrong items? Or do you find that the trend of the ballots agrees approximately with your own self-evaluation? Do these outside opinions cause you to modify your previous estimate of yourself?

Your fourth question: "What are the exceptions?" We have been thinking about the clusters of agreement; now let us think about items that have been checked by only one or a few of the listeners. How much scattering of comments is there? For example, on the rating scale, do the judgments range

---

[1] On the rating scale a *one* indicates highest effectiveness, a *five* indicates lowest effectiveness. If you had twenty ballots, half of them marked *three,* a fourth of them marked *two,* and the remaining fourth *four,* the arithmetical average would be *three.*

all up and down the scale? In the listing of general impressions, have a great variety of different items been given? As you consider the variety do you find that the impressions listed, even though different, tend to be consistent? For example, you can be friendly, animated, and sincere all at the same time. Or do some of the items checked by one listener flatly contradict those by another? For example, do some think you are aloof while others think you are friendly? Compare the male judgments of you with the female. Do there seem to be any consistent differences?

There is, of course, no hard and fast rule for interpreting scattered responses on the ballots. However, if your effectiveness ratings spread about evenly over three or four or even all five categories, that spread may suggest that some of the aspects of your speaking are contradicted by others. The same possibility is suggested if your ballots show inconsistent trait clusters.

### Personality pattern

As we pointed out in defining personality, many psychologists stress that personality must be viewed as an organized whole or pattern. This concept seems to be amply supported by both theory and practical tests.

All of us tend to see things as wholes or patterns. Suppose you put three dots on a chalkboard or sheet of paper like this:

•
•   •

What do you see? Not just three unrelated dots, but a triangle. When you go to a moving picture, you see people and things in motion, although you know, of course, that actually you are seeing a succession of still shots. The same phenomenon is true, not only of the visual but of all our sensory impressions. You can supply innumerable examples from your own daily observations.

Apply this principle to speech and personality. We have already noted that when you meet another person you summarize countless details about him into a few general impressions. These impressions are not simple sums of a number of items. They are combinations rather than sums, patterns rather than lists. Within the pattern you see in an individual you will emphasize certain details and disregard others. The important practical implication follows that in order to change the predominant pattern, the person does not have to change all the details. In fact, it is possible by changing one detail to alter the pattern of a hundred.

In trying to evaluate your own personality with the help of the class ballots, you will try to see yourself, not as a bundle of static traits or unrelated behaviors, but as an organized whole. You will realize that the innumerable details of your thought, emotion, voice, language, and bodily action are perceived as a few patterned general impressions. What are your basic personality patterns?

### Improving a personality pattern

Your personality is determined by your fundamental attitudes and values—your philosophy of life—plus your inherited physique, temperament, and intelligence. Around these you have gradually woven a pattern of numberless behavior details. How can you improve on this pattern?

## Adding details

There was a student who was basically an energetic, enthusiastic person but who had never learned to use bodily movement and gesture skillfully. On the platform, he seemed about to explode. He constantly jiggled, fidgeted, and made all sorts of abortive little gestures. He improved his personality pattern immensely by learning how to release that pent-up energy into purposeful bodily action.

Another student who was intelligent and hard-working nevertheless gave the impression of being only loosely informed on any subject. As a classmate said, "That guy knows more than anyone else in here, but he doesn't know anything for sure." The general impression the student gave was improved after he had learned systematic research methods, because he had gained assurance and showed it.

A girl gave the impression of being drab and colorless. Then she learned to smile when addressing the audience, and some of the drabness immediately disappeared. Next, she learned to choose subjects about which she was enthusiastic, and her natural enthusiasm, which had been previously hidden, began to be revealed through her facial animation. Her total effectiveness as a person shifted from mousy to lively.

All three of the students just described improved their personality patterns by *adding* details.

## Outlining details

Sometimes a speaker's total effectiveness is spoiled by one small but intensely irritating detail. A common example is the habit of vocalizing every pause with "and-uh."

One student, a sincere and excellent speaker, impressed many people as supercilious or haughty. It took a while for his instructor to discover the reason: The student had the habit of frequently cocking one eyebrow. This was so subtly done that it would seldom be noticed as a separate item, but its elimination proved that this one small mannerism could change the total impression of the student's personality.

There were two coeds who reduced their personal appeal because of their habits of laughter. One coed had a high-pitched giggle, the other a deep masculine-sounding honk. Both girls were unaware of how frequently and inappropriately they laughed; both were unaware of how distasteful the sounds were to others. It took time and hard work, but both coeds succeeded in eliminating the offending laughter, and by doing so, both succeeded in greatly improving their impressions upon other people. By omitting the one detail, the whole personality seemed different.

## Changing details

Sometimes details need to be changed, and many can be. Some of them are shadowy, hard to detect; others are obvious; and still others so blatant one can only wonder why they have not been changed long before. For example, among educated people we expect a minimum of expressions such as "ain't," "et," or "have saw." However pleasant a student's personality may be, his use of such locutions will make an unpleasant impression. Even one misuse of "lie-lay" can make an audience wince. So a little bit of change in English usage can often produce a great deal of change in total effectiveness.

Likewise, there should be a minimum of mispronunciations, such as "git," "jist," and "ketch." These are careless errors, and if they are sprinkled too liberally throughout your speech, you are likely to give other people the impression that you are a careless person, although you may not actually *be* a careless person.

There was a student who liked to gesture, but he used only a chopping motion with his right hand. He constantly chopped all through a talk. For some auditors the gesturing was mildly irritating; for others it was comical. Yet the speaker was essentially a friendly, serious, and thoughtful person. By enlarging his repertory of gestures, he vastly improved the general impression he made on his audiences.

A businessman taking a night class was criticized as bombastic. Actually he was not bombastic, but his voice was extraordinarily loud. As soon as he learned to control the loudness, he no longer seemed bombastic.

## Consistency of details

In the three preceding sections all the examples were of students with behavior details that departed from conventional norms. Anything you do which is markedly different from the way most other people do it, may attract unfavorable attention. And as we have seen, unfavorable effects are not always confined to the detail itself; a single detail may alter the effect of the pattern as a whole. Usually, your effectiveness is reduced by mannerisms other people consider eccentric.

However, if everything you do is completely conventional, your personality will become uninteresting, colorless, lacking in distinction. Therefore it is important to remember that eccentric behavior does not always produce unfavorable impressions, but may even improve the total effect. Mistakes are often virtues; faults can be very engaging.

Will Rogers was one of the best loved (and highest paid) speakers of his generation. He chewed gum when he talked, hesitated, made interminable waits, scratched his head, paused to grin in seeming embarrassment, mispronounced words—did everything wrong; yet the total result was the revelation of a charming and lovable personality. Will Rogers' variations from the rules revealed his individuality; his faults were his salvation. Perhaps in advising you, "Never say *ain't*," we should add, "well, hardly ever."

Immediately, however, we must stress that for *you* to adopt Will Rogers' mannerisms would prove disastrous. One speaker's meat is another's poison. For example, Winston Churchill's speaking rate is much slower than the accepted average, while a rapid-fire newscaster's is much faster. Both men are effective speakers, but try to imagine Churchill speaking as rapidly as a newscaster, or vice versa! It might be more interesting to imagine either or both of them speaking at the average rate!

Why is it that the same behavior can be bad for one speaker and good for another? The answer is that for one the detail fits in with the total personality pattern; for the other it does not. The ultimate test is consistency.

For example, when Colonel John Glenn returned from his pioneering space flight he was honored by an invitation to address a joint session of Congress. Such sessions are usually quite formal and are reserved for high-ranking foreign dignitaries or the like. Colonel Glenn appreciated these facts, yet to him it was just a homey, intimate gathering, and he provided a striking example of public speaking as enlarged conversation when he said in part:

> The flight of *Friendship 7* on February 20 involved much more than one man in the spacecraft in orbit.
>
> I can think of many people who were involved in this, but I think of none more than just a few sitting in the front row right up here.
>
> I'd like to have them stand up. If my parents would stand up, please. My dad and mother.
>
> My wife's mother is there. I don't believe Dr. Castor is there right now but —Mrs. Castor.

WIDE WORLD

Colonel John Glenn's homey, intimate talks, whether they be at a news conference or before a joint session of Congress, are appropriate and effective because everything he does or says is consistent with his total personality.

> I guess Dr. Castor is up there in the third row, I'm told here. There he is.
> My son and daughter, Dave and Lynn.
> And the real rock in our family, my wife Anne. I'm real proud of her.

. . . .

> The earlier flights of Alan Shepard and Gus Grissom, who are over here, were stepping stones. Their efforts were stepping stones toward my flight in *Friendship 7* and my flight in that spacecraft will, in turn, provide additional information for use in striving toward future flights which some of the other gentlemen you see here will take part in.
> Scott Carpenter here, who was my backup on this flight; Walt Schirra, Deke Slayton, and one missing member, who is still on his way back from Australia,

where he was on the tracking station, Gordon Cooper. A lot of direction is necessary for a project such as this, and the Director of Project Mercury since its inception has been Dr. Robert Gilruth, who certainly deserves a hand here.

I have been trying to introduce Walt Williams. I do not see him here. There he is up in the corner.[2]

Colonel Glenn's talk was universally praised. His down-to-earth speech was consistent with his total personality. But who else could have spoken in this special style to a joint session of the United States Congress and its distinguished guests, such as the members of the Cabinet, and of the Supreme Court?

## Summary

In a sense there are three "you's": what others think you are, what you think you are, and what you actually are. A speech class is not the place to change your basic personality; however, it is a place where you can improve self-evaluation and the impressions you make on other people.

You judge yourself and other people judge you in terms of general impressions which are composites of the many small details that comprise your behavior. These general impressions describe, not the list of details, but an organized sum total or pattern.

Generally, unusual behaviors detract from the effectiveness of the total personality pattern, but not always. The ultimate test of any specific detail is whether it is consistent with the whole pattern.

In evaluating the effects of your own personality upon other people, you may find certain details that contradict your true personality. You can improve yourself by adding, omitting, or changing details so as to make the total pattern of your personality more complete and more consistent.

[2] Delivered on February 26, 1962.

# 19

# THE SPEAKER'S ETHICAL RESPONSIBILITY

### "She's not my kind of a girl"

"I don't admire Barbara Graham at all—she's not my kind of a girl. But she's not on trial for that. She's on trial for murder." Thus spoke Attorney Jack Hardy to the jury, according to the Los Angeles *Times* of September 17, 1953. Mr. Hardy was the court-appointed lawyer defending the "beautiful blonde" with the "icy composure" who was accused of murdering and robbing an elderly lady. During the highly publicized trial the prosecution forced Barbara Graham to admit perjury and various other crimes and immoralities. While in jail she attempted to negotiate a false alibi, but the alibi man turned out to be a police officer who managed to get a voice recording of the negotiations. The recording revealed that Barbara Graham was asked if her lawyer knew about the attempt to fake an alibi. She said no, and added that she knew her lawyer would never approve. When the recording was played in court, Mr. Hardy was indignant that the police had questioned his integrity and had placed his professional reputation at the mercy of an admitted perjurer.

Now what would you say were Mr. Hardy's ethical responsibilities in that trial? He was outraged that anyone should even raise the question of his condoning false evidence. He knew, as all of us know, that a speaker's first responsibility is to speak the truth. Honesty is best because it is ethically right, but Mr. Hardy's experience illustrates also that honesty is best because it is practical. The penalties for false evidence are shattering. One detected instance can wreck the career of a lawyer, businessman, politician, teacher, or any other man. Dishonesty simply is not worth the risk.

Let us consider a second ethical question. Mr. Hardy was appointed by the court to defend Barbara Graham, a woman he did not "admire . . . at all." He was receiving no fee from his client, and he was endangering his professional reputation, as we have seen. Was not Mr. Hardy's first obligation to himself and his family? Should he not have feigned illness in order to avoid his duty? No. That would have been passing the buck to some other court-appointed attorney. In our country there are responsibilities that cannot be dodged by not speaking.

Here is a third question. What if Mr. Hardy had decided that his client was guilty? Should he then have pulled his punches in order that justice might prevail? No. In this country we believe that a person is innocent until proved guilty, and that he is entitled to have his case presented without prejudice in court. Mr. Hardy's responsibility was to present all the evidence there was in Mrs. Graham's favor, and to say everything that could

This is a moot court in which law students are practicing a basic principle of our judicial system, namely that the speakers' responsibility is shared by the opposing lawyers, judge, and jury. Simultaneously they are practicing responsible citizenship because cooperative responsibility is basic to American democracy.

honestly be said in her defense. The prosecution's responsibility was to present evidence and arguments against her. After hearing both sides, the jury's responsibility was to return a verdict. Such is the way of democracy. We extend the same principle to other controversies. We believe, for example, in the right of a minority to be heard. Usually, of course, a speaker defends people or causes in which he believes. Sometimes, however, it is necessary and ethical for a speaker to say, "I do not necessarily believe or disbelieve in this side of the controversy, but I do believe that its arguments should be heard."

It was Mr. Hardy's moral right and duty to introduce all the legitimate evidence he could find in his client's favor; to present legitimate reasoning in her behalf; and to try to relate his arguments to the legitimate motives of the jurors. "Motives?" you exclaim. Certainly. All speaking involves motives; our greatest and noblest speeches have motivated audiences. But notice that we said *legitimate* motives, *legitimate* evidence, *legitimate* reasoning. So you ask, "What is meant by legitimate?" There is no easy answer—each instance must be decided on its own merits, and often there is room for honest difference of opinion. For example, at one point in his closing plea Mr. Hardy was interrupted by a strenuous objection from the prosecution. Judge Fricke remarked mildly that "in the fervor of final argument" some allowances could be made. Mr. Hardy's responsibility for deciding upon the legitimacy of his words was shared by the judge, the opposing lawyers, and the jury. The ethical principles illustrated by Attorney Jack Hardy's defense of Barbara Graham apply to all public speaking.

In our nation freedom of speech is not only permitted, it is encouraged. A full discussion of common problems is necessary for the success of the democratic system. Each of us must expect to face situations where a failure to speak, and to speak well, will violate a moral obligation. Usually we can expect to speak only in defense of opinions in which we believe, but democracy sometimes requires that men present viewpoints that they do not necessarily share, but that would not otherwise be represented. Those of us who have the opportunity to secure sufficient training have an ethical responsibility to discharge the difficult task of the "court- (or conscience-) appointed" speaker.

Since we believe in this country that everyone has a right to speak his own thoughts, we expect in return that each person will respect the rights of others to be heard. We expect each group to check and balance opposing groups, but to do it responsibly, to uphold the principle of "Her Majesty's Loyal Opposition."

Finally, in this nation we impose on every citizen the obligation of being a vigilant listener. He must be willing to hear both sides. He must demand

Senator Margaret Chase Smith exemplifies sincerity, which most citizens rate as the number one requirement for effective speaking.

high standards of all the speakers. He must weigh the conflicting evidence and reasoning. He must decide whether motives are legitimate. He is the jury and must return the final verdict.

The trial of Barbara Graham suggests that the problem of a speaker's ethical responsibilities is complex. Nevertheless, many listeners simplify the problem into a single word, sincerity—a word which they think provides the principal standard that should guide both speakers and listeners.

## Sincerity

W. K. Clark conducted a survey of a number of typical community organizations and by means of an ingenious technique persuaded their members to list preferentially the characteristics of good public speaking.[1] The final question was: What is the "most essential" characteristic? "Sincerity" was the overwhelming choice; it was listed more than twice as often as the second highest standard. If Clark's sampling was at all typical of the adult general public, he might be said to have found the secret of successful public speech. However, this "secret" will require judicious examination.

### Sincerity alone is not enough

Sincerity is usually described as believing what one is saying. But sincerity alone is not enough. For example, a seventeen-year-old freshman student (whose proudest achievement, he later said, was that he had not missed

[1] W. K. Clark, "A Survey of Certain Audience Attitudes Toward Commonly Taught Standards of Public Speaking," *Speech Monographs,* XVIII (March 1951), 62–69.

Sunday school in ten years) gave a talk in which he reprimanded the women in the class for smoking. He was painfully sincere as he began explaining to them the evils of nicotine, but his very sincerity was comical because to his audience he was passionate about something they considered trivial. As his classmates broke out into uncontrollable mirth, he was sincerely puzzled. "What are you laughing at?" he shouted above the din. "The matter is serious!" The speech ended when one student became so convulsed that he fell out of his chair. Thus sincerity alone may be cruelly laughed at, or pitied. Moreover, sometimes a sincere but misinformed speaker is rightfully viewed as a dangerous fanatic.

## Distinguishing between sincerity and insincerity

Most people think that they can unerringly detect hypocrisy. R. A. Hildreth [2] undertook to test this belief. He secured the cooperation of twenty-four experienced public speakers, but he told them only that they were to participate in "an experiment involving extemporaneous speaking." On the day of the experiment each speaker was handed a list of current controversial questions. He was asked to study the list carefully and then to choose the topic and the side (pro or con) "in which he most sincerely believed." He was permitted thirty minutes to prepare a short talk defending his beliefs. After this preparation he was escorted to another room where he gave the talk in front of a sound motion picture camera and a small studio audience. The resulting speech was operationally defined as "sincere." Then came the shock: each speaker was told that his task was only partly completed. He was requested in the interests of science to take another thirty minutes to prepare a talk defending the *opposite* of his chosen side. The resulting speeches were called "insincere." Thus Hildreth secured sound motion pictures of forty-eight speeches, or twenty-four pairs, half of which were sincere and half insincere. The forty-eight speeches were made into two films which were shown to 159 judges who belonged to various typical adult community organizations similar to the ones surveyed by Clark. Before viewing the speeches the audiences were asked to indicate their personal beliefs on the controversial topics. After viewing, listeners rated each speaker on his effectiveness, as well as on his sincerity. Thus approximately 3,800 judgments were secured regarding both sincerity and effectiveness. After processing these data as a whole, Hildreth found that the audiences were surprisingly inaccurate in trying to distinguish between the sincere and the insincere speeches; statistically speaking, they would probably

[2] Richard A. Hildreth, "An Experimental Study of Audiences' Ability to Distinguish Between Sincere and Insincere Speeches," unpublished doctoral dissertation, University of Southern California, 1953.

An effective speaker must have a belief in something that transcends his selfish interests, but he must also have the speech skills by which sincerity is revealed.

UNIVERSITY OF SOUTHERN CALIFORNIA

have done better by flipping coins. Hildreth further discovered that there was no significant relationship between a speaker's *actual* sincerity and his rating on effectiveness. However, there was a significant tendency for the judges to rate a speaker as effective when they had rated him as sincere. But don't jump to hasty conclusions.

## Relation between sincerity and speech skills

J. W. Wills [3] studied Hildreth's data, and noticed that the forty-eight speeches could be roughly divided into three groups. First, there was the majority of speeches where judgments of sincerity disagreed widely; on one speech, for example, precisely half of the judges called it sincere and the other half called it insincere. Second, there were ten speeches which were consistently rated as sincere; and third, eight speeches consistently rated as insincere. Wills made an intensive analysis of the sound motion pictures during which he scored each speech on 120 items of delivery, language, organization, and content. Then he went back and compared the three groups of speeches with regard to their ratings on these 120 items. Wills reported twenty-three item ratings which were common to *all* ten of the speeches most often rated as sincere, and which were characteristic of *none* of the eight speeches most often rated as insincere:

[3] John W. Wills, "An Empirical Study of the Behavioral Characteristics of Sincere and Insincere Speakers," unpublished doctoral dissertation, University of Southern California, 1961.

1. Maintained relaxed but erect posture.
2. Used conventional gestures often.
3. Timed gestures well.
4. Reflected a pleasant mood.
5. Looked at camera (viewing audience) an average of 63.4 per cent of time.
6. Did not read speech.
7. Did not read last sentence of speech.
8. Had no tension in voice.
9. Had strong force level in voice.
10. Had some contrast in volume between sections of speech.
11. Used variety in volume often.
12. Averaged 150 words per minute.
13. Made some use of pause in speech.
14. Used variety of rate often.
15. Used some contrast in rate between sections.
16. Used great deal of variety in pitch.
17. Exhibited no pitch pattern.
18. Lowered pitch level of voice at end of sentences.
19. Exhibited excellent fluency.
20. Showed excellent opening enthusiasm.
21. Used no didactic tone in speaking.
22. Used clear transitions in content of speech.
23. Exhibited good variety in wording.

Wills also found eighteen item-ratings which applied to *all* of the "insincere" and *none* of the "sincere" speeches:

1. Maintained inferior posture.
2. Used no descriptive gestures.
3. Used ineffective or inconsistent gestures.
4. Used no facial expression for emphasis.
5. Reflected a serious or pained mood.
6. Looked at camera (viewing audience) an average of only 20.8 per cent of time.
7. Broke mood at the end of speech.
8. Had some tension in voice.
9. Used no intensity in voice for emphasis.
10. Used little variety in volume.
11. Averaged 124.8 words per minute.
12. Used little variety in rate.
13. Used little or no rate contrast between sections of speech.

14. Used little variety in pitch.
15. Exhibited inferior fluency.
16. Showed inferior opening enthusiasm.
17. Showed inferior closing enthusiasm.
18. Showed some lack of variety in wording.

Once again you may be tempted to jump to hasty conclusions. A study of the above two lists might lead you to conclude that, if you master certain speaking skills while avoiding certain other speech characteristics, then you will be judged by audiences to be sincere and therefore effective. Fortunately for us all, that conclusion is not justified by the evidence.

### Skill alone is not enough

All of the speakers in the Hildreth-Wills studies were chosen because they were above average in speaking skills and in speaking experience. But consider one of the speakers—code number 84. His insincere speech was correctly detected by approximately two-thirds of the listeners in spite of the fact that he was skillful. Consider also your own experience—listening to TV commercials, for example. Most announcers are highly skilled professionals. Yet do you suppose that every one of them believes in every sales message that he delivers? Of course not. Think about your judgments of other students in various classes. Are the best talkers always accepted as being sincere? Not if they are trying to apple polish, or show off, or dominate the class discussion periods.

### Broadening your concept of sincerity

Let us analyze the *insincere* speeches in Hildreth's experiments. We know that in all probability the speakers did not believe in the side of the question that they were "forced" to defend. But all of the topics were current controversies, which means that something could be said in favor of either side. Thus the speakers, just like a court-appointed attorney, could believe in the particular arguments they advanced without regard to side. Furthermore, as educated citizens of a democracy, they could strongly believe that both sides of true controversies should be heard. Many of the speakers had received intercollegiate forensic training in which they learned that usually the best way to reach a decision regarding a public problem is to study both sides with an open mind and to test the opposing arguments by debating on both sides.

The above analysis is consistent with Hildreth's findings. The audiences were correct more than 60 per cent of the time in identifying sincerity, but they were correct less than 25 per cent of the time in identifying insincerity. Does this mean that the audiences were gullible? Well, that possibility should be explored by further research. However, the nature of the topics, the training and experience of the speakers, suggest a more defensible explanation. The audiences may have thought that sincerity is believing in one side of a controversy, but apparently they judged sincerity (consciously or subconsciously) on broader grounds, such as that an effective speaker must have a belief in something that transcends his selfish interests.

The fact remains, however, that sincerity alone (regardless of its definition) is not enough. The young man who condemned the girls in his class for smoking was probably as sincere as one can be. And Wills' research strongly indicated that belief alone is not enough—the speaker must also have the knowledge and skill to let his belief shine through to his audience. Thus we make an important discovery. You might say that the emphasis in this textbook has been "practical." Now you find that every chapter contains a built-in ethical component; that practical skills and ethical responsibilities are subtly but surely interwoven; that in learning practical skills you have been simultaneously developing proper attitudes toward their use; that doing the right thing is usually the right thing to do.

## Accuracy

While discussing sincerity in the last several pages we have focused attention on the first stages of the communication process, the speaker, the "what you are." But the problem of ethical responsibilities involves the

David Brinkley is admired for the accuracy and the honesty of his radio and television talks.

entire process of communication. We must now examine ethics in relation to the message, the "what you say."

## Deliberate distortion

The most dangerous thing that a speaker can do is to distort the truth.

Consider plagiarism. A large Eastern university holds an annual contest with a cash prize for students who compete in "original oratory." One year a student won this contest because the ideas in his speech were stimulating and the language was smooth. About two weeks after the contest, however, somebody produced a printed article which was almost word for word a replica of the winner's speech. The scandal was reported in a series of articles in the student newspaper. The winner had already spent the prize money, but he withdrew from school in disgrace.

In February 1950 Senator Joseph R. McCarthy attracted national attention by a speech in which he said that fifty-seven known Communists were working in the State Department. During the next few years McCarthy made headlines repeatedly with additional accusations of communism in high places. But while McCarthy was investigating others, his speeches were also being investigated. Distinguished scholars, after comparing some of McCarthy's speeches with the ascertainable facts, reported dozens of examples where McCarthy had made false statements or had distorted the facts through such devices as omissions, quotations out of context, unwarranted inferences, and innuendo. In December 1954 McCarthy was censured in the United States Senate by a 67-22 vote.

## Unintentional distortion

Sometimes a speaker may be forgiven even when he seriously misstates, misrepresents, misquotes, or fails to acknowledge his sources; but such mistakes can be condoned only if they are rare and are clearly a result of such factors as the stress of the speaking situation, a slip of the tongue, or a failure of memory.

Unintentional distortions are usually the result of the speaker's ignorance or lack of preparation. In such cases the speaker merely substitutes one sin for another. He is ethically responsible for speaking only on subjects where he knows what he is talking about; he is ethically responsible for preparing every speech with thoroughness. Check this standard against your experience in this speech class. You have respected those students who presented well-chosen subjects, interesting and worthwhile ideas, facts drawn from personal experience and research; you have not respected those students who depended on a mixture of bluff, hot air, and platform gimmicks. You have appreciated the student who spoke because he had something to say, rather than the student who spoke because he had to say something. Misinformed or poorly prepared speakers raise the ancient question: Which is worse, the knave or the fool?

## Social standards

As we pointed out early in this chapter, the audience shares the speaker's ethical responsibilities. The career of Adolph Hitler provides a thought-provoking illustration. In 1923 Hitler made his first bid for power in the famous Munich beer hall *Putsch;* the attempt put Hitler in jail. Approximately ten years later the same Hitler, using the same public speaking skills with the same ethical standards, became *Der Führer* of his nation. During this decade Hitler did not change much, but apparently several million Germans did. In the early 1920's Hitler was viewed by most Germans as a dangerous demagogue who used the twisted facts and twisted logic of a twisted mind. In the early 1930's most of these same listeners viewed Hitler as a national savior. During this same period the listening standards of peoples all over the earth seemed to deteriorate. Hitler alone cannot be held responsible for his leadership into World War II; millions of listeners must share that responsibility.

While he was in jail in 1923–24 Hitler wrote *Mein Kampf,* a remarkably blunt statement of his goals and methods. He frequently discussed the importance of propaganda, and the reciprocal relationship between speaking and listening, between leadership and followership. For example:

> After my entrance into the German Workers' Party, I at once took over the management of propaganda. I regarded this department as by far the most important.[4]
>
> If propaganda has imbued a whole people with an idea, the organization can draw the consequences with a handful of men. Propaganda and organization, in other words, supporters and members, thus stand in a certain mutual relation. The better the propaganda has worked, the smaller the organization can be; and the larger the number of supporters, the more modest the number of members can be; and vice versa. . . .[5]

By now it should be clear that your ethical standards will in large measure determine your effectiveness as a speaker. In our democratic society you will have frequent opportunities to speak, but you will be a listener more often than a speaker. And your ethical standards will in large measure determine the effectiveness of the speakers to whom you listen. You can help

[4] Adolph Hitler, *Mein Kampf,* tr. by Ralph Mannheim (1943), p. 579. Reprinted by permission of Houghton Mifflin Company and Hurst & Blackett Ltd.
[5] *Mein Kampf,* pp. 582–83.

A dictator and his constituents.

*"In my country, as in yours, public men are proud to be the servants of the state, and would be ashamed to be its masters."* (Winston Churchill addressing the United States Congress, December 26, 1941)

A United States Senator and his constituents.

to stop a future McCarthy or Hitler; you can help encourage a future Lincoln or Churchill.

## Summary

Ethical responsibilities involve the entire process of communication: the speaker and his sincerity, the message and its accuracy, and the audience and its standards.

General audiences appear to list sincerity as the most essential characteristic of good speaking. Sincerity is usually defined as believing what one is saying. But personal sincerity alone does not always guarantee speech success. In fact, it has been demonstrated that audiences may be quite inaccurate in trying to distinguish between *actual* cases of sincerity and insincerity. Audiences do, however, tend to equate their ratings of speech effectiveness with their feelings of a speaker's apparent sincerity. Some of the audience bases for judging a speaker's apparent sincerity seem strongly related to certain speech skills. But neither is skill in itself enough. The best combination for speech success is a speaker who believes in his message and has the skill to let this belief shine through to the audience.

Ethical responsibilities in regard to the message are primarily those involving accuracy. Unintentional distortions may sometimes be forgiven if such mistakes are rare. But to deliberately distort is the most dangerous thing that a speaker can do. The speaker has an ethical responsibility to avoid both.

Audiences share in the ethical responsibilities of communication. When an unethical speaker is successful it may be as much a result of lack of audience standards as it is of speaker irresponsibility.

## TOPICAL PREVIEW

# 20

# THEORIES OF COMMUNICATION

You have already realized that in developing a philosophy of speech you must begin by systematizing your own personal attitudes toward the subject, a matter which was introduced by Chapter 18. However, a completely selfish philosophy can never suffice. You must also develop a sense of responsibility toward your listeners and toward other speakers, a problem which was discussed in Chapter 19. A sound philosophy of speech requires at least one more major element. You must study and reflect upon principles and theories which are basic to *all* communication. Some of these principles and theories will be introduced in the present chapter. They will provide a frame of reference for the better understanding of all the other chapters in this book; they will also suggest guidelines for continuing your study of speech.

To study theories of communication is to pursue knowledge that on the one hand dates back to the beginning of Western culture, and on the other hand includes hypotheses so recent that they are being tested and modified today. In general the classical tradition, still one of the richest fields for research, is called *rhetorical theory*, and the startling new developments of recent years are called *communication theory*. An over-all understanding of rhetorical theory provides perspective in terms of the depth and tradition which underlie the study of speech. An over-all understanding of communication theory provides perspective in terms of the constantly increasing scope and challenge of speech study.

### Classical rhetorical theory

It is ironic that the first great philosopher to write on the subject of speech-making was vehement in his condemnation of rhetoric. Plato branded rhetoric a false art, a "knack" comparable to "cookery," a skill especially susceptible to use for evil purposes. While scholars disagree as to whether Plato was mainly critical of the speechmaking of the day or for all time, it is clear that his treatment held a significant implication for any theory of speechmaking: there must be an inherent regard for truth. Isocrates, a contemporary of Plato, asserted that rhetoric was essential to citizenship. He headed a successful school which was founded on the principle of a union between oratory and statesmanship.

The Platonic regard for truth combined with the Isocratic tradition of active and responsible citizenship provided the background for the most comprehensive statement of public speaking principles ever written: Aristotle's *Rhetoric*.

Aristotle considered rhetoric to be a useful art and laid down a theory

PEPSI COLA

Modern theories of communication are not limited to speaking or writing. The basic process is analyzed in terms of all media, including, for example, abstract art.

of speechmaking that has endured for nearly 2,300 years as the basis of classical rhetorical theory. By treating the interrelated aspects of speaker, audience, and speech, Aristotle provided a guide for "finding the available means of persuasion in any given case." In Aristotelian terms, persuasion was accomplished by three modes of proof: *ethos,* the speaker's character; *pathos,* appeal to the emotions; and *logos,* appeal to reason. Although written in the fourth century before Christ, the principles of Aristotle are modern in the sense that the effectiveness of speech is measured by the reaction of an audience.

The brilliant Roman orator Cicero was an example of Aristotelian principles put into practice. He contributed to rhetorical theory both as a model speaker, and as a writer who amplified Aristotle's principles of speechmaking for Roman society. He was followed by Quintilian, who in the first century A.D. proposed a theory of education based on rhetoric.

Great scholars, teachers, and leaders have contributed to the preservation and growth of rhetorical theory through the ages. As a body of literature, rhetorical theory provides testimony of the high regard some of the most brilliant minds in intellectual history—Plato, Aristotle, Cicero, Quintilian, Saint Augustine, Francis Bacon—have had for the proper role of speech in society. The synthesis of these contributions has led to a philosophy of speechmaking that is centered on the principle of giving effectiveness to truth. Within its framework scholars have evaluated the methods and effectiveness of such great speakers as Demosthenes, Cicero, Edmund Burke, Patrick Henry, Abraham Lincoln, Franklin Delano Roosevelt, and Winston Churchill.

Classical rhetorical theory provides a rich heritage for any modern theory of communication. It provides guidelines for the understanding, criticism, and teaching of public address.

## Modern communication theory

The first step in the understanding of modern communication theory is to become familiar with several terms that are commonly used in this field of inquiry. You will recall that in the first paragraph of this book we defined speech as the communication of thought and emotion by means of voice, language, and/or bodily action. A key word in this definition is *communication.* Let us explore that word more thoroughly.

### Definition of communication

Communication between two or more persons is the process of transmitting and receiving ideas by means of language symbols.

You will notice that this definition is restricted to human communication between two or more persons. The reasons for this restriction will become clear as we consider the implications of all the terms in the definition, the first of which is *process*.

PROCESS    Basically a process is any continuous operation. It implies a complex mixture of objects, events, and relationships which is dynamic, ongoing, ever-changing. The importance of this concept to the study of communication has been stressed by the title of this book. Speech is viewed as dynamic (like a motion picture), not static (like a snapshot). This viewpoint was vividly expressed some 2,500 years ago by Heraclitus when he pointed out that you can never step in the same river twice—the river is constantly changing and so are you.

For purposes of study and analysis, the process of communication may usefully be subdivided into major steps. We must always remember, however, that such subdivisions are arbitrary and even artificial. It is like studying a motion picture by analyzing some of the individual frames. This analytical approach can help you understand how the process works or fails to work, but you must constantly remind yourself that the process of oral communication can be taken apart only in theory, never in actual practice. Do not study aspects of communication separately; study them *separately together*.

TRANSMITTING AND RECEIVING    By this time it is clear that communication is not something which the speaker or writer does all by himself. Nor should communication be viewed as two independent processes which occur in simple sequence: speaking→listening, or transmitting→receiving. Oral communication is almost always a single process in which the behavior of speaker and listener are inextricably interwoven. The nature of this interrelationship may be clarified by analyzing the process psychologically.

Essentially, when communication occurs, one person, object, or event is in the process of affecting another. The basic and simplest unit of this relationship is *stimulus-response*. We can use this unit to view a small isolated instance of relationship or an over-all complex relationship. For instance, suppose you accidentally touch the lighted end of a cigarette. The heat is a stimulus and your subsequent reaction is the response. Or we could define this over-all operation as a series of operations. Again the heat is a stimulus. The sense of heat as registered in your central nervous system serves as the first level of response. The perception of this heat in turn acts as a stimulus within your central nervous system to initiate the movement of jerking away your hand which again is a response. If you also cry "ouch," the response becomes more complex. The stimulus-response relationship is a unit basic to the theory of communication; it *is* the dynamic relationship between or among persons, objects, or events.

In oral communication the relationship takes place when stimulus material can bridge the gap between speaker and listener. Oral stimuli are in the form of sound waves generated by the speaker. These sound waves are symbols capable of arousing meaning in the mind of a listener. In most cases of oral communication the sound waves are supplemented by light waves which give the listener meaningful images of the speaker in action. Together these clusters of meaningful sound and light stimuli transmitted by the speaker and received by the listener give us a physical basis for explaining the oral communication process. Graphically, the elementary situation looks like this:

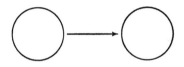

In most cases, however, oral communication is not a one-way operation; instead, the speaker, in addition to communicating to the audience, also receives meaningful stimuli from the audience, such as smiles, frowns, or nods. In conversation the listener and the speaker are constantly interchanging roles. Thus the above graph oversimplifies most speaking-listening since it restricts one person to transmitting and the other to receiving when, in actuality, humans are usually doing both. The human communicator should be considered as more than a transmitter or a receiver, he is really a "transceiver" capable of both operations in a single situation. We should modify our diagram to look like this:

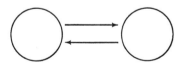

In public speaking when one speaker is attempting to communicate to a group of listeners, a new field of stimulus-response emerges among those transceivers who make up the audience. When you are a member of an audience the behavior of the other people affects your behavior. Think of how laughter rolls through an audience or how one cough can set a whole series of people to coughing. Members of audiences have a tendency to control their reactions in relation to the other listeners in the situation. To

Communication is a dynamic interaction between the speaker and the audience. Notice the interstimulation among listeners to this speaker (see diagram below and picture opposite).

FREDERICK WILLIAMS

realistically depict public speaking our diagram must include not only interstimulation between speaker and audience but additional interstimulation among the audience members:

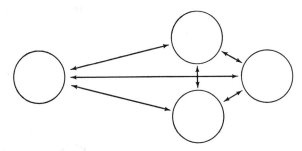

The above diagram is brought to life by the pictures on this and the opposite page.

**IDEAS**  In our definition of communication the term "ideas" is used broadly to indicate any experience, such as thoughts, perceptions, feelings, emotions, and attitudes, which can to any degree be put into the form of meaningful language symbols.

**LANGUAGE SYMBOLS**  You learned some of the implications of the term "language symbols" while studying Chapter 11. You know that words are symbols which stand for or represent objects, events, or relationships. Meanings

lie not in the words but in the people who use them. But let us pursue this matter further.

A symbol is anything that represents something else. Many symbols can be described as nonlinguistic. For example, the author has a mountain cabin to which he escapes whenever possible. After several hours of driving he nears the final curve and there beside the road is a huge boulder. To him that boulder symbolizes, "Home at last." There is no reason to suppose that the boulder symbolizes the same meaning for anybody else on earth; in fact, to other people it probably does not symbolize anything at all.

When two or more people, however, through mutual agreement or common usage attribute the same or similar meanings to given sounds, gestures, writings, or even smoke signals, then language symbols have been created. If common meanings for a considerable number of such symbols are arbitrarily agreed on, then a language has developed. An unusual example of this process was provided by a recent report from a public school speech therapist. He was called upon to visit a family with two boys, ages four and six. These brothers had invented a language all their own. They apparently could converse satisfactorily in their private language yet nobody, not even the parents, could break the code. The younger boy spoke no other language; the older one could also make himself understood in ordinary English. So the older youngster always had to translate what his brother said. The boys had created a new language by inventing or choosing an esoteric set of symbols and arbitrarily agreeing on the meanings of those symbols.

Language symbols are of two kinds: verbal and nonverbal. Verbal symbols are, of course, *words* which may be either spoken or written. The most common nonverbal symbols comprise "the language of gesture." You will recall from Chapter 9 that gestures include not only movements of the hands and arms, but also such bodily movements as facial expression, eye contact, posture, and walking. Students of language used to believe that some gestures had universal meanings, but modern research has severely shaken this belief. The meanings of many common gestures have been found to vary among cultures. Thus nodding the head means "yes" to you and me, but in some societies it means "no." The probabilities favor the viewpoint that most, if not all, gestures are language symbols because they require arbitrary agreements as to their meanings.

What is *meaning?* In simplest terms it is "the picture in your mind," which is one kind of response to various kinds of stimuli. When a dog perceives

Lyndon B. Johnson here illustrates nonverbal communication as he uses "the language of gesture."

UPI

food the subsequent salivation indicates the meaning (something to eat) in response to the stimulus (food). This is a "built-in" stimulus-response relationship within the dog; he is born with the ability to respond in this way when a food stimulus is perceived. Note that in this example the food is real, and not represented by a symbol.

Many stimulus-response relationships, especially those involving either language or nonlanguage symbols, are not built-in, but are learned. In a series of experiments the Russian physiologist Ivan Pavlov consistently rang a bell each time that he presented food to a dog. After several repetitions the dog would salivate (response) when he heard the bell (stimulus) even though no food was presented. Pavlov called this type of learning "conditioning." The dog had been conditioned to respond to an arbitrarily chosen symbol (the bell) as though it were the real thing (food). These experiments show how the meanings of words, vocal inflections, or gestures can be taught and learned. When a child is learning to talk the mother holds up a toy animal and says, "dog." After a number of repetitions the child learns the connection. Then if he wants to play with his favorite toy, he says, "dog" even though the actual object is in another room. His mother rewards him by bringing the toy. Eventually both mother and father are sorely tried by the ever-recurrent question, "What's *that?*"

## Cybernetics

Traditional rhetorical theories and research methods have been supplemented in recent years by new ones based upon twentieth century developments in the physical, biological, and social sciences.

One new and exciting approach to the study of communication is described in Norbert Wiener's *Cybernetics* (1948).[1] Cybernetics is defined as the science of control and communication in animals and machines. One implication of cybernetics is that a useful analogy may be drawn between the operations of a human nervous system and the operations of an electronic computer or "brain." This opens up a vast new field for experimental research, much of which will bear directly on the process of oral communication. For example, relatively little is known about the physiology of the brain and nervous system. Neurologists have long speculated that nerves are similar to electric wires and that nerve impulses are similar to electrical impulses. It is now possible to test such speculations by having a computer engineer construct electronic equipment in accordance with the neurologist's specifications. Ruch suggests one application:

[1] Wiener's later work, *The Human Use of Human Beings,* Houghton Mifflin, 1950, is written in language easier for the layman to understand.

For instance, it has been considered highly likely that the nerve nets involved in human visual imagery may be quite similar to the electronic connections which produce an image in the screen of a television set.[2]

Communication is, by definition, a central concept of cybernetics. But Wiener and other scientists in this field do not confine this concept to human communication. They have sought to describe the fundamental elements of the process (such as control, organization, and disorganization) and to apply these concepts to "communication" between or among animals, machines, social systems, systems in nature, and even to the organization of the universe. Thus they stress the key position of the communication process in explaining *any* known process; they give us a new perspective by which to view oral communication; and they provide advanced students and scholars of speech with the opportunity to create radically new hypotheses which can be scientifically checked.

## Information theory

Closely related to cybernetics is Shannon and Weaver's *information theory,* which postulates that communication (human or otherwise) requires the transmission of energy. They analyze all communication systems into five basic and common ingredients: (1) source, (2) encoder, (3) channel, (4) decoder, and (5) destination. Any interference with energy transmission is called *noise.*[3]

As you can see, this "model" might be adapted to many levels of communication. However, direct application of the model to human communication is likely to be confusing or even misleading. Such misunderstanding arises because of two major and related reasons. (1) The theory defines information in a way quite different from popular usage. The theory defines and measures "information" solely in terms of a series of *yes-no* or *on-off* decisions. You might think of this level as something like sending Morse code. The source can only transmit two signals to the destination: energy *on* or energy *off.* In other words this is the machine level of communication. (2) The theory does not account for *meaning* as it occurs in human beings. "Information" is not the perception of new facts or ideas; it is a mathematical measure of one's freedom of choice when selecting between *on-off* reactions in a time series. You probably find that last statement confusing. It was written technically on purpose to illustrate the danger of oversimplifying Shannon and Weaver's model.

Information theory furnishes us with a communication model that can be

[2] Floyd L. Ruch, *Psychology and Life,* 5th ed., Scott, Foresman, 1958, p. 370.
[3] Claude Shannon and Warren Weaver, *The Mathematical Theory of Communication,* Univ. of Illinois Press, 1949, p. 5.

usefully *adapted* to the analysis of human communication. More importantly, however, the theory provides a mathematical basis for measuring one level of communication; it provides new hypotheses that can be tested scientifically.

## Semantics

Cybernetics and information theory provide fresh approaches to understanding the process of communication, but neither takes into account man's behavioral use of language. Language and the process of meaning have already been discussed earlier in both Chapter 11 and in this chapter. The principles underlying both of those discussions come from the field of *semantics*, a study of "the meaning of meaning." Semantics emphasizes the study of meaning as a linguistic function.

A modern development which has had great impact upon the study of communication began when Korzybski published his theory of *general semantics*.[4] This theory drastically expands semantics to include the study of behavioral aspects of language and meaning. It examines how man's patterns of thinking, his emotions, and his attitudes influence his choice of symbols and language structure; then how man's language patterns influence his behavior patterns which in turn influence his social and physical environment. Many of man's problems are traced to the limitations of his language. The proper study and more accurate use of language and meaning are described as having therapeutic value for problems ranging from an individual's emotional maladjustments to international misunderstandings.

General semantics supplies us with a substantial list of suggested practical applications, some of which await experimental verification, but all of which have been described in highly readable form by several authors.[5] The theory also suggests many new hypotheses which can be and are being scientifically tested by advanced students of communication.

## A general communication model

In considering the various modern theories of communication you will note that they all treat communication as an occurrence rather than a thing. In cybernetics, communication is an occurrence whereby one thing affects another. From the mathematical theory of information we see an example

[4] Alfred Korzybski, *Science and Sanity: An Introduction to Non-Aristotelian Systems and General Semantics,* Inst. of General Semantics, 1933.

[5] See, for example, S. I. Hayakawa, *Language in Thought and Action,* Harcourt, Brace & World, 1949; Wendell Johnson, *People in Quandaries,* Harper, 1946; Irving J. Lee, *The Language of Wisdom and Folly,* Harper, 1949.

of this on the basic level of an electrical circuit. And in general semantics meaning, itself, is an occurrence, a response in the mind of the receiver.

If we want to construct a picture of communication we not only need the basic ingredients but we have to show how they affect each other. In short, we have to show a diagram or model of an occurrence.

The diagram of interstimulation (page 370) is one approach to showing communication in action. However it is restricted to situations where one source is communicating to many receivers. Shannon and Weaver's model (page 374) includes the basic ingredients for communication but is not focused on the process at the human level. We will, therefore, construct our own model, one that applies to any situation where two or more human beings are in the process of communication. This model will consider human communication to be purposive in the cybernetics sense; that is, people communicate when they want to affect other people. We will use ingredients from Shannon and Weaver's model but our model will go beyond the electrical circuit level of communication in order to include the concept of meaning. The construction of our model begins with three broad components: a *source,* a *channel,* and a *receiver.* But because the model focuses on human communication, we can consider both the source and receiver as *transceivers.* The transceivers are capable of having ideas, encoding, decoding, transmitting, receiving, and perceiving meaning. We will also include in the model the concept of feedback.

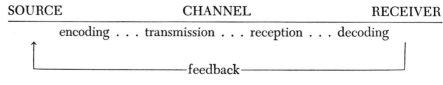

| SOURCE | CHANNEL | RECEIVER |
|---|---|---|

encoding . . . transmission . . . reception . . . decoding

feedback

OPERATIONS IN THE MODEL

**1. ENCODING** When the source translates his ideas into symbolic patterns that potentially can be transmitted, he is encoding. The encoding operation is preparatory to transmission; it takes place within the source.

**2. TRANSMISSION** The transmission operation involves the pattern of potentially meaningful stimuli from the time they leave the source until they impinge on the senses of a receiver. Transmission involves "bridging the gap" between source and receiver. It is like a radio broadcast.

**3. RECEPTION** When the receiver can lend his attention to the pattern of potentially meaningful stimuli, reception takes place. In short, reception is "closing the gap," it is "tuning in."

**4. DECODING** The basis of human decoding is a stimulus-response relationship that exists in the receiver. As the patterns of symbols (stimuli) are perceived, they elicit meaning (response). This is a further example of why it is useful to think of language as a code. Units of language do *not* themselves have meaning; they only "trigger" it in the mind of a receiver.

**5. FEEDBACK** As you remember from the interstimulation diagram, and certainly from experience, communication is not necessarily a one-way operation. When the capability for two-way transmission exists, we usually call such return communication "feedback" during which the source and receiver reverse their roles.

## Applications of the model

A communication model can provide new ways of analyzing and comparing almost all communication media or situations. Here are some applications:

|  | *Newspaper* | *Advertising* | *History* |
|---|---|---|---|
| SOURCE: | Editorial staff | Manufacturer | Past civilizations |
| CHANNEL: | Printed paper | Mass media | Records, artifacts |
| RECEIVER: | Subscribers | Public | Historians |
| *Feedback:* | Letters to the editor | Sales | None |

The model can be applied to dozens of other examples. Can you diagram the following: motion pictures, literature, public relations, government, a political campaign, phonograph recordings?

It is also useful to look at human communication from the standpoint of the respective number of humans that make up sources and receivers in various situations. In this respect we can classify human communication situations as interpersonal, centrifugal, centripetal, and cultural. For example: [6]

|  | *Interpersonal* | *Centrifugal* | *Centripetal* | *Cultural* |
|---|---|---|---|---|
| SOURCE: | One person | One person or organization | Many persons | Many persons |
| RECEIVER: | One person | Many persons | One person or organization | Many persons |
| *Example:* | Conversation | Mass communication | Public opinion | International relations |

[6] Adapted from: Jurgen Ruesch and Gregory Bateson, *Communication, The Social Matrix of Psychiatry*, W. W. Norton, 1951.

In Chapter 1 you studied a description of "the act of oral communication" in seven steps (pages 16–17). You should review that section now. When you first read it you perhaps thought that the seven steps were simply a common-sense analysis which had some practical values for practicing and improving your speaking skills. By this time, however, you can see that it is a speech model that fits into the broader concepts of cybernetics, information theory, and semantics. To see how it fits, study the following parallel lists.

| | |
|---|---|
| SOURCE: | 1. The speaker has an idea. |
| *Encoding:* | 2. The speaker puts his idea into words. |
| *Transmitting:* | 3. The speaker transmits. |
| CHANNEL: | (sound and light waves) |
| *Reception:* | 4. The listener hears and sees. |
| *Decoding:* | 5. The listener perceives. |
| RECEIVER: | 6. The listener reacts. |
| *Feedback:* | 7. The speaker responds to the listeners' reactions. |

In the beginning you may have had difficulty in visualizing the above seven steps as indivisible and interrelated parts of a single continuous process. By now this important concept is easier to grasp. The ongoing, dynamic continuity of the process is clarified when we analyze the first and the last steps. When a speaker has an idea, that idea is a response to something, that something was in response to something else, and so the cycle can be traced back and back. Thus we could say that the process has no determinable absolute beginning. Turning to the seventh and last step you will immediately observe that the end of every cycle of oral communication is the beginning of another cycle which may occur immediately or at some future time. Thus you may think of oral communication as a never-ending spiral.

By this time you will also recognize the continuity within the seven-step model. Analysis will quickly reveal that each step is dependent on the occurrence of the preceding steps. Furthermore, the over-all interdependence among the steps is demonstrated by the fact that the success of an entire communication cycle can be destroyed by a failure on any one of the steps. "Failure" does not mean that nothing was communicated. It may mean that too little was communicated or that the wrong meaning was communicated.

These fundamental questions may occur to you: Why is oral communication a single process? What binds the parts together? Why can't we divide it in two: (1) the process of speaking, and (2) the process of listening? The

Intelligent listening is an integral part of the communication process.

answer to these questions is suggested by the concept of *interactive thinking*. Two people sitting alone in different rooms can individually think about the same topic. In thinking about it, both of them use various tools of thought including language symbols in the form of electrochemical impulses. Communication between them requires an exchange of symbols, most of them in the form of sound or light waves. This exchange of symbols stirs up responses within each of them that modify the individual thinking of each of them. Thus human communication requires interactivity of thought in addition to intraindividual activity. This whole matter can be put into the following complex phrase: an inter-individual relationship between intra-individual processes.

### "The future enters into us"

The German lyric poet, Rainer Maria Rilke, wrote "The future enters into us, in order to transform itself in us, long before it happens." But it cannot transform itself in us if there is no communication among us. Man is both slave and master of his environment. And in mastering his environment no man is an island. The human urge to communicate is universal.

The importance of communication to the individual is more than matched by the importance of communication to groups of individuals even including whole nations.

We live in a democratic society where all of us have the right to speak, the right to be heard, the right to help choose. Throughout the history of our nation we have been opposed by authoritarian societies, and we have fought several wars with them in defense of our way of life. This conflict between dictatorship and democracy continues. In our generation, however, a new dimension has been added. Science has created weapons capable of destroying whole nations. The only way to stop this threatened destruction and eventually to dispose of these weapons, is by negotiation. Such negotiation is a problem in international communication. This problem includes the thinking-speaking-listening, not only of national leaders, but also of whole peoples so that they may influence their leaders. And in recent years science has given us the means for achieving mass communication—television, radio, motion pictures, recordings. Thus science has created potentially powerful deterrents to its potentially destructive weapons. And the future has posed the overwhelming question: Will our era become known as the "Age of Mass Communication" or the "Age of Mass Extermination"?

### Summary

To study theories of communication is to pursue knowledge that on the one hand dates back to ancient times, and on the other hand includes hypotheses that are being tested today. In general the classical tradition is called *rhetorical theory*, and recent developments are called *communication theory*.

The greatest single contribution to rhetorical theory has been Aristotle's *Rhetoric*. The study of the role of speech in society has attracted many other brilliant philosophers, statesmen, and teachers. Careful analyses have been made of hundreds of speeches; basic principles of effective content, organization, style, and delivery have been proposed. Modern scholars who follow the classical tradition study speechmaking as an art for giving effectiveness to truth.

In recent years new approaches to the study of communication have been provided by the physical, biological, and social sciences. These studies supplement traditional literary, artistic, and historical research; new approaches, dimensions, and methods have been added. Especially stimulating have been the contributions of cybernetics, information theory, and general semantics. Thus students of oral communication are challenged to do more than master skills. They are challenged to progress further into the principles and theories of a field which is both an art and a science.

# APPENDIXES

*To the instructor:*

Appendix A presents three suggested semester-sequences of assignments and classroom projects. All three have been successfully used as they stand (with only minor adjustments). They have also been successfully used by teachers who have made a number of modifications or adaptations. The assignments have been presented in a form intended to save time for both the instructor and the students. All three sequences assume a three-unit course with an enrollment of 18–25 students.

The first sequence suggests how the text has been applied to a terminal one-semester course. The second and third sequences show how the text has been used in two-semester courses. In the latter case the text can be fully supplemented by the following: (1) reading in depth on the subject matter of topics to be presented as classroom talks; (2) analyzing significant classical and contemporary speeches from anthologies and other sources; (3) using a workbook designed primarily to supplement a speech textbook. See, for example, Milton Dickens and James H. McBath, *Guidebook for Speech Practice* (Harcourt, Brace & World, 1961).

Appendixes B and C provide two sample speech outlines illustrating the six-step outlining procedure described in Chapter 7 and elsewhere in the text.

Appendix D contains suggestions to students for "Continuing the Study of Speech," a lecture which most instructors intend to give at the last class meeting but usually must omit because of lack of classroom time.

# APPENDIX A  *Class Assignments and Projects*

## One-semester program: Class schedule

| Assign-ment number | Approx-imate hours | Class projects | Remarks | Reading assign-ments |
|---|---|---|---|---|
| (1) | 1 | Informal lecture; introductions | Preview of course; grading; getting acquainted *Instructions, 1* | Chapter 1 |
| (2) | 1 | Class discussion | Subject: Chapter 1, "Approaching the Study of Speech" *Instructions, 2* | Chapter 2 |
| (3) | 1 | Organize and plan panel forums | *Instructions, 3* | Chapter 3 |
| (4) | 3–4 | Present panel forums | *Instructions, 3* | Chapters 4–5 |
| (5) | 1 | Lecture discussion | Subject: Planning the first speeches | |
| (6) | 2–3 | Student speeches and research | Demonstration talks *Instructions, 5* | Chapter 6 *Instructions, 6* |

| Assign-ment number | Approx-imate hours | Class projects | Remarks | Reading assign-ments |
|---|---|---|---|---|
| (7) | 1 | Lecture discussion | Subject: Chapter 6, "Speech Materials" | Chapter 7 |
| (8) | 3 | Student speeches | Anecdote talks *Instructions, 7* | Chapter 8 |
| (9) | 2 | Lecture discussion | Subject: "Speech Construction" | |
| (10) | 1 | Student speeches | Impromptu talks *Instructions, 17* | Chapter 9 |
| (11) | 2 | Demonstration-analysis | Tape recordings of students *Instructions, 12* | Chapter 10 |
| (12) | 1 | Demonstration-analysis | Professional recordings *Instructions, 13* | Chapter 11 |
| (13) | 3 | Student speeches | Informative talks *Instructions, 10* | Review of Chapters 1–11 |
| (14) | 1 | Written exam | Covering of the lectures and readings to date | Chapter 12 |
| (15) | 1 | Lecture and class poll | Subject: Chapter 12, "Audience Analysis" *Instructions, 4* | Chapter 13 |
| (16) | 3 | Student speeches | Talks adapted to audience interests *Instructions, 20* | Chapter 14 |
| (17) | 1 | Lecture discussion | Subject: Chapter 14, "Audience Under-standing" | Chapter 15 |
| (18) | 1 | Lecture discussion | Subject: Chapter 15, "Reinforcing Audience Attitudes" | |
| (19) | 3 | Student speeches | Talks for special occasions *Instructions, 23* | Chapter 16 |
| (20) | 1 | Lecture discussion | Subject: Chapter 16, "Building Audience Attitudes" | Chapter 17 |

| Assign-<br>ment<br>number | Approx-<br>imate<br>hours | Class projects | Remarks | Reading<br>assign-<br>ments |
|---|---|---|---|---|
| (21) | 4 | Student speeches | Direct argument<br>*Instructions, 24* | Chapters 18–19 |
| (22) | 1–2 | Lecture discussion | Subject: "Developing<br>a Philosophy<br>of Speech" | Chapter 20 |
| (23) | 5 | Student speeches | Talks to persuade<br>*Instructions, 27* | Review of<br>Chapters 1–20 |
| (24) | | Final exam | Covering of the entire<br>semester's work | |

### Two-semester program: Class schedule, first semester

| | | | | |
|---|---|---|---|---|
| (1) | 1 | Informal lecture;<br>introductions | Preview of course;<br>grading; getting<br>acquainted<br>*Instructions, 1* | Chapter 1 |
| (2) | 1 | Class discussion | Subject: Chapter 1,<br>"Approaching the<br>Study of Speech"<br>*Instructions, 2* | Chapter 2 |
| (3) | 1–2 | Organize and plan<br>panel forums | *Instructions, 3* | Chapter 3 |
| (4) | 1 | Lecture discussion | Subject: Chapter 3,<br>"Taking Part in<br>Group Discussion" | Chapter 4 |
| (5) | 3–6 | Present panel<br>forums | *Instructions, 3* | Chapter 5 |
| (6) | 1 | Class poll | Anonymous poll<br>of class traits,<br>interests, and<br>attitudes<br>*Instructions, 4* | |
| (7) | 3 | Student speeches | Demonstration talks<br>*Instructions, 5* | Chapter 6 |
| (8) | 1 | Research | *Instructions, 6* | Review of<br>Chapters 1–6 |
| (9) | 1 | Written exam | Covering of the lectures<br>and readings to<br>date | Chapter 7 |

| Assignment number | Approximate hours | Class projects | Remarks | Reading assignments |
|---|---|---|---|---|
| (10) | 3 | Student speeches | Anecdote talks<br>*Instructions, 7* | |
| (11) | 1 | Lecture discussion | Subject: Chapter 7,<br>"Speech Outlining" | Chapter 8 |
| (12) | 3 | Student speeches | Statistics-analogy talks<br>*Instructions, 8* | |
| (13) | 1 | Lecture discussion | Subject: Chapter 8,<br>"Conclusions, Introductions, Transitions" | Choosing of biographies for final talks<br>*Instructions, 9* |
| (14) | 4 | Student speeches | Informative talks<br>*Instructions, 10* | Review of Chapters 7–8 |
| (15) | 1 | Written exam | Covering of Chapters 7–8 | Chapter 9 |
| (16) | 1 | Lecture demonstration | Subject: Chapter 9,<br>"Visual Communication" | |
| (17) | 1 | Drills | Posture and bodily action<br>*Instructions, 11* | Chapter 10 |
| (18) | 1 | Demonstration | Voice recording equipment<br>*Instructions, 12* | |
| (19) | 1 | Lecture | Subject: Chapter 10,<br>"Vocal Communication" | |
| (20) | 1 | Demonstration-analysis | Professional recordings<br>*Instructions, 13* | Chapter 11 |
| (21) | 3 | Student speeches | Quotation talks<br>*Instructions, 14* | |
| (22) | 1 | Drills | Voice and articulation exercises<br>*Instructions, 15* | |
| (23) | 1 | Student contest | "Pronunciation Bee"<br>*Instructions, 16* | |

| Assign-<br>ment<br>number | Approx-<br>imate<br>hours | Class projects | Remarks | Reading<br>assign-<br>ments |
|---|---|---|---|---|
| (24) | 1 | Student speeches | Impromptu talks<br>*Instructions, 17* | |
| (25) | 5 | Student speeches | Biographical talks<br>*Instructions, 18* | Review of<br>Chapters 1–11 |
| (26) | 1 | Lecture | Review of Chapters<br>1–11 and preview<br>of next term | |
| (27) | | Final exam | Covering of the entire<br>semester's work | |

## Two-semester program: Class schedule, second semester

| | | | | |
|---|---|---|---|---|
| (1) | 1 | Informal lecture | Preview of course;<br>grading; getting<br>acquainted<br>*Instructions, 1* | Chapter 12 |
| (2) | 2 | Student speeches | Warm-up talks<br>*Instructions, 19* | |
| (3) | 2 | Lecture discussion | Subject: Chapter 12,<br>"Audience Analysis"<br>Optional: *Instruc-<br>tions, 4* | |
| (4) | 2 | Student speeches | Talks adapted to<br>audience interests<br>*Instructions, 20* | Chapter 13 |
| (5) | 2–3 | Student speeches | Heckling talks<br>*Instructions, 21* | |
| (6) | 1 | Lecture discussion | Subject: Chapter 13,<br>"Audience Attention" | |
| (7) | 3 | Student speeches | After-dinner talks;<br>mock banquets<br>*Instructions, 22* | Chapter 14 |
| (8) | 1 | Lecture discussion | Subject: Chapter<br>14, "Audience Un-<br>derstanding" | Review of<br>Chapters<br>12–14 |
| (9) | 1 | Written exam | Covering of Chapters<br>12–14 | |
| (10) | 4 | Student speeches | Talks to inform<br>*Instructions, 10* | Chapter 15 |

| Assignment number | Approximate hours | Class projects | Remarks | Reading assignments |
|---|---|---|---|---|
| (11) | 1 | Lecture discussion | Subject: Chapter 15, "Reinforcing Audience Attitudes" | |
| (12) | 3 | Student speeches | Talks for special occasions *Instructions, 23* | Chapter 16 |
| (13) | 1 | Lecture discussion | Subject: Chapter 16, "Building Audience Attitudes" | Chapter 17 |
| (14) | 1 | Lecture discussion | Subject: Chapter 17, "Releasing Audience Attitudes" | |
| (15) | 4 | Student speeches | Direct argument *Instructions, 24* | Review of Chapters 15–17 |
| (16) | 1 | Written exam | Covering of Chapters 15–17 | Chapter 18 |
| (17) | 1 | Lecture discussion | Subject: Chapter 18, "The Speaker's Personality" | |
| (18) | 2–3 | Student speeches | General impression talks *Instructions, 25* | Chapter 19 |
| (19) | 1 | Lecture discussion | Subject: Chapter 19, "The Speaker's Responsibility" | |
| (20) | 3–4 | Student speeches | Indirect argument *Instructions, 26* | Chapter 20 |
| (21) | 1 | Lecture discussion | Subject: Chapter 20, "Theories of Communication" | |
| (22) | 5–6 | Student speeches | Talks to persuade *Instructions, 27* | Review of Chapters 12–20 |
| (23) | 1 | Lecture | Subject: "Continuing the Study of Speech" | |
| (24) | | Final exam | Covering of the entire semester's work | |

## INSTRUCTIONS

### 1. Introductions

At the first or second class meeting each student will introduce himself, standing at his chair. He will give his name, a suggestion that may help others to remember his name, his home town, and his major field of study. Since the purpose is simply to get acquainted, these introductions can be put in the form of a memory game. After the first student introduces himself, the second student should name the first before introducing himself. The third student should name the first and the second, and so on. It is surprising how many names can be learned in this manner.

### 2. Class discussion

As a basis for class discussion you might administer this short test to yourself. Look over the statements and mentally indicate your present opinion as to whether each is true or false. Answers to this test can be found on page 392, but first try to answer them yourself.

1. The study of public speaking dates back to ancient times.
2. The most important test of speaking effectiveness is *always* in terms of audience response.
3. By and large, public speakers are born, not made.
4. The aim of a public speaking course is to teach the student to speak at any time, on any subject, with a minimum of preparation.
5. There are several fundamental differences between public speaking and conversation.
6. *How* you say a thing is more important than *what* you say.
7. There are five vowel sounds in the English language (and sometimes two more).
8. Most of our greatest speakers and actors still experience a great deal of stage fright.
9. There is only one correct pronunciation for any given word.
10. "Gestures" should be defined as movements of the arms and hands.
11. An extemporaneous speech is one given without preparation.
12. A good speaker should never lean on the rostrum or on other furniture.
13. In reading poetry aloud, the reader should pause at each comma, period, or end of a line.
14. The first step in the efficient preparation of a public speech is to write a manuscript or at least an outline.
15. The proper way to close any given speech is to say, "I thank you."

### 3. Panel forums

The class will be divided into about four groups of five or six students each. Each group will present a panel discussion before the other members of the class. This project will give the instructor a chance to hear the students "think out loud," and will give them practice in extemporaneously putting their thoughts into words in an informal, conversational situation.

The project will require from three to six class meetings to plan and to present, depending on how extensive the instructor wishes it to be.

*Planning for the panels.*    Each group will meet separately in a different part of the room and will immediately elect one of its members as the chairman. Their second task will be to choose a discussion topic, and each student should come prepared to suggest one or more topics which he would like to discuss or hear discussed. Topics should be timely, controversial, and interesting.

Each group will then plan its attack on its topic. One way of doing this is to subdivide the topic so that each member is responsible for one phase or aspect of it. The panel may plan to open by having each member give a brief (one-minute) summarizing statement of his phase of the topic. After these opening statements the whole group may engage in a give-and-take discussion on the topic as a whole.

*Presenting the panel discussion.*    Chairs for the panel should be placed in a semicircle facing the rest of the class. If a table is available, it should be placed in front of the semicircle. The names of the panel members may be written on the chalkboard behind the chairs. The chairman should sit at one end of the semicircle. During the discussion, members should remain seated. See Chapter 3 for further instructions.

*Open forum period.* .  If only one panel is to be heard at each meeting, the thirty-minute discussion may be followed by a ten-minute forum, permitting the rest of the class to join the panel with questions or brief comments. The chairman of the group should preside over the open forum and enforce the following rules: Questions should be addressed to a specified member of the panel through the chairman. The chairman may permit one or more members of the panel to answer, but a question and an answer together should be limited to one minute—he should not allow dialogues between a questioner and an answerer. He should encourage maximum participation, get questions from as many members of the audience and answers from as many members of the panel as possible. The chairman has the right to restate questions which he thinks should be made clearer, or to overrule questions which are irrelevant. Suggested topics:

Should we have censorship of the national press?
Should the American party system be changed to "liberal" and "conservative"?
Should we attend classes on a 12-months-a-year, 6-days-a-week basis?
How close can the United States come to having "free trade" policies?
What can be done about the narcotics problem?
Should all colleges and universities have compulsory chapel period?
How can the U.S. secondary school system be streamlined for more efficient college preparation?
Should we have more "how to do it" courses in college?
How might the draft system be made more equitable?
How can fraternities and sororities better contribute to campus life?

How can TV advertising be improved?

If we had a war with Russia, who would win?

## 4. Class poll

Mimeographed questionnaires similar to those appearing below will be distributed. To encourage frankness in answering, the poll will be anonymous. Fill out the questionnaire accurately and rapidly. When all students have filled in their answers, the papers will be collected and redistributed at random to keep the poll anonymous. The instructor will then read each item, and call for a show of hands—students voting according to the anonymous papers before them. The instructor will announce the count of hands for each item, and everyone can record the count on the margins of the ballot.

After the results have been tabulated each student will have a reasonably complete and accurate picture of the audience he will be addressing throughout the term. If time permits, immediately following the tabulation a class discussion of significant trends and exceptions may be conducted, together with a discussion of how these data can help each student in planning future talks. The record of the tabulation should be kept by every student, for it will be useful in future assignments.

This poll is anonymous. Do not write your name on this sheet.

---

### Part one—composition of audience

Place check marks in appropriate blanks. (*Code* _____)

1. My age.

   a _____under 18   b _____18–20      c _____21–25   d _____26 or over

2. Urban-rural background. I spent most of my life before 21 in:

   a _____farm community or village        c _____city of 25,000–100,000

   b _____town under 25,000 population      d _____city over 100,000

3. Geographical background. I spent most of my life before 21 in:

   a _____this immediate locality      e _____South; Southeast; Texas

   b _____Pacific Coast area           f _____East Coast or New England

   c _____Southwest; Mountain          g _____outside continental U.S.

   d _____Midwest

4. National background.

   a _____at least one parent or grandparent born outside U.S.

   b _____language other than English is native tongue for at least one person in immediate family or grandparents

Answers to true-false questions on page 390: The first two statements are true; the remaining thirteen statements are false.

5. Economic background. To the best of my knowledge, parental income up to time I was 21, except for unusual periods, probably averaged, on a yearly basis:

a _____$5,000 or less            c _____$10,000–$20,000
b _____$5,000–$10,000            d _____over $20,000

6. Military service. I spent some of the years 1941–53:

a _____serving in World War II or Korean war
b _____in peacetime military training

7. Marital, parental status. I am now:

a _____married                  c _____single
b _____parent                   d _____divorced or widowed

8. Political. preferences. Most of the time I tend to favor:

a _____Democrats                c _____third minor party
b _____Republicans              d _____none in particular

9. Religious preferences. (*Check one or more.*) I tend to favor:

a _____the Roman Catholic faith
b _____the Eastern Catholic faith
c _____a Protestant faith
d _____the Jewish faith
e _____the Moslem faith
f _____no church in particular (although I hold religious beliefs)
g _____agnostic, "free-thinking," or atheistic beliefs
h _____attending church regularly
i _____attending church irregularly
j _____attending seldom or never

10. Membership in certain groups.

a _____I am a member (or pledge) of a social fraternity or sorority
b _____I am or have been a member of a labor union
c _____I am or have been or hope to be a member of a recognized business or professional organization (such as The American Bar Association, The American Management Association, The National Association of Manufacturers, The American Medical Association, etc.)
d _____I am a member of a veterans' organization

11. Vocational aspiration or connection _____

---

## Part two—audience attitudes on contemporary affairs

*Directions*   The purpose of this poll is to supplement course materials on audience analysis. Its value depends on the frankness and accuracy of your answers. Please draw a circle around the *A* if you tend, in general, to *approve* of the ideas represented by the person, group, or statement; around the *D* if you tend to *disapprove;* around *P* if you are *uncertain* or your feelings are divided; and around the *X* if you *are not sure to whom or to what the item refers.*

A D X ?  1. John F. Kennedy        A D X ?  16. Jawaharlal Nehru
A D X ?  2. Dwight D. Eisenhower   A D X ?  17. Drew Pearson
A D X ?  3. Harry S. Truman        A D X ?  18. Fidel Castro
A D X ?  4. Mrs. Eleanor Roosevelt A D X ?  19. Walter Reuther
A D X ?  5. James Hoffa            A D X ?  20. Charles de Gaulle
A D X ?  6. Adlai Stevenson        A D X ?  21. American Legion
A D X ?  7. Earl Warren            A D X ?  22. the NAACP
A D X ?  8. Norman Thomas          A D X ?  23. Movie censorship
A D X ?  9. Konrad Adenauer        A D X ?  24. NATO
A D X ? 10. Richard Nixon          A D X ?  25. the WCTU
A D X ? 11. Gamal Nasser           A D X ?  26. the DAR
A D X ? 12. Nelson Rockefeller     A D X ?  27. the NAM
A D X ? 13. Winston Churchill      A D X ?  28. the AFL–CIO
A D X ? 14. Linus Pauling          A D X ?  29. the AMA
A D X ? 15. Hubert Humphrey        A D X ?  30. the United Nations

A D X ? 31. The present administration has been successful in its domestic policy.
A D X ? 32. The Voice of America is a waste of money.
A D X ? 33. The United States should reduce its defense budget by at least ten billion dollars.
A D X ? 34. Negroes, on the whole, have a square deal in the United States.
A D X ? 35. Russia apparently intends to conquer the world.
A D X ? 36. College fraternities and sororities are, in general, satisfactory.
A D X ? 37. A re-emphasis on traditional religion is greatly needed in the world today.
A D X ? 38. Medical care today is too expensive for most Americans.
A D X ? 39. The Communist party in the United States should be outlawed.
A D X ? 40. There is too much emphasis on ballistic missiles in present defense plans.
A D X ? 41. Labor unions, in general, are beneficial to the American way of life.
A D X ? 42. There is an overemphasis on big college athletic programs.
A D X ? 43. The United States should extend reciprocal trade agreements to cover more nations and more products.
A D X ? 44. Congressional investigating committees are doing a very good job.
A D X ? 45. The American public-school systems are doing an adequate job of educating American youth.
A D X ? 46. Farm price supports are unnecessary and wasteful.
A D X ? 47. The present administration has been successful in its foreign policy.
A D X ? 48. The average American is overtaxed.

A D X ?  49. Voting in the United States should be made compulsory.
A D X ?  50. The Kinsey reports have made a valuable contribution to American life.
A D X ?  51. The present policy of student draft deferment is fair.

---

## 5. Demonstration talk

In this four- to five-minute talk you will present one point and then support it, largely by means of visual aids. Supplement what you *say* with something the audience can *see*. Don't rely entirely on the chalkboard—consider the list of possible visual aids in Chapter 6 and try to make an ingenious choice.

Follow this sequence:
1. *Opening.* State the main point of the talk.
2. *Transition.* Get from the statement of your point into the supporting materials.
3. *Development.* Your main task is to clarify, reinforce, or prove your point. If you use some explanation or description, keep both brief, simple, concrete, and interesting. Weave in your visual aids so that they are an integral part of the talk.
4. *Transition.* Get from developmental materials into your concluding statements.
5. *Conclusion.* Summarize or restate your point.

Your delivery of this talk should be concerned with just three things.

1. *Handling visual aids.* Try to handle them easily and meaningfully without excess or random movements. Be sure the audience can see them.
2. *Directness.* Talk *with* your classmates. Look at them. Think in terms of their reactions. Be friendly and communicative.
3. *Animation.* Show by facial expression, mood, and manner that you are alert, interested, enthusiastic.

You may use notes but do not rely upon them too heavily. You will find that the visual aids themselves become "a set of notes," reminding you of your planned ideas. Study Criticism Chart 5. Suggested topics:

Brushing the teeth correctly
Surfing
Making basic football formations
Practicing to be a drum major
Performing magic tricks
Painting with the fingers
Taking a picture
Setting a table
Hitting a baseball

Polishing a car
Arranging flowers
Modeling in clay
Making pizza
Using good form in bowling
Demonstrating a printing process
Handling a firearm
Practicing proper form in tennis or golf

## Criticism chart 5    *Demonstration talk*

Name_____Time____to____Total_____
Topic_____Visual Aid_____

OPENING   1   2   3   4   5 [1]

*Main point:* stated—not stated; clear—not clear enough; too brief—wordy, abstract, technical, involved

TRANSITION   1   2   3   4   5

Adequate—fair—lacking; brief, smooth, appropriate—wordy, awkward, inappropriate

DEVELOPMENT OF POINT   1   2   3   4   5

*Explanation and/or description:* brief, simple, clear, adequate—wordy, complicated, hard to understand, inadequate; concrete, specific—abstract, vague; interesting—dull; compact—rambling

*Use of visual aid:* an integral part of the talk—partially appropriate—mostly superfluous; clearly visible to audience—not clearly visible to audience; helped clarify the point—distracted from the point—too complex or detailed

CONCLUSION   1   2   3   4   5

*Summary or restatement:* adequate—fair—lacking; appropriate—inappropriate; smooth—too abrupt

DELIVERY   1   2   3   4   5

*Handling of visual aids:* skillful—fair—distracting; too much physical movement—too little physical movement; appropriate—inappropriate, awkward, blocked view of visual aid; movements coordinated—jerky; relaxed—tense; vigorous—limp—too vigorous; meaningful—random; "fiddled" with _____

*Directness:* excellent, partial, lacking; looked at audience, at floor, ceiling, walls, out of window, over the heads, at notes, at visual aids, at one person or part of audience; eyes shifty, faraway look; general manner: aloof, condescending, reserved, passive, impersonal, uncertain—friendly, poised, communicative, forceful, intense

*Animation:* facial expression: excellent—fair—lacking—overdone—inappropriate; general manner: lively, enthusiastic, alert—listless, colorless, stolid

## 6. Research assignment

Following the suggestions given in Chapter 6 begin collecting materials on a speech topic of your choice. Bring to class ten pieces of information on this topic. Record the information according to the instructions on pages 111–12. You should have one card each from the following sources: a book, a periodical, a newspaper, a pamphlet, an encyclopedia, a book of quotations, an almanac, an atlas, *Who's Who,* and either the *Statesman's Yearbook* or the *Statistical Abstract of the United States.*

[1] On the rating scale, 1 means far below average; 2, somewhat below average; 3, average; 4, somewhat above average; 5, superior.

## 7. Anecdote talk

In this three- to four-minute talk you will develop one point, principally by means of anecdote. You may include either one or two anecdotes, depending on time limits. If two are used, each should develop the same point. Follow this sequence:

1. *Opening.* Just start telling the anecdote. Don't state your point.
2. *Anecdote.* Review the suggestions regarding the choosing of anecdotes, pages 93–95. While telling the anecdote(s), imply your point, but don't state it.
3. *Transitions.* Get from the anecdote into the second anecdote if you have one. Lead into your statement of the main point.
4. *Conclusion.* State your point.

Four aspects of delivery will be practiced. Directness and animation remain the same as in the previous criticism chart. Appearance and bodily action will be added. Study Criticism Chart 7 regarding these additional aspects of delivery. Try to include the appropriate details as you practice your talk aloud. Don't memorize and don't overuse your notes.

### Criticism chart 7 *Anecdote talk*

Name_____*Time*____*to*____*Total*_____
*Topic*_____

OPENING  1  2  3  4  5
  *Began with illustration:* well done—fair—weak; stated the point—used extraneous materials—"hemmed and hawed"
ANECDOTE  1  2  3  4  5
  *Style:* narrative—not narrative
  *Detail:* well done—too many—too few
  *Arrangement:* clear, easy to follow—unclear, vague, confused; built to climax—"ran down"—no climax—anticlimax
  *General effect:* pointed, appropriate, interesting, in good taste—pointless, inappropriate, insufficiently interesting, in poor taste, tended to "drag" in places
TRANSITIONS  1  2  3  4  5
  Adequate—fair—lacking; brief—too brief; smooth, appropriate—wordy, awkward, inappropriate, abrupt
CONCLUSION  1  2  3  4  5
  *Main point:* stated—not stated; clear—not clear enough; brief—too brief—wordy, abstract, technical, involved; appropriate—inappropriate; smooth—too abrupt
DELIVERY  1  2  3  4  5
  *Directness:* see Criticism Chart 5
  *Animation:* see Criticism Chart 5
  *Appearance:* dress appropriate, well-groomed—distracting; posture alert, at ease—tense, stiff, formal, slouchy, stooped, listless, swayed, leaned on _____

BODILY ACTION:

*Platform position:* no change—paced, restless; moved about easily—awkwardly—mechanically; moved at appropriate times—at inappropriate times

*Feet:* well-managed—fair—distracting; jiggled, teetered—straddled—at attention—weight on one foot—shifting

*Basic hand positions:* satisfactory—constantly shifted—the same; behind back —at sides—in pockets—in front of body—on lectern—twisted or rubbed together; fiddled with _____

*Gestures:* lacking—seldom—frequent—too many; natural—appropriate—not carried through—lacked variety

## 8. Statistics-analogy talk

In this three- to four-minute talk you will again develop one point, this time by means of statistics and analogy. Review the section in Chapter 6 on statistics. A leading suggestion was that the meaning of statistics must frequently be clarified by analogy. In this talk clarify your statistics by using at least one analogy. The talk provides a good opportunity to practice handling of notes—you may want to read some of the statistics. Visual aids may be used to supplement the figures. Study Criticism Chart 8. Suggested topics:

Show the comparative size of the planets by relating them to some well-known objects of everyday life.

Show the major divisions of the national budget by dividing up one dollar.

Show the effects of inflation by the change in price of one particular food item.

Show some of the vast distances in space by scaled comparison with some distances on the earth.

Show the consumption of water, oil, or gasoline by referring to the size lake (length, width, depth) it would make.

**Criticism chart 8**  *Statistics-analogy talk*

Name_____ *Time_____ to_____ Total_____*

*Topic_____*

CONTENT

*Speech structure*   1   2   3   4   5
*Suggestions:*

*Statistics*   1   2   3   4   5

| | | | |
|---|---|---|---|
| Did they support a main point? | Yes_____ | Partly_____ | No_____ |
| Were they impressive? | Yes_____ | Partly_____ | No_____ |
| Were they clearly understandable? | Yes_____ | Partly_____ | No_____ |
| Were they easily remembered? | Yes_____ | Partly_____ | No_____ |

*Analogies*   1   2   3   4   5
    Did they explain the statistics?        Yes_____Partly_____No_____
    Were they appropriate?              Yes_____Partly_____No_____
    Were they vivid?                    Yes_____Partly_____No_____
DELIVERY   1   2   3   4   5
    See Criticism Chart 7
SUGGESTIONS:

## 9. Choosing biography for final speech

Probably it seems to you that the end of the semester is still far away. Nevertheless, it is time to begin preparing for your final speech. Your final speech will be the longest of the semester—seven to eight minutes—and it should be the most carefully prepared. Thorough preparation requires an early choice of subject and ample time for gathering the speech materials.

Each student in the class will choose as the subject for his final speech the life of some important or unusual man or woman. The man or woman must be one about whom a book has been written or about whom an equivalent amount of material is available. First, you should immediately consider a list of prominent people in whom you have a personal interest. Second, you should find biographies or autobiographies of these people and scan these books in order to determine which ones seem to be the most interestingly written. Third, you should ask yourself which one of these possible subjects would be of the greatest interest to the members of your audience. Upon these three bases you will make your final choice of subject.

As soon as you have chosen your subject you should notify your instructor. In order that each final speech may be of maximum interest to the class, no more than one speech will be given about any one person. The first student to request a certain personality will be given preference.

As soon as your subject has been approved by the instructor you should begin reading the biography of the person you have chosen. Read it not as a textbook, but as you would read a novel. Be on the alert for supporting materials, anecdotes, quotations, explanations, descriptions, instances, statistics, and visual aids. You will be expected to use at least five forms of support in your final speech.

You cannot condense an entire book into eight minutes. Therefore, as you read your biography you should be considering some particular angle or aspect by which you can narrow the topic to suit your time limits.

The use of condensed biographies such as those contained in the *Reader's Digest* provides an unpermitted short cut. It is not permitted because it denies you the experience of speaking from an adequate background of information. It is to give you this experience that the assignment is made.

**399**

## 10. Informative talk

Prepare a six-minute talk with the general purpose to inform. Emphasis should be put on clear organization. The materials of this speech should be outlined in accordance with the suggestions in Chapter 7. Study Criticism Chart 10 for a sample of how the success of the speech may be evaluated by the instructor. Suggested topics:

Interesting aspects of a foreign language
Splitting the atom
Famous discoveries in history
People who almost became President
Some aspect of law enforcement
The status of capital punishment
Famous hoaxes in history
Famous "con" games
Unsolved crimes
What's next in space?
Reading music
Interesting customs of ancient civilization
The characteristics of a sports car
The effects of atomic bombs
What is fallout?
The typical bomb shelter
A famous battle in history
Vitamin pills
Trends in car styling
The roots of Christianity
The roots of democratic theory
Speed reading
Points on income tax
Investing money
Methods of shorthand
Extra ways to make money
Scholarships you might be interested in
What is classical music?
First aid
Reports on the Peace Corps
Our city government

## Criticism chart 10  *Talk to inform*

Name_____Time____to _____Total_____
Topic_____

INTRODUCTION   1   2   3   4   5

    Did the opening catch audience attention?
    Did the speaker establish his right to inform upon this subject?
    Was the audience motivated to want to learn?
    Did the speaker lead into subject matter effectively?
    Was a preview of main points given?

BODY   1   2   3   4   5

    Was the central idea clear?
    Did the main points and subpoints clarify the central idea adequately?
    Did the main points and subpoints form an easy-to-remember pattern?
    Did the body of the speech employ aids to learning?

CONCLUSION   1   2   3   4   5

    Was the entire speech focused on the central idea?
    Were the main points summarized?
    Did the closing words give an appropriate, rounded-out effect?

DELIVERY   1   2   3   4   5

    See Criticism Chart 7.

## 11. Drills for posture and bodily action

In your demonstration talk you should have experienced how spontaneity can be achieved. Outside the class you should have been practicing posture and bodily actions that can and should be made habitual. These class drills will provide the instructor with a chance to check up on your progress toward acquiring these habits. The basic idea of the drills is to have all students, individually or together, practice posture, conventional gestures, and moving about the platform. One drill sequence may proceed as follows:

    Student is introduced by a chairman.
    Rises at chair.
    Nods head toward chairman. (Don't bow with body.)
    Says, "Mr. Chairman."
    Smiles.
    Walks to platform. (How do you habitually walk?)
    Faces audience, pauses, smiles. (What about your posture?)
    Says, "Fellow students."
    Makes a one-sentence statement requiring the use of one of the conventional gestures (pages 173–75).
    Says, "And now I would like to introduce . . . [naming next classmate]."
    Gestures with hand and arm toward classmate.

Returns to seat.
Classmate repeats above sequence.

Another alternative is to present pantomimes as a drill in visual communication. The class can be divided into teams of two or three. Each team should agree on a situation or setting to be presented as a brief pantomime. They will prepare and rehearse beforehand in accordance with the instructor's suggestions. In practicing and presenting the pantomime strive for free uninhibited movement. Put yourself into the mood and spirit of the skit. Be alert and responsive to the actions of others and do your own part wholeheartedly. Try to avoid jerky, incomplete gestures and random, purposeless, distracting movements. Suggested topics:

In the dentist's office
A conductor rehearsing the orchestra
A high school dance
A high pressure salesman on a used car lot
Eating a huge meal
Exercising in a reducing salon
Giving travel directions

### 12. The use of tape-recording equipment

If your instructor decides to use this class project, he will demonstrate in class one or more types of recording equipment.

On this assignment you will (1) find out how recording equipment can be used for voice practice, and (2) try to hear yourself as others hear you. One way of doing this involves the dividing of the class into pairs of students: The instructor interviews each pair, and the interview is recorded and played back.

Your instructor may also wish to have you give an oral reading which he will tape-record and use for purposes of analyzing and criticizing your voice, articulation, and pronunciation.

### 13. Analysis of professional recordings

The instructor may play for the class a recording by an unknown student from some other class. You will listen carefully and fill out a chart similar to Criticism Chart 14. The instructor may then see how much you have heard and how well you judged. He may call attention to a good many things that you failed to hear.

The instructor may next play records or tape recordings of one or more professional speakers, readers, or actors. Contrast these professional voices with the student voice you have just heard, and also with your own recorded voice. Make critical notes to indicate new ideas of *what can be done*. You may not plan to become a professional, but by listening carefully to examples of excellence you should be able to set higher personal goals for improving your audibility, distinctness and accuracy, meaningfulness, and pleasantness of voice and articulation.

## 14. Quotation talk

In this three- to four-minute talk you will develop one point, chiefly by means of quotations. Approximately half your speaking time should be devoted to the quotations. The quoted portions should be *read* from your notes. For suggestions on reading from manuscript, study pages 224–26.

Criticism of this talk will be concentrated on voice, articulation, and pronunciation. Your instructor may wish to use Criticism Chart 14.

**Criticism chart 14**   *Vocal communication*

*Name*_____*Time*____*to*____*Total*_____
*Topic*_____

AUDIBILITY   1   2   3   4   5
  *Suggestions*
  _____ faulty breathing (see page 194)
  _____ inattention to audibility (see pages 194–95)
  _____ poorly adapted to acoustics (see page 195)
  _____ endings trailed away (see page 195)
  _____ muffled (see page 195)
  _____ pitch level too low (see pages 195–96)
  _____ other difficulties of audibility (consult instructor)
DISTINCTNESS AND PRONUNCIATION   1   2   3   4   5
  *Suggestions*
  _____ careless, lip-lazy (see pages 197–98)
  _____ slurred, mumbled (see pages 197–98)
  _____ muffled (see page 195)
  _____ too precise, affected (see pages 198–99)
  _____ regional or foreign accent (consult instructor)
  _____ faulty sounds (see pages 197–98)


  mispronounced words (see page 190)


  other inaccuracies (consult instructor)


MEANINGFULNESS   1   2   3   4   5
  *Suggestions*
  _____ insensitive to meanings (see pages 199–200)
  _____ rate too fast (see pages 200–02)
  _____ rate too slow (see pages 200–02)

_____ rate monotonous (see pages 200–01)
_____ phrasing jerky, illogical (see pages 201–02)
_____ volume monotonous (see page 202)
_____ pitch monotonous (see page 202)
_____ general vocal quality monotonous (see page 203)
_____ other difficulties of meaningfulness (consult instructor)
*Additional comments*

## 15. Drill: voice and articulation

Your instructor may devote a class hour to the voice and articulation exercises described in Chapter 10 or he may add exercises of his own choice. This is a good chance for you to make sure you understand how to practice the exercises you need as indicated by your criticism chart (see preceding project). Some exercises may be done individually, some in unison.

## 16. "Pronunciation Bee"

The class may be divided into two or more teams. The instructor will provide lists of commonly mispronounced words—similar to the list provided below. A "pronouncing bee" will then be held. The exact rules for scoring may be agreed on in advance. If time permits, the contest may be extended to include the tongue twisters on pages 405–06. Successive members of each of the teams can attempt a tongue twister; the instructor can act as referee of the contest.

*Do you pronounce these correctly?*

| | |
|---|---|
| 1. regime | 17. metal |
| 2. something | 18. later |
| 3. eleven | 19. latter |
| 4. chimney | 20. garage |
| 5. pumpkin | 21. slovenly |
| 6. length | 22. prestige |
| 7. era | 23. get |
| 8. gesture | 24. instead |
| 9. pantomime | 25. again |
| 10. chasm | 26. catch |
| 11. architect | 27. just |
| 12. diphtheria | 28. I'm |
| 13. relevant | 29. alias |
| 14. naphtha | 30. genuine |
| 15. tremendous | 31. theater |
| 16. notice | 32. piano |

33. wrestle
34. deaf
35. zoology
36. penalize
37. strength
38. perform
39. experiment
40. heroine
41. discretion
42. complacent
43. guarantee
44. pronunciation
45. consul
46. unless
47. undo
48. soda
49. idea
50. egg
51. measure
52. kettle
53. fellow
54. potato
55. cow
56. pretty
57. children
58. hundred
59. brethren
60. prepare

61. professor
62. protect
63. introduce
64. represent
65. aggravate
66. geography
67. perspiration
68. with
69. modern
70. aluminum
71. cavalry
72. larynx
73. diphthong
74. usual
75. mutual
76. escape
77. diary
78. medieval
79. temperature
80. arctic
81. adjective
82. asked
83. understand
84. picture
85. accessory
86. government
87. chocolate
88. poem

## *Can you handle these tongue twisters?*

1. The sea ceaseth and sufficeth us.
2. Amidst the mists and coldest frosts,
   With barest wrists and stoutest boasts,
   He thrusts his fists against the posts,
   And still insists he sees the ghosts.
3. Bring me some ice, not some mice.
4. Many a wit is not a whit wittier than Whittier.
5. Three thousandths is less than six hundredths.
6. My good blade carves the casques of men,
   My tough lance thrusteth sure.
7. Around the rough and rugged rock the ragged rascal ran.
8. Everywhere in the country one saw the bright broom blossoms.

9. Shave a cedar shingle thin.
10. Better buy better rubber buggy bumpers.
11. Six long slim slick slender saplings.
12. Susan sells sea shells on the seashore.
13. The sun shines on the shop signs.
14. The clumsy kitchen clock click-clacked.
15. Rich gifts wax poor when givers prove unkind.
16. Thou wouldst not play false, yet wouldst wrongly win.
17. Suddenly seaward swept the squall.
18. Six thick thistle sticks; six thick thistles stick.
19. The Cataract strong then plunges along,
    Striking and raging as if a war waging,
    Rising and leaping, sinking and creeping,
    Showering and springing, flying and flinging,
    Writhing and ringing.
20. Are our cars here?
21. National Shropshire Sheep Association.
22. "Are you copper bottoming them, my man?" "No, I'm aluminuming 'em, mum."
23. Linger longer, Lemuel Lister, lilting limitless lullabies.
24. Dick twirled the stick athwart the path.
25. The Red Cross lady led the parade across the corner, interrupting a wedding party.


### 17. Impromptu talk

This exercise provides you with a chance to try out the suggestions for impromptu speaking from Chapter 11. Time limit for these talks: one minute.

One way of proceeding is as follows: The instructor can conceal in a large sack a number of small objects in common use, such as a pen, key, ruler, button, safety pin, or what have you. A student can draw an object at random from the sack. He can be given one minute in which to plan a talk about the object he chooses; then just as he starts his impromptu talk, a second student can draw an object from the sack. In this way, each student prepares his talk during the one minute in which his predecessor is speaking.

Instead of having students draw objects from a sack, the instructor may prefer to have them draw cards on which topics have been written—possibly in the form of maxims, quotations, or the like.

After all students have given impromptu talks, the class may vote for the best speaker. Each student turns in a list of the five best speakers (himself excepted, of course) in the order of his preference. Votes can be tallied by instructor, possibly on the chalkboard during the class hour. You may find a surprising variation of opinion among the students regarding the ranking of some of the talks. It will be instructive to analyze why some of the speeches received rather consistent ratings, while others may have been scored all the way from first to last.

## 18. Biography speech

The final class speeches will be based on the biographies or autobiographies of prominent or unusual people. In accordance with Instructions, 9, you have already chosen the life of some man or woman, and have read a biography of that person. Your next job is to narrow these materials down to the time limit, which is seven to eight minutes. Do not do this by merely giving a chronological condensation of the events in the life of the subject. Such a listing of names, dates, places, and accomplishments is usually boring to the audience and contains so many details that none of them is remembered. Therefore, try to choose one particular aspect of the person's life and use only those materials which are particularly adapted to the chosen aspect. For example, it is impossible in eight minutes to cover all aspects of the life of Abraham Lincoln. However, you might talk on "Lincoln the Lawyer," or "Lincoln the Public Speaker," or "Lincoln as a Husband," or any one of a dozen other aspects of his life and career. As another example, one student successfully narrowed a topic by choosing the subject, "Tom Paine Was Not an Atheist."

If you have decided on the particular aspect of the subject's life that you want to discuss, your next task will be to build an outline following the suggestions in Chapters 7 and 8.

Having prepared your outline, you will practice aloud from it before the date assigned for your class performance. Do not try to memorize a particular set of words. In your delivery you will attempt to practice all of the skills that have been studied during the semester. These are summarized by Criticism Chart 18, below.

You should make two copies of your outline and turn in one copy to your instructor before speaking. He may then wish to criticize the content of the speech by writing notations in the margins of the outline.

### Criticism Chart 18    *Biography Speech*

*Name*_____*Time*____*to*____*Total*_____
*Topic*_____

CONTENT

*Introduction*    1    2    3    4    5
  Was the opening interesting?
  Was it appropriate?
  Did it lead smoothly into the body of the speech?
*Body*    1    2    3    4    5
  Was there a single central idea?
  Was the central idea clear enough?
  Were there two to five main points?
  Were the main points interrelated?
  Were the several speech units well organized? Statements? Supports? Transitions?

Were at least five forms of support used? Explanation? Description? Anecdote? Instances? Quotations? Statistics? Visual aids?

*Conclusion*   1   2   3   4   5

Was the conclusion appropriate?

Did it round off the speech?

Did it ramble?

Was it too abrupt?

DELIVERY

*Appearance*   1   2   3   4   5

Dress; posture

*Bodily communication*   1   2   3   4   5

Change of position on platform; basic position of hands; gestures

*Vocal communication*   1   2   3   4   5

Audibility; distinctness; pronunciation; meaningfulness

*Language*   1   2   3   4   5

Meaningfulness; simplicity and precision; concreteness; figurative language; fluency

*General impressions*   1   2   3   4   5

Directness; animation; friendliness; sincerity; poise; other

### 19. Warm-up talk

Prepare a three-minute talk on "How to Lose Friends and Alienate People," or some other subject if your instructor so prescribes. The purpose of the assignment is to get back into the feel of speechmaking after a lapse of time since the first semester's work, and simultaneously to illustrate from your own experience some of the principles of audience analysis discussed in Chapter 12.

### 20. Audience interest talk

Prepare a three-minute talk on "What This College (or University, or Community) Needs More Than Anything Else." Adapt the talk to the immediate interests of the audience, and make that adaptation clear by references to places, persons, or events within the personal experience of the audience. Be guided by the class poll (Instructions, 4) in choosing a topic and planning the talk.

### 21. Heckling talk

Prepare a two-minute talk on a subject likely to arouse the antagonism of some members of the class.

During the presentation of these talks, audience members will be permitted to heckle the speakers. Each student speaker will have a student chairman, and the heckling will be conducted in accordance with rules previously agreed on, enforced by the student chairman.

The assignment provides practice for the speaker in adapting to immediate audience response, and provides a revealing cross section of some of the thoughts that run through listeners' minds while they listen to a speech. Suggested topics:

I came here from the greatest state in the Union
Most of you were spoiled by your overindulgent parents
Taxes (or tuition) should be increased
Our football team doesn't deserve to win a game
Shakespeare's plays were written by someone else
Women are inferior to men (or vice versa)
The grades being given in this class are too high
You ought to vote Democratic (or Republican)
Let's take Santa out of Christmas
The United States would be better off under a dictatorship
You are all downright conformists
All special school vacations should be eliminated
Weeknight dating should be eliminated
We should abolish all college athletics

## 22. After-dinner talk

The class will be divided into groups, and each group will prepare and present a mock banquet. Each group will elect one of its members as toastmaster, select a suitable imaginary occasion, determine a theme, and decide on an appropriate sequence of topics for its speakers.

The general purpose of these talks will be to entertain, and practice will be given in using the suggestions in Chapter 13. Emphasis will be upon studying the factors of attention.

## 23. Talk for special occasion

The class will be divided into teams of three. Each team will plan a program of welcome (or farewell) and response; or presentation and acceptance. Although the programs will represent hypothetical situations, they must be plausible and serious. Talks should be planned in accordance with suggestions in Chapter 15. Criticism Charts 23a, b, and c are suggested as one way of evaluating the success of this assignment. There are three charts numbered 23–a for the chairman; b for a talk of welcome, farewell, or presentation; and c for a talk of acceptance or response.

### Criticism chart 23a  *Speech of introduction*

Name_____ Time_____to_____Total_____

INTRODUCTION   1   2   3   4   5
    Was the hypothetical occasion plausible?
    Did the opening remarks set an appropriate atmosphere?

Did the opening remarks lead smoothly into the introduction itself?

BODY  1  2  3  4  5

Did the introducer "humanize" his speaker?

Did the introducer make the audience want to hear the speaker?

Did the introducer overpraise the speaker?

Did the introducer state the speaker's subject properly?

Was interest aroused in the topic?

Was the topic accurately announced?

Did the introducer "steal the speaker's thunder" by saying too much about the topic?

CONCLUSION  1  2  3  4  5

Were the final words climactic?

Did the introducer lead the applause?

Did the introducer remain standing until the speaker reached lectern?

DELIVERY  1  2  3  4  5

See Criticism Chart 18.

### Criticism chart 23b  *Welcome, farewell, and presentation*

Name_____Time_____to_____Total_____

---

INTRODUCTION  1  2  3  4  5

Did the speaker refer to the chairman's remarks?

Did he refer to the occasion?

Was the hypothetical occasion plausible?

Was the opening appropriate?

BODY  1  2  3  4  5

Did the speaker give appropriate praise to the recipient?

Was the praise overdone?

Were there enough illustrative supports, such as anecdotes, instances, and quotations?

CONCLUSION  1  2  3  4  5

Did final words round off the talk?

Did the conclusion focus attention on the main theme or subject?

Was the conclusion climactic?

DELIVERY  1  2  3  4  5

See Criticism Chart 18.

### Criticism chart 23c  *Response or acceptance*

Name_____Time_____to_____Total_____

---

INTRODUCTION  1  2  3  4  5

Did the opening words express sincere thanks?

Did the speaker refer to remarks made by previous speakers?

Did he refer to the occasion?

Was the hypothetical occasion plausible?

Was the opening appropriate?

BODY   1   2   3   4   5

Did the speaker reply to praise tactfully, by return praise, by sharing credit with others?

Were there enough illustrative supports, such as anecdotes, instances, and quotations?

CONCLUSION   1   2   3   4   5

Did the speaker's final words round off the talk?

Did the speaker restate his appreciation?

DELIVERY   1   2   3   4   5

See Criticism Chart 18.

## 24. Direct argument

The class will be divided into pairs. The students of each pair will take opposing sides on a controversial question, giving six-minute talks in immediate succession. Each pair will thus present a semi-debate. Each speech will be presented as a direct argument, following the suggestions in Chapter 16 but with particular attention to pages 317–19. Criticism Chart 24 shows more precisely the specific details that may be evaluated in each speech. Suggested propositions:

We should have pay-TV

Athletic scholarships are unethical

We should send economic aid to every nation that requests it

We should teach the theory of communism in our schools

Federal aid to education is desirable

All students should take a final major examination before a college degree is awarded

Strict attendance rules in college classes are unrealistic

Physical education courses should be expanded

Tax money should be allotted to private schools

All colleges and universities should have compulsory military training programs

A university degree should be granted after three years of study

Marriage and divorce laws should be enacted by the federal government

Recipients of welfare payments should be put to work for the state or city

Personal income tax can be abolished

The minimum voting age should be reduced to 18 in all states

### Criticism chart 24   *Direct argument*

Name_____ Time____to ____Total_____

Topic_____

INTRODUCTION   1   2   3   4   5

Did the opening words get favorable attention?

Did the speaker state his point of view early?

Did he give a preview of his main points?
Was the transition into the body of the speech smooth?
BODY   1   2   3   4   5
Was the central idea (proposition) clear?
Were the purpose and central idea sufficiently narrowed?
Did the main points suffice to prove the central idea?
Were there too many or too few main points?
Were the main points persuasively worded?
Was each main point supported by evidence?
Did the evidence include authorities, instances, and statistics?
Was the reasoning from the evidence sound?
Was the speech adapted to audience interests?
Was the speech adapted to audience drives and motives?
Was the speech adapted to existing audience attitudes toward related topics?
CONCLUSION   1   2   3   4   5
Were the main points restated?
Did the conclusion focus the whole speech on the central idea?
DELIVERY   1   2   3   4   5
See Criticism Chart 18.


### 25. General impression talk

Thus far in your class projects attention has been directed toward selected aspects or details of speechmaking. In Chapter 18, however, it was shown that most speaking is judged by laymen not in terms of details, but in terms of general impressions. Therefore, in this assignment we will turn from particulars to your total effectiveness.

Prepare a three- to four-minute talk adapted to your major subject field or proposed future vocation. Thus, if you are an education major, you might prepare a talk appropriate for a PTA meeting, or a high school assembly program, or a faculty meeting, or a student club, or a classroom lecture. The instructor will provide more explicit directions on this aspect of the assignment.

Criticism of this talk may be provided by classmates. A suggested ballot is provided in Criticism Chart 25. Unless your instructor provides different instructions, follow this procedure.

1. Study the ballot carefully before the assignment begins. Familiarize yourself with the descriptive words in the first part of the ballot, as well as with the five levels of total effectiveness in the second part.

2. Cut some ordinary 8½ x 11 paper into quarters. You will need one of these quarter-sheets for each of your classmates.

3. When a classmate is called upon to speak, write his name at the top of one of the quarter-sheets; do not write your own name on the sheet.

4. While he is talking indicate your general impressions of him by jotting down appropriate words or phrases, using part one of the ballot as a check list. Write

down as many of the words as you think are applicable. Feel free to write brief additional comments if the lists fail to express some of your reactions to the speech. Be honest.

5. At the conclusion of his talk, a brief pause will be provided during which you will rate his total effectiveness in accordance with the rating scale, which is the second part of the ballot. Judge him in terms of all the speeches you have heard in this class to date. Decide which of the five steps on the scale best describes his total effectiveness, and record your decision by writing the number for that step at the bottom of the quarter-sheet.

6. At the end of the class hour, clip together all your completed quarter-sheets. Write your own name on a slip of paper and clip it to the top of the pack. Your instructor will then collect all the ballots.

7. At a class meeting after the assignment is completed the instructor will return the quarter-sheet ballots to the students about whom they were written. When you receive the ballots written by your classmates on your own speech, analyze them as suggested in Chapter 18.

### Criticism chart 25    *General impression talk*

Name_____ Time_____to_____Total_____
Topic _____

GENERAL IMPRESSIONS OF THE SPEAKER

| *Too little* | *About right* | *Too much* |
|---|---|---|
| aloof | friendly | fawning |
| colorless | animated | showing off |
| insincere | sincere | fanatical |
| nervous | confident | arrogant |
| ill at ease | poised | condescending |
| tactless | courteous | oily |
| listless | alert | tense |
| weak | forceful | bombastic |
| grim | humorous | clownish |
| poorly informed | knows the subject | displays his knowledge |
| fumbling | fluent | gushy |
| passive | enthusiastic | boisterous |
| evasive | direct | fixed stare |
| empty-headed | thoughtful | ponderous |
| dogmatic | open-minded | vacillating |
| banal | original | eccentric |

TOTAL EFFECTIVENESS OF SPEECH AND SPEAKER

| 1 | 2 | 3 | 4 | 5 |
|---|---|---|---|---|
| Almost complete ineffective-ness | Below average effectiveness | Average effectiveness | Above average effectiveness | Almost complete effectiveness |

## 26. Indirect argument

Prepare an eight- to ten-minute talk in which you take a side on a controversial question. A subject must be chosen so that some of the audience will be undecided or opposed to your point of view. Your general purpose will be to convince, that is, to build new attitudes in those classmates who are undecided or opposed. The talk should be of indirect design, following suggestions in Chapter 16 with particular reference to pages 317 and 319–20. Study Criticism Chart 26 for more detailed reminders on how the talk should be constructed. Suggested subjects:

Depressed areas of the United States
Traffic congestion
Juvenile delinquency
The plight of the unskilled laborer
Earning money for college
Combating communism
Unwed mothers
The threat of nuclear war
The training of engineers
School dropouts
Improving postal service
The high cost of textbooks
Television commercials
The European Common Market
Patent medicines
The overcrowding of schools
The draft system

### Criticism chart 26 *Indirect argument*

Name_____ Time____to____Total_____
Topic_____

INTRODUCTION   1   2   3   4   5
    Did the opening words get favorable attention?
    Did the speaker establish personal prestige?
    Did he begin on common ground?
    Did he reveal his purpose and central idea too soon?
    Was the transition into the body of the speech smooth?
BODY   1   2   3   4   5
    Was the central idea revealed gradually and tactfully?
    Were the purpose and central idea sufficiently narrowed?
    Was the problem-solution sequence followed?
    Was the idea sequence adapted to audience opposition?
Review other criteria, Criticism Chart 24.

CONCLUSION 1 2 3 4 5
See Criticism Chart 24.
DELIVERY 1 2 3 4 5
See Criticism Chart 18.

## 27. Persuasive speech

The term *persuasive speech* customarily includes any speech where the purpose is to stimulate (reinforce attitudes), to convince (build attitudes), or to actuate (release attitudes). For this final speech your instructor may grant wide individual latitude in choosing the purpose and subject. On the other hand, he may wish to provide detailed instructions for one or more specific types of persuasive speeches. In any case your ultimate goal is to influence behavior through speech.

### Criticism chart 27 *Persuasive speech*

Name_____ Time_____ to _____ Total_____
Topic_____

THE ATTENTION STEP 1 2 3 4 5
  Did the opening get attention?
  Was the attention favorable?
  Was the attention directed naturally and quickly toward the subject?
THE NEED STEP 1 2 3 4 5
  Did the speaker give the audience reasons for believing or acting?
  Were the reasons logically adequate?
  Were the reasons presented in terms of audience motivation?
  Was this step effective, that is, did the speaker actually arouse feelings of need?
  If not, what may have been his trouble?
  If so, were his psychological techniques ethical?
THE SATISFACTION STEP 1 2 3 4 5
  Did the speaker present a proposal or plan?
  Was it directly and clearly related to the "needs"?
  Was the proposal logically adequate?
  Was it psychologically sound?
THE ACTION STEP 1 2 3 4 5
  Did the speaker give a specific and concrete picture of what each individual should do, think, or feel?
  Did he include a definite "call for action" appropriate to the audience, the occasion, and the speaker's goal?

# APPENDIX B  *Sample Speech Outline*

The following sample outline is more detailed than is necessary for an ordinary speech. The parts, the forms of support, and the transitions have been labeled in italics, and the gist of anecdotes is given. These details were added to enable you to follow the thought more readily, to show the relationships among ideas, and to show the logical relationships between the thought and the mechanics of the outline form.

*Title:* "Is Silence Golden?"
*Subject:* Speech training
*Purpose:* To convince my listeners that they should take speech courses

### INTRODUCTION

  I. *Quotation:* The other day in my speech class Professor W. Charles Redding raised this question for discussion, "Is silence golden?"
   *Transition:* That question struck a chord in my memory.
 II. *Brief anecdote:* Last summer the boss gave a dinner party . . . Jack Reader was tongued-tied . . . Leaving party, Jack was discouraged. I said, "Well, silence is golden." "Golden!" Jack snorted, "It's humiliating!"
III. *Brief anecdote:* My Uncle Luther, a businessman . . . his chance to run for president of Chamber of Commerce . . . turned down chance because afraid of public speaking . . . his silence isn't golden—it's expensive.

IV. *Brief anecdote:* Mrs. Warner, a neighbor . . . children now grown up . . . she needs constructive community activities . . . she has money, talent, education but no speech training . . . her silence isn't golden—it's a penalty on her community.

> *Transition:* People like Jack, and Uncle Luther, and Mrs. Warner are typical. They demonstrate that silence is often not golden. With most people the problem is not how to remain silent but how to talk effectively. This semester I have discovered that effective talking can be learned. I got my nerve up and enrolled in a speech class. And tonight I want to recommend that class to all of you.

BODY

*Central idea:* Tonight I want to show that speech training is golden. It makes you a more effective person, a more effective wage earner, and a more effective citizen.

> *Transition:* Let us consider the first of these.

I. *Main point:* Speech training makes you a more effective person.
   A. *Quotation:* Lowell Thomas once remarked, "I can think of nothing that is more likely to add cubits to your stature than well-rounded training in public speaking . . ."
   > *Transition:* The truth of his words is well illustrated in an actual speech class.
   B. *Anecdote:* At the beginning of the term Tom was a social hermit . . . he has now learned to like people.
   > *Transition:* Tom is no isolated case. A dozen others in the class have obviously improved their personalities. For example . . .
   C. *Instances:* Loreine is less gushy; Paul has been developing confidence and poise; etc.
   > *Transition:* But speech training not only makes you a more effective person . . .

II. *Main point:* Speech training makes you a more effective wage earner.
   A. *Statistics:* According to the *Statistical Abstract,* here are the professions and vocations which pay the highest incomes . . . Notice in how many of them public speaking is a necessity for success.
   B. *Statistics:* The National Council of Teachers of English made a survey of 2,615 adults from 253 different occupations . . . etc.
   C. *Quotations:* The national societies of such professions as engineering and medicine have recommended that public speaking be . . . etc.
   > *Transition:* Thus speech training is golden in a literal sense—it means money. That brings us to the third and final value.

III. *Main point:* Speech training makes you a more effective citizen.
   A. *Explanation:* In a democracy free public discussion is the basic technique . . . contrast Russia where basic technique is propaganda . . . under a dictator silence often *is* golden . . . but democracy . . . etc.
   B. *Anecdote:* A group of taxpayers in my home town held a meeting last year . . . etc.

C. *Quotation:* Woodrow Wilson summed up the importance of speech to responsible citizenship when he said . . . etc.

   *Transition:* And now to summarize . . .

CONCLUSION

I. *Summary:* I have shown that speech training makes you a more effective person, a more effective wage earner, and a more effective citizen.
II. *Quotation:* John Morley has said, "I hope that your professors of rhetoric will teach you to cultivate that golden art—the steadfast use of a language in which truth can be told; a speech that is strong by natural force, and not merely effective by declamation; an utterance without trick, without affectation, without mannerism."
III. I am sure our professors can teach that golden art. The only question is: Are you and I, the students, willing to learn it?

18    **Appendixes**

# APPENDIX C   *Sample Speech Outline*

The following sample outline is quoted from Milton Dickens and James H. McBath, *Guidebook for Speech Practice* (Harcourt, Brace & World, 1961), page 37.[1] See this guidebook, pages 33–36, for a description of how this outline was developed according to the recommended six-step procedure.

*Title:* "I'm a Rock Hound"
*Subject:* Collecting rocks and minerals
*Purpose:* To inform my audience of the personal values of the hobby of collecting rocks and minerals

### INTRODUCTION

Here is a remarkable piece of rock—just look at it. I found this rock right here on our own campus, and there's a story behind this piece of rock which I will presently tell. Maybe that story will interest you in the hobby of rock-collecting. You will discover that this hobby is enjoyable, inexpensive, and instructive. You might even make a fortune from it!

### BODY

*Central idea:* Collecting rocks and minerals is a desirable hobby.

I. It is enjoyable.
   A. You will enjoy hiking.

[1] Quoted by special permission of Harcourt, Brace & World, Inc.

1. Last weekend two friends and I enjoyed some beautiful scenery, a mineral find, and a mild adventure with some wild animals.
2. After our return we found that we were relaxed, refreshed, and pleasantly tired.

B. You will enjoy identifying and mounting specimens at home.
1. Here is an interesting specimen; let's identify it together.
2. Here is a mounted collection—let me tell you about it.

II. It is inexpensive.
A. You can buy the needed tools for as little as $5.
1. Here is an inexpensive rock pick.
2. Probably you already own these other tools—magnifying glass, pocket-knife, a penny, etc.

B. You can buy a beginning book for from $1 to $4.
1. Here is a paperback by Zim, Shaffer, and Perlman which sells for only $1.
2. Here are two longer books by Pough and by Pearl; each is authoritative; each sells for less than $4.

III. It is instructive.
A. You will immediately acquire a new and useful topic for conversation. [Have we time for subpoints? Or shall we just support by an illustration?]
B. You will soon acquire some surprising information about local geology.
1. The soil is . . .
2. Our water supply depends upon . . .

CONCLUSION

This morning I have sought to show that collecting rocks and minerals is a desirable hobby. It is enjoyable; it is inexpensive; it is instructive. Why not give it a try? Almost every weekend I go rock hunting. Let me invite you one and all to go along. Maybe we'll discover a uranium treasure. More certain and more important—we'll have a wonderful time.

# APPENDIX  D  *Continuing the Study of Speech*

You have now completed this basic course but you have only begun to master the art of public speaking. Probably you will agree that you need additional courses, additional practical experience, and additional study. How long will this take? Daniel Webster was once asked how long it took him to prepare his famous speech, "Reply to Hayne."

"All my life," Webster replied.

In looking ahead, however, a student usually thinks about the immediate future; he wants to make the most of the once-in-a-lifetime opportunities offered during his college career. So the question is frequently asked, "What is the best speech course for me to take next?" The answer depends on your personal interests and talents, and your proposed future career. To acquaint you with the breadth and variety of speech offerings, and to assist you in planning a future program of studies, we will devote the next section to a brief description of some courses commonly offered by colleges and universities. Later we will discuss nonclassroom opportunities for speech practice and speech evaluation.

## Breadth and variety of areas

*Public speaking.* At some schools the beginning course in public speaking is followed by one or more advanced courses in which you may explore much further such topics as audience analysis, psychology of motivation, applied semantics, basic and special types of speeches. At the same time you continue to improve your mastery of platform skills through guided practice. Typical course titles include persuasion, advanced public speaking, forms of public address, speech for radio-television, business and professional speaking.

*Group discussion.* You were briefly introduced to group discussion in Chapter 3. An entire course is needed to more fully understand the nature of the discussion process, basic principles and theories, and methods of leadership or participation. Review pages 41–42 to refresh your memory on the many types and forms. A discussion class also provides opportunities for practical practice projects.

*Voice and diction.* During this semester you have been trying to improve your speaking voice along the lines suggested by Chapter 10. This may be enough. But if your intended career requires that you make an ordinary voice good or a good voice better, then a special course with special equipment and expert guidance is needed. Only by intensive work can you change faulty habits of voice, articulation, and pronunciation.

*Argumentation and debate.* Courses in this area are often misevaluated. Students may think that the materials studied are difficult and dull, or may be frightened by the prospect of debating against other students. A review of Chapter 16 should help remove such misconceptions or fears. The analysis of a controversial question, the gathering of evidence, the process of reasoning and constructing a case, the planning of rebuttal—these stimulate an inquiring mind. And practice debates provide enjoyable as well as valuable training for many professions or vocations.

*Oral reading.* As we suggested in Chapter 11, this area offers further development in the skills of reading communicatively from manuscript. It also offers another dimension to the understanding and appreciation of literature, including prose, poetry, drama, and stories for children.

*Parliamentary procedure.* Students who have been elected to office in a fraternity, a campus club, or the student government soon realize the importance of knowing their parliamentary procedure. Most of us in our democratic society will become members of various organizations that try to conduct meetings according to parliamentary rules. Therefore we need to understand these rules and the principles underlying them. We also need practice in conducting meetings and participating from the floor.

*Speech science and correction.* Many schools have courses in such subjects as phonetics, mechanics of voice production, audiology, and speech correction. These courses are not restricted to students who plan to become speech therapists—consider music majors, for example.

*Communication.* Chapter 20 gave a brief introduction to the process and theories of communication. In recent years a growing number of schools have initiated courses in communication theory and its application to the study of speech, mass communication, propaganda, audio-visual education, and public opinion.

*History, theory, and criticism of public address.* The continued study of speech, especially on the graduate level, is often centered on this area. The history of public address includes the study of great speeches, as models of composition and as contributions to intellectual history. The study of rhetorical theory (see pages 365–67) covers the contributions of the ancients, the evolution of theory through subsequent eras, and modern interpretations. Criticism of public address means applying rhetorical theory and research methods to the evaluation of significant public speeches.

## Speech and your career

Here is a check list of some of the major fields of college and university study. See what areas of speech might be of further benefit to your interests and career:

Broadcasting: oral reading, communication, voice and diction, persuasion
Business: advanced speaking, discussion, parliamentary procedure, persuasion
Classics: rhetorical theory
Drama: advanced speaking, oral reading, voice and diction
Economics: discussion, communication
Education: advanced speaking, discussion, oral reading, speech science
Engineering: advanced speaking, discussion, communication
English: advanced speaking; oral reading; history, theory, and criticism of public address
History: history of public address
Humanities: oral reading; history, theory, and criticism of public address
International relations: advanced speaking, argumentation and debate, discussion, parliamentary procedure, communication
Journalism: discussion, persuasion, criticism of public address, communication
Law: advanced speaking, argumentation and debate, parliamentary procedure, persuasion
Library science: discussion, oral reading
Mathematics: discussion, communication
Medicine: advanced speaking, discussion, speech science
Music: phonetics, oral reading, voice and diction
Nursing: discussion, speech science
Physical education: oral reading, discussion
Physical sciences: discussion, communication
Political science: advanced speaking, argumentation and debate, discussion, parliamentary procedure, persuasion, communication
Psychology: speech science, persuasion, communication
Public administration: communication, argumentation and debate, discussion, parliamentary procedure, persuasion
Religion: advanced speaking, oral reading, voice and diction, persuasion
Sociology: discussion, communication

## Further opportunities for speaking

Do not forget that your everyday conversation can be a speech laboratory in which you deliberately practice to enlarge your vocabulary, improve animation and directness, eliminate careless habits of articulation and pronunciation, and develop more vocal variety. But you must also find opportunities to speak before groups. You have improved during this semester by speaking to your speech class. You will continue to improve by continuing to speak to campus and community audiences.

## Campus

Your future courses in a variety of subjects are likely to provide for class discussions, student panels, chalk talks, or oral reports. Welcome such assignments and make them do double duty—you can learn the subject matter and also practice systematically to improve your speaking effectiveness.

Training in both speech and leadership is provided by many student organizations. What campus groups does your school have? Perhaps YMCA, YWCA, First-time Voters, Young Republicans, Young Democrats, student religious groups, departmental clubs (such as National Collegiate Players, English Literature Society, or Geology Club), service clubs or committees, professional and social fraternities. Or how about running for an office in your student government?

Most schools maintain a forensic program where you may participate in campus or intercollegiate speaking contests in debate, oral interpretation, extemporaneous and impromptu speaking, or oratory. Perhaps you should try out for a campus theater production, or for the staff of the campus radio or television station.

## Community

Even while you are a student, you may have opportunities to participate in off-campus groups. After graduation you will probably join a few organizations which, in addition to their other benefits, will furnish occasions for the continuing practice of speechmaking. There are many worthy community groups; among them are taxpayers leagues, church groups, PTA, Toastmasters, Toastmistresses, Red Cross, Community Chest Speakers Bureau, League of Women Voters, fraternal organizations, businessmen's clubs.

# INDEX

Delivery of speeches: adjusting the, 244–45; beginning advice on, 59–63; bodily action in, 61–62, 165–80; extemporaneous method, 220–23; of humorous material, 255–58; impromptu, 223–24; language in, 205–27; from manuscripts, 224–26; of memorized speeches, 227; personality and, 335–49; practicing of, 59–63, 220–27; of speech to entertain, 263–65; using visual aids, 177–79; voice in, 183–203; *see also* Verbal, Visual, *and* Vocal communication

Demonstration talk, 395–96; criticism chart for, 396

Demosthenes, 29, 367

Description, 92–93

Development of speech, *see* Body of speech

De Voto, Bernard, *quoted,* 86

Dewey, John, 320

Dewey, Thomas E., *quoted,* 154, 258

Diaphragm, 184–86, *pictured,* 185

Dickens, Milton, 27–29

Dictionaries, 206, 212–13

Direct argument, 318–19; assignment in, 411–12; criticism chart for, 411–12; design for, 318

Directness, 17–18, 167–71; *see also* Communicativeness

Discussion: assignments in, 390–91; duties in guiding, 47–48; duties of a leader, 46–48; duties of a participant, 43–46; leader's advance preparations, 47; open forum, 42–43; panel, 42–43; participant's advance preparation for, 43; participation in, 43–46; purposes of, 41–43; sample leading questions in, 48; stock outline for, 47; types of, 41–43

Discussions, class, 390; panel forum, 390–91

Distinctness, *see* Articulation

Divisions of speech, 56–59, 119–20

Dress (for speaking), 166–71

Drives, 310

Dullness, 251–53

Earnest, Ernest, *quoted,* 90–91

Effectiveness (speech), 232

Eisenhower, Dwight D., *pictured,* 65; *quoted,* 91, 330

Emotion and reasoning, 302–03

Emotional maladjustment, 10, 183

Encyclopedias, 110

English usage, 213–15; *see also* Language

Enthusiasm, 36

Ethical responsibility, 351–63; and accuracy, 359–61; in Barbara Graham trial, 351–54; and sincerity, 354–59; and social standards, 361–63

Evidence, 303–07; kinds of, 304–05; tests of, 305–07

Ewing, Oscar R., *quoted,* 145, 321–23

Exhalation, 186

Explanation, 88–91

Extemporaneous speaking, 220–23; how to practice, 60–61; use of notes in, 60

Extended analogy, 132–34

Eye contact, 17–18, 166–71; *see also* Communicativeness

Facial expression, 166–71

Factors of attention: *see* Attention, factors of

Facts: defined, 304; as evidence, 304–05

Fairbanks, Grant, 197

Fairless, Benjamin F., *quoted,* 97

Flesch, Rudolf, *quoted,* 213

Fluency, 60, 220–23

Ford, Henry, 242; *quoted,* 15

Forgetting, 36

Forms of support, 88–105; anecdotes as, 93–95; audio-visual, 100–01; combinations of, 101–05; description as, 92–93; explanation as, 88–91; first use of, 57–58; functions of, 87–88; instances as, 95–97; quotations as, 97–100; statistics as, 100; *see also* Functions of supports

Fosdick, Harry Emerson, *quoted,* 90, 296

Fowler, H. W., 215

Franklin, Benjamin, 288, 317

Frost, Robert, *pictured,* 2–3

Fulbright, J. William, *quoted,* 96–97

Functions of supports: to clarify, 87; to prove, 87–88; to reinforce, 87

**431**

Speech preparation (Cont.)
55–56, 71–74; outlining, 56–59, 115–40; practicing delivery, 59–63; six-step procedure, 51
Speech purpose, *see* Purpose
Speech sounds, 196–97
Speech subjects: choice of, 53–55; slanting, 240–41; suitability of, 53–55; tests for, 55; *see also* Speeches, subjects for
Speech unit, 57–59, 115–17; definition of, 57; elaborations of, 58–59; examples of, 58, 115–17
Speeches, subjects for: demonstration talk, 395; direct argument, 411; discussion, 390–91; heckling talk, 409; indirect argument, 414; information talk, 400; persuasive speech, 415; statistics-analogy talk, 398
Speeches to convince, 299–323; conclusion for, 323; definition of, 301–02; design of, 316–20; direct approach in, 318–19; ethical responsibility in, 351–63; indirect approach in, 319–20; introduction for, 322–23; logic versus psychology, 302–03; logical validity, 303–09; outlining, 316–23; psychological validity of, 309–16; reasoning in, 307–09; supports for, 320–22
Speeches to entertain, 263–67; attention in, 263; delivery of, 263–65; example of outline of, 265–66; organization of, 265–67
Speeches to inform, 271–83; aids to learning in, 275–80; assignment for, 400; and audience analysis, 274–75; complaints about, 272–73; criticism chart for, 401; motivation in, 275–78; occasions for, 271–72; organization of, 280–83; tests for success of, 271
Speeches of response, 295–96
Speeches for special occasions, 292–97; assignments for, 409–11; criticism chart for, 409–12; introductions, 293–94; presentations, 295; responses, 295–96; welcomes, 294
Speeches to stimulate, 285–97; assignment for, 409–11; and central idea,

287; main points and subpoints of, 287–88; occasions for, 292–97; outlining, 287–91; as reinforcement of attitudes, 285–86; supports for, 288–91
Stage fright: aspects of, 27; and bodily action, 35; and breathing, 34; and "butterflies," 34; control of, 31–32; description of, 27–29; a diminishing phenomenon, 29–31; extent of, 25–27; and forgetting, 36; physiological aspects of, 27–29; in prominent speakers, 29–30
Statistics, as form of support, 100
Statistics-analogy talk, 398–99; criticism chart for, 398–99
Steichen, Edward, *pictured*, 338–39
Stengel, Casey, *pictured*, 254–55
Stevenson, Adlai, 83–86; *pictured*, 85; *quoted*, 83–85, 256
Stimulus-response, 368–70, 372–73
Stock designs: adapting to subject matter, 132–33; check list of, 132; for direct argument, 318–19; in discussion, 47; how to use, 133–34; for indirect argument, 319–20
Style, *see* Language *and* Words
Subordinate ideas, 121–22
Subpoints, 86–87, 136–39
Summary, 144–48
Supporting materials, 87–105, 136–39; *see also* Forms of support *and* Functions of supports
Syllogisms, 308
Symbols, words as, 207–09
Synonyms, 209–10, 212–13

Television, *see* Radio and television
Theories of communication, 366–80; cybernetics, 373–74; general communication model, 375–79; information theory, 374–75; modern theory, 367–75; rhetorical theory, 366–67
Thinking: as core of outlining, 115; reasoning and, 307–09; transitions as test of, 155–61
Thorax, 184–86; *pictured*, 185
Thought and language, 16–17, 205–06
Time limits, 45, 47, 232
Timing: of gestures, 179–80; of speech, 60

E
F
G
H
I
J

6
7
8
9
0
1
2
3